COLLEGE FOOTBALL ALMANAC

COLLEGE FOOTBALL ALMANAC

Robert M. Ours

Barnes & Noble Books
A Division of Harper & Row, Publishers
New York, Cambridge, Philadelphia, San Francisco,
London, Mexico City, São Paulo, Singapore, Sydney

FIRST EDITION

Designer: Jane Weinberger

Library of Congress Cataloging in Publication Data

Ours, Robert M.
    College football almanac.

    1. Football—United States—Miscellanea. 2. College
sports—United States—Miscellanea. 3. Football—United
States—Records. I. Title.
GV959.O87 1984   796.332'63'0973   84–47660
ISBN 0-06-464091-4 (pbk.)

---

84 85 86 87 88 10 9 8 7 6 5 4 3 2 1

Contents

Acknowledgments

I would like to thank the numerous sports information directors whose cooperation made the task of putting this almanac together an easier one. I am indebted to Pete Nevins of East Stroudsburg St. and Fred Nuesch of Texas A & I, librarian and secretary, respectively, of the College Sports Information Directors of America, for providing a complete list of Academic All America selections. Appreciation also goes to two members of the National Collegiate Athletic Association staff, publications editor Timothy J. Lilley and researcher Steve Boda, for their assistance. Special thanks go to Daniel Bial for his editorial suggestions and encouragement.

My gratitude also goes to my parents. My father, the late Henry M. Ours of Buckhannon, W.Va., took me to my first football games and bought me my first football magazines, thus instilling at an early age the seeds of this project. My mother, Grace Ours, had the prescience not to throw out all the books, clippings and notes that took up storage space in the early years, and remains a football fan to this day. Finally, I thank my daughters, Dorothy and Linda, for their constant encouragement and my wife, Ann, who has had to put up with being a football widow in more than the usual sense.

Introduction ▬▬▬▬▬

College football is 115 years old this fall, but modern fans would hardly recognize the sport as played in the first game November 13, 1869, at New Brunswick, N.J. When Princeton and Rutgers lined up to play on a field 120 yards long and 75 yards wide, there were 25 players on each side—and no officials. Using a round, soccer-style ball, Rutgers scored 6 goals to 4 for the visitors, after which the teams had dinner together and Princeton issued a challenge for a return match. A week later, Princeton got revenge by blanking Rutgers 8 goals to none, then entertained the visitors with dinner accompanied by speeches and songs.

The sport spread slowly at first, with Columbia, Yale, Harvard and Stevens Tech fielding teams by 1875. In that year a leather-covered, egg-shaped rugby ball was adopted and normal procedure was to have three officials on hand, a judge from each team plus a referee to settle disputes.

In 1876 a crossbar, 10 feet above the ground, was added to the goal posts and the field was reduced to 110 yards by 53⅓ yards. The number of players on each side also was reduced to 15.

Still, the game did not really begin to resemble the modern one until Walter Camp, a former Yale back who had recently graduated, revised the rules in the early 1880s. In 1880 Camp's revisions limited players to 11 on a side and established a scrimmage system for putting the ball into play. Two years later Camp instituted the system of downs for advancing the ball, requiring a team to make 5 yards in 3 downs. (The present system of 4 downs to make 10 yards was not adopted until 1912). The first-down rule of 1882 caused the initial marking of yard lines on the field, leading to the term "gridiron." It also inspired the first planned play strategy and verbal signals.

With these changes, the game spread more rapidly and some 250 colleges were participating in the sport by the beginning of the 20th century.

The 19th century game was primarily one of brute strength. There was no such thing as a pass and strategy centered on formations such as the "flying wedge," in which the ball carrier was surrounded by a wedge of teammates (often clasping hands). The only way to break through the wedge was for a defensive player to throw himself into the legs of the oncharging foes, a particularly dangerous practice in the days in which a stocking cap or a heavy thatch of hair was considered adequate head protection.

The first real uniform, devised in 1877 by a Princeton player aptly named L.P. Smock, consisted of a tightly laced canvas jacket (difficult for opponents to get a grip on), along with black knee pants, stockings and jersey —the latter trimmed in orange with an orange *P*. Other than extra cloth padding sometimes added to shoulders and over the thighs and knees, there was little in the way of protection for players in the first decades of the game.

So many serious injuries and occasional deaths occurred that the flying wedge and similar formations were outlawed in 1894, and by 1896 only 1 offensive back was allowed to be in motion at the snap of the ball—and he could not be running forward. The rule requiring 7 offensive players to be on the line of scrimmage at the snap was experimented with as early as 1895 but was not finally adopted until 1910.

By 1894 the officiating crew had grown from a single referee (first required in 1885) to a referee, an umpire and a linesman. The field judge was not added until 1907 and the back judge not until 1955. The modern crew includes a line judge and a clock operator as well.

Keeping an eye on all of the players undoubtedly was difficult for the small officiating crews of the 19th century, but identifying their gridiron heroes was even more difficult for the fans.

Although Walter Camp had formulated the first All America team in 1889, numerals to identify individual players were not authorized until 1915 and it was 1937 before numbers were required on both the front and back of jerseys. A further modification of the rules in 1967 required numbering according to position, with players ineligible to receive forward passes to be numbered in the 50–79 range.

Cries of extravagance erupted as early as 1878, when Princeton and Yale rented a field for $300 at Hoboken, N.J., to play before a crowd of 4,000 (Princeton won, 1–0). But the sport was really becoming "big time" in 1903, when Harvard unveiled the first huge stadium designed for football.

Despite its rapidly growing popularity, though, college football was in serious trouble in the early 20th century. The rules changes in the 1890s led to only a brief decrease in the injury and death rate on the playing field. By 1905 the public outcry against the brutality of the sport was so great that several schools (including Columbia) banned football and others threatened to do so. Even President Theodore Roosevelt, hardly known as a pantywaist, demanded that reforms be made.

The movement led to the creation of a body which 5 years later, in 1910, became known as the National Collegiate Athletic Association. The NCAA since then has been the major impetus in rule changes and in setting up and policing the procedures under which member colleges operate their football programs.

The reform movement led to many changes in the rules and in player equipment which created the immensely popular sport of college football as known in the 1980s. Nearly 650 4-year colleges and universities (505 of them members of the NCAA) fielded teams in 1983, and home attendance records have increased for Division I-A teams in 29 of the past 30 years.

Probably the biggest change that opened up the game was the rule adopted in 1906 that legalized the forward pass. Passing could be done only under very narrow restrictions at first and it was not until liberalization of the rules in 1910 and 1912 allowed more freedom that the pass became a real offensive weapon.

Notre Dame, then an excellent but little-known team, called the nation's attention to the new weapon in 1913, when it utilized the pass to shock powerful Army 35–13 at West Point, the only defeat the Cadets suffered that year.

Various restrictions continued to discourage many coaches from developing a passing attack throughout the 1920s, but by the late 1930s the rules had changed sufficiently and the ball had been modified enough to allow for effective passing.

A prolate spheroid had been required as the shape of the football as early as 1896, but specific measurements did not go into effect until 1912. Further specifications in the late 1920s and early 1930s led to slightly narrower balls and also allowed the use of white or other colored balls for night games.

Scoring changes in the early 20th century also helped popularize the game by increasing the value of touchdowns. When the first real football scoring system was devised in 1883 (as opposed to the single point per goal system used earlier), kicking was emphasized. Field goals counted 5 points and conversions after TDs counted 4, while the touchdown itself counted only 2. That was changed the following year.

From 1884 until 1898, TDs counted 4 points and conversions counted 2, but the field goal still was king at 5 points. Safeties were increased from 1 to 2 points in 1884 and have remained so since.

In 1898 the value of a touchdown was raised to 5 points and the conversion was reduced to 1. The field goal was equal to the TD in point value from then until 1904, when it was reduced to 4. In 1909 it was further lowered to its modern value of 3 points. The touchdown was given its modern 6-point value in 1912. No further point modifications were made until 1958, when teams were given the option of trying to run or pass the ball across the goal line for 2 points after a TD, while a successful kicked conversion remained worth one point. At the same time the scrimmage line for conversion attempts was moved from the 2-yard line to the 3-yard line.

Goal posts, originally placed right on the goal line, were moved back 10 yards, to the rear of the end zone, in 1927 in an effort to avert injuries by ball carriers or other players running into the uprights. That move, of course, also increased the distance for field goal tries.

Other safety factors during the 20th century have included improvements in pads and headgear. Leather helmets came into common use after World War I, although head protectors were not required by the rules until 1939. Plastic helmets came into wide use after World War II. Shoulder pads, knee pads, hip pads, etc., also evolved in this century, becoming larger and stronger in recent decades. Face masks were not common until the 1950s and required mouthpieces are a recent development.

The modern gladiator, nearly hidden by his protective equipment, has become largely a specialist playing either offense or defense, or perhaps coming onto the field just to punt or kick field goals and extra points. Few if any substitutions were allowed in the early years of the game until the rules of the late 1880s permitted substitutions for injured or disqualified players. Except for a brief time of unlimited allowable substitution in the 1898–1905 period, it was a game for players who participated in all aspects. Two-platoon football was made possible under rules established in 1941, but was not put into practice much until the late stages of World War II. Single-platoon football was reestablished under the rules of 1953 and it was not until 1965 that free substitution and 2-platoon football returned in full flower.

World War II was a watershed in college football, with many schools dropping the sport for at least 1 or 2 years and others competing with a mixture of 4F students, youngsters waiting to go into the service or servicemen attending Army, Navy, or Air Force programs at the colleges.

The post-war period was a transitional era in which returning war veterans, many of them in their middle or late 20s, mixed with younger team members. It was also a time in which leather equipment gradually began to give way to plastic. And it saw the continuing change from the tried and true single wing, double wing and Notre Dame box formations of the prewar period to the glamorous T formation that had been introduced just before the war and had taken the coaching profession by storm.

The straight T, usually with a man in motion, was the forerunner of the split T, the winged T, the triple option, the I, the wishbone and other modern, fast-moving offenses.

Attachments are often formed at a young age, and my love of college football dates to the first year following World War II when such storied players as Doc Blanchard and Glenn Davis of Army, Johnny Lujack of Notre Dame, Bobby Layne of Texas and Charlie (Choo Choo) Justice of North Carolina were drawing the headlines. I was already beginning to form a lifelong attachment to my home-state West Virginia University team, but I also was a big fan of the great Army team that had been undefeated national champion for two consecutive years.

The sunny autumn afternoon of November 9, 1946, still stands out vividly in my mind. That was the day on which Army, once more unbeaten, faced undefeated Notre Dame before more than 74,000 fans in Yankee Stadium in one of those "game of the century" contests that crop up every decade or so. In those pre-television days, millions of fans throughout the nation listened to big games on the radio, and I had expected to be one of those eager listeners on November 9th.

However, I spent much of the day playing sandlot football and time sped by. When I raced home and warmed up the big livingroom radio set, I found that I was in time to hear only the last 2 plays of that now-famous 0–0 tie. My disappointment was great, but my curiosity concerning college football had only begun. Over the next 3½ decades I watched thousands of games on all levels (live and on TV), covered a number for the Associated Press and several newspapers, read numerous histories of the college game and swam in statistics.

Yet many of the questions I had about the various teams (and I became interested in all of the major college teams and many other teams as well) could not be answered by any one source. I found it necessary to go to the various NCAA sources, individual school media guides, old newspaper accounts, etc., to find the answers. Even then I found many documents unreliable because of typographical errors or other mistakes. So I began to collect my own set of statistics and to formulate my own lists, checking and double-checking to try to make them as accurate as possible. In discussions with friends, other football fans and sportswriters and sportscasters, it became clear that others would be interested in the type of information I had collected. Thus was born the idea of a college football almanac.

The project outgrew the space limitations of a practical handbook, so I had to pare the list to 105 teams representing the majority of the NCAA Division I-A schools along with some Division I-AA schools (such as those in the Ivy League) with notable football pasts. In addition to the Ivy League, I was able to include all members of the Atlantic Coast Conference, Big 8, Big 10, Pacific Coast Athletic Association, Pacific 10, Southeastern Conference, Southwest Conference and Western Athletic Conference in addition to the 20 Division I-A independents. Also selected were Miami of Ohio, to represent the Mid-American Conference; Tulsa, to represent the Missouri Valley Conference; Virginia Military Institute, to represent the Southern Conference; Holy Cross, to represent Division I-AA independents with a major past; and William and Mary, to represent those outstanding academic institutions that go into nearly every football battle outmanned but unbowed.

Each listing is divided into several sections to allow both leisurely browsing and a quick check of basic information. The "Notable Teams" section for each school lists all the teams that won at least 70 percent of their regular season games (in a minimum 5-game schedule) or were chosen to play in the Rose, Orange, Sugar or Cotton Bowls. Bowl records are listed under the year in which regular season games were played (thus, a game played on January 1, 1950, would be listed with the 1949 season). Season records in all cases pertain to the regular season, with bowl results listed separately. Bowls include only those certified by the NCAA.

Conference championships are listed for each school, with co-championships designated with an asterisk. Top 10 rankings date from 1936 for the Associated Press (sportswriters' poll) and from 1950 for United Press International (coaches' poll), with *U* designating when a team was unranked in one poll while attaining top 10 ranking in the other.

The "Major Rivals" section lists won-lost records against foes met at least 15 times, although fewer games were required for a half-dozen schools that did not take up the game until after World War II. This section has a few inconsistencies because of different records of a given rivalry by the schools involved (and old newspaper accounts and media guides do not always resolve the problem).

The section on coaches includes those with the best won-lost records and those with the longest tenure.

"Miscellanea" includes a hodgepodge of facts, including the first game played, the longest winning or unbeaten string, longest losing or winless string, highest point total and biggest margin for and against (including the largest since World War II as well as all-time) and individual national awards. Not all of the All America players are included for some schools, such as Notre Dame (where All America players are legion). However, there is a complete listing of each school's Academic All America first stringers. The Academic team, selected each year since 1952 by the College Sports Information Directors of America, is the all-star team most representative of the student athlete as it is based on grade point average as well as football ability.

Robert M. Ours
Morgantown, W.Va.

Abbreviations

B—Back

C—Center

DB—Defensive Back

DE—Defensive End

DL—Defensive Lineman

DT—Defensive Tackle

E—End

FB—Fullback

FL—Flanker

G—Guard

HB—Halfback

K—Kicker

LB—Linebacker

MG—Middle Guard

OG—Offensive Guard

OL—Offensive Lineman

OT—Offensive Tackle

P—Punter

QB—Quarterback

RB—Running Back

S—Safety

T—Tackle

TB—Tailback

WR—Wide Receiver

COLLEGE
FOOTBALL
ALMANAC

College Football Almanac

Air Force (Falcons; Silver & Blue) (WAC)

NOTABLE TEAMS

1956—6-2-1. Coach Buck Shaw directed Falcons to wins in 1st 6 games in initial varsity season. 1958—9-0-1. Ben Martin's 1st team won 4 by TD or less behind T Brock Strom (1st Air Force consensus All America) and soph QB Rich Mayo (1,019 yards passing); tied Iowa 13–13 in 2nd game and TCU 0–0 in Cotton Bowl. 1963—7-3-0. QB Terry Isaacson passed for 946 yards and ran for 801 as Falcons lost no game by more than 10 points; lost to North Carolina in Gator Bowl 35-0. 1968—7-3-0. Charlie Longnecker caught 45 passes; 2 of losses by less than TD. 1970—9-2-0. Scored 353 as Bob Parker passed for 2,789 yards and 21 TDs and Ernie Jennings caught 74 for 17 TDs; lost to Tennessee in Sugar Bowl 34-13. 1983—9-2-0. Scored 32.5 points a game behind nation's 2nd best rushing attack as QB Marty Louthan scored 16 TDs; beat Mississippi 9-3 in Independence Bowl.

BOWL RECORD

Cotton 0–0–1; Gator 0–1–0; Hall of Fame 1–0–0; Independence 1–0–0; Sugar 0–1–0.

CONFERENCE TITLES

None.

TOP 10 AP & UPI RANKING

1958   6–8

MAJOR RIVALS

Air Force has played at least 10 games with Army (9–8–1), Colorado (4–12–0), Colorado St. (13–8–1), Navy (8–8–0), Notre Dame (3–11–0), Oregon (4–6–1), UCLA (4–6–1) and Wyoming (10–9–3).

COACHES

Dean of Air Force coaches was Ben Martin with record of 96–103–9 for 1958–77, including 3 bowl teams and 1 unbeaten team. The only other coach with a tenure of at least 5 years was Ken Hatfield with a record of 26–32–1 with 2 bowl champions for 1979–83.

MISCELLANEA

First varsity game was 46–0 win over San Diego U. in 1956 . . . highest score was 69–0 over Colorado St. in 1963 . . . worst defeat was 49–0 by Notre Dame in 1977 . . . highest against Falcons was 53–17 by Colorado in 1971 . . . longest unbeaten string of 14 in 1958–59 ended by Oregon 20–3 . . . longest losing string of 11 in 1978–79 broken with 28–7 win over Army . . . longest winless string of 12 in 1974–75 broken with 33–3 win over Army . . . consensus All America players were Brock Strom, T, 1958; and Ernie Jennings, E, 1970 . . . Academic All America choices were Strom, T, 1958; Rich Mayo, B, 1959–60; Jennings, E, 1970; Darryl Haas, K, 1971; Bob Homburg, DE, and Mark Prill, LB, 1972; Joe Debes, OT, 1973–74; Steve Hoog, WR, 1978; Mike France, LB, 1981; and Jeff Kubiak, P, 1983.

Alabama (Crimson Tide; Crimson & White) (SEC)

NOTABLE TEAMS

1904—7–3–0. Shut out 5 foes. 1906—5–1–0. Shut out 4; lost to Vanderbilt 78–0. 1907—5–1–2. Shut out 5; lost to Sewanee 54–4. 1908—6–1–1. Lost to Georgia Tech 11–6 and tied Georgia 6–6. 1909—5–1–2. J.W.H. Pollard's last team shut out 6; lost to LSU in finale 12–6. 1915—6–2–0. Shut out 5 as W. T. VandeGraaff starred at FB. 1919—8–1–0. Outscored foes 280–22; lost to Vanderbilt 16–12. 1920—10–1–0. Outscored foes 377–35, losing only to Georgia 21–14, as Riggs Stephenson starred at FB. **1923—7-2-1.** Wallace Wade's 1st team shut out 6. **1924—8-1-0.** Outscored foes 290–24 and won Southern Conference, losing only to Centre 17–0. **1925—9-0-0.** Tide's 1st bowl team outscored foes 277–7 behind B Johnny Mack Brown and QB Pooley Hubert; beat undefeated Washington in Rose Bowl 20–19. **1926—9-0-0.** Yielded just 20 points while winning 3rd straight Southern Conference title; tied unbeaten national champion Stanford in Rose Bowl 7–7. **1930—9-0-0.** Wade's last team outscored foes 247–13 as T Fred Sington became Tide's 1st consensus All America choice; beat undefeated Washington St. in Rose Bowl 24–0. **1931—9-1-0.** Frank W. Thomas's 1st team scored 370 behind B Johnny Cain, losing only to Tennessee 25–0. **1932— 8-2-0.** Lost only to Tennessee 7–3 and Georgia Tech 6–0 as Cain starred again. **1933—7-1-1.** Won initial SEC championship behind G Tom Hupke and HB Dixie Howell (1,437 yards total offense); lost only to Fordham 2–0 and tied Mississippi 0–0. **1934—9-0-0.** Howell (1,157 yards total offense), E Don Hutson and T Bill Lee starred as Tide outscored foes 287–32, then beat undefeated Stanford in Rose Bowl 29–13. **1935—6-2-1.** QB Riley Smith led team to wins over all but Howard (7–7 in opener), Mississippi St. (20–7) and Vanderbilt (14–6 in finale). **1936—8-0-1.** Shut out 5 of first 6 as G Arthur White starred; tie was with Tennessee 0–0. **1937—9-0-0.** Outscored foes 225–20, shutting out 6 behind linemen James Ryba and Leroy Monsky and HB Joe Kilgrow; lost to unbeaten California 13–0 in Rose Bowl for 1st bowl loss. **1938—7-1-1.** Led nation in total defense, losing only to unbeaten Tennessee 13–0 and tying Georgia Tech 14–14. **1940—7-2-0.** One of losses was to unbeaten Tennessee. **1941—8-2-0.** E Holt Rast and B Jimmy Nelson starred; beat Texas A&M in Cotton Bowl 29–21. **1942— 7-3-0.** Shut out 5 behind T Don Whitmire and C Joe Domnanovich; beat Boston College in Orange Bowl 37–21. **1944—5-1-2.** Lost only to Georgia 14–7 after year's layoff because of W.W. II; lost to Duke in Sugar Bowl 29–26. **1945—9-0-0.** Scored 396 behind HB Harry Gilmer (1,457 yards total offense) and C Vaughn Mancha and led nation in total defense and rushing defense; gave Southern California 1st Rose Bowl defeat, 34–14. **1947—8-2-0.** Red Drew's 1st team won last 7 behind Gilmer; lost to Texas in Sugar Bowl 27–7. **1950—9-2-0.** Scored 328 behind HB Ed Salem (1,252 yards total offense) and E Al Lary (35 receptions for 756 yards); won last 6 after losses to Vanderbilt 27–22 and Tennessee 14–9. **1952—9-2-0.** Bobby Marlow ran for 950 yards and Cecil Ingram led nation with 10 interceptions; beat Syracuse 61–6 in Orange Bowl for largest margin ever in major bowl. **1953—6-2-3.** Lost to Southern Mississippi 25–19 in opener and to unbeaten national champion Maryland; lost to Rice in Cotton Bowl 28–6. **1959—**

7–1–2. Bear Bryant's 2nd 'Bama team led nation in pass defense and lost only to Georgia 17–3 in opener; lost inaugural Liberty Bowl to Penn State 7–0. 1960—8–1–1. Won last 6 after 20–7 loss to Tennessee; tied Texas in Bluebonnet Bowl 3–3. 1961—10–0–0. Outscored foes 287–22 behind T Billy Neighbors, QB Pat Trammell (1,314 yards total offense) and C Lee Roy Jordan while leading nation in total defense and scoring defense; beat Arkansas 10–3 in Sugar Bowl for 1st national championship. 1962—9–1–0. Defense anchored by Jordan gave no foe more than 7 points and Joe Namath had 1,421 yards total offense as Tide lost only to Georgia Tech 7–6; beat Oklahoma in Orange Bowl 17–0. 1963—8–2–0. Lost only to Florida 10–6 and Auburn 10–8; beat undefeated Mississippi in Sugar Bowl 12–7. 1964—10–0–0. Namath, HB David Ray and G Wayne Freeman led Tide to share of national title despite 21–17 loss to Texas in Orange Bowl. 1965—8–1–1. Lost only to Georgia 18–17 in opener and tied Tennessee 7–7 as Steve Sloan passed for 1,453 yards behind C Paul Crane; beat undefeated Nebraska in Orange Bowl 39–28 to again earn share of national title. 1966—10–0–0. Led nation in scoring defense, shutting out 6, while scoring all in double figures behind T Cecil Dowdy, E Ray Perkins (33 receptions for 490 yards) and QB Ken Stabler (1,353 yards total offense); beat Nebraska in Sugar Bowl 34–7. 1967—8–1–1. Stabler passed for 1,214 yards and Dennis Homan caught 54 for 820 yards as Tide lost only to Tennessee 24–13; lost to Texas A&M in Cotton Bowl 20–16. 1968—8–2–0. Lost only to Mississippi 10–8 and Tennessee 10–9 as LB Mike Hall led defense and Scott Hunter passed for 1,471 yards to direct offense; lost to Missouri in Gator Bowl 35–10. 1971 —11–0–0. Scored 362 as Johnny Musso ran for 1,088 yards behind G John Hannah; lost to unbeaten national champion Nebraska in Orange Bowl 38–6. 1972—10–1–0. Scored 393 behind line led by Hannah, losing only to Auburn 17–16 in finale; lost to Texas in Cotton Bowl 17–13. 1973— 11–0–0. Wilbur Jackson (752 yards rushing) and Gary Rutledge (1,150 yards total offense) led offense to 454 points while LB Woody Lowe sparked defense; lost to unbeaten Notre Dame in Sugar Bowl 24–23 but shared national title with Fighting Irish. 1974—11–0–0. Lowe and DE Leroy Cook led another tough defense as Tide lost only to Notre Dame 13–11 in Orange Bowl. 1975—10–1–0. Cook and Lowe starred again as Tide led nation in scoring defense while Richard Todd (1,090 yards total offense) and Johnny Davis (820 yards rushing) led offense; lost only to Missouri 20–7 in opener but won 5th straight SEC title and beat Penn State in Sugar Bowl 13–6. 1976 —8–3–0. Lost 2 by 3-point margins as Jeff Rutledge had 1,018 yards total offense and DT Bob Baumhower led defense; beat UCLA in Liberty Bowl 36–6. 1977—10–1–0. Scored 345 behind Rutledge (1,518 yards total offense), Johnny Davis (931 yards rushing) and Ozzie Newsome (36 receptions for 804 yards) while losing only to Nebraska 31–24; beat Ohio State in Sugar Bowl 35–6. **1978—10-1-0.** Rutledge teamed with Tony Nathan (770 yards rushing) to lead Tide to 331 points as DT Marty Lyons led defense; lost only to Southern California 24–14 and beat undefeated Penn State in Sugar Bowl 14–7 to earn share of national championship. **1979—11-0-0.** Bryant's 7th unbeaten team scored 359 behind T Jim Bunch and QB Steadman Shealy (1,508 yards total offense) while leading nation in scoring defense; beat Arkansas 24–9 in Sugar Bowl to earn 6th national title. **1980—9-2-0.** Scored 322 and DL E.J. Junior led tough defense as Tide lost only to Mississippi St. 6–3 and Notre Dame 7–0; beat Baylor in Cotton Bowl 30–2. **1981—9-1-1.** Scored all in double figures but lost to Georgia Tech 24–21 and tied Southern Mississippi 13–13 as DB Tommy Wilcox starred on defense; lost to Texas in Cotton Bowl 14–12.

BOWL RECORD

Bluebonnet 0–0–2; Cotton 2–4–0; Gator 0–1–0; Liberty 2–2–0; Orange 4–3–0; Rose 4–1–1; Sugar 7–3–0; Sun 1–0–0.

CONFERENCE TITLES

Southern 1924, 1925, 1926, 1930*. Southeastern 1933, 1934*, 1937, 1945, 1953, 1961*, 1964, 1965, 1966*, 1971, 1972, 1973, 1974, 1975, 1977, 1978, 1979, 1981*.

TOP 10 AP & UPI RANKING

1936	4	1960	9–10	1967	8–7	1977	2–2
1937	4	1961	1–1	1971	4–2	1978	1–2
1942	10	1962	5–5	1972	7–4	1979	1–1
1945	2	1963	8–9	1973	4–1	1980	6–6
1947	6	1964	1–1	1974	5–2	1981	7–6
1952	9–9	1965	1–4	1975	3–3		
1959	10–U	1966	3–3	1976	U–9		

MAJOR RIVALS

Alabama has played at least 15 games with Auburn (28–19–1), Florida (16–5–0), Georgia (31–20–4), Georgia Tech (28–20–3), Howard (20–0–1), Kentucky (28–1–1), LSU (32–11–4), Miami (Fla.) (13–2–0), Mississippi (30–5–2), Mississippi St. (54–11–3), Sewanee (17–10–3), Southern Mississippi (18–3–2), Tennessee (34–25–7), Tulane (23–10–3) and Vanderbilt (40–17–4).

COACHES

The legendary Paul (Bear) Bryant compiled record of 232–46–9 in 1958–82, including 13 SEC titles, 6 national championships, 23 bowl teams and 7 teams unbeaten in regular season. He was national coach of the year in 1961, 1971 and 1973. Bryant ranks first in all-time victories and 17th in winning percentage. Frank Thomas was 2nd in wins with record of 115–24–7 for 1931–46, including 4 SEC titles, 6 bowl teams and 4 teams unbeaten in regular season. He ranks in top 15 in winning percentage. Wallace Wade was 61–13–3 for 1923–30, including 4 conference titles and 3 unbeaten Rose Bowl teams. Others with outstanding records included J.W.H. Pollard, 20–4–5 for 1906–09; Xen C. Scott, 29–9–3 for 1919–22; and Harold D. (Red) Drew, 55–29–7 for 1947–54 with one SEC title and 3 bowl teams.

MISCELLANEA

First game was 56–0 win over Birmingham H.S. in 1892 . . . first win over college opponent was 18–6 over Tulane in 1894 . . . highest score was 110–0 over Marion Institute in 1922 . . . highest since W.W. II was 89–0 over Delta State in 1951 . . . worst defeat was 78–0 by Vanderbilt in 1906 . . . worst since W.W. II was 40–0 by Auburn in 1957 . . . highest against Tide since W.W. II was 41–34 by Tennessee in 1983 . . . longest winning streak of 28 in 1978–80 broken by Mississippi St. 6–3 . . . 26-game unbeaten string in 1960–62 ended by Georgia Tech 7–6 . . . 24-game unbeaten string in 1924–27 ended by Georgia Tech 13–0 . . . longest winless string of 20 in 1954–56 broken with 13–12 win over Mississippi St. . . . Alabama has had 26 consensus All America players, but only multi-year choice was Leroy Cook, DL, 1974–75 . . . unanimous choices were Fred Sington, T, 1930; Billy Neighbors, T, 1961; Lee Roy Jordan, C, 1962; Cecil Dowdy, T, 1966; John Hannah, G, 1972; and E.J. Junior, DL, 1980 . . . others selected since 1970 were Johnny Musso, B, 1971; Buddy Brown, G, 1973; Woodrow Lowe, LB, 1974; Ozzie Newsome, WR, 1977; Marty Lyons, DL, 1978; Jim Bunch, T, 1979; and Tommy Wilcox, DB, 1981 . . . Academic All America choices were Tommy Brooker, E, and Pat Trammell, B, 1961; Gaylon McCollough, C, 1964; Steve Sloan, QB, and Dennis Homan, HB, 1965; Steve Davis, K, and Bob Childs, LB, 1967; Musso, RB, 1970–71; Randy Hall, DT, 1973–74; Danny Ridgeway, K, 1975; Major Ogilvie, RB, 1979; and Mike Pitts, DL, 1982 . . . Alabama ranks in top 5 in all-time winning percentage and in top 10 in total victories.

Arizona (Wildcats; Navy Blue & Cardinal Red) (Pacific-10)

NOTABLE TEAMS

1901—4–1–0. Lost to Phoenix Indian School 13–0. 1902—5–0–0. Outscored foes 134–0 but played only one college opponent. 1908—5–0–0. Outscored foes 136–5, but only one college opponent.1910—5–0–0. Gave up just 8 points. 1914—4–1–0. Lost to Occidental 14–0. 1919—7–1–0. Shut out 7; lost to Pomona 19–7. 1920—6–1–0. Scored 381; lost to Pomona 31–0. 1921—7–1–0. Scored 418 and lost only to Texas A&M 17–13; lost to unbeaten Centre in San Diego East-West Classic 38–0. 1926—5–1–1. Won first 5 before losing to Occidental 9–7 and tying Colorado St. 3–3. 1928—5–1–2. Lost only to Southern California 78–7. 1929—7–1–0. Shut out 6 but lost to Pomona 15–12. 1930—6–1–1. J.F. McKale's last team lost only to Rice 21–0, then shut out last 6 foes. 1934—7–2–1. Lost close ones to Loyola (Calif.) 6–0 and Texas Tech 13–7. 1935—7–2–0. Won last 5 behind QB Ted Bland after 7-point losses to Centenary and Loyola (Calif.). 1937—8–2–0. Won last 6 behind Little All America FB Walter Nielsen. 1940—7–2–0. B John Black sparked team for 2nd straight year. 1941—7–3–0. E Henry Stanton caught 50 passes for 820 yards as Wildcats scored 253 and won 3rd Border Conference title. 1945—5–0–0. Outscored slate of minor foes 193–12 after 2-year layoff caused by W.W. II. 1954—7–3–0. Art Luppino led nation's rushers with 1,359 yards and led in scoring with 166 of Wildcats' 385 points. 1960—7–3–0. Bobby Lee Thompson ran for 732 yards and Joe Hernandez scored 12 TDs; won last 6. 1961—8–1–1. Thompson ran for 752 yards and Eddie Wilson passed for 1,294 as team lost only to West Texas St. 27–23 and tied Nebraska 14–14. 1968—8–2–0. Ron Gardin caught 48 passes for 892 yards and Rich Moriarty intercepted 8 passes; lost to Auburn in Sun Bowl 34–10. 1973—8–3–0. Jim Young's 1st team scored 295 and won Western Athletic Conference title as Bruce Hill ran and passed for 1,915 yards and Jim Upchurch ran for 1,184. 1974—9–2–0. Hill had 2,118 yards total offense, Upchurch 1,004 yards rushing and Theopolis ("T") Bell caught 53 passes for 700 yards and scored 11 TDs. 1975—9–2–0. Hill had 2,021 yards total offense, Bell was 3rd in nation in kickoff returns and Lee Pistor kicked 15 FGs as Wildcats scored 330.

BOWL RECORD

Fiesta 0–1–0; Salad 0–1–0; San Diego East-West 0–1–0; Sun 0–1–0.

CONFERENCE TITLES

Border 1935, 1936, 1941*. Western Athletic 1964*, 1973*.

TOP 10 AP & UPI RANKING

None.

MAJOR RIVALS

Arizona has played at least 15 games with Arizona St. (31–26–0), Brigham Young (10–8–1), Colorado St. (12–2–1), New Mexico (40–18–3), New Mexico St. (29–5–1), Texas-El Paso (34–11–2), Texas Tech (3–25–2), Utah (13–16–2) and Wyoming (12–10–0).

COACHES

Dean of Wildcat coaches was J.F. (Pop) McKale with record of 60–31–6 for 1914–30. Second in wins was Miles W. Casteel with record of 45–26–3 for 1939–48, including one conference title and one unbeaten team. G.A. (Tex) Oliver was 32–11–4 for 1933–37 with 2 conference titles; and James C. Young was 31–13–0 for 1973–76 with one conference title. Other winning coaches included Jim LaRue, 41–37–2 for 1959–66 with one conference title; and Warren Woodson, 26–22–2 for 1952–56. Woodson, who also coached at 4 other schools, is tied for fifth in all-time coaching victories.

MISCELLANEA

First game was 0–0 tie with Tucson town team in 1899 . . . first win was 22–5 over Tucson Indians same year . . . first win over college foe was 12–0 over Arizona St. in 1902 . . . highest score was 167–0 over Camp Harry Jones in 1920 . . . highest since W.W. II was 67–0 over Arizona St. in 1946 and 67–13 over New Mexico St. in 1951 . . . worst defeat was 75–0 by Michigan St. in 1949 . . . highest against Wildcats was 78–7 by Southern California in 1928 . . . longest unbeaten string of 11 in 1960–61 ended by West Texas St. 27–23 . . . longest winless string of 10 in 1956–57 broken with 17–14 win over Marquette . . . Ricky Hunley, LB, was consensus All America in 1983 . . . Academic All America choices were Mike Moody, OG, 1968; Jon

Abbott, LB, 1975–77; Jeffery Whitton, DL, 1979; and Ricky Hunley, LB, 1982–83.

Arizona State (Sun Devils; Maroon & Gold) (Pacific-10)

NOTABLE TEAMS

1924—7-0-1. Scored in double figures all games; tie was with Sherman Indians 12–12. 1925—6-2-0. Lost to Arizona and Texas-El Paso. 1926—4-1-1. Shut out 4; lost to Arizona 35–0. 1931—5-2-0. HB Norris Steverson led team to 1st Border Conference title. 1939—8-2-0. Won Border Conference behind G Al Sanserino, HB Joe Hernandez and FB Wayne Pitts; tied Catholic U. in Sun Bowl 0–0. 1940—7-1-2. Won conference again, losing only to Hardin-Simmons 17–0; lost to Western Reserve in Sun Bowl 26–13. 1949—7-2-0. Scored 342 as Wilford White ran for 935 yards and caught 17 passes for another 334; lost to Xavier (Ohio) in Salad Bowl 33–21. 1950 —9-1-0. Scored 383 as White ran for 1,502 yards to lead nation, and Sun Devils led nation in total offense and rushing while Hank Rich led country with 12 interceptions; lost only to Hardin-Simmons in regular season and to Miami (Ohio) in Salad Bowl 34–21. 1955—8-2-1. Dan Devine's 1st team scored 343 as Dave Graybill passed for 1,079 yards and Leon Burton scored 10 TDs; lost to San Jose St. 27–20 and Arizona 7–6. 1956—9-1-0. Scored 306 as Bobby Mulgado rushed for 721 yards; lost only to Texas-El Paso. 1957—10-0-0. Outscored foes 397–66 as Sun Devils led nation in total offense and scoring in Devine's last year; Burton led nation's rushers with 1,126 yards and scored 16 TDs. 1958—7-3-0. Frank Kush's 1st team won last 5; Burton rushed for 642 yards and 11 TDs. 1959—10-1-0. Nolan Jones scored 100 points (including 11 TDs) and team lost only to San Jose St. 24–15. 1960—7-3-0. Lost 2 by TD or less. 1961—7-3-0. Again lost 2 by TD or less while winning 7th Border Conference title. 1962—7-2-1. Led nation in total offense as John Jacobs passed for 1,263 yards and 14 TDs and Joe Zuger led nation with 10 interceptions; lost only to West Texas St. 15–14 and Arizona 20–17. 1963—8-1-0. Lost opener to Wichita St. but scored in double figures all games as Tony Lorick rushed for 805 yards. 1964—8-2-0. John Torok passed for 2,356 yards and 20 TDs while receivers included Ben Hawkins (42 catches for 719 yards) and Jerry Smith (42 receptions for 618 yards). 1967—8-2-0. Scored 350 as Max Anderson ran for 1,183 yards and 12 TDs while MG Curley Culp led defense. 1968—8-2-0. Scored 414 as

Art Malone ran for 1,431 yards and 16 TDs and Fair Hooker caught 42 passes for 665 yards. 1969—8-2-0. Scored 383 behind QB Joe Spagnola (1,488 yards passing) and Dave Buchanan (908 yards rushing and 15 TDs) while Seth Miller led nation with 11 pass interceptions; won last 6 to take 1st Western Athletic Conference title. 1970—10-0-0. Led nation in total offense and scored 379 as Bob Thomas ran for 900 yards, Spagnola passed for 1,991 yards and 18 TDs and J. D. Hill caught 58 passes for 908 yards and 10 TDs; beat North Carolina in Peach Bowl 48-26. 1971—10-1-0. Scored 417 as Woody Green ran for 1,209 yards and Danny White passed for 1,393 yards and 15 TDs; lost only to Oregon St. 24-18, and beat Florida St. in inaugural Fiesta Bowl 45-38. 1972—9-2-0. Led nation in total offense and scoring (513 points) as Green ran for 1,363 yards and 15 TDs and became Sun Devils' 1st consensus All America player, White passed for 1,930 yards and 21 TDs and Steve Holden caught 38 passes for 848 yards and 12 TDs; lost close ones to Wyoming 45-43 and Air Force 39-31, but beat Missouri in Fiesta Bowl 49-35. 1973—10-1-0. Again led nation in total offense and scoring (491 points) as Green ran for 1,182 yards, White passed for 2,609 yards and 23 TDs and Morris Owens caught 50 passes for 1,076 yards and 9 scores; lost only to Utah 36-31 but won 5th straight WAC title and beat Pittsburgh in Fiesta Bowl 28-7. 1975—11-0-0. Scored 347 as Fred Williams ran for 1,316 yards and John Jefferson caught 44 passes for 808 yards; beat Nebraska in Fiesta Bowl 17-14. 1977—9-2-0. Scored 369 behind QB Dennis Sproul and Jefferson (53 catches for 912 yards) and won 7th and last WAC title; lost to Penn State in Fiesta Bowl 42-30. 1978—8-3-0. Scored 313 as Mark Malone passed for 1,305 yards and ran for 705 while DL Al Harris anchored defense; beat Rutgers in Garden State Bowl 34-18. 1981—9-2-0. Scored 394 and led nation in total offense behind Mike Pagel (2,484 yards and 29 TD's passing) as Luis Zendejas kicked 16 FGs and 45 extra points. 1982—9-2-0. Led nation in total defense behind DL Vernon Maxwell and DB Mike Richardson as Zendejas kicked 21 FGs; won 9 straight before losing to Washington 17-13 and Arizona, but beat Oklahoma in Fiesta Bowl 32-21.

BOWL RECORD

Fiesta 5-1-0; Garden State 1-0-0; Peach 1-0-0; Salad 0-2-0; Sun 0-1-1.

CONFERENCE TITLES

Border 1931, 1939, 1940, 1952, 1957, 1959, 1961. Western Athletic 1969, 1970, 1971, 1972, 1973*, 1975, 1977*.

TOP 10 AP & UPI RANKING

1970	6–8	1975	2–2
1971	8–6	1982	6–6
1973	9–10		

MAJOR RIVALS

Sun Devils have played at least 15 games with Arizona (26–31–0), Brigham Young (18–5–0), Colorado St. (16–1–0), Hardin-Simmons (8–13–0), New Mexico (22–5–1), New Mexico St. (20–6–1), Northern Arizona (16–14–4), San Jose St. (15–11–0), Texas-El Paso (30–13–3), Utah (12–6–0), West Texas St. (13–7–0) and Wyoming (9–6–0).

COACHES

Dean of ASU coaches was Frank Kush with record of 179–58–1 (5 wins later forfeited) for 1958–79, including 7 conference titles, 7 bowl teams (6 winners) and 2 unbeaten teams. Kush was national coach of the year in 1975. He ranks in top 20 in all-time victories. Other outstanding records were by Dan Devine, 27–3–1 for 1955–57 with 1 conference title and 1 unbeaten team; Darryl Rogers, 32–12–1 for 1980–83 with 1 bowl champion; Aaron McCreary, 26–16–4 for 1923–29 with 1 unbeaten team; Dixie Howell, 23–15–4 for 1938–41 with 2 bowl teams; and Ed Doherty, 25–17–0 for 1947–50 with 2 bowl teams.

MISCELLANEA

First game was 38–20 loss to Phoenix Indians in 1897 . . . first win was 6–0 over same team in 1899 . . . first win over college foe was 11–2 over Arizona in 1899 . . . highest score was 79–7 over Colorado St. in 1969 . . . worst defeat was 74–2 by Nevada-Reno in 1946 . . . longest winning streak of 21 in 1969–71 ended by Oregon St. 24–18 . . . longest winless string of 11 in 1937–38 broken with 13–0 win over Cal-Davis . . . consensus All America players were Woody Green, B, 1972–73; John Jefferson, WR, 1977; Al Harris, DL, 1978; Mike Richardson, DB, 1981–82; Vernon Maxwell, DE, 1982; and Luis Zendejas, K, 1983 . . . Ken Dyer, E, made Academic All America in 1966 . . . Arizona State ranks in top 20 in all-time winning percentage.

Arkansas (Razorbacks; Cardinal & White) (Southwest)

NOTABLE TEAMS

1909—7–0–0. Scored in double figures each game, outscoring foes 186–18 behind FB Clinton Milford. 1910—7–1–0. Shut out 5; lost to Kansas St. 5–0. 1911—6–2–1. Again shut out 5. 1913—7–2–0. Shut out all 4 home game foes. 1917—5–1–1. Shut out 5, losing only to Texas 20–0 and tying Oklahoma 0–0. 1923—6–2–1. Shut out 6, losing only to Baylor and unbeaten SMU 13–6. 1924—7–2–1. Scored 227 behind HB Herman Bagby. 1927— 8–1–0. George Cole scored 11 TDs; lost only to Texas A&M 40–6. 1928 —7–2–0. Francis Schmidt's last team shut out 5 behind G Clyde Van Sickle as Garland Beavers scored 14 TDs. 1929—7–2–0. Fred Thomsen's 1st team won last 5. 1933—7–3–0. Won 1st Southwest Conference title behind FB Tom Murphy; tied Centenary 7–7 in Dixie Classic. 1936—7–3–0. Jim Benton caught 35 passes for 489 yards; won last 5 to take SWC title. 1937— 6–2–2. Lost only to Baylor 20–14 and Rice 26–20 as Benton caught 48 passes for 814 yards and 7 TDs and team led nation in passing. 1946—6–3–1. Lost 2 by total of 3 points and won share of SWC title; tied LSU in Cotton Bowl 0–0. 1954—8–2–0. G Bud Brooks led offense as Razorbacks lost only to SMU 21–14 and LSU 7–6 and won SWC; lost to Georgia Tech in Cotton Bowl 14–6. 1959—8–2–0. HB Jim Mooty led team to 5th SWC title; beat Georgia Tech in Gator Bowl 14–7. 1960—8–2–0. Repeated as SWC champion but lost to Duke in Cotton Bowl 7–6. 1961—8–2–0. Won last 5 to take 3rd straight SWC title; lost to unbeaten national champion Alabama in Sugar Bowl 10–3. 1962—9–1–0. Scored 286, as Billy Moore scored 14 TDs, and lost only to Texas 7–3; lost to unbeaten Mississippi in Sugar Bowl 17–13. 1964—10–0–0. Led nation in scoring defense, shutting out last 5 foes; beat Nebraska in Cotton Bowl 10–7 to earn share of national championship as Frank Broyles won coach of year honors. 1965—10–0–0. Led nation in scoring average (32.4) as Bobby Burnett ran for 947 yards and 16 TDs while DT Loyd Phillips anchored defense; lost to LSU in Cotton Bowl 14–7. 1966 —8–2–0. Lost only to Baylor 7–0 and Texas Tech 21–16 as Phillips starred again and Gary Adams intercepted 7 passes. 1968—9–1–0. Scored 334 and lost only to Texas 39–29 as Bill Montgomery ran and passed for 1,834 yards and Bill Burnett ran for 859 yards and 16 TDs; beat Georgia in Sugar Bowl 16–2. 1969—9–1–0. Scored 331 behind C Rodney Brand, Burnett (900 yards rushing and 20 TDs) and Chuck Dicus (42 receptions for 688 yards) while leading nation in scoring defense; lost only to unbeaten national champion Texas in finale 15–14, then lost to Mississippi in Sugar Bowl 27–22. 1970—9-2-0. Scored 395 as Montgomery ran and passed for 1,819 yards and DT Dick Bumpas anchored defense; lost opener to Stanford and finale to unbeaten Texas. 1971—8-2-1. Joe Ferguson ran and passed for 2,242 yards and Mike Reppond caught 56 for 986 yards as Razorbacks lost only to Tulsa 21–20 and Texas A&M 17–9; lost to Tennessee in Liberty Bowl 14–13. 1975—9-2-0. Won last 5 to earn share of SWC title as Ike Forte ran for 983 yards; lost only to Oklahoma St. 20–13 and Texas 24–18, and beat Georgia in Cotton Bowl 31–10. 1977—10-1-0. Lou Holtz's 1st team scored 358 as Ben Cowins ran for 1,192 yards and 14 TDs and Steve Little kicked 19 FGs; lost only to unbeaten Texas 13–9, and whipped Oklahoma in Orange Bowl 31–6. 1978—9-2-0. Cowins ran for 1,006 yards; won last 5, then tied UCLA in Fiesta Bowl 10–10. 1979—10-1-0. Scored all in double figures behind QB Kevin Scanlon, T Greg Kolenda and Ish Ordonez (18 FGs), losing only to Houston 13–10; won SWC but lost to unbeaten national champion Alabama in Sugar Bowl 24–9. 1981—8-3-0. Two losses by less than TD as DL Billy Ray Smith starred; lost to North Carolina in Gator Bowl 31–27. 1982—8-2-1. Led nation in scoring defense behind Smith as OL Steve Korte led offense; beat Florida in Bluebonnet Bowl 28–24.

BOWL RECORD

Bluebonnet 1–0–0; Cotton 2–3–1; Dixie 1–0–1; Fiesta 0–0–1; Gator 1–1–0; Hall of Fame 1–0–0; Liberty 0–1–0; Orange 1–0–0; Sugar 1–4–0.

CONFERENCE TITLES

Southwest 1933, 1936, 1946*, 1954, 1959*, 1960, 1961*, 1964, 1965, 1968*, 1975*, 1979*.

TOP 10 AP & UPI RANKING

1954	10–8	1962	6–6	1969	7–3	1979	8–9
1959	9–9	1964	2–2	1975	7–6	1982	9–8
1960	7–7	1965	3–2	1977	3–3		
1961	9–8	1968	6–9	1978	U–10		

MAJOR RIVALS

Arkansas has played at least 15 games with Baylor (30–30–2), Drury (13–5–2), Hendrix (15–0–2), LSU (12–23–2), Mississippi (15–15–0), Missouri-Rolla (15–4–0), Oklahoma St. (30–15–1), Rice (28–28–3), SMU (28–26–

5), Texas (16–50–0), Texas A&M (34–20–3), TCU (37–21–2), Texas Tech (23–4–0) and Tulsa (43–15–3).

COACHES

Dean of Arkansas coaches was Frank Broyles with record of 144–58–5 for 1958–76, including 7 conference titles, 10 bowl teams, 2 teams unbeaten in regular season and 1 national champion. He was national coach of the year in 1964, as was Lou Holtz in 1977. Holtz was 60–21–2 for 1977–83, with 1 conference title and 6 bowl teams. Other outstanding records were by Hugo Bezdek, 29–13–1 for 1908–12 with 1 unbeaten team; Francis Schmidt, 42–20–3 for 1922–28; and John Barnhill, 22–17–3 for 1946–49 with 1 conference title and 2 bowl teams. Second to Broyles in tenure was Fred Thomsen, 56–61–10 for 1929–41 with 2 conference titles.

MISCELLANEA

First game was 42–0 win over Fort Smith H.S. in 1894 . . . first win over college foe was 24–0 over Ouachita in 1897 . . . highest score was 100–0 over S.W. Missouri St. in 1911 . . . highest since W.W. II was 64–0 over N.W. Louisiana St. in 1947 . . . worst defeat was 103–0 by Oklahoma in 1918 . . . worst since W.W. II was 47–0 by Rice in 1953 . . . longest winning streak of 22 in 1963–65 ended by LSU 14–7 in Cotton Bowl . . . longest losing string of 7 in 1952–53 broken with 13–6 win over TCU . . . consensus All America players were Clyde Scott, B, 1948; Bud Brooks, G, 1954; Glen Ray Hines, T, 1965; Loyd Phillips, DT, 1965–66; Jim Barnes, G, 1968; Rodney Brand, C, 1969; Dick Bumpas, DT, 1970; Leotis Harris, G, and Steve Little, K, 1977; Greg Kolenda, T, 1979; Billy Ray Smith, DL, DE, 1981–82; and Steve Korte, OG, 1982 . . . Academic All America selections were Gerald Nesbitt, FB, 1957; Lance Alworth, B, 1961; Ken Hatfield, B, 1964; Randy Stewart, C, Jim Lindsey, HB, and Jack Brasuell, DB, 1965; Bob White, K, 1968; Bill Burnett, HB, and Terry Stewart, DB, 1969; and Brad Shoup, DB, 1978 . . . Outland Trophy winners were Bud Brooks, G, 1954; and Loyd Phillips, T, 1966.

Army (Black Knights, Cadets; Black, Gold & Gray) (Independent)

NOTABLE TEAMS

1891—4-1-1. Lost only to Rutgers 27–6; beat Navy for first time 32–16. 1895—5-2-0. Lost to Harvard and Yale, but shut out others. 1897—6-1-1. Lost only to Harvard and tied Yale. 1901—5-1-2. Lost only to unbeaten Harvard 6–0 as T Paul Bunker and B Charles Daly starred. 1902—6-1-1. Shut out 5, losing only to Harvard 14–6. 1903—6-2-1. Lost successive games to Harvard and Yale. 1904—7-2-0. B Henry Torney and C Arthur Tipton starred as Cadets lost only to Harvard 4–0 and Princeton 12–6. 1907 —6-2-1. Shut out 6 behind G William Erwin, losing only to Cornell 14–10 and Navy 6–0. 1908—6-1-2. Shut out 5, losing only to Yale 6–0. 1910— 6-2-0. Lost to Harvard 6–0 and Navy 3–0. 1911—6-1-1. Yielded just 11 points, tying Georgetown 0–0 and losing finale to Navy 3–0. 1913—8-1-0. Scored 253 and shut out 5, losing only to passing attack of unbeaten Notre Dame 35–13. 1914—9-0-0. Beat Notre Dame 20–7 and outscored foes 219–20 to win 1st national championship. 1916—9-0-0. Outscored foes 235–36 behind HB Elmer Oliphant. 1917—7-1-0. Oliphant starred again as Cadets lost only to Notre Dame 7–2. 1920—7-2-0. Scored 318 and shut out 5, losing only to unbeaten Notre Dame and Navy. 1922—8-0-2. Charles Daly's last team shut out 7 as C Ed Garbisch starred; ties were with Yale 7–7 and Notre Dame 0–0. 1923—6-2-1. Lost only to Notre Dame and unbeaten Yale.1924—5-1-2. Lost only to unbeaten national champion Notre Dame 13–7 as Garbisch starred again. 1925—7-2-0. HB Harry Wilson led Army attack. 1926—7-1-1. Lost only to Notre Dame 7–0 and tied Navy 21–21. 1927—9-1-0. Shut out 6 and lost only to Yale 10–6 in Wilson's last year as leading Army runner. 1928—8-2-0. Chris Cagle ran and passed for 1,229 yards. 1930—8-1-1. Lost only to unbeaten Notre Dame 7–6 and shut out 7 behind T Jack Price; beat Navy 6–0 in New York City Charity Bowl. 1931—8-2-1. Price starred again. 1932—8-2-0. Shut out 8 behind line led by G Milt Summerfelt. 1933—9-1-0. Shut out 7, losing only to Notre Dame 13–12 in finale. 1934—7-3-0. No loss by more than 7 points as Jack Buckler led running attack. 1935—6-2-1. Won first 4 and last 2. 1937—7-2-0. Gar Davidson's last team lost only to Yale 15–7 and Notre Dame 7–0. 1938—8-2-0. Lost to Columbia 20–18 and Notre Dame 19–7. 1943—7-2-1. Shut out 5 as C Cas Myslinski starred; lost only to Notre Dame and Navy. 1944—9-0-0. Set NCAA scoring record of 56 points a game behind HB Glenn Davis and FB Felix (Doc) Blanchard and also led nation in rushing and in scoring defense while outscoring foes 504–35; beat Notre Dame 59–0 (worst defeat in Irish history) en route to national championship. 1945—9–0–0. Led nation in total offense, rushing and scoring average while outscoring foes 412–46 behind Heisman winner Blanchard (718 yards rushing), Davis (944 yards rushing), T Tex Coulter and G John Green; repeated as national champion. 1946—9–0–1. Red Blaik's 3rd consecutive unbeaten team saw record marred only by unbeaten national champion Notre Dame in epic 0–0 tie as Davis (712 yards rushing) won Heisman and other stars included Blanchard (613 yards rushing) and E Hank Foldberg. 1948—8–0–1. Gil Stephenson ran for 887 yards as soph as Cadets scored 294; tie was with Navy 21–21 in finale. 1949—9–0–0. Blaik's 5th unbeaten team outscored foes 354–68 behind QB Arnold Galiffa and won Lambert Trophy for 5th time in 6 years. 1950—8–1–0. Shut out 5 and led nation in scoring defense behind E Dan Foldberg, but was shocked by Navy 14–2 in finale. 1953—7–1–1. First winning team after "cribbing" scandal lost only to Northwestern in early season. 1954—7–2–0. Led nation in rushing as Tommy Bell ran for 1,020 yards; lost opener to South Carolina and finale to Navy 27–20. 1957—7–2–0. Soph Bob Anderson ran for 983 yards as Cadets lost only to Notre Dame 23–21 and Navy 14–0. 1958— 8–0–1. Blaik's last team led nation in passing behind QB Joe Caldwell and G Bob Novogratz while HB Pete Dawkins won Heisman; tie was with Pittsburgh 14–14. 1963—7–3–0. Won 3 by less than TD in Paul Dietzel's 2nd year. 1966—8–2–0. Tom Cahill's 1st team lost only to unbeaten Notre Dame and Tennessee as Steve Lindell passed for 1,035 yards and Terry Young caught 37 for 539 yards. 1967—8–2–0. Young caught 41 passes for 516 yards as Cadets lost only to Duke 10–7 and Navy 19–14. 1968—7–3–0. Charlie Jarvis ran for 1,110 yards as Cadets' losses were by total of only 12 points.

BOWL RECORD

New York City Charity 1–0–0.

CONFERENCE TITLES

None. Won Lambert Trophy in 1944, 1945, 1946, 1948, 1949, 1953, 1958.

TOP 10 AP & UPI RANKING

1944	1	1948	6	1954	7–7
1945	1	1949	4	1958	3–3
1946	2	1950	2–5		

MAJOR RIVALS

Army has played at least 15 games with Air Force (8–9–1), Boston College (10–9–0), Colgate (15–4–2), Columbia (14–4–3), Harvard (15–19–2), Holy Cross (11–3–1), Navy (37–40–7), Notre Dame (8–33–4), Pennsylvania (11–4–2), Penn State (10–13–2), Pittsburgh (6–19–2), Rutgers (12–5–0), Syracuse (9–7–0), Tufts (20–0–0), Villanova (18–3–0) and Yale (12–21–8).

COACHES

Dean of Army coaches was Earl (Red) Blaik with record of 121–33–10 for 1941–58, including 7 Lambert Trophy winners, 6 unbeaten teams and 2 national champions. He was national coach of the year in 1946. Charles Daly was 58–13–3 for 1913–16 and 1919–22 with 3 unbeaten teams. Other winning records for at least 4 years of coaching were by Herman Koehler, 20–11–3 for 1897–1900; Biff Jones, 30–8–2 for 1926–29; Gar Davidson, 35–11–1 for 1933–37; Paul Dietzel, 21–18–1 for 1962–65; and Tom Cahill, 40–39–2 for 1966–73. Cahill won national coach of the year honors in 1966.

MISCELLANEA

First game was 24–0 defeat by Navy in 1890 . . . first win was 10–6 over Fordham in 1891 . . . highest score was 90–0 over Bowdoin in 1920 . . . highest since W.W. II was 81–0 over Furman in 1955 . . . worst defeat was 77–7 by Nebraska in 1972 . . . longest unbeaten string of 32 in 1944–47 ended by Columbia 21–20 . . . winning streak of 25 in 1944–46 ended by Notre Dame 0–0 . . . longest winless string of 11 in 1970–71 broken with 16–13 win over Georgia Tech . . . Army has had 28 consensus All America players since 1898 . . . multi-year choices were Paul Bunker, T, 1901, and HB, 1902; Henry Torney, B, 1904–05; Elmer Oliphant, HB, 1916–17; Chris (Red) Cagle, HB, 1927–29; Glenn Davis, HB, and Felix (Doc) Blanchard, FB, 1944–46 . . . unanimous choices for one year were Casimir Myslinski, C, 1943; Dan Foldberg, E, 1950; and Pete Dawkins, HB, 1958 . . . other recent selections were Bob Anderson, B, 1957; and Bill Carpenter,

E, 1959 . . . Academic All America selections were Ralph Chesnauskas, E, 1955; James Kernan, C, 1957; Dawkins, HB, 1957–58; Don Usry, E, 1959; Sam Champi, DE, 1967; and Theodore Shadid, C, 1969 . . . Heisman Trophy winners were Blanchard, FB, 1945; Davis, HB, 1946; and Dawkins, HB, 1958 . . . Outland Trophy went to Joe Steffy, G, 1947 . . . Army ranks in top 20 in both all-time total victories and winning percentage.

Auburn (Tigers; Burnt Orange & Navy Blue) (SEC)

NOTABLE TEAMS

1893—3-0-2. Ties with Sewanee 14–14 and Georgia Tech 0–0. 1900— 4-0-1. Shut out 4; tie was with Georgia 0–0. 1904—5-0-0. Mike Donahue's 1st team blanked first 3 foes. 1907—6-2-1. Shut out first 5; lost to Sewanee 12–6 and Georgia 6–0. 1908—6-1-0. Lost to unbeaten LSU 10–2; blanked other foes 156–0. 1909—5-2-0. Lost successive games to Vanderbilt and Sewanee. 1910—6-1-0. Lost to Texas 9–0; blanked others 176–0. 1912— 6-1-1. Tied Vanderbilt 7–7 and lost to Georgia 12–6 in last 2 games. 1913 —8-0-0. Donahue's 2nd unbeaten team outscored foes 223–13. 1914— 8-0-1. Outscored foes 193–0, tying Georgia 0–0. 1915—6-2-0. Shut out first 6 before losing to Vanderbilt and Georgia Tech. 1916—6-2-0. Shut out 5 but again lost last 2. 1917—6-2-1. One of losses was to unbeaten national champion Georgia Tech. 1919—7-1-0. Yielded just 20 points behind line led by T Pete Bonner; lost to Vanderbilt 7–6. 1920—6-2-0. Shut out 5 as C.C. Warren and N.W. Caton starred on line. 1922—8-2-0. Donahue's last team blanked 5, losing only to Army and Georgia Tech. 1932—9-0-1. Scored 275 as HB Jimmy Hitchcock became Tigers' 1st consensus All America choice; tie was 20–20 with South Carolina in finale. 1935—8-2-0. Lost only to Tennessee 13–6 and LSU 6–0. 1936—7-2-1. Walter Gilbert and Joel Eaves starred on line; tied Villanova 7–7 in Bacardi Bowl in Cuba. 1937— 5-2-3. Shut out 6 while losing only to Rice 13–7 and LSU 9–7; beat Michigan St. in Orange Bowl 6–0. 1953—7-2-1. Frank D'Agostino and Jim Pyburn starred on line in Shug Jordan's 3rd year; lost to Texas Tech in Gator Bowl 35–13. 1954—7-3-0. Each loss by 1 TD and Joe Childress ran for 836 yards; won last 6 before beating Baylor in Gator Bowl 33–13. 1955—8-1-1. Fob James ran for 879 yards as Tigers lost only to Tulane 27–13; lost to Vanderbilt in Gator Bowl 25–13. 1956—7-3-0. Soph RB Tommy Lorino starred along with senior QB Howell Tubbs. 1957—10-0-0. Led nation in total defense, rushing defense and scoring defense while outscoring foes 207–28 as Jimmy Phillips starred at end; won SEC and earned share of national championship. 1958—9–0–1. Again led nation in total defense and rushing defense behind T Zeke Smith and LB Jackie Burkett; tie was with Georgia Tech 7–7. 1959—7–3–0. Lost 2 by total of 4 points as Smith and Burkett starred again. 1960—8–2–0. Lost only to Tennessee 10–3 in opener and Alabama 3–0 in finale as Ken Rice starred at T and Ed Dyas led nation with 13 FGs. 1963—9–1–0. Jimmy Sidle ran for 1,006 yards and passed for 706 and Tucker Frederickson starred at FB as Tigers lost only to Mississippi St. 13–10; lost to Nebraska in Orange Bowl 13–7. 1969—8–2–0. Scored 363 as soph Pat Sullivan passed for 1,686 yards while Buddy McClinton intercepted 9 passes; lost to Houston in Bluebonnet Bowl 36–7. 1970—8–2–0. Scored 355 as Sullivan passed for 2,586 yards and led nation in total offense (2,856 yards) while DB Larry Willingham sparked defense; beat Mississippi in Gator Bowl 35–28. 1971—9–1–0. Heisman winner Sullivan passed for 2,012 yards and Terry Beasley caught 55 for 12 TDs as Tigers scored 313 and lost only to unbeaten Alabama 31–7 in finale; lost to Oklahoma in Sugar Bowl 40–22. 1972—9–1–0. Terry Henley ran for 843 yards as Tigers lost only to LSU 35–7; beat Colorado in Gator Bowl 24–3. 1974—9–2–0. Secdrick McIntyre ran for 839 yards and Phil Gargis for 687 while LB Ken Bernich sparked defense as team lost only to Florida and unbeaten Alabama; beat Texas in Gator Bowl 27–3. 1979—8–3–0. James Brooks ran for 1,208 yards and Joe Cribbs for 1,120 as Tigers scored 330. 1982—8–3–0. Lost 2 by less than FG as Bo Jackson ran for 829 yards and David King intercepted 6 passes; beat Boston College in Tangerine Bowl 33–26. 1983—10–1–0. Jackson ran for 1,213 yards as soph and scored 14 TDs as Tigers lost only to unbeaten Texas 20–7 in 2nd game; won SEC and beat Michigan in Sugar Bowl 9–7.

BOWL RECORD

Bacardi 0–0–1; Bluebonnet 0–1–0; Gator 4–2–0; Liberty 0–1–0; Orange 1–1–0; Sugar 1–1–0; Sun 1–1–0; Tangerine 1–0–0.

CONFERENCE TITLES

Southeastern 1957, 1983.

TOP 10 AP & UPI RANKING

1955	10–8	1963	5–6	1972	5–7
1957	1–2	1970	10–9	1974	8–6
1958	4–4	1971	U–5	1983	3–3

MAJOR RIVALS

Auburn has played at least 15 games with Alabama (19–28–1), Birmingham-Southern (13–3–0), Chattanooga (18–0–0), Clemson (31–11–2), Florida (34–24–2), Georgia (39–41–7), Georgia Tech (43–39–4), Howard (23–0–1), Kentucky (18–5–1), LSU (9–14–1), Mississippi St. (39–16–2), Tennessee (19–15–1) and Vanderbilt (8–19–1).

COACHES

Dean of Auburn coaches was Ralph (Shug) Jordan with record of 176–83–6 for 1951–75, including 1 SEC and national champion, 12 bowl teams and 2 unbeaten teams. Mike Donahue had record of 89–26–4 for 1908–22 with 2 unbeaten teams. Other winning records for at least 3 years of coaching were by John Heisman, 12–4–2 for 1895–99; Chet Wynne, 22–15–2 for 1930–33 with 1 unbeaten team; Jack Meagher, 48–37–10 for 1934–42 with 2 bowl teams; Doug Barfield, 29–25–1 for 1976–80; and Pat Dye, 25–10–0 for 1981–83 with 1 conference title and 2 bowl champions.

MISCELLANEA

First game was 10–0 win over Georgia in 1892 . . . highest score was 94–0 over Georgia Tech in 1894 . . . highest since 1900 was 92–0 over Mercer in 1916 . . . highest since W.W. II was 63–14 over Florida in 1970 . . . biggest margin of victory since W.W. II was 57–0 over Wake Forest in 1969 . . . worst defeat was 64–0 by North Carolina in 1892 . . . worst since 1900 was 68–7 (also highest total against Tigers) by Georgia Tech in 1917 . . . worst since W.W. II was 55–0 by Alabama in 1948 . . . longest unbeaten string of 24 in 1956–58 ended by Tennessee 3–0 in 1959 opener . . . unbeaten string of 23 in 1913–15 ended by Vanderbilt 17–0 . . . longest winless string of 16 in 1926–28 broken with 25–6 win over Howard . . . consensus All America players were Jimmy Hitchcock, B, 1932; Jimmy Phillips, E, 1957; Zeke Smith, G, 1958; Ken Rice, T, 1960; Tucker Frederickson, B, 1964; Buddy McClinton, DB, 1969; Larry Willingham, DB, 1970; Pat Sullivan, QB, and Terry Beasley, E, 1971; Ken Bernich, LB, 1974; and Bo Jackson, RB, 1983 . . . Academic All America choices were Phillips, E, 1957; Jackie

Burkett, C, 1959; Ed Dyas, B, 1960; Bill Cody, LB, 1965; McClinton, DB, 1969; Bobby Davis, LB, 1974; Chuck Fletcher, DT, 1975; and Chris Vacarella, RB, 1976 . . . Heisman Trophy went to Pat Sullivan, QB, in 1971 . . . Outland Trophy went to Zeke Smith, G, in 1958.

Baylor (Bears; Green & Gold) (Southwest)

NOTABLE TEAMS

1910—6-1-1. Loss was forfeit to Texas. 1915—7-1-0. Shut out 6 and won 1st Southwest Conference title; lost only to Sewanee 16-3. 1916—9-1-0. Outscored foes 314-27, losing only to Texas A&M 3-0. 1917—6-2-1. Shut out 7; one of losses was to unbeaten Texas A&M 7-0. 1921—8-3-0. Shut out 5 behind T Russell Blailock and Wesley Bradshaw scored 119 points (including 14 TDs and 6 FGs). 1922—8-3-0. Won 8 of first 9. 1923—5-1-2. Lost only to unbeaten SMU in finale 16-0. 1924—7-2-1. Lost close ones to Austin College 7-3 and Central Oklahoma 13-6 but won 3rd SWC title. 1928—8-2-0. Virgil Gilliland starred at HB as Bears lost only to Arkansas and Texas 6-0. 1935—8-3-0. Shut out 6. 1937—7-3-0. No loss by more than a TD. 1938—7-2-1. Lost only to unbeaten national champion TCU and SMU behind QB Billy Patterson and E Sam Boyd. 1939—7-3-0. Lost only to SMU in last 5. 1949—8-2-0. Adrian Burk led nation in passing (1,428 yards and 14 TDs) and J.D. Ison caught 42 for 457 yards as Bears lost only to Texas and Rice. 1950—7-3-0. George Sauer's 1st team lost only to Texas 27-20 in last 5. 1951—8-1-1. Lost only to TCU 20-7 as Larry Isbell passed for 1,430 yards while Robert Reid had 11 interceptions and Red Donaldson 7; lost to unbeaten Georgia Tech in Orange Bowl 17-14. 1953—7-3-0. L.G. Dupre was top runner as Bears won first 6. 1954—7-3-0. Del Shofner was star runner as Bears lost only to Rice 20-14 in last 6; lost to Auburn in Gator Bowl 33-13. 1956—8-2-0. Lost only to unbeaten Texas A&M 19-13 and to TCU 7-6 as G Bill Glass starred; upset unbeaten Tennessee in Sugar Bowl 13-7. 1960—8-2-0. FB Ronnie Bull starred as Bears lost only to TCU 14-6 and Texas 12-7; lost to Florida in Gator Bowl 13-12. 1963—7-3-0. Don Trull led nation's passers for 2nd season in row with 2,157 yards and Lawrence Elkins caught 70 for 873 yards and 8 TDs; beat LSU in Bluebonnet Bowl 14-7. 1974—8-3-0. Steve Beaird ran for 1,104 yards and 16 TDs as Bears won first SWC title in 50 years; lost to Penn State in Cotton Bowl 41-20. 1980—10-1-0. Mike Singletary anchored defense while Walter Abercrombie ran for 1,187 yards and Dennis Gentry for

883 as Bears scored 315 and lost only to San Jose St. 30–22; lost to Alabama in Cotton Bowl 30–2.

BOWL RECORD

Bluebonnet 1–1–0; Cotton 0–2–0; Dixie 1–0–0; Gator 0–2–0; Gotham 1–0–0; Orange 0–1–0; Peach 1–0–0; Sugar 1–0–0.

CONFERENCE TITLES

Southwest 1915*, 1922, 1924, 1974, 1980.

TOP 10 AP & UPI RANKING

1951	9–9

MAJOR RIVALS

Baylor has played at least 15 games with Arkansas (30–30–2), Houston (7–8–1), Rice (34–28–2), SMU (25–34–7), Southwestern (13–6–1), TCU (40–43–8), Texas (15–54–4), Texas A&M (27–42–8), Texas Tech (23–17–1) and Trinity (15–6–1).

COACHES

Dean of Baylor coaches was Morley Jennings with record of 83–60–6 for 1926–40. Grant Teaff had record of 67–64–5 for 1972–83 with 2 conference titles and 4 bowl teams. He was national coach of the year in 1974. Other top records were by C.P. Mosley, 30–16–4 for 1914–19 with one conference title; Frank Bridgers, 35–18–6 for 1920–25 with 2 conference titles; and George Sauer, 38–21–3 for 1950–55 with 2 bowl teams.

MISCELLANEA

First game was 33–0 loss to Texas A&M in 1899 . . . first win was 6–0 over Toby's same year . . . first win over college opponent was 11–0 over Austin College in 1900 . . . highest score was 103–0 over Simmons in 1917 . . . highest since W.W. II was 55–0 over Army in 1979 . . . worst defeat was 89–0 by LSU in 1908 . . . worst since W.W. II was 63–8 by LSU in 1969 . . . longest winning streak of 10 in 1936–37 ended by Texas 9–6 . . . longest losing string of 11 in 1969–70 broken with 10–7 win over Army . . . consensus All America players were Barton Koch, G, 1930; Bill Glass, G, 1956; Lawrence Elkins, E, B, 1963–64; Gary Green, DB, 1976; and Mike

Singletary, LB, 1979–80 . . . Academic All America choices were Ronnie Bull, B, 1961; Don Trull, B, 1962–63; and Cris Quinn, DE, 1976.

Boston College (Eagles; Maroon & Gold) (Independent)

NOTABLE TEAMS

1896—5–2–0. Won 5 of last 6. 1899—8–1–1. Lost to Brown 18–0; shut out all others, tying Bates 0–0. 1916—6–2–0. Lost to Dartmouth and Tufts. 1917—6–2–0. Lost close ones to Brown 7–2 and Army 14–7. 1918—5–2–0. Lost successive games to Fordham 14–0 and Harvard 14–6. 1920—8–0–0. Outscored foes 161–16, shutting out 6, as E Luke Urban became Eagles' 1st consensus All America player. 1922—6–2–1. Unbeaten in last 5. 1923— 7–1–1. Shut out 7, losing only to Marquette 7–6. 1925—6–2–0. Lost successive games to West Virginia and West Virginia Wesleyan. 1926—6–0–2. Frank Cavanaugh's 2nd unbeaten team shut out 5 and Al Weston scored 12 TDs; ties were with Haskell 21–21 and Holy Cross 0–0. 1928—9–0–0. Joe McKenney's 1st team outscored foes 263–39 as Weston starred. 1929— 7–2–1. Lost to Fordham 7–6 and Marquette. 1933—8–1–0. Shut out 6, losing only to Fordham (32–6). 1936—6–1–2. Lost only to Temple 14–0 in 2nd game. 1938—6–1–2. Lost finale to Holy Cross 29–7. 1939—9–1–0. Frank Leahy's 1st team shut out 5 and lost only to Florida 7–0; lost to Clemson in Cotton Bowl 6–3. 1940—10–0–0. Shut out 6 and led nation in scoring (outscored foes 320–52) behind Mike Holovak (11 TDs) and E Gene Goodreault; beat undefeated Tennessee in Sugar Bowl 19–13. 1941 —7–3–0. Denny Myers's 1st team lost only to Tennessee 14–7 in last 7 games. 1942—8–1–0. Shut out 5 and led nation in rushing defense while Holovak ran for 893 yards; lost finale to Holy Cross 55–12, then lost to Alabama in Orange Bowl 37–21. 1943—4–0–1. Tied Harvard 6–6 in only major game in war-curtailed schedule. 1954—8–1–0. Ed DeSilva ran for 635 yards as Eagles lost only to Xavier (O.) 19–14. 1957—7–2–0. Lost opener to Navy and finale to Holy Cross; won 4 by TD or less. 1958—7–3–0. Lost only to Clemson in last 7. 1962—8–2–0. Jack Concannon passed for 1,452 yards and 15 TDs and Art Graham caught 41 for 823 yards; won last 5. 1970 —8–2–0. Joe Yukica's 3rd team scored 307 as Fred Willis ran for 1,007 yards and 11 TDs and Red Harris passed for 1,595 yards. 1971—9–2–0. Tom Bougus ran for 1,058 yards; won last 5 after losses to West Virginia and Texas Tech. 1974—8–3–0. Scored 375 as Keith Barnette ran for 1,097 yards and scored 22 TDs and Mike Kruczek passed for 1,275 yards. 1976—8–3–0. Glen Capriola ran for 1,003 yards and Tim Moorman kicked 12 FGs and was perfect on 29 extra points. 1982—8–2–1. Jack Bicknell's 2nd team lost only to West Virginia 20–13 and national champion Penn State; lost to Auburn in Tangerine Bowl 33–26. 1983—9–2–0. Scored 333 as Doug Flutie passed for 2,724 yards and Brian Brennan caught 67 for 1,168 yards; lost to West Virginia and Syracuse, then to Notre Dame in Liberty Bowl, 19–18.

BOWL RECORD

Cotton 0–1–0; Liberty 0–1–0; Orange 0–1–0; Sugar 1–0–0; Tangerine 0–1–0.

CONFERENCE TITLES

None. Won Lambert Trophy 1942, 1983.

TOP 10 AP & UPI RANKING

1940	5
1942	8

MAJOR RIVALS

BC has played at least 15 games with Army (9–10–0), Boston University (27–4–1), Detroit (12–7–0), Fordham (14–11–2), Georgetown (11–5–1), Holy Cross (45–31–3), Massachusetts (16–5–0), Navy (10–9–0), St. Anselm's (11–3–3), Syracuse (10–14–0), Temple (11–3–2) and Villanova (29–15–1).

COACHES

Dean of BC coaches was Joe Yukica with record of 68–37–0 for 1968–77. Frank Cavanaugh was 48–14–5 for 1919–26 with 2 unbeaten teams. Joe McKenney was 44–18–3 for 1928–34 with 1 unbeaten team. Frank Leahy, 20–2–0 for 1939–40 at BC, ranks 2nd in all-time winning percentage for college coaches; Gil Dobie, 16–6–5 for 1936–38 at BC, ranks in top 15 in all-time winning percentage and in top 20 in total victories. Other top records were by Dennis Myers, 35–27–4 for 1941–42 and 1946–50 with 1 bowl team; Mike Holovak, 49–29–3 for 1951–59; Jim Miller, 34–24–0 for 1962–67; and Jack Bicknell, 22–12–1 for 1981–83 with 2 bowl teams.

MISCELLANEA

First game was 4–0 win over St. John's Institute in 1893 . . . first win over college foe was 10–6 over Boston University in same year . . . highest score was 78–0 over St. Anselm's in 1941 . . . highest since W.W. II was 76–0 over Holy Cross in 1949 . . . worst defeat was 55–0 by Colby in 1912 . . . worst since W.W. II was 54–0 by Mississippi in 1950 . . . highest ever against Eagles was 58–25 by Army in 1968 . . . longest unbeaten streak of 17 in 1927–29 ended by Fordham 7–6 . . . longest winless string of 18 in 1910–12 broken with 13–0 win over Connecticut . . . consensus All America players were Luke Urban, E, 1920; Gene Goodreault, E, 1940; and Mike Holovak, B, 1942 . . . BC has had no Academic All America first stringers.

Brigham Young (Cougars; Royal Blue & White) (WAC)

NOTABLE TEAMS

1932—8–1–0. Lost to Utah 29–0 but outscored others 188–21. 1966—8–2–0. Virgil Carter led nation in total offense (2,545 yards) as Phil Odle caught 60 passes for 920 yards and John Ogden ran for 906. 1976—9–2–0. LaVell Edwards's 5th team scored 352 and led nation in passing as Gifford Nielsen threw for 3,192 yards and 29 TDs and Todd Christensen caught 51 for 510 yards; won WAC but lost to Oklahoma St. in Tangerine Bowl 49–21. 1977—9–2–0. Again led nation in passing and scored 433 as Marc Wilson threw for 2,418 yards and 24 TDs and Christensen caught 50 for 603 yards. 1978—9–3–0. Mike Chronister caught 52 passes for 850 yards and Cougars lost only to Utah 23–22 in last 7; won 3rd straight WAC title but lost to Navy 23–16 in inaugural Holiday Bowl. 1979—11–0–0. Led nation in total offense, passing and scoring average (40.6) as Wilson (Cougars' 1st consensus All America), led in total offense (3,580 yards) and passed for 3,720 yards and 29 TDs; lost to Indiana in Holiday Bowl 38–37. 1980—11–1–0. Led nation again in same 3 offensive categories (averaging 46.7 per game on 560 points) as Jim McMahon led in total offense (4,627 yards) and passing (4,571 yards and 47 TDs) and Scott Phillips caught 60 for 689 yards; lost only to New Mexico, 25–21 in opener, but beat SMU in Holiday Bowl 46–45. 1981—10–2–0. Scored 465 and led nation in passing and scoring as McMahon again led in total offense (3,458 yards) and passing (3,555 yards and 30 TDs) while TE Gordon Hudson caught 67 for 960 yards and 10 TDs; beat Washington St. in Holiday Bowl 38–36. 1982—8–3–0. Lost none by more than 3 points (including 17–14 loss to unbeaten Georgia) as Steve Young passed for 3,100 yards and 18 TDs and Hudson caught 67 for 928 yards; lost to Ohio State in Holiday Bowl 47–17. 1983—10–1–0. Led nation in total offense and passing while scoring 484 as Young passed for 3,902 yards and 33 TDs and led nation in total offense (4,346 yards) and passing efficiency while Casey Tiumalu caught 60 for 583 yards; won 8th straight WAC title and beat Missouri in Holiday Bowl 21–17.

BOWL RECORD

Fiesta 0–1–0; Holiday 3–3–0; Tangerine 0–1–0.

CONFERENCE TITLES

Western Athletic 1965, 1974, 1976*, 1977*, 1978, 1979, 1980, 1981, 1982, 1983.

TOP 10 AP & UPI RANKING

1983	7–7

MAJOR RIVALS

BYU has played at least 15 games with Arizona (8–10–1), Arizona St. (5–17–0), Colorado St. (21–22–3), Denver (7–15–0), Montana St. (10–7–0), New Mexico (21–11–1), Texas-El Paso (16–5–1), Utah (16–38–4), Utah St. (24–32–3), Western State (20–0–0) and Wyoming (25–26–3).

COACHES

Best record was by LaVell Edwards with 105–37–1 for 1972–83, including 9 conference titles, 8 bowl teams and 1 team unbeaten in regular season. Edwards ranks in top 10 in winning percentage among active coaches. G. Ott Romney was 42–31–5 for 1928–36 and Eddie Kimball was 34–32–8 for 1937–48. Tom Hudspeth was 39–42–1 for 1964–71 with 1 conference title.

MISCELLANEA

First game was 42–3 defeat by Utah St. in 1922 . . . first win was 7–0 over Wyoming same year . . . highest score was 83–7 over Texas-El Paso in 1980 . . . worst defeat was 56–6 by Denver in 1951 . . . highest against Cougars was 58–34 by Denver in 1956 . . . longest winning streak of 17 in 1980–81 ended by Nevada-Las Vegas 45–41 . . . longest winless string of 14 in 1955–56 broken with 33–12 win over New Mexico . . . consensus All America choices were Marc Wilson, QB, 1979; Nick Eyre, OL, 1980; Jim McMahon, QB, 1981; Gordon Hudson, TE, 1982–83; and Steve Young, QB, 1983 . . . Academic All America players were Steve Stratton, RB, 1973; Scott Phillips, RB, 1980; and Dan Platter, WR, 1981.

Brown (Bruins, Bears; Brown, Cardinal & White) (Ivy)

NOTABLE TEAMS

1907—7–3–0. Shut out 6. 1909—7–3–0. Shut out 5 behind E Adrian Regnier. 1910—7–2–1. Shut out 6 and B Earl Sprackling led offense. 1915—5–3–1. Invited to Rose Bowl but lost to unbeaten Washington St. 14–0. 1916—8–1–0. Shut out 6 and B Fritz Pollard led offense; loss was to Colgate 28–0 in finale. 1917—8–2–0. Lost successive games to Syracuse 6–0 and USN Reserve. 1922—6–2–1. Won first 5. 1926—9–0–1. D.O. McLaughry's 1st team, the famous 60-minute "iron men," shut out 7; tie was with Colgate 10–10 in finale. 1928—8–1–0. Won last 6 after 32–14 loss to Yale. 1931—7–3–0. Won first 5; lost 2 by TD or less. 1932—7–1–0. Yielded only 21 points before losing finale to unbeaten, unscored-on Colgate 21–0. 1948—7–2–0. Scored in double figures in all, losing only to Yale and Harvard. 1949—8–1–0. Rip Engle's last team scored 263, losing only to Princeton 27–14 in 3rd game. 1954—6–2–1. Scored in double figures in all but lost close ones to Yale 26–24 and Temple 19–14. 1975—6–2–1. Bob Farnham led nation in pass receiving with 56 catches for 701 yards. 1976—8–1–0. Won 3 by TD or less and lost only to Pennsylvania 7–6; got share of 1st modern Ivy title. 1977—7–2–0. Won last 5 after losses to Yale 10–9 and Penn 14–7.

BOWL RECORD

Rose 0–1–0.

CONFERENCE TITLES

Ivy (unofficial) 1916, 1926, 1932. Ivy 1976*.

TOP 10 AP & UPI RANKING

None.

MAJOR RIVALS

Brown has played at least 15 games with Colby (15–1–0), Colgate (19–25–7), Columbia (26–20–2), Cornell (14–16–1), Dartmouth (16–42–1), Harvard (21–60–2), Holy Cross (18–21–2), New Hampshire (14–1–0), Pennsylvania (12–39–1), Princeton (14–36–0), Rhode Island (56–11–2), Syracuse (3–9–3), Tufts (25–2–0), Vermont (15–0–1) and Yale (20–64–4).

COACHES

Dean of Brown coaches was E.N. Robinson with record of 140–82–12 for 1898–1901, 1904–07 and 1910–25, including a Rose Bowl team. D.O. McLaughry had a record of 76–58–5 for 1926–40, including one unbeaten team. John Anderson had record of 60–39–3 for 1973–83, with one Ivy title; and C.A. (Rip) Engle was 28–20–4 for 1944–49.

MISCELLANEA

First game (informal) was loss to Amherst in 1878 . . . first win was 70–0 over Providence H.S. in 1886 . . . first formal game was 14–0 win over Pawtucket C.C. in 1889 . . . first win over college foe was 16–0 over Tufts in 1889 . . . highest score was 70–0 over Providence H.S. in 1886 and over Colby in 1905 . . . highest since W.W. II was 55–6 over Rhode Island in 1947 and 55–13 over same team in 1950 . . . worst defeat was 62–0 by Dartmouth in 1903 . . . worst since W.W. II was 52–0 by Princeton in 1961 . . . highest against Bruins since W.W. II was 54–21 by Princeton in 1960 . . . longest unbeaten string of 14 in 1925–27 ended by Penn 14–6 . . . longest losing string of 12 in 1966–67 broken with 7–0 win over Colgate . . . consensus All America players were Thomas Barry, B, 1902; John Mayhew, B, 1906; Adrian Regnier, E, 1909; Earl Sprackling, B, 1910; George Crowther, B, 1912; and Fritz Pollard, B, 1916 . . . Academic All America choices were Travis Holcombe, OG, 1981; and Dave Folsom, DB, 1982.

California (Golden Bears; Blue & Gold) (Pacific-10)

NOTABLE TEAMS

1885—4–0–1. Unscored on; tie was 0–0 with Wasps. 1886—6–2–1. Lost to Orions 12–10 and Reliance 7–4. 1888—6–1–0. Lost to Volunteers 10–6; shut out all others. 1893—5–1–1. Lost to Reliance Club 16–4 and tied Stanford 6–6 in last 2 games. 1896—6–2–2. Shut out 5. 1898—8–0–2. Shut out all but Olympic Club (5–5). 1899—7–1–1. Shut out 8, losing only to Carlisle Indians 2–0 in finale. 1901—9–0–1. Shut out 8; tie was 0–0 with Reliance in opener. 1902—8–0–0. Outscored foes 168–12, shutting out 7. 1903—6–1–2. Shut out 7, losing only to Nevada 6–2. 1904—6–1–1. Shut out first 6 before losing to Stanford 18–0 and tying Washington 6–6. 1905 —4–1–2. Shut out first 6 but lost finale to unbeaten Stanford 12–5. 1909— 12–3–1. James Schaeffer's 1st team lost 3 by total of 11 points. 1910— 12–0–2. Shut out 9; ties were both with Victoria All Stars as team continued to play mostly club foes. 1911—11–2–1. Both losses were to Victoria All Stars. 1912—10–2–1. Lost both to Australian Waratahs. 1914—14–1–0. Lost only to Stanford 26–8 as only 5 games played with college opponents. 1918—7–2–0. Lost to 2 of 5 service teams played but won 1st Pacific Coast Conference title. 1919—6–2–1. Losses only to Washington St. and Washington. 1920—8–0–0. Outscored foes 482–14 en route to national championship; beat undefeated Ohio State in Rose Bowl 28–0. 1921—9–0–0. Andy Smith's 2nd straight unbeaten team outscored foes 312–33 behind E Brick Muller and T Dan McMillan (Bears' 1st All America choices); tied unbeaten Washington & Jefferson in Rose Bowl 0–0. 1922—9–0–0. Muller led team to 3rd straight PCC title as foes were outscored 398–34. 1923—9–0–1. Shut out 9, tying Nevada 0–0. 1924—8–0–2. Smith's 5th consecutive unbeaten team tied Washington 7–7 and Stanford 20–20 as C Edwin Horrell starred. 1927—7–3–0. Lost 2 by TD or less. 1928—6–1–2. Shut out 6, losing only to Olympic Club 12–0; lost to unbeaten Georgia Tech in Rose Bowl 8–7. 1929—7–1–1. Lost only to Stanford in finale 21–6. 1931—8–2–0. Won last 5 after losses to St. Mary's and Southern California. 1935—9–1–0. Stub Allison's 1st team shut out 7 behind T Larry Lutz, losing only to Stanford 13–0 in finale. 1937—9–0–1. Shut out 6, including 0–0 tie with Washington as B Sam Chapman led offense; beat undefeated Alabama in Rose Bowl 13–0 for Tide's first bowl defeat in 5 trips. 1938—10–1–0. Shut out 5 and lost only to USC 13–7; won 3rd PCC title behind B Vic Bottari. 1947— 9–1–0. Pappy Waldorf's 1st team scored 275 and lost only to USC (39–14). 1948—10–

0–0. Scored 291 behind B Jackie Jensen; lost to Northwestern in Rose Bowl 20–14. 1949—10–0–0. Scored 319 as Rod Franz starred at G; lost to Ohio State in Rose Bowl 17–14. 1950—9–0–1. Johnny Olszewski ran for 950 yards and Pete Schabarum scored 11 TDs as Bears beat all but Stanford (7–7 in finale); lost to Michigan in Rose Bowl 14–6. 1951—8–2–0. Scored 307 behind G Les Richter but lost to USC and UCLA. 1952—7–3–0. Olszewski ran for 845 yards; won first 5. 1958—7–3–0. Lost only to Oregon St. 14–8 in last 8 as Joe Kapp (1,231 yards total offense) led Bears to PCC title; lost to Iowa in Rose Bowl 38–12. 1975—8–3–0. Scored 330 as Joe Roth passed for 1,880 yards and Chuck Muncie led running attack; won 8 of last 9 to share PAC-8 title.

BOWL RECORD

Garden State 0–1–0; Rose 2–5–1.

TOP 10 AP & UPI RANKING

1937	2
1948	4
1949	3
1950	5–4

CONFERENCE TITLES

Pacific Coast 1918, 1920, 1921, 1922, 1923, 1928*, 1935*, 1937, 1938*, 1948*, 1949, 1950, 1958. Pacific 8 1975*.

MAJOR RIVALS

California has played at least 15 games with Nevada-Reno (21–1–1), Oregon (31–17–2), Oregon St. (25–15–0), St. Mary's (28–8–2), San Jose St. (19–3–0), Santa Clara (17–5–0), Southern California (23–44–4), Stanford (36–40–10), UCLA (19–34–1), Washington (32–30–4) and Washington St. (32–13–4).

COACHES

Leading Cal coaches were Andy Smith, 74–16–7 for 1916–25 with 5 conference titles, 2 Rose Bowl teams, 5 unbeaten teams and 1 national champion; and James Schaeffer, 73–16–8 for 1909–15 with 1 unbeaten team. Lynn (Pappy) Waldorf was 67–32–4 for 1947–56, with 3 conference titles, 3 Rose Bowl teams and 3 unbeaten teams. Other winning records were by Nibs

Price, 27–17–3 for 1926–30 with 1 Rose Bowl team; Bill Ingram, 27–14–4 for 1931–34; Stub Allison, 58–42–2 for 1935–44 with 3 conference titles and 1 unbeaten Rose Bowl team; and Mike White, 35–30–1 for 1972–77 with 1 conference title.

MISCELLANEA

First game was 7–4 loss to Phoenix Club in 1882 . . . first game with college opponent was 14–10 loss to Stanford in 1892 (spring game) . . . first win over college foe was 51–0 over St. Mary's in 1898 . . . highest score was 127–0 over St. Mary's in 1920 . . . highest since W.W. II was 60–14 over Montana in 1947 . . . biggest margin since W.W. II was 52–3 over San Jose St. in 1977 . . . worst defeat was 74–0 by USC in 1930 . . . worst since W.W. II was 66–0 by Alabama in 1973 . . . longest unbeaten string of 50 in 1920–25 ended by Olympic Club 15–0 . . . unbeaten string of 18 in 1937–38 ended by USC 13–7 . . . 14-game winning streak in 1947–48 ended by Northwestern 20–14 in Rose Bowl . . . longest losing string of 8 in 1962 broken with 15–8 win over Iowa St. in 1963 opener . . . Cal has had 17 consensus All America players since 1921 . . . repeaters were Brick Muller, E, 1921–22 and Les Richter, G, 1950–51 . . . others selected since W.W. II were Jackie Jensen, B, 1948; Rod Franz, G, 1949; Ed White, MG, 1968; Sherman White, DT, 1971; Steve Bartkowski, QB, 1974; Chuck Muncie, RB, and Steve Rivera, E, 1975; and Ron Rivera, LB, 1983 . . . Academic All America choices were Bob Crittenden, MG, 1967; Robert Richards, OT, 1970; and Harvey Salem, OT, 1982.

Clemson (Tigers; Orange & Purple) (ACC)

NOTABLE TEAMS

1900—6–0–0. John Heisman's first Tiger team outscored foes 222–10. 1902 —6–1–0. Lost only to South Carolina 12–6. 1903—4–1–1. Heisman's last team lost only to North Carolina 11–6. 1906—4–0–3. Shut out all but Auburn (6–4); all ties scoreless. 1917—6–2–0. Scored in double figures except in losses. 1918—5–2–0. Lost 1 to service team. 1919—6–2–2. Shut out 5 behind guards L.M. Lightsey and R.C. Potts. 1928—8–3–0. Shut out 7. 1929—8–3–0. Won first 6 behind TB Goat McMillan. 1930—8–2–0. Again won first 6 as Maxcy Welch scored 10 TDs. 1938—7–1–1. Won last 5 after loss to unbeaten Tennessee 20–7 and tie with VMI 7–7. 1939— 8–1–0. Jess Neely's last team lost only to Tulane 7–6 behind backs Banks

McFadden and Charlie Timmons; beat Boston College in Cotton Bowl 6–3. 1940—6–2–1. Frank Howard's 1st team won first 5 and took Southern Conference title behind E Joe Blalock. 1941—7–2–0. Scored 233 behind Timmons and Blalock. 1948—10–0–0. Outscored foes 250–53 as Bobby Gage starred at TB and S and Ray Mathews scored 13 TDs; won Southern Conference and beat Missouri in Gator Bowl 24–23. 1950—8–0–1. Scored 329 as Fred Cone ran for 845 yards and 15 TDs; tied South Carolina 14–14 and beat undefeated Miami (Fla.) in Orange Bowl 15–14. 1951—7–2–0. Billy Hair passed for 1,004 yards and ran for 698 and Glenn Smith caught 39 passes for 632 yards while Fred Knoebel intercepted 7 passes; lost to Miami (Fla.) in Gator Bowl 14–0. 1955—7–3–0. Joel Wells ran for 782 yards. 1956—7–1–2. Won 1st Atlantic Coast Conference title as Wells ran for 803 yards; lost only to Miami (Fla.) 21–0, then to Colorado in Orange Bowl 27–21. 1957—7–3–0. Harvey White passed for 841 yards; lost only to Duke 7–6 in last 7. 1958—8–2–0. White and Doug Cline led Tigers to ACC title; lost to unbeaten national champion LSU in Sugar Bowl 7–0. 1959 —8–2–0. Won 3rd ACC title in 4 years as T Lou Cordileone starred and Bill Mathis scored 11 TDs; beat TCU in Bluebonnet Bowl 23–7. 1977—8–2–1. Steve Fuller passed for 1,655 yards and Jerry Butler caught 47 for 824 yards as Tigers lost only to Maryland 21–14 and Notre Dame 21–17; lost to Pittsburgh in Gator Bowl 34–3. 1978—10–1–0. Scored 351 as Fuller passed for 1,515 yards, Butler caught 58 for 908 yards and Lester Brown ran for 1,022 yards and 17 TDs; lost only to Georgia 12–0 in 2nd game, and beat Ohio State in Gator Bowl 17–15. 1979—8–3–0. Danny Ford's 1st team lost 2 by less than TD as DL Jim Stuckey anchored defense; lost to Baylor in Peach Bowl 24–18. 1981—11–0–0. Scored 316 as Homer Jordan passed for 1,630 yards and Perry Tuttle caught 52 for 883 yards while LB Jeff Davis and DB Terry Kinard led defense; beat Nebraska in Orange Bowl 22–15 to nail down 1st national championship. 1982—9–1–1. Won 2nd straight ACC title as Kinard starred again but lost to unbeaten Georgia 13–7 and tied Boston College 17–17. 1983—9–1–1. Scored 338 as Mike Eppley passed for 1,410 yards and 13 TDs; ineligible for bowl 2nd straight year.

BOWL RECORD

Bluebonnet 1–0–0; Cotton 1–0–0; Gator 2–2–0; Orange 2–1–0; Peach 0–1–0; Sugar 0–1–0.

CONFERENCE TITLES

Southern 1940, 1948. Atlantic Coast 1956, 1958, 1959, 1965*, 1966, 1967, 1978, 1981, 1982.

TOP 10 AP & UPI RANKING

1950	10–U
1978	6–7
1981	1–1
1982	8–U

MAJOR RIVALS

Clemson has played at least 15 games with Auburn (11–31–2), The Citadel (27–5–1), Davidson (11–5–4), Duke (15–12–1), Furman (34–10–4), Georgia (14–34–4), Georgia Tech (12–34–2), Maryland (14–17–1), North Carolina (19–12–1), N.C. State (33–18–1), Presbyterian (32–3–4), South Carolina (48–30–3), Tennessee (5–11–2), Virginia (23–0–0), Virginia Tech (12–6–1) and Wake Forest (37–11–1).

COACHES

Dean of Clemson coaches was Frank Howard with record of 165–118–12 for 1940–69, including 8 conference titles, 6 bowl teams and 2 unbeaten teams. Danny Ford was 45–11–2 for 1978–83 with 2 ACC titles, 2 bowl teams and an unbeaten national champion. Ford was national coach of the year in 1981. Second in tenure and wins was Jess Neely with 43–35–7 for 1931–39, including a Cotton Bowl champion. Neely ranks in top 5 in all-time coaching victories. Other outstanding records were by John Heisman, who ranks in top 15 in all-time coaching victories, and was 19–3–2 for 1900–03 with 1 unbeaten team; E.A. Donahue, 21–12–3 for 1917–20; and Josh Cody, 29–11–1 for 1927–30.

MISCELLANEA

First game was 14–6 win over Furman in 1896 . . . highest score was 122–0 over Guilford in 1901 . . . highest since W.W. II was 82–24 over Wake Forest in 1981 . . . biggest margin since W.W. II was 66–0 over Presbyterian in 1957 . . . worst defeat was 74–7 by Alabama in 1931 . . . worst since W.W. II was 56–0 by Alabama in 1975 . . . longest unbeaten string of 16 in 1949–51 ended by Pacific 21–7 . . . winning streak of 15 in 1947–49 ended by Rice 33–7 . . . longest losing string of 11 in 1924–25 broken with 6–0 win over The Citadel . . . consensus All America players were Harry Olszewski, G, 1967; Bennie Cunningham, TE, 1974; Jim Stuckey, DL, 1979; Jeff Davis, LB, 1981; Terry Kinard, DB, 1981–82; and William Perry, DL, 1983 . . . Academic All America selections were Lou Cordileone, T, 1959; and Steve Fuller, QB, 1978.

Colorado (Golden Buffaloes; Silver, Gold & Columbine Blue) (Big 8)

NOTABLE TEAMS

1894—8–1–0. Outscored foes 288–32, losing only to Denver A.C. 20–6. 1895—5–1–0. Fred Folsom's 1st team lost only to Denver A.C. 22–10. 1896 —5–0–0. Outscored foes 171–6, beating Denver A.C. 8–6. 1897—7–1–0. Lost to Denver A.C. 8–0 but outscored others 288–2. 1899—7–2–0. Shut out first 6. 1901—5–1–1. Shut out 5 and won 1st Rocky Mountain Conference title; lost only to Denver A.C. in finale 29–0. 1902—5–1–0. Lost only to unbeaten Nebraska 10–0. 1903—8–2–0. Shut out 6 and won 3rd straight Rocky Mountain title. 1904—6–2–1. Shut out 5. 1905—8–1–0. Scored 359 and shut out 6, losing only to Nebraska 18–0. 1908—5–2–0. Shut out 5 but lost to Utah 21–14 and Denver 14–10. 1909—6–0–0. Blanked foes 141–0. 1910—6–0–0. Outscored foes 121–3 and won Rocky Mountain title. 1911 —6–0–0. Folsom's 4th unbeaten team outscored foes 88–5 and took conference again. 1913—5–1–1. Lost only to Oklahoma 14–3 and won 6th Rocky Mountain title. 1914—5–1–0. Lost only to Colorado Mines 6–2. 1917— 6–2–0. One of losses was to unbeaten Denver 7–0. 1920—4–1–2. Myron Witham's 1st team lost only to Utah 7–0. 1921—4–1–1. Lost only to Chicago 35–0. 1923—9–0–0. Outscored foes 280–27 and won Rocky Mountain title. 1924—8–1–1. Blanked 9 foes 237–0 (tying Denver 0–0) but lost at Hawaii on New Year's Day 13–0. 1928—5–1–0. Lost only to Utah 25–6. 1929— 5–1–1. Won 3 by TD or less, losing only to unbeaten Utah 40–0. 1930— 6–1–1. Tied Utah St. 0–0 and lost only to unbeaten Utah 34–0. 1933— 7–2–0. Shut out 5. 1934—6–1–2. Won 9th Rocky Mountain title, losing only to Northern Colorado 13–7. 1937—8–0–0. Byron (Whizzer) White (1st Colorado All America) led nation in total offense (1,596 yards), rushing (1,121 yards), scoring (122 points) and all-purpose running (1,970 yards) as Buffs took 11th and last Rocky Mountain title; team outscored foes 248–26 and led nation in total offense, rushing and scoring average, but lost to Rice in Cotton Bowl 28–14. 1942—7–2–0. Won 2nd Mountain States Conference title. 1943—5–2–0. Both losses to Colorado College in war-curtailed schedule. 1944—6–2–0. Both losses to service teams; won 4th and last Mountain States title. 1951—7–3–0. Scored 289 as Merwin Hodel led running attack. 1952—6–2–2. Don Branby starred at E, Zack Jordan in backfield. 1954—7–2–1. Scored 283 as Carroll Hardy scored 9 TDs; one of losses was to unbeaten Oklahoma. 1956—7–2–1. Again lost to unbeaten Oklahoma but John Bayuk ran for 659 yards and 11 TDs; beat Clemson in Orange Bowl 27–21. 1961—9–1–0. Won 1st Big 8 title, losing only to Utah 21–12, as Joe Romig and Jerry Hillebrand starred on line; lost to LSU in Orange Bowl 25–7. 1965—6–2–2. Bernie McCall passed for 1,175 yards; one of losses was to unbeaten Nebraska. 1966—7–3–0. Lost only to Nebraska 21–19 in last 6. 1967—8–2–0. Monte Huber caught 45 passes and soph Bobby Anderson ran for 625 yards; beat Miami (Fla.) in Bluebonnet Bowl 31–21. 1969—7–3–0. Anderson ran for 954 yards and 18 TDs while DE Bill Brundige sparked defense; beat Alabama in Liberty Bowl 47–33. 1971—9–2–0. Scored 341 as Charlie Davis ran for 1,386 yards and DE Herb Orvis led defense; lost to Oklahoma and unbeaten national champion Nebraska, but beat Houston in Bluebonnet Bowl 29–17. 1972—8–3–0. Scored 310 as Davis ran for 926 yards and 12 TDs while DB Cullen Bryant starred on defense; lost to Auburn in Gator Bowl 24–3. 1975—9–2–0. Lost to Oklahoma and Nebraska but scored 310 as David Williams passed for 1,282 yards; lost to Texas in Bluebonnet Bowl 38–21. 1976—8–3–0. Tony Reed ran for 1,210 yards and caught 19 passes for 128 more and Jim Kelleher scored 15 TDs; won 5 of last 6 to get share of Big 8 title but lost to Ohio St. in Orange Bowl 27–10.

BOWL RECORD

Bluebonnet 2–1–0; Cotton 0–1–0; Gator 0–1–0; Liberty 1–1–0; Orange 1–2–0.

CONFERENCE TITLES

Rocky Mountain 1901, 1902, 1903, 1910, 1911, 1913, 1923, 1924, 1934*, 1935*, 1937. Mountain States 1939, 1942*, 1943, 1944. Big 8 1961, 1976*.

TOP 10 AP & UPI RANKING

1961	7–7
1971	3–7

MAJOR RIVALS

Colorado has played at least 15 games with Air Force (12–4–0), Colorado College (32–14–3), Colorado Mines (36–14–1), Colorado St. (44–14–2), Denver (26–14–4), Denver AC (3–13–0), Iowa St. (26–12–1), Kansas (25–17–3), Kansas St. (28–12–0), Missouri (13–33–3), Nebraska (11–31–1), Oklahoma (8–30–1), Oklahoma St. (14–11–2), Utah (30–24–3), Utah St. (10–6–1) and Wyoming (21–3–1).

COACHES

Dean of Colorado coaches was Fred Folsom with record of 77–23–2 for 1895–99, 1901–02 and 1908–15, including 5 conference titles and 4 perfect records. He ranks in top 20 in all-time winning percentage. Eddie Crowder was 67–49–2 for 1963–73 with 5 bowl teams. Others with outstanding records included Myron Witham, 63–26–7 for 1920–31, including 2 conference titles and 1 perfect record; Bunnie Oakes, 25–15–1 for 1935–39 with 3 conference titles and a bowl team unbeaten in regular season; Jim Yeager, 24–17–2 for 1941–43 and 1946–47 with 2 conference titles; Dallas Ward, 63–41–6 for 1948–58 with 1 Orange Bowl champion; and Bill Mallory, 35–21–1 for 1974–78 with 1 Big 8 title and 2 bowl teams.

MISCELLANEA

First game was 20–0 loss to Denver AC in 1890 . . . first win was 24–4 over Colorado College in 1891 . . . highest score was 109–0 over Regis in 1905 . . . highest since W.W. II was 65–12 over Arizona in 1958 . . . biggest margin since W.W. II was 61–0 over Colorado St. in 1952 and over Drake in 1954 . . . worst defeat was 103–0 by Colorado Mines in 1890 . . . worst since 1900 was 76–0 by Texas in 1946 . . . highest against Buffaloes since 1900 was 82–42 by Oklahoma in 1980 . . . longest winning streak of 21 in 1908–12 ended by Colorado St. 21–0 . . . unbeaten string of 19 in 1922–24 ended by Hawaii 13–0 on New Year's Day 1925 . . . longest losing string of 10 in 1963–64 broken with 14–7 win over Iowa State . . . consensus All America players were Whizzer White, B, 1937; Joe Romig, G, 1960–61; Dick Anderson, DB, 1967; Mike Montler, G, 1968; Bob Anderson, B, 1969; Don

Popplewell, C, 1970; and Cullen Bryant, DB, 1972 . . . Academic All America choices were Romig, G, 1960–61; Kirk Tracy, OG, 1967; Jim Cooch, DB, 1970; Rick Stearns, LB, 1973–74; and Steve Young, DT, 1975.

Colorado State (Rams; Green & Gold) (WAC)

NOTABLE TEAMS

1903—5–1–0. Lost only to Colorado 5–0 in opener. 1915—7–0–0. Outscored foes 243–31 and won 1st Rocky Mountain Conference title. 1916—6–0–1. E Ralph Robinson and C Charles Shepardson led team to 2nd straight conference title; tie was 0–0 with Colorado Mines. 1919—7–1–0. Won 3rd Rocky Mountain title, losing only to Colorado College 13–0 in finale. 1920 —6–1–1. Shut out 6, losing only to Nebraska 7–0. 1925—9–1–0. Won 5th conference title while shutting out 5; lost finale at Hawaii 41–0. 1926—6–2–1. One of losses was to unbeaten Utah 10–6. 1927—7–1–0. Backs Rollie Caldwell and Fay Rankin led Rams to conference title; lost to Denver 6–0. 1928—6–2–0. Lost close ones to Utah 6–0 and Colorado 13–7. 1933 —5–1–1. Lost only to Utah 13–0 in finale. 1934—6–2–1. Won 8th and last Rocky Mountain title, losing only to Arizona 7–3 and Colorado. 1948—8–2–0. Lost only to Drake 31–29 and Utah 12–3; lost to Occidental in Raisin Bowl 21–20. 1949—9–1–0. Linemen Dale Dodrill and Thurman McGraw led Rams to wins over all but Wyoming 8–0 loss. 1955—8–2–0. Gary Glick ran and passed for 827 yards and returned punts and kickoffs for 310 more (besides intercepting 5 passes) as Rams won Skyline 8 title. 1966—7–3–0. Scored 275 as Oscar Reed ran for 946 yards and 10 TDs; won 6 of last 7. 1977—9–2–1. Scored 310 as Dan Graham passed for 1,692 yards and 17 TDs and Mark Bell caught 40 for 797 yards and 9 scores.

BOWL RECORD

Raisin 0–1–0.

CONFERENCE TITLES

Rocky Mountain 1915, 1916, 1919, 1920, 1925, 1927, 1933*, 1934*. Skyline 8 1955.

TOP 10 AP & UPI RANKING

None.

MAJOR RIVALS

Colorado St. has played at least 15 games with Air Force (8–12–1), Arizona (2–12–1), Arizona St. (1–16–0), Brigham Young (22–21–3), Colorado (15–44–2), Colorado College (20–6–5), Colorado Mines (27–16–2), Denver (28–26–5), Montana (10–6–0), New Mexico (17–16–0), Northern Colorado (14–0–1), Texas-El Paso (14–6–0), Utah (13–39–2), Utah St. (32–30–2) and Wyoming (39–31–5).

COACHES

Dean of CSU coaches was Harry Hughes with record of 125–92–18 for 1911–41, including 8 conference titles and 2 unbeaten teams. Bob Davis was 54–33–2 for 1947–55 with 1 conference title and 1 bowl team. Sark Arslanian was 46–52–3 for 1973–81.

MISCELLANEA

First game was 12–8 loss to Longmont Academy in 1893 . . . first win was 24–16 over same team same year . . . first win over college opponent was 60–10 over Denver in 1893 . . . highest score was 77–0 over Kansas Teachers College in 1967 . . . worst defeat was 79–7 by Arizona St. in 1969 . . . longest unbeaten string of 14 in 1915–16 broken by Wyoming 6–0 in 1917 . . . longest losing string of 26 in 1960–62 broken with 20–0 win over Pacific in 1963 . . . only consensus All America player was Mike Bell, DL, 1978 . . . Academic All America choices were Gary Glick, B, 1955; and Tom French, OT, 1969.

Columbia (Lions; Light Blue & White) (Ivy)

NOTABLE TEAMS

1875—4–1–1. Tied Rutgers 1–1 and lost only to Princeton 6–2. 1899—8–3–0. Shut out 8 but got shut out in losses. 1903—9–1–0. Shut out 7 and lost only to Yale 25–0 as B Richard Smith starred. 1904—7–3–0. Shut out first 6. 1915—5–0–0. Outscored foes 126–28 in first varsity season in 10 years after faculty banned sport for violence. 1918—5-1-0. Gave up only 7 points before losing finale to Syracuse 20-0. 1931—7-1-1. Shut out 6, losing only to Cornell 13-0. 1932—7-1-1. Lost to Brown 7-6 and tied Syracuse 0-0 in last 2 games. 1933—7-1-0. Joe Ferrara and Cliff Montgomery starred as Lions lost only to unbeaten Princeton 20-0; upset Stanford 7-0 in Rose Bowl. 1934—7-1-0. Lou Little's 5th straight winning team lost only to Navy 18-7 in 3rd game. 1945—8-1-0. Scored 251 but lost to Pennsylvania 32-7. 1947—7-2-0. Swept last 5, giving Army first defeat since 1943, as Gene Rossides had 1,062 yards total offense and E Bill Swiacki caught 31 passes for 517 yards.

BOWL RECORD

Rose 1-0-0.

CONFERENCE TITLES

Ivy 1961*.

TOP 10 AP & UPI RANKING

None.

MAJOR RIVALS

Lions have played at least 15 games with Army (4-14-3), Brown (20-26-2), Colgate (4-15-1), Cornell (23-45-0), Dartmouth (11-42-1), Harvard (10-31-1), Lafayette (8-10-1), Navy (9-13-1), Pennsylvania (17-45-1), Princeton (8-44-1), Rutgers (21-23-5), Stevens (10-5-2), Syracuse (9-11-4), Union (13-1-1), Wesleyan (16-5-1), Williams (14-5-2) and Yale (14-45-2).

COACHES

Dean of Columbia coaches was Lou Little with record of 110-116-10 for 1930-56, including a Rose Bowl champion and a 29-4-2 mark for 1931-34. Aldo T. (Buff) Donelli was 30-67-2 for 1957-67 with 1 conference title. Winning records were compiled by William F. Morley, 26-11-1 in 1902-05; and Charles F. Crowley, 26-16-4 in 1925-29.

MISCELLANEA

Columbia was 3rd college to play football, losing first game to Rutgers 6–3 in 1870 . . . first win was 6–0 over Stevens in 1872 . . . highest score was 70–0 over Hobart in 1917 . . . highest since W.W. II was 59–21 over Syracuse in 1946 . . . biggest margin since W.W. II was 50–0 over Brown in 1961 . . . worst defeat was 93–0 to Yale in 1883 . . . worst since 1900 was 69–0 to Rutgers in 1978 . . . highest against Lions since 1900 was 77–28 by Holy Cross in 1983 . . . longest winning streak of 8 in 1903 ended by Yale 25–0 and in 1933–34 ended by Navy 18–7 . . . longest unbeaten string of 10 in 1902–03 ended by Yale and in 1931–32 ended by Brown 7–6 . . . Columbia has lost 11 in a row 4 times, the most recent in 1973–74 broken with 38–33 win over Bucknell . . . consensus All America players were Bill Morley, B, 1900–01; Harold Weekes, B, 1901; Richard Smith, B, 1903; Paul Governali, B, 1942; and Bill Swiacki, E, 1947 . . . Academic All America choices were Mitch Price, B, 1952; John Gasella, T, 1953; Claude Benham, B, 1956; and John Sefcik, HB, 1971 . . . Governali won Maxwell Award as player of year in 1942.

Cornell (Big Red; Carnelian & White) (Ivy)

NOTABLE TEAMS

1889—7–2–0. Scored 354 and shut out 6; both losses to Yale. 1891—7–3–0. Scored 298 and shut out 6. 1892—10–1–0. Scored 434 and shut out 7; lost to Harvard 20–14. 1898—10–2–0. Pop Warner's 2nd Cornell team shut out 8; lost to Princeton 6–0 and Penn 12–6. 1899—7–3–0. Shut out 7 under coach Percy Haughton. 1900—10–2–0. Shut out 8 as HB Ray Starbuck made All America. 1901—11–1–0. Outscored foes 333–14, losing only to Princeton 8–6. 1902—8–3–0. Scored 324 and shut out 7 behind G Bill Warner. 1904—7–3–0. Won 7 of first 8 as Pop Warner returned to helm. 1906—8–1–2. Warner's last Cornell team, led by linemen Elmer Thompson and Bill Newman, lost only to national champion Princeton 16–5. 1907—8–2–0. Lost close ones to Penn State 8–6 and Penn 12–5. 1908—7–1–1. G Bernie O'Rourke starred as Big Red lost only to national champion Penn 17–4 in finale. 1911—7–3–0. Lost only to Penn State 5–0 in first 8 games. 1914—8–2–0. Won last 7 after successive losses to Pitt 9–3 and Colgate 7–3. 1915—9–0–0. Outscored foes 287–50 behind QB Charles Barrett and E

Murray Shelton and won 1st national championship. 1916—6-2-0. Lost to Harvard and Penn. 1920—6-2-0. Gil Dobie's 1st Cornell team won first 5. 1921—8-0-0. Outscored foes 392-21 behind HB Edgar Kaw and won 2nd national title. 1922—8-0-0. Repeated as national champions, outscoring foes 339-27 as Kaw starred at FB. 1923—8-0-0. QB George Pfann and T Frank Sundstrom led Big Red to 3rd straight unbeaten season, outscoring foes 320-33. 1925—6-2-0. Shut out 5, but lost to Penn and unbeaten national champion Dartmouth. 1926—6-1-1. Lost only to Columbia 17-9 and tied Penn 10-10. 1929—6-2-0. Lost final 2 to Dartmouth 18-14 and Penn. 1930—6-2-0. Scored 273 but lost close ones to Columbia 10-7 and Dartmouth 19-13. 1931—7-1-0. Shut out 6, losing only to Dartmouth 14-0. 1938—5-1-1. Lost only to Syracuse 19-17 as Brud Holland starred at E. 1939—8-0-0. Carl Snavely's best Cornell team scored all in double figures behind T Nick Drahos. 1940—6-2-0. Led nation in passing but lost final 2 to Dartmouth 3-0 and Penn 22-20. 1948—8-1-0. Lost only to unbeaten Army 27-6. 1949—8-1-0. Scored 284 as Jeff Fleischmann scored 10 TDs and Pete Dorset passed for 7; lost only to Dartmouth 16-7. 1950 —7-2-0. Rocco Calvo led offense as Big Red lost only to unbeaten Princeton 27-0 and to Columbia 20-19 in successive games. 1967—6-2-1. Bill Robertson passed for 1,347 yards and Bill Murphy caught 50 for 853 and 9 scores. 1971—8-1-0. Ed Marinaro led nation in rushing (1,881 yards), scoring (148 points) and all-purpose running (1,932 yards) as Big Red won 1st formal Ivy League title; lost only to Dartmouth 24-14.

BOWL RECORD

None.

CONFERENCE TITLES

Ivy (informal) 1914, 1915, 1921, 1922, 1931, 1938, 1939, 1948, 1949, 1953, 1954*. Ivy 1971*.

TOP 10 AP & UPI RANKING

1939	4

MAJOR RIVALS

Cornell has played at least 15 games with Brown (16-14-1), Bucknell (27-3-0), Colgate (43-24-3), Columbia (45-23-3), Dartmouth (25-41-1), Harvard (18-28-2), Lafayette (9-5-1), Lehigh (12-3-2), Michigan (12-

6–0), Pennsylvania (35–50–5), Princeton (23–41–2), Syracuse (23–11–0), Williams (13–5–3) and Yale (14–30–2).

COACHES

Dean of Cornell coaches was Gil Dobie with record of 82–36–7 for 1920–35, including 3 conference titles, 3 unbeaten teams and 2 national champions. Dobie is 16th in all-time winning percentage and tied for 15th in all-time coaching victories with Carl Snavely. George (Lefty) James was 66–58–2 for 1947–60 with 4 conference titles. Other winning records were by Glenn (Pop) Warner, 36–13–3 for 1897–98 and 1904–06; Al Sharpe, 34–21–1 for 1912–17 with 2 conference titles and an unbeaten national champion; Carl Snavely, 46–26–3 for 1936–44 with 2 conference titles and 1 unbeaten team; and Jack Musick, 45–33–3 for 1966–74 with 1 conference title.

MISCELLANEA

First game was 24–10 loss to Union in 1887 . . . first win was 26–0 over Palmyra in 1888 . . . first win over college opponent was 20–0 over Williams in 1888 . . . highest score was 124–0 over Rochester in 1889 . . . highest since 1900 was 110–0 over Western Reserve in 1921 . . . highest since W.W. II was 57–20 over Columbia in 1964 . . . largest margin since W.W. II was 54–0 over Columbia in 1949 . . . worst defeat was 77–0 by Harvard in 1890 . . . worst since W.W. II was 55–0 by Syracuse in 1958 . . . highest against Cornell since 1900 was 62–13 by Dartmouth in 1925 . . . highest since W.W. II was 60–7 by Colgate in 1983 . . . longest winning streak of 26 in 1921–24 ended by Williams 14–7 . . . winning streak of 19 in 1914–16 ended by Harvard 23–0 . . . unbeaten string of 18 in 1938–40 ended by Dartmouth 3–0 . . . longest losing string of 10 in 1975–76 broken with 9–3 win over Harvard . . . Cornell has had 15 consensus All America players since 1895 . . . multi-year choices were William Warner, G, 1901–02; Charles Barrett, B, 1914–15; Edgar Kaw, B, 1921–22; and Nick Drahos, T, 1939–40 . . . Ed Marinaro, B, was unanimous choice in 1971 . . . Academic All America selections were Joseph Holland, RB, 1977–78; and Derrick Harmon, RB, 1982–83 . . . Cornell ranks in top 25 in all-time total victories.

Dartmouth (Big Green; Green & White) (Ivy)

NOTABLE TEAMS

1889—7–1–0. Scored 239; lost to Harvard 38–0. 1901—9–1–0. Shut out 6, losing only to unbeaten Harvard 27–12. 1902—6–2–1. E Allen Farmer starred as team shut out 5. 1903—9–1–0. F.G. Folsom's 1st team shut out 8 as C Henry Hooper and B Myron Witham became 1st Dartmouth players to make consensus All America; lost only to unbeaten national champion Princeton 17–0. 1904—7–0–1. Shut out 5, including 0–0 tie with Harvard, as Joseph Gilman and Ralph Glaze starred on line. 1905—7–1–2. Shut out 6, losing only to Colgate 16–10, as Glaze starred again. 1907—8–0–1. Shut out all but Amherst (15–10) behind linemen Edward Rich and Benjamin Lang; tie was 0–0 with Vermont. 1908—6–1–1. Tied Williams 0–0 and lost finale to Harvard 6–0. 1909—5–1–2. Shut out first 6 but lost finale to Harvard 12–3. 1910—5–2–0. Lost to Princeton and Harvard. 1911—8–2–0. HB David Morey starred as Indians swept first 8. 1912—7–2–0. Shut out 6 behind T Wesley Englehorn; 1 of losses was to unbeaten Harvard 3–0. 1913 —7–1–0. E Robert Hogsett starred as Big Green lost only finale to Carlisle Indians 35–10. 1914—8–1–0. Outscored foes 359–25, losing only to Princeton 16–12. 1915—7–1–1. Clarence Spears starred at G as team shut out 6 and lost only to Princeton 30–7. 1919—6–1–1. Tied Colgate 7–7 and lost finale to Brown 7–6. 1920—7–2–0. Won last 5 after losses to Penn St. 14–7 and Syracuse 10–0. 1921—6–2–1. One of losses was to unbeaten national champion Cornell. 1923—8–1–0. Shut out 5, losing only to unbeaten Cornell 32–7. 1924—7–0–1. Outscored foes 225–31 as Swede Oberlander scored 10 TDs; tie was with Yale 14–14. 1925—8–0–0. J.B. Hawley's 2nd straight unbeaten team outscored foes 340–29 as Myles Lane scored 17 TDs and Big Green won national championship. 1927—7–1–0. Lane scored 125 points as team lost only to Yale 19–0. 1929—7–2–0. Scored 305, with Al Marsters scoring 109; lost close ones to Yale 16–12 and Navy 13–6. 1930 —7–1–1. Scored 301 and shut out 5 while losing only to Stanford 14–7 in finale. 1935—8–2–0. Scored 302 and swept 8 straight before losing to unbeaten Princeton. 1936—7–1–1. Lost only to Holy Cross 7–0 in 3rd game. 1937—7–0–2. Red Blaik's 1st unbeaten team had ties with Yale 9–9 and Cornell 6–6. 1938—7–2–0. Scored 254 and led nation in scoring average behind All America B Bob MacLeod; lost last 2 to Cornell 14–7 and Stanford 23–13. 1943—6–1–0. Lost only to Penn 7–6. 1948—6–2–0. Lost to Penn in opener and to Cornell 27–26. 1949—6–2–0. Tom Rowe caught 36 passes as Big Green lost only to Penn in opener and Princeton 19–13 in finale. **1957** —7–1–1. Tied Yale 14–14 and lost only to Princeton 34–14 in finale. **1958** —7–2–0. Lost close ones to Holy Cross 14–8 and Harvard 16–8 in successive games, but won 1st formal Ivy title. **1962**—9–0–0. Bill King passed for 1,043 yards and 14 TDs as team outscored foes 236–57. **1963**—7–2–0. Won 6 by TD or less, with losses to Yale 10–6 and Harvard 17–13 in successive games. **1965**—9–0–0. Scored 271 led by Pete Walton's 10 TDs and Mickey Beard's passing; won 3rd Ivy title in 4 years and took Lambert Trophy as well. **1966** —7–2–0. Beard passed for 1,079 yards and 13 TDs as team scored 273 but lost to Holy Cross 7–6 and Harvard 19–14. **1967**—7–2–0. Lost to Yale and Cornell. **1969**—8–1–0. Scored 282 and lost only to Princeton 35–7 in finale. **1970**—9–0–0. Bob Blackman's 3rd unbeaten team and 2nd Lambert Trophy winner outscored foes 311–42 as John Short ran for 787 yards and scored 15 TDs; shut out 6 (including last 4 foes) to lead nation in scoring defense. **1971**—8–1–0. Scored double figures in all, losing only to Columbia 31–29. **1972**—7–1–1. Scored 260 and won 4th straight Ivy title, losing only to Yale 45–14.

BOWL RECORD

None.

CONFERENCE TITLES

Ivy (informal) 1920, 1925*, 1929, 1936, 1937. Ivy 1958, 1962, 1963*, 1965, 1966*, 1969*, 1970, 1971*, 1972, 1973, 1978, 1981*, 1982*.

TOP 10 AP & UPI RANKING

1937	7

MAJOR RIVALS

Dartmouth has played at least 15 games with Amherst (24–3–3), Brown (42–16–3), Columbia (42–11–1), Cornell (41–25–1), Harvard (38–45–4), Holy Cross (28–19–4), Massachusetts (20–3–1), New Hampshire (17–2–1), Norwich (26–0–0), Pennsylvania (26–23–2), Princeton (31–29–3), Tufts (13–1–1), Vermont (24–1–3), Williams (20–4–2) and Yale (24–38–5).

COACHES

Dean of Dartmouth coaches was Robert L. (Bob) Blackman with record of 104–37–3 for 1955–70, including 7 conference titles, 2 Lambert Trophies and 3 unbeaten teams. Second in wins was Earl (Red) Blaik with record of 45–15–4 for 1934–40, including 2 conference titles and 1 unbeaten team. Other outstanding coaches were Fred Folsom, 29–5–4 for 1903–06 with 1 unbeaten team; Frank Cavanaugh, 42–9–3 for 1911–16; Clarence Spears, 21–9–1 for 1917–20; Jackson Cannell, 39–19–4 for 1921–22 and 1929–33; Jesse Hawley, 39–10–1 for 1923–28 with 2 unbeaten teams; John (Jake) Crouthamel, 41–20–2 for 1971–77 with 3 conference titles; and Joseph M. Yukica, 29–27–2 for 1978–83 with 3 conference titles.

MISCELLANEA

First game was 1–0 win over Amherst in 1881 . . . highest score was 91–0 over Vermont in 1886 . . . highest since 1900 was 79–0 over Norwich in 1930 . . . highest since W.W. II was 56–6 over New Hampshire in 1965, 56–14 over Columbia in 1966 and 56–41 over Columbia in 1982 . . . biggest margin since W.W. II was 55–0 over Columbia in 1970 . . . worst defeat was 113–0 by Yale in 1884 . . . worst since 1900 was 64–0 by Notre Dame in 1944 . . . worst since W.W. II was 60–6 by Army in 1954 . . . longest winning streak of 15 in 1961–63 ended by Yale 10–6 . . . longest unbeaten string of 22 in 1923–26 ended by Yale 14–7 and similar string in 1936–38 ended by Cornell 14–7 . . . longest losing string of 7 in 1952–53 broken with 32–0 win over Yale . . . Dartmouth has had 15 consensus All America players since 1903 . . . multi-year choices were Clarence Spears, G, 1914–15; and Carl Diehl, G, 1924–25 . . . Andy Oberlander, B, was unanimous choice in 1925 . . . most recent selection was Bob MacLeod, B, 1938 . . . Academic All America players were Willie Bogan, DB, 1970; and Michael Patsis, DB, 1983 . . . Dartmouth ranks in top 15 both in number of all-time wins and in winning percentage.

Duke (Blue Devils; Blue & White) (ACC)

NOTABLE TEAMS

1920—4–0–1. Tie was 0–0 with Wofford in finale. 1921—6–1–2. Lost to William & Mary 12–0 but shut out all but New York University (7–7) in last 7 games. 1922—7–2–1. Shut out 5. 1930—8–1–2. Shut out 5 after losing opener to South Carolina 22–0. 1932—7–3–0. Shut out 7, with 2 losses by TD or less. 1933—9–1–0. Won 1st Southern Conference title and T Fred Crawford became First Duke All America as no foe scored more than 7; lost finale to Georgia Tech 6–0. 1934—7–2–0. Ace Parker gained notice as Blue

Devils lost only to Tennessee 14–6 and North Carolina 7–0. 1935—8–2–0. Lost close ones to Georgia Tech 6–0 and Auburn 7–0 in successive games. 1936—9–1–0. Shut out 7 and lost only to Tennessee 15–13 as Parker made All America. 1937—7–2–1. Lost to North Carolina 14–6 and to national champion Pittsburgh 10–0. 1938—9–0–0. Bob O'Mara ran for 703 yards and team blanked foes 114–0 to lead nation in scoring defense but lost to Southern California 7–3 in Rose Bowl. 1939—8–1–0. Won last 6 after 14–13 loss to Pittsburgh. 1940—7–2–0. Steve Lach caught 26 passes for 335 yards; one of losses was to unbeaten Tennessee. 1941—9–0–0. Scored 311 and led nation in total offense as Tom Davis ran for 569 yards and passed for 506 more; lost to Oregon St. 20–16 in Rose Bowl transplanted to Durham, N.C., because of W.W. II. 1943—8–1–0. Buddy Luper ran and passed for 871 yards as team lost only to Navy 14–13; led nation in scoring average, total defense, rushing defense and scoring defense. 1944—5–4–0. Won last 4, then upset Alabama 29–26 in Sugar Bowl. 1945—6–2–0. Lost to Navy and to Army's unbeaten national champions but won 9th Southern Conference title. 1950—7–3–0. Wallace Wade's last team saw Billy Cox pass for 1,428 yards and run for 567 more while Corren Youmans caught 40 passes. 1952—8–2–0. Won 10th and last Southern Conference title. 1953—7–2–1. Won share of 1st Atlantic Coast Conference title, losing only to Army 14–13 and Georgia Tech 13–10. 1954—7–2–1. Bob Pascal scored 10 TDs as Blue Devils lost only to Army and Navy; beat Nebraska in Orange Bowl 34–7. 1955—7–2–1. Sonny Jurgensen led team to 3rd straight ACC title. 1957— 6–2–2. Wray Carlton ran for 833 yards and scored 74 points; lost to Oklahoma in Orange Bowl 48–21. 1960—7–3–0. Tee Moorman caught 54 passes as team won ACC title; beat Arkansas 7–6 in Cotton Bowl. 1961—7–3–0. Lost only to Michigan in last 5 games. 1962—8–2–0. Won 4 by TD or less and took 3rd straight ACC crown; lost to unbeaten national champion Southern California 14–7 in opener.

BOWL RECORD

Cotton 1–0–0; Orange 1–1–0; Rose 0–2–0; Sugar 1–0–0.

CONFERENCE TITLES

Southern 1933, 1935, 1936, 1938, 1939, 1941, 1943, 1944, 1945, 1952. Atlantic Coast 1953*, 1954, 1955*, 1960, 1961, 1962.

TOP 10 AP & UPI RANKING

1938	3	1943	7
1939	8	1960	10–U
1941	2		

MAJOR RIVALS

Duke has played at least 15 games with Clemson (12–15–1), Davidson (16–4–1), Georgia Tech (25–25–1), Maryland (14–12–0), Navy (9–14–5), North Carolina (30–35–4), North Carolina St. (35–20–4), Pittsburgh (8–9–0), South Carolina (24–13–2), Tennessee (12–11–2), Virginia (23–11–0) and Wake Forest (45–17–2).

COACHES

Dean of Duke coaches was Wallace Wade with record of 110–36–7 for 1931–41 and 1946–50, including 6 conference titles, 2 bowl teams and 2 teams unbeaten in regular season. Bill Murray was 93–51–9 for 1951–65 with 7 conference titles and 3 bowl teams. Eddie Cameron was 25–11–1 for 1942–45 with 3 conference titles and 1 bowl champion.

MISCELLANEA

First game was 16–0 win over North Carolina in 1888 in first football game played south of Mason-Dixon line . . . highest score was 96–0 over Furman in 1891 . . . highest since 1900 was 76–0 over Bogue Field in 1945 . . . highest since W.W. II was 67–0 over Richmond in 1949 . . . worst defeat was 64–0 by Notre Dame in 1966 . . . longest winning streaks of 11 in 1932–33 ended by Georgia Tech 6–0 and in 1940–41 ended by Oregon St. 20–16 in Rose Bowl . . . longest losing string of 11 in 1979–80 broken with 34–17 win over Clemson . . . consensus All America players were Fred Crawford, T, 1933; Ace Parker, B, 1936; and Ernie Jackson, DB, 1971 . . . Mike McGee, T, won Outland Trophy in 1959 . . . Academic All America choices were Roger Hayes, DE, 1966; Bob Lasky, DT, 1967; and Curt Rawley, DT, 1970.

East Carolina (Pirates; Purple & Gold) (Independent)

NOTABLE TEAMS

1941—7–0–0. Outscored opponents 159–20. 1950—7–3–0. Lost only to unbeaten Appalachian St. 20–0 in last 6 games. 1952—6–2–2. Won last 7 after losses to Norfolk Navy 13–7 and Lenoir Rhyne 7–6; lost to Clarion St. in Lions Bowl 13–6. 1953—8–1–0. Scored 292 while losing only to Tampa 18–13; lost to Morris Harvey in Elks Bowl 12–0. 1960—7–3–0. Won first 6. 1963—8–1–0. Lost opener to Richmond 10–7; beat Northeastern in Eastern Bowl 27–6. 1964—8–1–0. Scored 265 while losing only to Richmond 22–20; beat Massachusetts in Tangerine Bowl 14–13. 1965—8–1–0. Scored 268 and lost only to Furman 14–7 as Dave Alexander ran for 1,029 yards; beat Maine in Tangerine Bowl 31–0. 1967—8–2–0. Butch Colson ran for 1,135 yards and 15 TDs. 1972—9–2–0. Carlester Crumpler ran for 1,309 yards and scored 17 TDs to lead Pirates to Southern Conference title; losses were to North Carolina and North Carolina St. 1973—9–2–0. Scored 352 as Crumpler ran for 1,042 yards and Carl Summerell passed for 1,222. 1975—8–3–0. Scored 296 and Jim Bolding led nation with 10 interceptions; lost only to Richmond 17–14 in last 9 games. 1976—9–2–0. Eddie Hicks ran for 897 yards as Pirates won 4th and last Southern Conference title; lost to North Carolina 12–10 and Furman 17–10. 1977—8–3–0. Lost close ones to South Carolina 19–16, Southwestern Louisiana 9–7 and William & Mary 21–17. 1978—8–3–0. Lost only to Southern Mississippi 17–16 in last 8 games; beat Louisiana Tech in Independence Bowl 35–13. 1983—8–3–0. Henry Williams led nation in kickoff returns with average of 31.1 and OL Terry Long became Pirates' 1st consensus All America; lost close games to Florida St. 47–46, Florida 24–17 and national champion Miami (Fla.) 12–9.

BOWL RECORD

Independence 1–0–0; Tangerine 2–0–0.

CONFERENCE TITLES

Southern 1966*, 1972, 1973, 1976.

TOP 10 AP & UPI RANKING

None.

MAJOR RIVALS

Pirates have played at least 12 games with Appalachian St. (10–19–0), Catawba (8–3–1), The Citadel (13–4–0), Elon (9–9–0), Furman (11–3–0), Guilford (9–5–1), Lenoir Rhyne (6–15–0), North Carolina St. (4–10–0), Richmond (13–11–0), Western Carolina (17–13–0) and William & Mary (11–4–1).

COACHES

Most victories under Clarence Stasavich with record of 50–27–1 for 1962–69, including 1 conference title and 3 bowl champions. Jack Boone had longest tenure with record of 49–45–5 for 1952–61 with 2 minor bowl teams. Pat Dye was 48–18–1 for 1974–79 with 1 league title and a bowl champion. Sonny Randle was 22–10–0 for 1971–73 with 2 conference titles; and Ed Emory was 24–20–0 for 1980–83.

MISCELLANEA

First game was 39–0 loss to Presbyterian in 1932 . . . first win was 6–0 over Campbell in 1933 . . . highest score was 66–23 over East Tennessee St. in 1981 . . . biggest margin was 61–10 over Virginia in 1975 . . . worst defeat was 79–0 by Guilford in 1932 . . . worst since W.W. II was 65–0 by Southern Mississippi in 1968 . . . longest winning streak of 14 in 1963–64 ended by Richmond 22–20 . . . longest losing string of 10 in 1969–70 broken with 7–0 win over Furman . . . Terry Long, OL, was a consensus All America selection for 1983 . . . Pirates have had no Academic All America choices.

Florida (Gators; Orange & Blue) (SEC)

NOTABLE TEAMS

1907—4–1–1. Lost only to Mercer 6–0. 1909—6–1–1. Shut out 5, losing only to Stetson 26–0 (tied same team in rematch 5–5). 1910—6–1–0. Shut out 5, losing only to Mercer. 1911—5–0–1. Outscored foes 84–14, tying

South Carolina 6–6. 1914—5–2–0. Shut out 5. 1922—7–2–0. Scored 240 and shut out 5; lost to Furman 7–6 and Harvard. 1923—6–1–2. Lost only to Army 20–0 in opener. 1924—6–2–2. Shut out 5; lost successive games to Army 14–7 and Mercer. 1925—8–2–0. Shut out 5; 1 of losses was to unbeaten Alabama. 1927—7–3–0. Lost only to Georgia in last 5. 1928—8–1–0. Charles Bachman's 1st team scored 336; lost only to Tennessee in finale 13–12. 1929—8–2–0. Lost only to Harvard in last 6. 1952—7–3–0. Scored 290 as Rick Casares led running attack; beat Tulsa in Gator Bowl 14–13. 1957—6–2–1. HB Jim Rountree starred as Gators lost only to Mississippi St. and unbeaten national champion Auburn. 1960—8–2–0. Ray Graves' 1st team lost only to Rice 10–0 and Auburn 10–7; beat Baylor in Gator Bowl 13–12. 1964—7–3–0. Soph QB Steve Spurrier ran and passed for 1,089 yards; one of losses was to unbeaten national champion Alabama 17–14. 1965—7–3–0. Two of losses by less than TD as Spurrier had 2,123 yards in total offense; lost to Missouri in Sugar Bowl 20–18. 1966—8–2–0. Spurrier (1st Gator consensus All America) passed for 2,012 yards in final year and won Heisman; beat Georgia Tech in Orange Bowl 27–12. 1969—8–1–1. Graves' last team scored 329 as John Reaves led nation in passing with 2,896 yards; lost to North Carolina 22–7 but beat Tennessee in Gator Bowl 14–13. 1974—8–3–0. Scored in double figures in all as Tony Green ran for 856 yards; lost to Nebraska in Sugar Bowl 13–10. 1975—9–2–0. Scored 302 as Jimmy DuBose ran for 1,307 yards, but lost close ones to North Carolina St. 8–7 and Georgia 10–7; lost to Maryland in Gator Bowl 13–0. 1976—8–3–0. Scored 314 behind QB Jimmy Fisher; lost to Texas A&M in Sun Bowl 37–14. 1982—8–3–0. Lost only to unbeaten Georgia in last 6 games; lost to Arkansas in Bluebonnet Bowl 28–24. 1983—8–2–1. Lost successive close games to Auburn 28–21 and Georgia 10–9; Charley Pell's 4th bowl team at Florida defeated Iowa in Gator Bowl 14–6.

BOWL RECORD

Bluebonnet 0–1–0; Gator 5–2–0; Orange 1–0–0; Peach 0–1–0; Sugar 0–2–0; Sun 0–1–0; Tangerine 1–1–0.

CONFERENCE TITLES

None.

TOP 10 AP & UPI RANKING

1983   6–6

MAJOR RIVALS

Florida has played at least 15 games with Alabama (5–15–0), Auburn (24–34–2), Florida St. (19–6–1), Georgia (20–39–2), Georgia Tech (9–23–6), Kentucky (18–16–0), LSU (12–16–2), Maryland (11–6–0), Mercer (10–6–1), Miami (Fla.) (24–21–0), Mississippi (6–8–1), Mississippi St. (22–13–2), Rollins (13–2–1), Stetson (15–2–2), Tennessee (4–13–0), Tulane (12–6–2) and Vanderbilt (13–8–2).

COACHES

Most victories were by Ray Graves with record of 70–31–4 for 1960–69, including 5 bowl teams (4 winners). Other outstanding records were by G.E. Pyle, 26–7–3 for 1909–13 with 1 unbeaten team; Charles Bachman, 27–18–3 for 1928–32; Bob Woodruff, 53–42–6 for 1950–59 with 2 bowl teams; Doug Dickey, 58–43–2 for 1970–78 with 4 bowl teams; and Charley Pell, 32–25–2 for 1979–83 with 4 bowl teams.

MISCELLANEA

First game was 16–6 win over Gainesville AC in 1906 . . . first win against college foe was 6–0 over Rollins in same year . . . highest score was 144–0 over Florida Southern in 1913 . . . highest since W.W. II was 77–14 over West Texas St. in 1982 . . . worst defeat was 75–0 by Georgia in 1942 . . . worst since W.W. II was 51–0 by Georgia in 1968 . . . highest against Gators since W.W. II was 63–14 by Auburn in 1970 . . . longest unbeaten string of 13 in 1923–24 ended by Army 14–7 . . . longest losing string of 13 in 1945–47 broken with 7–6 win over North Carolina St. . . . winless string of 13 in 1978–79 broken with 41–13 win over California in 1980 . . . consensus All America players were Steve Spurrier, B, 1966; Carlos Alvarez, E, 1969; Sammy Green, LB, 1975; David Little, LB, 1980; and Wilber Marshall, LB, 1982–83 . . . Academic All America choices were Charles Casey, E, 1965; Carlos Alvarez, WR, 1969 and 1971; David Posey, K, 1976; Wes Chandler, B, 1977; and Cris Collinsworth, WR, 1980 . . . Steve Spurrier, QB, won Heisman Trophy in 1966.

Florida State (Seminoles; Garnet & Gold) (Independent)

NOTABLE TEAMS

1948—7-1-0. Don Veller's 1st team lost only to Erskine 14–6. 1949—
8–1–0. Scored 272 while losing only to Livingston St. 13–6; beat Wofford
in Cigar Bowl 19–6. 1950—8–0–0. Outscored foes 219–54 behind Little All
America T Jerry Morrical. 1951—6–2–0. Lost to first major opponent,
Miami (Fla.) 35–13 and to Tampa 14–6. 1954—8–3–0. Lost only to Auburn
in last 9 games; lost to Texas-El Paso in Sun Bowl 47–20. 1958—7–3–0. Tom
Nugent's last team played Florida for first time (losing 21–7); lost to Oklahoma St. in Bluegrass Bowl 15–6. 1964—8–1–1. Lost only to Virginia Tech
20–11 as Steve Tensi passed for 1,681 yards and Fred Biletnikoff (1st Seminole consensus All America) caught 57 for 987 yards and 11 TDs; beat
Florida for first time 16–7 and beat Oklahoma in Gator Bowl 36–19. 1967
—7–2–1. Kim Hammond passed for 1,991 yards and Ron Sellers caught 70
for 1,228; tied Penn State in Gator Bowl 17–17. 1968—8–2–0. Bill Capple-
man passed for 2,410 yards and 25 TDs and Sellers led nation with 86 catches
for 1,496 yards and 12 TDs; lost to LSU in inaugural Peach Bowl 31–27.
1971—8–3–0. Gary Huff led nation in total offense, passing for 2,736 yards
and 23 TDs, and team lost no game by more than 7 points; lost to Arizona
St. in Fiesta Bowl 45–38. 1977—9–2–0. Scored in double figures in all as
Larry Key ran for 1,117 yards; beat Texas Tech in Tangerine Bowl 40–17.
1978—8–3–0. Scored 312 and lost 2 by TD or less. 1979—11–0–0. Scored
319 as Mark Lyles ran for 1,011 yards and K Dave Cappelen ended fine
career with 71 points; lost to Oklahoma in Orange Bowl 24–7. 1980—
10–1–0. Scored 335 and led nation in scoring defense while losing only to
Miami (Fla.) 10–9; lost to Oklahoma in Orange Bowl 18–17. 1982—8–3–0.
Scored 388 as Greg Allen led nation with 126 points; Bobby Bowden's 5th
Seminole bowl team beat West Virginia in Gator Bowl 31–12.

BOWL RECORD

Bluegrass 0–1–0; Fiesta 0–1–0; Gator 2–0–1; Orange 0–2–0; Peach 1–1–0;
Sun 0–2–0; Tangerine 1–0–0.

CONFERENCE TITLES

None.

TOP 10 AP & UPI RANKING

1979	6–8
1980	5–5
1982	U–10

MAJOR RIVALS

FSU has played at least 10 games with Auburn (1–10–1), Florida (6–19–1), Houston (2–12–2), Memphis St. (6–7–0), Miami (Fla.) (12–15–0), North Carolina St. (8–4–0), South Carolina (9–2–0), Southern Mississippi (9–7–1), Tampa (9–2–0), Virginia Tech (14–10–1) and Wake Forest (7–2–1).

COACHES

Bobby Bowden was most successful FSU coach with record of 66–27–0 for 1976–83 with 5 bowl teams and 1 team unbeaten in regular season. Dean of Florida St. coaches was Don Peterson with record of 62–42–11 for 1960–70, including 4 bowl teams. Other top records were by Don Veller, 31–12–1 for 1948–52 with 1 unbeaten team and 1 minor bowl appearance; and Tom Nugent, 34–28–1 for 1953–58 with 2 bowl teams.

MISCELLANEA

First game was 14–6 loss to Stetson in 1947 . . . first win was 30–0 over Cumberland in 1948 . . . highest score was 74–0 over Whiting Field in 1949 . . . worst defeat was 49–0 by Florida in 1973 . . . highest against Seminoles was 58–14 by Southern Mississippi in 1981 . . . longest winning streak of 15 in 1978–79 ended by Oklahoma 24–7 in Orange Bowl . . . longest losing string of 20 in 1972–74 broken with 21–14 win over Miami (Fla.) . . . consensus All America players were Fred Biletnikoff, E, 1964; Ron Sellers, E, 1967; Ron Simmons, MG, 1979–80; and Greg Allen, RB, 1983 . . . Academic All America choices were Gary Huff, QB, 1972; Phil Williams, WR, 1979; William Keith Jones, DB, 1979–80; and Rohn Stark, P, 1981.

Fresno State (Bulldogs; Cardinal, White & Blue) (PCAA)

NOTABLE TEAMS

1922—7-1-2. Shut out 6; lost to Stanford freshmen 27-3. 1923—7-2-0. Won 2nd straight California Coast title. 1924—7-2-0. Shut out 5. 1930—8-0-0. Won 4 by TD or less and won Far Western title. 1934—7-2-1. Won Far Western title. 1937—7-1-1. Won 4th Far Western title, losing only to Hardin-Simmons 14-7; beat Arkansas St. 27-26 in Little All American Honors Bowl. 1938—7-3-0. Scored 227 and won first 5. 1939—9-1-0. Lost only to San Jose St. 42-7 as C Bob Burgess and E Jack Mulkey starred. 1940 —8-2-1. Burgess and Mulkey starred again; beat Hawaii in Pineapple Bowl 3-0. 1942—9-1-0. James Bradshaw's last team scored 362 and shut out 7; lost only to San Francisco 33-13. 1952—8-2-0. Clark Van Galder's 1st team scored 331 as Larry Willoughby ran for 1,092 yards. 1954—7-3-0. Won 6 of first 7 behind G Willard Whitaker and T Lyman Ehrlich. 1955—9-1-0. Scored 273 as FB Dean Philpott led attack; lost only to Utah St. 39-13. 1956 —8-2-0. Lost only to Pacific 21-14 and Idaho as Philpott ran for 807 yards. 1959—7-3-0. Cecil Coleman's 1st team lost only to Pacific 18-13 in last 6 games. 1960—9-1-0. Scored 298 as Dale Messer ran for 811 yards; lost only to Montana St. 22-20. 1961—9-0-0. Scored 256 and won 9th California College Conference title; beat Bowling Green in Mercy Bowl 36-6. 1962 —7-3-0. Scored 284 and had 2 losses by FG or less. 1966—7-3-0. Darryl Rogers' 1st team won all 7 by TD or less. 1968—7-3-0. Won 7 of last 8 to take 10th and last Calif. College crown; lost to Humboldt St. in Camellia Bowl 29-14. 1977—9-2-0. Scored 354 and won last 8 to take 1st PCAA title. 1982—10-1-0. Scored 352, losing only to Nevada-Reno 40-26, and won PCAA; beat Bowling Green in California Bowl 29-28.

BOWL RECORD

California 1-0-0; Mercy 1-0-0; Raisin 0-1-0.

CONFERENCE TITLES

California Coast 1922, 1923. Far Western 1930, 1934, 1935, 1937. California College 1941, 1942, 1954, 1955, 1956, 1958*, 1959, 1960, 1961, 1968. Pacific Coast Athletic Association 1977, 1982.

TOP 10 AP & UPI RANKING

None.

MAJOR RIVALS

Fresno State has played at least 15 games with Cal Poly-SLO (29–10–2), UC Davis (10–5–1), Hawaii (13–8–0), Long Beach St. (13–13–0), Los Angeles St. (15–3–0), Montana St. (10–15–0), Nevada-Reno (16–10–1), Pacific (33–24–2), San Diego St. (16–22–4), San Jose St. (20–28–3) and UC Santa Barbara (15–4–1).

COACHES

Most wins compiled by Jimmy Bradshaw with record of 59–18–5 for 1936–42 and 1946, including 3 conference titles and 2 minor bowl appearances. Clark Van Galder was 46–22–2 for 1952–58 with 4 conference titles. Other outstanding records were by Cecil Coleman, 37–13–0 for 1959–63 with 3 conference titles and 1 unbeaten bowl champion; Darryl Rogers, 43–32–1 for 1966–72 with one conference title and 1 minor bowl appearance; and Jim Sweeney, 41–26–0 for 1976–77 and 1980–83 with 2 conference titles and 1 bowl champion. Fresno's first coach, Arthur Jones, was 36–26–7 for 1921–28 with 2 conference titles.

MISCELLANEA

First game was 12–0 win over Cal Tech in 1921 . . . highest score was 80–0 over Fort Ord in 1942 . . . highest since W.W. II was 60–7 over Pepperdine in 1952 and 60–0 over San Diego St. in 1960 . . . worst defeat was 62–0 by North Texas St. in 1951 . . . highest against Bulldogs was 65–33 by San Jose St. in 1981 . . . longest winning streak of 13 in 1960–62 ended by Abilene Christian 26–14 . . . longest winless string of 13 in 1928–29 broken with 20–6 win over Pacific . . . Fresno State has had no consensus All America players and no Academic All America first stringers.

Fullerton, California State University (Titans; Blue, Orange & White) (PCAA)

NOTABLE TEAMS

In 14 years of varsity football, Fullerton State has had no team that won 70% or more of its games in regular season, but has had 4 teams that finished 7–4, including the 1983 conference champions.

BOWL RECORD

California 0–1–0.

CONFERENCE TITLES

Pacific Coast Athletic Association, 1983.

TOP 10 AP & UPI RANKING

None.

MAJOR RIVALS

Fullerton State has played at least 8 games with Cal Poly-Pomona (5–3–1), Cal Poly-SLO (5–6–0), Fresno St. (6–5–0), Long Beach St. (3–9–0), Nevada-Las Vegas (1–7–0), Northridge St. (9–1–0), Pacific (3–6–0) and San Jose St. (2–8–0).

COACHES

Winning coaches have been Dick Coury, 13–8–1 for 1970–71, and Pete Yoder, 18–15–0 for 1972–74. Jim Colletto was 19–36–1 for 1975–79 and Gene Murphy was 17–29–0 for 1980–83 with 1 conference champion and bowl team.

MISCELLANEA

First game was 31–0 win over Cal Poly-Pomona in 1970 . . . highest score was 58–14 over Santa Clara in 1976 . . . biggest margin of victory was 48–0 over Cal Poly-Pomona in 1977 . . . worst defeat was 70–0 by Southern Mississippi in 1975 . . . longest unbeaten string of 5 in 1970 ended by Nevada-Las Vegas 20–10 . . . longest losing string of 9 in 1974–75 broken with 32–31 win over UC Riverside . . . Fullerton State has had no consensus All America players and no Academic All America choices.

Georgia (Bulldogs; Red & Black) (SEC)

NOTABLE TEAMS

1894—5–1–0. Lost opener to Sewanee 12–8 but outscored others 148–8. 1910—6–2–1. Scored 281 and shut out 5. 1911—7–1–1. Shut out 5, losing only to Vanderbilt 17–0. 1912—6–1–1. Again lost only to Vanderbilt, 46–0. 1913—6–2–0. HB Bob McWhorter starred as Bulldogs lost only to Virginia 13–6 and unbeaten Auburn 21–7. 1920—8–0–1. Outscored foes 250–17; tied Virginia 0–0. 1921—7–2–1. Shut out 6 but lost close ones to Harvard 10–7 and Dartmouth 7–0. 1924—7–3–0. Shut out 6; lost only to Yale 7–6 in first 8 games. 1927—9–1–0. George Woodruff's last team shut out 5 with Chick Shiver and Tom Nash (Georgia's 1st consensus All America player) starring at ends; lost finale to Georgia Tech 12–0. 1930—7–2–1. Lost successive late-season games to Tulane and unbeaten Alabama. 1931—8–2–0. Catfish Smith starred at end as Bulldogs lost only to unbeaten Tulane and Southern California. 1933—8–2–0. Lost late-season games to Auburn and USC. 1934—7–3–0. Shut out 5 and won last 5. 1941—8–1–1. Frank Sinkwich led nation in rushing with 1,103 yards as Bulldogs lost only to Alabama 27–14; beat TCU in Orange Bowl 40–26. 1942—10–1–0. Heisman winner Sinkwich topped nation in total offense (as did team) with 2,187 yards and Bulldogs scored 367 while losing only to Auburn 27–13; won 1st SEC title and beat UCLA in Rose Bowl 9–0. 1944—7–3–0. Reid Moseley led nation's pass receivers with 32 catches for 506 yards. 1945—8–2–0. Scored 294 as Moseley again led nation's pass receivers with 31 catches for 662 yards; beat Tulsa in Oil Bowl 20–6. 1946—10–0–0. Led nation in scoring with 372 points behind TB Charlie Trippi and G Herb St. John; beat North Carolina in Sugar Bowl 20–10. 1948—9–1–0. Scored 278 behind QB John Rauch and took 3rd SEC title while losing only to North Carolina 21–14; lost to Texas in Orange Bowl 41–28. 1959—9–1–0. Wally Butts' last outstanding team won SEC while losing only to South Carolina 30–14; beat Missouri in Orange Bowl 14–0. 1966—9–1–0. Lost only to Miami (Fla.) 7–6 as George Patton starred at DT; beat SMU in Cotton Bowl 24–9. 1967—7–3–0. Had successive single-point losses to Houston and Florida; lost to North Carolina St. in Liberty Bowl 14–7. 1968—8–0–2. Vince Dooley's 1st unbeaten team led nation in scoring defense and starred DT Bill Stanfill and S Jake Scott; tied

Tennessee and Houston, then lost to Arkansas 16–2 in Sugar Bowl. 1971— 10–1–0. Scored 353 behind line led by G Royce Smith and lost only to Auburn 35–20; beat North Carolina in Gator Bowl 7–3. 1975—9–2–0. Won last 6 behind G Randy Johnson; lost to Arkansas in Cotton Bowl 31–10. 1976 —10–1–0. Scored 324 as Kevin McLee ran for 1,058 yards; lost only to Mississippi 21–17 but lost to unbeaten national champion Pittsburgh in Sugar Bowl 27–3. 1978—9–1–1. Lost only to South Carolina 27–10; lost to Stanford in Bluebonnet Bowl 25–22. 1980—11–0–0. Scored 316 as freshman Herschel Walker ran for 1,616 yards and 15 TDs and Scott Woerner and Jeff Hipp (8 interceptions) starred on defense; beat Notre Dame 17–10 in Sugar Bowl to claim 1st national championship. 1981—10–1–0. Scored 352 behind Walker's 1,891 yards and 18 TDs and Buck Belue's passing; lost only to unbeaten national champion Clemson 13–3 but lost to Pittsburgh in Sugar Bowl 24–20. 1982—11–0–0. Dooley's 3rd unbeaten team scored 315 as Heisman winner Walker ran for 1,752 yards and 16 TDs while Terry Hoage led nation with 12 interceptions; lost to national champion Penn State 27–23 in Sugar Bowl. 1983—9–1–1. Lost only to Auburn 13–7 as DB Hoage sparked defense and Kevin Butler kicked 18 FGs; upset unbeaten Texas 10–9 in Cotton Bowl.

BOWL RECORD

Bluebonnet 0–1–0; Cotton 2–1–0; Gator 1–0–1; Liberty 0–1–0; Oil 1–0–0; Orange 2–1–0; Peach 1–0–0; Presidential Cup 0–1–0; Rose 1–0–0; Sugar 2–4–0; Sun 1–1–0; Tangerine 0–1–0.

CONFERENCE TITLES

Southeastern 1942, 1946*, 1948, 1959, 1966*, 1968, 1976, 1980, 1981*, 1982.

TOP 10 AP & UPI RANKING

1942	2	1959	5–5	1971	7–8	1981	6–5
1946	3	1966	4–4	1976	10–10	1982	4–4
1948	8	1968	8–4	1980	1–1	1983	4–4

MAJOR RIVALS

Georgia has played at least 15 games with Alabama (20–31–4), Auburn (41–39–7), Clemson (34–14–4), Florida (39–20–2), Furman (20–2–0), Georgia Tech (42–31–5), Kentucky (28–7–2), Louisiana St. (6–9–1), Mercer (22–0–0), Mississippi (14–7–1), Mississippi St. (10–5–0), North Carolina (16–12–2), South Carolina (30–6–2), Tennessee (9–8–2), Tulane (13–10–1), Vanderbilt (28–15–1) and Virginia (6–6–3).

COACHES

Dean of Georgia coaches was Wallace Butts with record of 140–86–9 for 1939–60, including 4 conference titles, 8 bowl teams and 1 unbeaten team. However, Vince Dooley has compiled most victories with record of 161–60–7 for 1964–83, including 6 conference titles, 15 bowl teams, 3 teams unbeaten in regular season and 1 national champion. He was national coach of the year in 1980. Other outstanding records were by W.A. Cunningham, 43–18–9 for 1910–19; H.J. Stegeman, 20–6–3 for 1920–22 with 1 unbeaten team; George Woodruff, 30–16–1 for 1923–27; and Harry Mehre, 59–34–6 for 1928–37.

MISCELLANEA

First game was 50–0 win over Mercer in 1892 . . . highest score was 108–0 over Alabama Presbyterian in 1913 . . . highest since W.W. II was 76–0 over The Citadel in 1958 . . . worst defeat was 55–0 by North Carolina in 1900 . . . worst since W.W. II was 48–6 by Georgia Tech in 1951 . . . longest winning streak of 19 in 1981–82 ended by Penn State 27–23 in Sugar Bowl . . . winning streaks of 15 in 1945–47 ended by North Carolina 14–7 and in 1979–81 ended by Clemson 13–3 . . . longest losing string of 8 in 1904–05 broken with 16–12 win over Dahlonega . . . Georgia has had 12 consensus All America players since 1927 . . . multi-year choices were Frank Sinkwich, B, 1941–42, Herschel Walker, RB, 1980–82; and Terry Hoage, DB, 1982–83 . . . other unanimous choices were Charley Trippi, B, 1946, and Royce Smith, G, 1971 . . . others selected since 1965 were Ed Chandler, T, 1967; Bill Stanfill, DT, and Jake Scott, DB, 1968; Randy Johnson, G, 1975; and Joel Parrish, G, 1976 . . . Academic All America selections were Francis Tarkenton, B, 1960; Bob Etter, K, 1965–66; Stanfill, DT, 1968; Tom Nash, OT, and Mixon Robinson, DE, 1971; Jeff Lewis, LB, 1977; and Terry Hoage, DB, 1982–83 . . . Heisman Trophy winners were Frank Sinkwich, HB, 1942, and Herschel Walker, RB, 1982 . . . Bill Stanfill, T, won Outland Trophy in 1968 . . . Georgia ranks in top 20 in all-time winning percentage and in top 25 in total victories.

Georgia Tech (Yellow Jackets; Old Gold & White) (ACC)

NOTABLE TEAMS

1901—4-0-1. Shut out 4; tied Furman 5-5. 1904—8-1-1. John Heisman's 1st team scored 287 and shut out 6, losing only to unbeaten Auburn 12-0. 1905—6-0-1. Scored 207; tie was with Sewanee 18-18. 1909—7-2-0. Lost to Sewanee and Auburn. 1911—6-2-1. Shut out 6 as Roy Goree starred at E. 1913—7-2-0. Scored 248; one of losses was to unbeaten Auburn. 1914 —6-2-0. Jim Senter starred at E. 1915—7-0-1. Outscored foes 231-24 behind backs Wooch Fielder and Froggy Morrison; tie was 0-0 with Georgia. 1916—8-0-1. Outscored foes 421-20 behind line led by Six Carpenter, Bob Lang and Pup Phillips; tie was 7-7 with Washington & Lee. 1917 —9-0-0. Heisman's 4th unbeaten team outscored foes 494-17 and won national championship as back Everett Strupper became first Tech consensus All America. 1918—6-1-0. Lost only to national champion Pittsburgh 32-0; outscored others 462-0. 1919—7-3-0. Heisman's last team shut out 7. 1920 —8-1-0. William A. Alexander's 1st team outscored foes 312-16, losing only to Pittsburgh 10-3. 1921—8-1-0. Scored 360 and shut out 5 but lost to Penn State 28-7 in New York City. 1922—7-2-0. Won Southern Conference and lost only to Navy and Notre Dame as Red Barron starred in backfield. 1925—6-2-1. Lost successive games to unbeaten Alabama 7-0 and to Notre Dame 13-0. 1927—8-1-1. Shut out 7, losing only to Notre Dame 26-7. 1928—9-0-0. Outscored foes 213-40 behind HB Warner Mizzell, C Peter Pund and T F.R. Speer; got share of national championship and beat California in Rose Bowl 8-7. 1939—7-2-0. Lost close ones to Notre Dame 17-14 and Duke 7-6; won 1st SEC title and beat Missouri in Orange Bowl 21-7. 1942—9-1-0. G Harvey Hardy was All America; lost finale to Georgia 34-0 and lost to Texas in Cotton Bowl 14-7. 1943—7-3-0. Scored 280 behind G John Steber; beat Tulsa in Sugar Bowl 20-18. 1944 —8-2-0. B Frank Broyles and E Phil Tinsley starred; won 2nd straight SEC title but lost to Tulsa in Orange Bowl 26-12. 1946—8-2-0. Lost opener to Tennessee 13-9 and finale to unbeaten Georgia; beat St. Mary's in Oil Bowl 41-19. 1947—9-1-0. Shut out 6 and lost only to Alabama 14-7 behind T Bobby Davis; beat undefeated Kansas in Orange Bowl 20-14. 1948—7-3-0. Led nation in total defense and rushing defense, with no loss by more than 8 points. 1949—7-3-0. Won 4 of first 5. 1951—10-0-1. Linemen Ray Beck on offense and Lamar Wheat on defense starred as record was marred only by mid-season 14–14 tie with Duke; beat Baylor in Orange Bowl 17–14. 1952—11–0–0. Bobby Dodd's 2nd straight unbeaten team scored 301 behind B Leon Hardeman, took 5th SEC title and earned share of national championship; beat undefeated Mississippi in Sugar Bowl 24–7. 1953—8–2–1. LB Larry Morris led defense as Tech lost only to Notre Dame and Alabama; beat West Virginia in Sugar Bowl 42–19. 1954—7–3–0. Lost close games to Florida 13–12, Kentucky 13–6 and Duke 21–20; beat Arkansas in Cotton Bowl 14–6. 1955—8–1–1. Lost only to Auburn 14–12 while leading nation in scoring defense; beat Pittsburgh in Sugar Bowl 7–0. 1956 —9–1–0. Again led nation in scoring defense while shutting out 5 and losing only to unbeaten Tennessee 6–0; beat Pitt in Gator Bowl 21–14. 1961— 7–3–0. Lost only to LSU in first 7 games; lost to Penn St. in Gator Bowl 30–15. 1962—7–2–1. Lost close ones to LSU 10–7 and Auburn 17–14 as Billy Lothridge led attack and kicked for 35 points as well; lost to Missouri in Bluebonnet Bowl 14–10. 1963—7–3–0. QB Lothridge led nation in kicking with 12 FGs and 15 extra points. 1964—7–3–0. Won first 7, 3 by TD or less. 1966—9–1–0. Jim Breland was All America C as Tech lost only to Georgia 23–14 in finale; lost to Florida in Orange Bowl 27–12. 1970— 8–3–0. Rock Perdoni starred at DT; lost only to Notre Dame 10–7 in last 5, then beat Texas Tech in Sun Bowl 17–9.

BOWL RECORD

Bluebonnet 0–1–0; Cotton 1–1–0; Gator 2–2–0; Liberty 1–0–0; Oil 1–0–0; Orange 3–2–0; Peach 0–2–0; Rose 1–0–0; Sugar 4–0–0; Sun 1–0–0.

CONFERENCE TITLES

Southern 1922, 1927, 1928. Southeastern 1939*, 1943, 1944, 1951*, 1952.

TOP 10 AP & UPI RANKING

1942	5	1952	2–2	1956	4–4
1947	10	1953	8–9	1966	8–8
1951	5–5	1955	7–7		

MAJOR RIVALS

Georgia Tech has played at least 15 games with Alabama (20–28–3), Auburn (39–43–4), Clemson (34–12–2), Duke (25–25–1), Florida (24–9–6), Georgia (31–42–5), Kentucky (11–7–1), LSU (12–5–0), Navy (13–8–0),

North Carolina (10–7–2), Notre Dame (4–25–1), South Carolina (10–7–0), Tennessee (16–22–1), Tulane (35–13–0) and Vanderbilt (16–15–3).

COACHES

Dean of Georgia Tech coaches was William A. Alexander with record of 134–95–15 for 1920–44, including 6 conference titles, 5 bowl teams and 1 unbeaten national champion. Alexander was national coach of the year in 1942. Most wins, however, came under Bobby Dodd with record of 165–64–8 for 1945–66, including 2 conference titles, 13 bowl teams, 2 unbeaten teams and 1 national champion. John Heisman was 102–29–7 for 1904–19 with 4 undefeated teams and a national champion. Pepper Rodgers was 34–31–2 for 1974–79 with 1 bowl team.

MISCELLANEA

First game was 12–0 loss to Mercer in 1892 . . . first win was 28–6 over Georgia in 1893 . . . highest score was 222–0 (NCAA record) over Cumberland in 1916 . . . highest since W.W. II was 54–0 over The Citadel in 1948 and 54–6 over same school in 1952 . . . worst defeat was 94–0 by Auburn in 1894 . . . worst since 1900 was 73–0 by Clemson in 1903 . . . worst since W.W. II was 69–14 by Notre Dame in 1977 . . . longest unbeaten string of 33 in 1914–18 ended by Pittsburgh 32–0 . . . unbeaten string of 31 in 1950–53 ended by Notre Dame 27–14 . . . unbeaten string of 16 in 1927–29 ended by North Carolina 18–7 . . . longest winless string of 15 in 1896–1901 broken with 29–0 win over Gordon . . . Georgia Tech has had 15 consensus All America players since 1917 . . . only multi-year choice was Bill Fincher, E, 1918 and 1920 . . . selections since 1950 were Hal Miller, T, 1952; Larry Morris, C, 1953; Maxie Baughan, C, 1959; Jim Breland, C, 1966; Rock Perdoni, DT, 1970; and Randy Rhino, DB, 1973 . . . Academic All America selections were Ed Gossage, G, Cecil Trainer, E, and George Morris, LB, 1952; Wade Mitchell, B, 1955; Allen Ecker, G, 1956; Breland, C, and W.J. Blaine, LB, 1966; Bill Eastman, DB, 1966–67; and Sheldon Fox, LB, 1980 . . . Georgia Tech ranks in top 25 in both all-time victories and winning percentage.

Harvard (Crimson; Crimson) (Ivy)

NOTABLE TEAMS

1881—6–1–1. Lost to Yale and tied Princeton. 1882—7–1–0. Lost to unbeaten Yale. 1883—8–2–0. Lost to Princeton and to unbeaten Yale. 1886—12–2–0. Outscored foes 765–41 (highest total of points ever scored in one season); lost to Princeton and Yale. 1887—10–1–0. Outscored foes 660–23, losing only to unbeaten Yale 17–8 in finale. 1888—12–1–0. Outscored foes 635–32, losing only to Princeton 18–6. 1889—9–2–0. Scored 419 as E Arthur Cumnock, G John Cranston and B James Lee made 1st All America team; lost to unbeaten national champion Princeton and to Yale. 1890—11–0–0. Won 1st national championship, outscoring foes 555–12 behind 5 All America players. 1891—13–1–0. Outscored foes 588–26, losing only to unbeaten national champ Yale 10–0 in finale. 1892—10–1–0. Scored 365 and shut out 7 behind 5 All America players; lost only to unbeaten national champion Yale 6–0 in finale. 1893—12–1–0. George A. Stewart's last team outscored foes 418–15, losing only to Yale 6–0. 1894—11–2–0. One of losses was to unbeaten national champ Yale. 1895—8–2–1. Shut out 8 as B Charles Brewer made All America for 3rd time; 1 of losses was to unbeaten national champion Penn 17–14. 1897—10–1–1. Shut out 10, losing only to unbeaten national champion Penn 15–6. 1898—11–0–0. Outscored foes 257–19 behind backs Charles Daly and Benjamin Dibblee and won national title. 1899—10–0–1. Repeated as national champ despite 0–0 tie with Yale in finale as Daly starred again. 1900—10–1–0. Daly made All America 3rd straight year as Crimson shut out 7 and lost only to unbeaten national champion Yale 28–0 in finale. 1901—12–0–0. Outscored foes 254–24 as 8 players made All America (all of linemen except center). 1902—11–1–0. Shut out 7 as E Edward Bowditch and B Thomas Graydon starred; lost only to Yale 23–0 in finale. 1903—9–3–0. Lost only to Amherst 5–0 in first 10 games. 1904—7–2–1. Shut out 7; 1 of losses was to unbeaten national champion Penn. 1905—8–2–1. Led by 4 All America players; 1 of losses was to unbeaten Yale 6–0. 1906—10–1–0. Shut out 7, losing only to Yale 6–0 in finale. 1907—7–3–0. Won first 7 as B John Wendell starred. 1908—9–0–1. Percy Haughton's 1st team shut out 8 behind T Hamilton Fish; tie was with Navy 6–6. 1909—8–1–0. Shut out 6 as Fish starred again; lost only to unbeaten national champion Yale 8–0 in finale. 1910—8–0–1. Won national championship despite 0–0 tie with Yale behind line led by T Robert McKay and G Robert Fisher; shut out all but Cornell (27–5). 1911—6–2–1. Lost successive games to Princeton 8–6 and Carlisle 18–15. 1912—9–0–0. Won national championship, outscoring foes 176–22 as Charles Brickley starred in backfield. 1913—9–0–0. Retained national title, outscoring foes 225–21 behind Brickley and B Edward Mahan. 1914—7–0–2. Haughton's 5th unbeaten team shut out 6 as Mahan starred again; ties were with Penn State 13–13 and Brown 0–0. 1915—8–1–0. Lost only to unbeaten national champion Cornell 10–0 in mid-season as Mahan and Richard King starred in backfield. 1916—7–3–0. Shut out 7. 1919—8–0–1. Scored 222 and shut out 7 behind B Edward Casey; tied Princeton 10–10 but beat Oregon 7–6 in Rose Bowl in Crimson's only bowl appearance.1920—8–0–1. Shut out 7 behind line led by G Tom Woods; tie was with Princeton 14–14. 1921— 7–2–1. Lost successive close ones to Centre 6–0 and Princeton 10–3. 1922 —7–2–0. G Charles Hubbard starred as Crimson lost only to Princeton 10–3 and Brown 3–0 in successive games. 1931—7–1–0. B Barry Wood led team to wins in all except finale, a 3–0 loss to Yale. 1944—5–1–0. Lost only to Melville P.T. Boat 13–0 in informal W.W. II schedule. 1946—7–2–0. Chip Gannon starred in backfield as Crimson lost only to Rutgers and Yale. 1953 —6–2–0. Lost pair of 6–0 games to Columbia and Princeton. 1966—8–1–0. Led nation in rushing as Bobby Leo ran for 827 yards; lost only to Princeton 18–14. 1968—8–0–1. Vic Gatto and Ray Hornblower led rushers as Crimson won 3rd formal Ivy League title; tied Yale in finale 29–29. 1970— 7–2–0. One of losses was to unbeaten Dartmouth. 1973—7–2–0. Jim Stoeckel passed for 1,391 yards and Bruce Tetirick kicked 9 FGs and 25 extra points. 1974—7–2–0. Milt Holt passed for 1,456 yards and 16 TDs and Pat McInally caught 46 for 655 yards. 1975—7–2–0. Won 2nd straight Ivy title, losing only to Boston U. 13–9 and Princeton 24–20. 1980—7–3–0. Won 3 by less than TD as Dave Cody kicked 10 FGs. 1982—7–3–0. Lost close ones to Army 17–13, Dartmouth 14–12 and Penn 23–21 but won share of Ivy title. 1983—6–2–2. Unbeaten in last 5 games; again earned share of Ivy title.

BOWL RECORD

Rose 1–0–0.

CONFERENCE TITLES

Ivy (informal) 1901, 1902, 1908, 1912, 1913, 1946*. Ivy 1961*, 1966*, 1968*, 1974*, 1975, 1982*, 1983*.

TOP 10 AP & UPI RANKING

None.

MAJOR RIVALS

Harvard has played at least 15 games with Amherst (24–1–0), Army (19–15–2), Bates (23–0–0), Bowdoin (17–0–0), Brown (60–21–2), Columbia (31–10–1), Cornell (28–18–2), Dartmouth (45–38–4), Holy Cross (25–11–2), Massachusetts (10–6–1), MIT (15–0–0), Pennsylvania (35–17–2), Princeton (27–42–7), Tufts (17–5–0), Wesleyan (17–1–0), Williams (30–0–0) and Yale (38–54–8).

COACHES

Dean of Harvard coaches was John M. Yovicsin with record of 78–42–5 for 1957–70, including 3 conference titles and 1 unbeaten team. Percy D. Haughton was 71–7–5 for 1908–16 with 3 conference titles, 5 unbeaten teams and 3 national champions. He ranks in top 5 in all-time winning percentage. Joseph Restic was 72–44–5 for 1971–83 with 4 conference titles. Other top records were by Robert T. Fisher, 43–14–5 for 1919–25 with 1 Rose Bowl champion and 2 unbeaten teams; Arnold Horween, 21–17–3 for 1926–30; and Edward L. Casey, 20–11–1 for 1931–34. Dick Harlow was national coach of the year in 1936.

MISCELLANEA

First game was 3–0 win over McGill in 1874 . . . highest score was 158–0 over Exeter in 1886 . . . highest since 1900 was 69–6 over Tufts in 1926 and 69–0 over Coast Guard in 1946 . . . worst defeat was 54–0 by Yale in 1957 . . . highest against Crimson was 63–26 by Princeton in 1950 . . . longest unbeaten string of 33 in 1911–15 ended by Cornell 10–0 . . . unbeaten string of 32 in 1898–1900 ended by Yale 28–0 . . . unbeaten string of 25 in 1919–21 ended by Centre 6–0 . . . winning streak of 24 in 1890–91 ended by Yale 10–0 . . . winning streak of 23 in 1901–02 ended by Yale 23–0 . . . longest losing string of 9 in 1949–50 broken with 14–13 win over Brown . . . Harvard has had 60 consensus All America players since 1889 . . . multi-year choices were John Cranston, G, 1889, C, 1890; Frank Hallowell, E, 1890, 1892; Marshall Newell, T, 1890–93; Bertram Waters, G, 1892, T, 1894; William Lewis, C, 1892–93; Charles Brewster, B, 1892–93, 1895; Norman Cabot, E, 1895–96; Benjamin Dibblee, B, 1897–98; John

Hallowell, E, 1898, 1900; Charles Daly, B, 1898–1900; David Campbell, E, 1899–1901; Edward Bowditch, E, 1901–02; Thomas Graydon, B, 1901–02; Daniel Hurley, B, 1904–05; Francis Burr, G, 1905–06; Hamilton Fish, T, 1908–09; Robert Fisher, G, 1910–11; Percy Wendell, B, 1910–11; Stanley Pennock, G, 1912–14; Charles Brickley, B, 1912–13; Edward Mahan, B, 1913–15; Charles Hubbard, G, 1922–23; and Ben Ticknor, C, 1929–30 . . . most recent selection was Endicott Peabody, G, 1941 . . . Harvard has had no Academic All America selections . . . Harvard ranks 2nd in all-time total victories and in top 10 in winning percentage.

Hawaii (Rainbow Warriors; Green & White) (WAC)

NOTABLE TEAMS

1915—5-1-1. Lost only to Kamehameha H.S. 7–0 in opener. 1917—4-0-1. Shut out 4, tying Punahou Academy 0–0 in opener. 1919—4-0-1. Tied Outrigger Canoe Club 6–6 in opener. 1920—6-2-0. Shut out 5 but lost to Outrigger Canoe Club 3–0 and Nevada-Reno 14–0 (first game played with continental U.S. team). 1922—5-1-1. Lost to a Navy service team 13–10. 1923—5-1-2. Lost to Pomona 14–7 in first game on U.S. continent but beat Oregon St. 7–0 on New Year's Day for first win over continental team. 1924 —8-0-0. Outscored foes 188–12, including New Year's win over Colorado 13–0. 1925—10-0-0. Otto Klum's 2nd straight unbeaten team outscored foes 421–17, shutting out 8 and beating Washington St. 20–11 in New Year's game. 1927—5-2-0. Lost to Alumni 3–2 in opener and Santa Clara 18–12 in finale. 1930—5-2-0. Lost successive games to Town Team and Southern California. 1934—6-0-0. Klum's 3rd unbeaten team outscored foes 142–21. 1941—8-1-0. Lost only to Healani 26–6 in mid-season. 1946 —7-2-0. Won 7 straight after 4-year layoff during W.W. II; beat Utah in Pineapple Bowl 19–16. 1949—6-2-0. Scored 342 as Harry Kahuanui starred at E; lost to Stanford in Pineapple Bowl 74–20. 1956—7-3-0. Scored 291 points. 1962—6-2-0. Returned to varsity football after 1-year layoff. 1968—7-3-0. Dave Holmes' 1st team scored 312 as Larry Arnold passed for 1,821 yards and 19 TDs, and Rich Leon caught 56. 1970—9-2-0. Scored 286 as Larry Sherrer ran for 722 yards and Bill Massey for 708. 1972— 8-3-0. Albert Holmes ran for 1,146 yards and 12 TDs. 1973—9-2-0. Dave Holmes' last team saw Casey Ortiz pass for 1,385 yards and Allen Brown catch 46 for 735 yards. 1980—8-3-0. Gary Allen ran for 884 yards and

caught 26 passes for 257 more; lost only to Brigham Young in last 7. **1981**
—9–2–0. Scored 328 as Allen ran for 1,006 yards and caught 21 passes for
367 more.

BOWL RECORD

None.

CONFERENCE TITLES

None.

TOP 10 AP & UPI RANKING

None.

MAJOR RIVALS

Hawaii has played at least 12 games with Cal State (L.A.) (6–6–0), Fresno
State (8–13–0), Pacific (7–15–0), San Jose St. (6–11–0) and Utah (4–11–0).

COACHES

Dean of Hawaii coaches was Otto (Proc) Klum with record of 84–51–7 for
1921–39, including 3 unbeaten teams. Dave Holmes was 46–17–1 for 1968–
73. Other top records were by Tommy Kaulukukui, 34–18–3 for 1946–50;
and Dick Tomey, 45–31–1 for 1977–83.

MISCELLANEA

First game was 6–5 win over McKinley H.S. in 1909 . . . first win over college
foe was 3–2 over Oahu College (Punahou) in 1910 . . . first win over
continental U.S. foe was 7–0 over Oregon St. in 1923 season . . . highest
score was 101–0 over Field Artillery and over Healani, both in 1926 . . .
highest since W.W. II was 98–7 over Islanders in 1949 . . . worst defeat was
75–0 by Pacific in 1949 . . . longest unbeaten string of 21 in 1923–26 ended
by Alumni 2–0 . . . longest winless string of 8 in 1964–65 broken with 10–8
win over Cal Western . . . Hawaii has had no consensus All America players
and no Academic All America selections.

Holy Cross (Crusaders; Royal Purple) (Independent)

NOTABLE TEAMS

1901—7–1–1. Lost opener to Massachusetts 17–0 and tied Brown 6–6. 1902 —6–2–1. Maurice Connor's last team shut out 6. 1903—8–2–0. Shut out 5; lost to Dartmouth and Yale before winning final 6. 1922—7–2–1. Lost to Harvard and Boston College. 1923—8–2–0. Shut out 7, again losing to Harvard and Boston College. 1924—7–1–1. Lost to Harvard 12–6 and tied Lehigh 3–3. 1925—8–2–0. Won first 6. 1926—7–1–2. Lost only to Boston U. 3–0. 1930—8–2–0. John McEwen's 1st team shut out 7. 1931—7–2–1. Lost close ones to Dartmouth 14–7 and Harvard 7–0. 1932—6–2–2. McEwen's last team lost successive games to Brown 10–7 and Harvard 7–0. 1933—7–2–0. Dr. Eddie Anderson's 1st team lost only to Detroit and Boston College. 1934—8–2–0. Lost successive games to Colgate and Temple. 1935—9–0–1. Scored 260 and shut out 8; tie was with Manhattan 13–13. 1936—7–2–1. Lost squeakers to Temple 3–0 and Boston College 13–12. 1937—8–0–2. Anderson's 2nd unbeaten team shut out 7; ties were 0–0 with Temple and Carnegie Tech. 1938—8–1–0. Scored 225 in last year of Anderson's 1st term; lost only to Carnegie Tech 7–6. 1939—7–2–0. Shut out 6. 1943—6–2–0. Stan Koslowski led nation in all-purpose running. 1945— 8–1–0. Ox DaGrosa's 1st team led nation in pass defense and lost only to Temple 14–6 as Koslowski starred in backfield; lost to Miami (Fla.) in Orange Bowl 13–6. 1951—8–2–0. Scored 362 in 2nd year of Anderson's 2nd term; lost close ones to Tulane 20–14 and Boston College 19–14. 1952— 8–2–0. Charlie Maloy passed for 1,514 yards and 13 TDs and John Carroll caught 46 for 609 yards; lost to Syracuse 20–19 and Quantico Marines. 1961 —7–3–0. Pat McCarthy passed for 1,081 yards and ran for 512 more. 1982 —8–3–0. Scored all in double figures; 2 of losses by TD or less. 1983— 9–1–1. Scored 304 as Gill Fenerty ran for 1,039 yards and 14 TDs; lost only to Boston College 47–7, but lost to Western Carolina 28–21 in Division I-AA playoffs.

BOWL RECORD

Orange 0–1–0.

CONFERENCE TITLES

None.

TOP 10 AP & UPI RANKING

1938   9

MAJOR RIVALS

Crusaders have played at least 15 games with Army (3–11–1), Boston College (32–44–3), Boston U. (21–9–5), Brown (21–18–2), Colgate (22–19–5), Connecticut (18–7–1), Dartmouth (19–28–4), Fordham (15–9–3), Harvard (11–25–2), Massachusetts (17–14–4), Providence (17–0–0), Rutgers (11–8–0), Springfield (12–4–1), Syracuse (5–23–0), Temple (12–9–2), Tufts (11–3–1), and Villanova (7–12–0).

COACHES

Dean of Holy Cross coaches was Dr. Eddie Anderson with record of 129–67–8 for 1933–38 and 1950–64, including 2 unbeaten teams. Anderson ranks 7th in all-time college victories with 201. Cleo A. O'Donnell was 69–27–4 for 1919–29. Other top records were by Maurice Connor, 23–11–3 for 1899–1902; John J. McEwen, 21–6–3 for 1930–32; John (Ox) DaGrosa, 17–10–2 for 1945–47 with 1 bowl team; and Rick Carter, 23–10–1 for 1981–83 with 1 Division I-AA playoff team.

MISCELLANEA

First game was 10–0 loss to Worcester Tech in 1896 . . . first win was 14–0 over Worcester Academy same year . . . first win over college foe was 6–4 over Boston College in 1896 . . . highest score was 79–0 over Bates in 1935 . . . highest since W.W. II was 77–28 over Columbia in 1983 . . . worst defeat was 76–0 by Boston College in 1949 . . . longest unbeaten string of 18 in 1934–36 ended by Temple 3–0 . . . longest winless string of 14 in 1968–70 broken with 21–16 win over Harvard in 1971 . . . Only consensus All America choice was John Provost, DB, 1974 . . . Bruce Kozerski, OT, was chosen Academic All America in 1983.

Houston (Cougars; Cougar Red & White) (Southwest)

NOTABLE TEAMS

1952—8-2-0. Lost to Texas A&M 21-13 and Mississippi 6-0 but won 1st Missouri Valley Conference title. 1956—7-2-1. Won last 5 and won MVC championship. 1966—8-2-0. Led nation in total offense and Ken Hebert led country in scoring with 113 of Cougars' 335 points; Dick Post ran for 1,061 yards. 1967—7-3-0. Scored 322 and led nation in total offense and rushing as Paul Gipson ran for 1,100 yards and G Rich Stotter became Cougars' 1st consensus All America. 1968—6-2-2. Led nation in total offense, rushing and scoring (42.5 average) as Gipson ran for 1,550 yards and 13 TDs. 1969 —8-2-0. Scored 386 and won last 8 as Jim Strong ran for 1,293 yards and Elmo Wright caught 63 passes for 1,275 yards and 14 TDs; beat Auburn in Bluebonnet Bowl 36-7. 1970—8-3-0. Scored 307 as Wright caught 47 passes for 874 yards. 1971—9-2-0. Scored 322 as Robert Newhouse ran for 1,757 yards and 12 TDs; lost to Colorado in Bluebonnet Bowl 29-17. 1973 —10-1-0. Scored 316 as FB Leonard Parker ran for 1,123 yards; lost only to Auburn 7-0 and beat Tulane in Bluebonnet Bowl 47-7. 1974—8-3-0. Lost only to Tulsa in last 8; tied North Carolina St. in Bluebonnet Bowl 31-31. 1976—9-2-0. Won 1st Southwest Conference title as Wilson Whitley starred at DT and Anthony Francis led nation with 10 interceptions; beat undefeated Maryland in Cotton Bowl 30-21. 1978—9-2-0. Emmett King ran for 1,095 yards and Randy Love for 1,019 as Cougars lost only to Texas Tech 22-21 in conference; lost to Notre Dame in Cotton Bowl 35-34. 1979 —10-1-0. Won 6 by TD or less and lost only to Texas 21-13 as Terald Clark ran for 1,063 yards; Bill Yeoman's 10th bowl team beat Nebraska in Cotton Bowl 17-14.

BOWL RECORD

Bluebonnet 2-1-1; Cotton 2-1-0; Garden State 1-0-0; Salad 1-0-0; Sun 0-1-0; Tangerine 1-0-0.

CONFERENCE TITLES

Missouri Valley 1952, 1956, 1957, 1959*. Southwest 1976*, 1978, 1979*.

TOP 10 AP & UPI RANKING

1973	9–U
1976	4–4
1978	10–U
1979	5–5

MAJOR RIVALS

Houston has played at least 10 games with Arkansas (5–5–0), Baylor (8–7–1), Cincinnati (11–2–0), Florida St. (12–2–2), Miami (Fla.) (7–8–0), Mississippi (3–15–0), Mississippi St. (6–6–0), North Texas St. (4–7–0), Oklahoma St. (7–7–1), Rice (10–3–0), Texas (4–4–2), Texas A&M (10–9–3), Texas Tech (12–4–0), and Tulsa (14–11–0).

COACHES

Dean of Houston coaches is Bill Yeoman with record of 148–86–8 for 1962–83, including 10 bowl teams and 3 conference titles. Clyde Lee was 37–32–2 for 1948–54 with 1 conference title and 1 bowl champion. Harold Lahar was 24–23–2 for 1957–61 with 2 conference titles.

MISCELLANEA

First game was 13–7 loss to Southwestern Louisiana in 1946 . . . first win was 14–12 over West Texas St. same year . . . highest score was 100–6 (modern NCAA record) over Tulsa in 1968 . . . worst defeat was 50–0 by Texas in 1982 . . . highest against Cougars was 61–14 by Texas Tech in 1954 . . . longest winning streak of 10 in 1969–70 ended by Oklahoma St. 26–17 and in 1972–73 ended by Auburn 7–0 . . . longest losing string of 8 in 1947 broken with 14–0 win over Texas A&I, and in 1975 broken with 42–30 win over Tulsa . . . consensus All America players were Rich Stotter, G, 1967; Bill Bridges, G, 1969; Elmo Wright, E, 1970; Wilson Whitley, DT, 1976; and Leonard Mitchell, DL, 1980 . . . Academic All America choices were Horst Paul, E, 1964; Mark Mohr, DB, 1976; and Kevin Rollwage, OT, 1976–77 . . . Whitley, DT, won Lombardi Trophy in 1976.

Illinois (The Fighting Illini; Orange & Blue) (Big 10)

NOTABLE TEAMS

1891—6–0–0. One game won by forfeit after losing on field. 1897—6–2–0. Shut out 5; lost to Chicago and Carlisle Indians. 1901—8–2–0. Shut out 6. 1902—10–2–1. Scored 380 and shut out 8; lost to Chicago 6–0 and Minnesota 17–5. 1904—9–2–1. Shut out 7; lost to Northwestern 12–6 and Nebraska 16–10. 1908—5–1–1. Tied Marquette 6–6 and lost to Chicago 11–6 in successive games as F.C. VanHook starred at G. 1909—5–2–0. Lost tough ones to Kentucky 6–2 and Chicago 14–8. 1910—7–0–0. Scored only 89 but blanked all foes behind C J.F. Twist and G G.D. Butzer; won 1st Big 10 title. 1914—7–0–0. Robert C. Zuppke's 2nd team outscored foes 224–22 as G Ralph Chapman and E Perry Graves became Illinois' 1st All America players. 1915—5–0–2. HB Bart Macomber led Illini to 2nd straight Big 10 title; ties were with Ohio State 3–3 and Minnesota 6–6. 1918—5–2–0. Shut out 5 and won Big 10 behind C John Depler; lost successive 7–0 games to Great Lakes and Municipal Pier. 1919—6–1–0. Won 4 by TD or less, losing only to Wisconsin 14–10. 1920—5–2–0. Lost final 2 to Wisconsin 14–9 and unbeaten Ohio State 7–0. 1923—8–0–0. Zuppke's 3rd unbeaten team blanked last 5 foes and won national title behind G Jim McMillen and soph RB Red Grange (723 yards rushing and 12 TDs). 1924—6–1–1. Grange ran for 743 yards and passed for 433 as Illini lost only to Minnesota 20–7 after tying Chicago 21–21. 1926—6–2–0. Lost to Michigan and Ohio State (7–6). 1927—7–0–1. Zuppke's 2nd national champion starred Russ Crane at G and Robert Reitsch at C; tie was with Iowa St. 12–12. 1928—7–1–0. Shut out 5 and won 2nd straight Big 10 title while losing only to Michigan 3–0. 1929 —6–1–1. Lost only to Northwestern 7–0 as Lou Gordon starred at T. 1934 —7–1–0. Won 5 by TD or less, losing only to Wisconsin 7–3. 1946—7–2–0. Won last 5 after losses to unbeaten national champion Notre Dame and Indiana (14–7) to win Big 10; beat undefeated UCLA in Rose Bowl 45–14. 1950—7–2–0. Dick Raklovits ran for 709 yards; lost only to Wisconsin 7–6 and Northwestern 14–7. 1951—8–0–1. Johnny Karras led running attack and S Al Brosky and LB Charles Boerio sparked defense as Illini won 4 by TD or less and tied Ohio State 0–0; beat Stanford in Rose Bowl 40–7. 1953 —7–1–1. J.C. Caroline led nation in rushing (1,256 yards) and all-purpose running (1,470 yards) as Illini won 11th Big 10 title; tied Nebraska 21–21 and lost only to Wisconsin 34–7. 1963—7–1–1. C and LB Dick Butkus led team to Big 10 title, losing only to Michigan 14–8 and tying Ohio State

20–20; beat Washington in Rose Bowl 17–7. **1983**—10–1–0. Scored 338 as Jack Trudeau passed for 2,446 yards and Tim Brewster caught 59 for 628 yards; lost only to Missouri 28–18 in opener, then to UCLA 45–9 in Rose Bowl.

BOWL RECORD

Liberty 0–1–0; Rose 3–1–0.

CONFERENCE TITLES

Big 10 1910*, 1914, 1915*, 1918*, 1919, 1923*, 1927, 1928, 1946, 1951, 1953*, 1963, 1983.

MAJOR RIVALS

Illinois has played at least 15 games with Chicago (23–17–4), Indiana (28–14–2), Iowa (30–16–2), Michigan (19–50–0), Michigan St. (11–11–1), Minnesota (19–24–2), Northwestern (40–33–5), Ohio St. (20–48–4), Purdue (31–28–6) and Wisconsin (25–23–6).

TOP 10 AP & UPI RANKING

1946	5	1963	3–4
1951	4–3	1983	10–10
1953	7–7		

COACHES

Dean of Illinois coaches was Robert C. Zuppke with record of 131–81–13 for 1913–41, including 7 conference titles, 4 unbeaten teams and 2 national champions. Ray Eliot was 83–73–11 for 1942–59 with 3 conference titles, 2 Rose Bowl champions and 1 unbeaten team. Other top records were by Arthur R. Hall, 27–10–3 for 1907–12 with 1 conference title and 1 unbeaten team; Pete Elliott, 31–34–1 for 1960–66 with 1 conference title and 1 Rose Bowl champion; and Mike White, 27–18–1 for 1980–83 with 1 conference title and 2 bowl teams.

MISCELLANEA

First game was 16–0 defeat by Illinois Wesleyan in 1890 . . . first win was 12–6 over same team same year . . . highest score was 87–3 over Illinois Wesleyan in 1912 . . . highest since W.W. II was 60–14 over Western Michigan in 1947 . . . biggest margin since W.W. II was 51–0 over Wisconsin in 1965 . . . worst defeat was 63–0 by Chicago in 1906 . . . worst since W.W. II was 57–0 by Michigan in 1969 . . . highest against Illini was 70–21 by Michigan in 1981 . . . longest unbeaten string of 15 in 1914–16 ended by Colgate 15–3 . . . winning streak of 13 in 1909–11 ended by Chicago 24–0 . . . longest losing string of 15 in 1960–62 broken with 14–10 win over Purdue . . . Illinois has had 14 consensus All America players since 1914 . . . multi-year choices were Harold (Red) Grange, B, 1923–25; and Dick Butkus, C, 1963–64; . . . others since W.W. II were Alex Agase, G, 1946; Johnny Karras, B, 1951; J.C. Caroline, B, 1953; Bill Burrell, G, 1959; and Jim Grabowski, B, 1965 . . . Academic All America selections were Bob Lenzini, T, 1952; Grabowski, B, 1964–65; John Wright, E, 1966; Jim Rucks, DE, 1970; Bob Bucklin, DE, 1971; and Dan Gregus, DL, 1980–82.

Indiana (Fightin' Hoosiers; Cream & Crimson) (Big 10)

NOTABLE TEAMS

1896—6–2–0. Lost first 2 to DePauw and Noblesville. 1897—6–1–1. Shut out 5, losing only to Purdue 20–6. 1898—4–1–2. James Horne's 1st team lost only to Purdue 14–0. 1899—6–2–0. Shut out 5 but lost to Notre Dame and Northwestern. 1905—8–1–1. Shut out 6 and tied Purdue 11–11; lost only to unbeaten Chicago's national champions 16–5. 1910—6–1–0. Shut out 5; lost only to unbeaten, unscored-on Illinois 3–0. 1917—5–2–0. Scored 225 and blanked 5. 1920—5–2–0. Guards William McCaw and Elliott Risley starred as Hoosiers lost only to Iowa 14–7 and to unbeaten Notre Dame 13–10. 1942—7–3–0. Scored 256 and shut out 6 as HB Bill Hillenbrand became Hoosiers' 1st consensus All America. 1944—7–3–0. Scored 292 and shut out 5 behind C John Tavener. 1945—9–0–1. Scored 269 and won 1st Big 10 title as backs Pete Pihos and George Taliaferro and ends Bob Ravensberg and Ted Kluszewski starred; tie was with Northwestern 7–7 in 2nd game. 1967—9–1–0. Won 7 by TD or less as Jade Butcher caught 38 passes for 10 TDs; lost only to Minnesota 33–7 and lost to Southern California in Rose Bowl 14–3.

BOWL RECORD

Holiday 1–0–0; Rose 0–1–0.

CONFERENCE TITLES

Big 10 1945, 1967*.

TOP 10 AP & UPI RANKING

1945	4
1967	4–6

MAJOR RIVALS

Indiana has played at least 15 games with Chicago (5–20–1), DePauw (23–7–3), Illinois (15–28–2), Iowa (19–28–4), Kentucky (11–5–1), Michigan (8–32–0), Michigan St. (9–23–2), Minnesota (15–27–3), Nebraska (9–7–3), Northwestern (22–33–1), Notre Dame (5–22–1), Ohio State (10–47–4), Purdue (27–53–6), Wabash (14–6–0) and Wisconsin (11–23–2).

COACHES

Dean of Indiana coaches was A.N. (Bo) McMillin with record of 63–48–11 for 1934–47, including an unbeaten Big 10 champion. He was national coach of the year in 1945. Second in tenure and wins was Lee Corso with record of 41–68–2 for 1973–82 with 1 bowl champion. Other top records were by James H. Horne, 33–21–5 for 1898–1904; and James M. Sheldon, 35–26–3 for 1905–13. John Pont was national coach of the year in 1967.

MISCELLANEA

First recorded game was 10–8 loss to Franklin in 1888 . . . first recorded win was 30–0 over Louisville AC in 1891 . . . first recorded win over college foe was 11–10 over Butler in 1892 . . . highest score was 76–0 over Franklin in 1901 . . . highest since W.W. II was 58–30 over Kentucky in 1969 . . . biggest margin since W.W. II was 48–6 over Marquette in 1947 and 49–7 over Colorado in 1980 . . . worst defeat was 68–0 by Purdue in 1892 . . . worst since 1900 was 63–0 by Michigan in 1925 . . . worst since W.W. II was 56–0 by Ohio State in 1957 . . . highest ever against Hoosiers was 69–17 by Nebraska in 1978 . . . longest unbeaten string of 12 in 1944–45 ended by Cincinnati 15–6 in 1946 . . . longest losing strings of 11 in 1948–49 broken with 48–14 win over Pitt and in 1973–74 broken with 34–3 win over Minnesota . . . consensus All America players were Billy Hillenbrand, B, 1942; John Tavener, C, 1944; and Bob Ravensberg, E, 1945 . . . Academic

All America choices were Harry Gonso, HB, 1967; Glenn Scolnik, RB, 1972; and Kevin Speer, C, 1980.

Iowa (Hawkeyes; Old Gold & Black) (Big 10)

NOTABLE TEAMS

1896—7-1-1. Shut out 7; lost to Chicago 6-0 and tied Nebraska 0-0. 1899 —8-0-1. Tied Chicago 5-5 in 2nd game; outscored others 216-0. 1900— 7-0-1. Alden Knipe's 2nd straight unbeaten team outscored foes 311-12 and won 1st Big 10 title; tie was with Northwestern 5-5 in finale. 1903— 9-2-0. Lost only to Minnesota and to unbeaten Nebraska. 1905—8-2-0. Scored 305 and shut out 7; 1 of losses was to unbeaten national champion Chicago. 1910—5-2-0. Jess Hawley's 1st team shut out 5; lost close ones to Northwestern 10-5 and Missouri 5-0. 1913—5-2-0. Scored 310 behind FB Ralph McGinnis; lost to unbeaten teams Chicago and Nebraska. 1918— 6-2-1. Shut out 6. 1919—5-2-0. Lost only to Illinois 9-7 and Chicago 9-6 as E Les Belding became 1st Iowa All America. 1920—5-2-0. Led by Belding and T Fred Slater. 1921—7-0-0. Outscored foes 185-36 and won Big 10 as Slater starred again. 1922—7-0-0. Howard Jones' 2nd straight unbeaten team outscored foes 212-33 behind FB Gordon Locke. 1924—6-1-1. Burt Ingwersen's 1st team lost only to Illinois 36-0. 1928—6-2-0. Won first 6 behind T Peter Westra and HB Willis Glassgow. 1939—6-1-1. Lost only to Michigan 27-7 and tied Northwestern 7-7 as HB Nile Kinnick won Heisman. 1956—8-1-0. Lost only to Michigan 17-14 as T Alex Karras and QB Kenneth Ploen starred; beat Oregon St. in Rose Bowl 35-19. 1957 —7-1-1. Scored 263 as Randy Duncan passed for 1,124 yards and Jim Gibbons caught 36 for 587 yards; lost only to national champion Ohio State 17-13 and tied Michigan 21-21. 1958—7-1-1. Led nation in total offense as Duncan ran and passed for 1,406 yards and 15 TDs; lost only to Ohio State 38-28 and tied unbeaten Air Force 13-13, but beat California in Rose Bowl 38-12 to earn share of national championship. 1960—8-1-0. Forest Evashevski's last team scored all in double figures behind G Mark Manders and HB Larry Ferguson; lost only to Minnesota 27-10. 1981—8-3-0. Got share of Big 10 title for first time since 1960 as DL Andre Tippett and P Reggie Roby made All America; lost to Washington in Rose Bowl 28-0. 1983— 9-2-0. Scored 374 as Chuck Long passed for 2,434 yards; won 6 of last 7 but lost to Florida in Gator Bowl 14-6.

BOWL RECORD

Gator 0–1–0; Peach 1–0–0; Rose 2–1–0.

CONFERENCE TITLES

Big 10 1900*, 1921, 1922*, 1956, 1958, 1960*, 1981*.

TOP 10 AP & UPI RANKING:

1939	9	1957	6–5
1953	9–10	1958	2–2
1956	3–3	1960	3–2

MAJOR RIVALS

Iowa has played at least 15 games with Grinnell (11–5–1), Illinois (16–30–2), Indiana (28–19–4), Iowa State (19–12–0), Michigan (5–27–3), Michigan St. (10–10–1), Minnesota (24–51–2), Nebraska (12–24–3), Northwestern (30–14–3), Notre Dame (8–13–3), Ohio State (11–29–2), Purdue (18–40–2) and Wisconsin (26–34–1).

COACHES

Dean of Iowa coaches was Forest Evashevski with record of 52–27–4 for 1952–60, including 3 conference titles, 2 Rose Bowl champions and 1 national title. Howard Jones was 42–17–1 for 1916–23 with 2 conference titles and 2 perfect seasons. Other top records were by Alden Knipe, 29–11–4 for 1898–1902 with 1 conference title and 2 unbeaten teams; Jess Hawley, 24–18–0 for 1910–15; Burt Ingwersen, 33–27–4 for 1924–31; Dr. Eddie Anderson, 35–33–2 for 1939–42 and 1946–49; and Hayden Fry, 34–24–0 for 1979–83 with 1 conference title and 3 bowl teams. Eddie Anderson was coach of the year in 1939. Anderson ranks in top 10 and Howard Jones in top 15 in all-time coaching victories.

MISCELLANEA

First game was 24–0 loss to Grinnell in 1889 . . . first win was 91–0 over Iowa Wesleyan in 1890 . . . highest score was 95–0 over Iowa Teachers in 1914 . . . highest since W.W. II was 70–14 over Utah St. in 1957 . . . biggest margin since W.W. II was 64–0 over Northwestern in 1981 . . . worst defeat was 107–0 by Michigan in 1902 . . . worst since W.W. II was 83–21 by Ohio State in 1950 . . . longest unbeaten string of 23 in 1898–1901 ended by

Minnesota 16–0 . . . winning streak of 20 in 1920–23 ended by Illinois 9–6 . . . longest losing string of 12 in 1973–74 broken with 21–10 win over UCLA . . . Iowa has had 9 consensus All America players since 1919 . . . only multi-year choice was Calvin Jones, G, 1954–55 . . . most recent selections were Alex Karras, T, 1957; Randy Duncan, B, 1958; and Andre Tippett, DL, and Reggie Roby, P, 1981 . . . Academic All America choices were Bill Fenton, E, 1952–53; and Bob Elliott, DB, 1975 . . . Nile Kinnick, HB, won Heisman Trophy in 1939 . . . Outland Trophy winners were Calvin Jones, G, 1955; and Alex Karras, T, 1957.

Iowa State (Cyclones; Cardinal & Gold) (Big 8)

NOTABLE TEAMS

1894—6–1–0. Lost only to Grinnell 12–6. 1896—8–2–0. Scored 303; lost to Minnesota and Nebraska. 1903—8–1–0. Shut out 5; lost only to Minnesota 46–0. 1904—7–2–0. Shut out 6. 1906—9–1–0. A.W. Ristine's last team scored 268 and shut out 7; lost to Minnesota 22–4. 1907—7–1–0. Clyde Williams' 1st team lost only to Minnesota 8–0. 1911—6–1–1. End A.K. Chappell starred as Cyclones lost only to Minnesota 5–0 in opener. 1912—6–2–0. Williams' last team lost only to Minnesota 5–0 and Iowa 20–7. 1915—6–2–0. Lost to Minnesota 9–6 and to unbeaten Nebraska. 1917— 5–2–0. Lost close ones to Kansas 7–0 and Iowa 6–3. 1938—7–1–1. G Ed Bock became 1st Cyclone consensus All America as team won first 7 before 13–13 tie with Kansas St. and 10–0 loss to unbeaten Oklahoma. 1944— 6–1–1. Shut out 5, losing only to Oklahoma 12–7. 1959—7–3–0. TB Dwight Nichols ended fine career. 1960—7–3–0. Led nation in pass defense and Tom Watkins starred at FB. 1971—8–3–0. Scored 322 as Dean Carlson passed for 1,637 yards; lost to LSU in Sun Bowl 33–15. 1976—8–3–0. Scored 369 as Dexter Green ran for 1,074 yards. 1977—8–3–0. Lost 2 by less than TD and Green ran for 1,240 yards; lost to North Carolina St. in Peach Bowl 24–14. 1978—8–3–0. Earle Bruce's last team starred Green and DT Mike Stensrud; lost to Texas A&M in Hall of Fame Bowl 28–12.

BOWL RECORD

Hall of Fame 0–1–0; Liberty 0–1–0; Peach 0–1–0; Sun 0–1–0.

CONFERENCE TITLES

None.

TOP 10 AP & UPI RANKING

None.

MAJOR RIVALS

Iowa St. has played at least 15 games with Coe (16–2–0), Colorado (11–26–1), Cornell (Iowa) (14–3–1), Drake (47–16–4), Grinnell (20–10–3), Iowa (12–19–0), Kansas (24–34–5), Kansas St. (40–24–3), Minnesota (2–19–1), Missouri (23–46–8), Nebraska (14–62–2), Oklahoma (4–50–2), Oklahoma St. (10–14–1) and Simpson (15–1–1).

COACHES

Dean of Iowa St. coaches was Clay Stapleton with record of 42–53–4 for 1958–67. Best winning percentage was by A.W. Ristine with record of 36–10–1 for 1902–06. Other top records were by Glen Warner, 24–8–0 for 1894–98; Clyde Williams, 33–14–2 for 1907–12; Charles Mayser, 21–11–2 for 1915–19; and Earle Bruce, 36–32–0 for 1973–78 with 2 bowl teams.

MISCELLANEA

First game was 6–6 tie with State Center in 1892 . . . first win was 30–0 over Des Moines YMCA same year . . . first win over college foe was 16–8 over Iowa in 1894 . . . highest score was 87–0 over Simpson in 1904 . . . highest since W.W. II was 69–0 over Colorado St. in 1980 . . . worst defeat was 63–0 by Oklahoma in 1946 . . . highest against Cyclones since W.W.II was 72–29 by Nebraska in 1983 . . . longest unbeaten string of 10 in 1937–38 ended by Oklahoma 10–0 . . . longest losing string of 16 in 1929–30 broken with 6–0 win over Simpson in 1931 . . . only consensus All America player was Ed Bock, G, in 1938 . . . Academic All America choices were Max Burkett, S, 1952; and Mark Carlson, LB, 1982.

Kansas (Jayhawks; Crimson & Blue) (Big 8)

NOTABLE TEAMS

1891—7-0-1. Tie was with Washington (Mo.) 6-6 in finale. 1892—7-1-0. Lost only to Baker 18-0. 1895—6-1-0. Shut out first 5; lost to Missouri 10-6 in finale. 1896—7-3-0. Gave up only 14 points in games won. 1897—8-2-0. Shut out 7; lost to Nebraska 6-5 and KC Medical 2-0 in successive games. 1898—7-1-0. Shut out 6; lost to Nebraska 18-6. 1899—10-0-0. Outscored foes 280-37 in only season under Fielding H. Yost. 1904—8-1-1. Bert Kennedy's 1st team won last 6 after loss to Haskell 23-6 and tie with Colorado 6-6. 1905—10-1-0. Shut out 9; lost only to Colorado 15-0. 1906—7-2-2. Shut out 6. 1908—9-0-0. Won Missouri Valley title, outscoring foes 131-20 with 5 shutouts. 1909—8-1-0. Shut out 6, losing only to Missouri 12-6 in finale. 1910—6-1-1. Kennedy's last team featured G Ellis Davidson and E Earl Ammons; lost only to Nebraska 6-0 and tied Missouri 5-5. 1915—6-2-0. HB Ad Lindsey led attack. 1917—6-2-0. Led by T George Nettels, E Dutch Lonborg and QB Stem Foster. 1923—5-0-3. Won MVC title while shutting out 6, including successive 0-0 ties with Nebraska and Kansas St. 1930—6-2-0. Won 1st Big 6 title, losing only to Pennsylvania and Nebraska. 1946—7-2-1. Won Big 7 as Ray Evans starred at HB and Don Fambrough at G. 1947—8-0-2. Scored 290 as Evans ran and passed for 1,018 yards; tied by TCU and Oklahoma and lost to Georgia Tech in Orange Bowl 20-14. 1948—7-3-0. J.V. Sikes' 1st team won 7 straight after 14-13 loss to TCU in opener. 1951—8-2-0. Scored 316 behind G George Mrkonic. 1952—7-3-0. Two of losses by 1 point each (to Nebraska and Missouri). 1960—7-2-1. John Hadl ran and passed for 941 yards to lead Jayhawks to Big 8 title; conference title and 2 games forfeited, however, to drop record to 5-4-1. 1968—9-1-0. Scored 380 as Bobby Douglass had 1,811 yards of total offense and John Riggins ran for 866; lost only to Oklahoma 27-23 but lost also to unbeaten Penn State in Orange Bowl 15-14. 1981—8-3-0. Won 4 by less than TD; lost to Mississippi St. in Hall of Fame Bowl 10-0.

BOWL RECORD

Bluebonnet 1-0-0; Hall of Fame 0-1-0; Liberty 0-1-0; Orange 0-2-0; Sun 0-1-0.

CONFERENCE TITLES

Missouri Valley 1908, 1923*. Big 6 1930. Big 7 1946*, 1947*. Big 8 1960 (but later forfeited), 1968*.

TOP 10 AP & UPI RANKING

1960	U–9
1968	7–6

MAJOR RIVALS

Kansas has played at least 15 games with Colorado (16–24–3), Drake (10–6–1), Emporia St. (16–1–1), Iowa State (34–24–5), Kansas St. (56–21–4), Missouri (40–43–9), Nebraska (21–66–3), Oklahoma (22–53–6), Oklahoma St. (22–17–3), TCU (5–15–4), Washburn (28–5–4) and Washington (Mo.) (12–0–3).

COACHES

Dean of Kansas coaches was Jack Mitchell with record of 44–42–5 for 1958–66, including 1 conference title (later forfeited) and 1 bowl champion. Most successful was A.R. (Bert) Kennedy with record of 58–9–4 for 1904–10 with 1 conference title and 1 unbeaten team. J.V. Sikes was 35–25–0 for 1948–53. Don Fambrough was 2nd in tenure with record of 36–49–5 for 1971–74 and 1979–82, including 2 bowl teams.

MISCELLANEA

First game was 22–9 loss to Baker in 1890 . . . first win was 14–12 over Baker same year . . . highest score was 86–6 over South Dakota St. in 1947 . . . biggest margin of victory was 83–0 over Washington (Mo.) in 1923 . . . worst defeat was 65–0 by Oklahoma in 1954 . . . highest against Jayhawks was 69–21 by Missouri in 1969 . . . longest winning string of 18 in 1907–09 ended by Missouri 12–6 . . . unbeaten string of 15 in 1890–92 ended by Baker 18–0 . . . longest losing string of 17 in 1953–55 broken with 13–0 win over Washington State . . . consensus All America choices were Gale Sayers, B, 1963–64; John Zook, DE, 1968; and Dave Jaynes, QB, 1973 . . . Academic All America choices were Fred Elder, T, 1964; Mike Sweatman, LB, 1967; Dave Morgan, LB, 1968; Mike McCoy, C, 1971; and Tom Fitch, S, 1976.

Kansas State (Wildcats; Purple & White) (Big 8)

NOTABLE TEAMS

1905—6–2–0. Mike Ahearn's 1st team lost only to Washburn 12–5 and to Kansas. 1906—5–2–0. Lost successive games to Washburn 5–4 and Wichita St. 12–6. 1908—6–2–0. Won last 5 after losses to unbeaten Kansas and to Oklahoma. 1909—7–2–0. Scored 320 and shut out 6, but lost close ones to Missouri 3–0 and Kansas 5–3. 1910—10–1–0. Ahearn's last team scored 336 and shut out 7, losing only to Colorado College 15–8. 1912—8–2–0. Won last 5 as T Jacob Holmes starred. 1916—6–1–1. Z.G. Clevenger's 1st team lost only to Nebraska 14–0 and tied Kansas 0–0 behind E Lee Randels and B Eddie Wells. 1917—6–2–0. Scored 215 and shut out 5, losing only to Kansas 9–0 and Iowa St. 10–7. 1918—4–1–0. Lost only to Kansas 13–7 in finale. 1922—5–1–2. Lost only to Nebraska 21–0 as G Ray Hahn starred. 1931—8–2–0. Lost successive games to Iowa St. 7–6 and Nebraska 6–3 but won others behind E Henry Cronkite and backs Ralph Graham and Eldon Auker. 1933—6–2–1. Graham and G Homer Hanson starred as Wildcats shut out 6. 1934—7–2–1. Won last 5 behind T George Maddox and won Big 6 title. 1954—7–3–0. Led by linemen Ron Nery and Ron Marciniak and B Corky Taylor; one of losses was to unbeaten Oklahoma.

BOWL RECORD

Independence 0–1–0.

CONFERENCE TITLES

Big 6 1934.

TOP 10 AP & UPI RANKING

None.

MAJOR RIVALS

Wildcats have played at least 15 games with Colorado (11–28–0), Iowa St. (24–40–3), Kansas (21–56–4), Kansas St. Teachers (Emporia St.) (13–8–3), Missouri (16–48–5), Nebraska (10–56–2), Oklahoma (11–54–4), Oklahoma St. (12–26–0), Tulsa (6–9–1), Washburn (18–10–2) and Wichita St. (17–3–2).

COACHES

Best record was compiled by Mike Ahearn with 39–12–0 for 1905–10. Longest tenures were by Charles Bachman, 33–23–9 for 1920–27; and Vince Gibson, 33–52–0 for 1967–74. Other top records were by Guy Lowman, 17–15–3 for 1911–14; Z.G. Clevenger, 19–9–2 for 1916–19; and A.N. McMillin, 29–21–1 for 1928–33.

MISCELLANEA

First game was 14–0 loss to Ft. Riley in 1896 . . . first win was 4–0 over Dickinson County H.S. in 1897 . . . first win over college foe was 17–5 over Kansas Wesleyan in 1899 . . . highest score was 75–5 over Drury in 1910 . . . highest since W.W. II was 59–21 over Oklahoma in 1969 . . . biggest margin since W.W. II was 55–0 over Ft. Hays St. in 1949 and over Baker in 1950 . . . biggest margin ever was 71–0 over Wichita St. in 1909 . . . worst defeat was 76–0 by Oklahoma in 1942 . . . worst since W.W. II was 66–0 by Oklahoma in 1956 . . . longest winning streak of 13 in 1909–10 ended by Colorado College 15–8 . . . longest losing string of 28 in 1945–48 broken with 37–6 win over Arkansas St. . . . only consensus All America player was Gary Spani, LB, 1977 . . . Academic All America choices were Don Lareau, LB, 1974; Floyd Dorsey, OG, 1977; Darren Gale, DB, 1981–82; and Mark Hundley, RB, 1982.

Kentucky (Wildcats; Blue & White) (SEC)

NOTABLE TEAMS

1894—5–2–0. Scored 218; lost to Cincinnati and Centre. **1898**—7–0–0. Blanked opponents 180–0. **1903**—7–1–0. Shut out first 6; lost finale to Transylvania 17–0. **1904**—9–1–0. Scored 276 and shut out 8, losing only to Cincinnati 11–0. **1907**—9–1–1. Shut out 9, losing only to Vanderbilt 40–0 and tying Tennessee 0–0. **1909**—9–1–0. Scored 261 and shut out 6, losing only to North Carolina St. 15–6. **1910**—7–2–0. Won first 7 before losing to St. Louis and Centre. **1911**—7–3–0. Shut out 6. **1912**—7–2–0. Lost close games to Miami (O.) 13–8 and VMI 3–2. **1913**—6–2–0. Lost to Illinois and Tennessee. **1915**—6–1–1. Lost only to Mississippi St. 12–0 as T C.C. Schrader and B William Rodes starred. **1916**—4–1–2. Rodes led team again; lost only to Vanderbilt (45–0). **1929**—6–1–1. Lost only to Alabama 24–13 and tied Tennessee 6–6. 1939—6–2–1. Lost to Georgia Tech 13–6 and to unbeaten, unscored-on Tennessee 19–0. 1946—7–3–0. Bear Bryant's 1st Wildcat team starred basketball ace Wallace Jones at E. 1947—7–3–0. Two losses by 7-point margins; beat Villanova in Great Lakes Bowl 24–14. 1949 —9–2–0. Scored 304 and led nation in total defense and scoring defense behind T Bob Gain and C Harry Ulinski; lost to Santa Clara in Orange Bowl 21–13. 1950—10–1–0. Scored 380 behind Gain and QB Babe Parilli (Kentucky's 1st consensus All America players) but lost finale to Tennessee 7–0; upset unbeaten national champion Oklahoma in Sugar Bowl 13–7. 1951— 7–4–0. Three early-season losses were by TD or less; Parilli (with 1,643 yards passing), C Doug Moseley and G Gene Donaldson led rally climaxed by 20–7 win over TCU in Cotton Bowl. 1953—7–2–1. Bryant's last team won last 6 behind HB Steve Meilinger and G Ray Correll. 1954—7–3–0. Blanton Collier's 1st team won last 5 behind QB Bob Hardy. 1976—7–4–0 (8–3–0 by forfeit). Starred T Warren Bryant and E Art Still; beat North Carolina in Peach Bowl 21–0. 1977—10–1–0. QB Derrick Ramsey ran and passed for 1,510 yards and Still starred again as Wildcats lost only to Baylor 21–6 in 2nd game.

BOWL RECORD

Cotton 1–0–0; Great Lakes 1–0–0; Hall of Fame 0–1–0; Orange 0–1–0; Peach 1–0–0; Sugar 1–0–0.

CONFERENCE TITLES

Southeastern 1950.

TOP 10 AP & UPI RANKING

1950	7–7
1977	6–U

MAJOR RIVALS

Kentucky has played at least 15 games with Alabama (1–28–1), Auburn (5–18–1), Central U. (4–10–1), Centre (11–18–1), Cincinnati (17–7–3), Florida (16–18–0), Georgetown (Ky.) (22–1–0), Georgia (7–28–2), Georgia Tech (7–11–1), Indiana (4–11–1), LSU (9–24–1), Maryville (19–0–1), Mississippi (10–19–1), Mississippi St. (10–5–0), Tennessee (22–48–9), Transylvania (15–5–1), Vanderbilt (25–28–4), VMI (12–4–0), Virginia Tech (10–5–2), Washington & Lee (11–7–2), West Virginia (11–8–1) and Xavier (O.) (18–2–0).

COACHES

Top record was by Paul (Bear) Bryant with record of 60–23–5 for 1946–53, including 1 conference title and 4 bowl teams (3 winners). Longest tenure was by Fran Curci with record of 47–51–2 for 1973–81, including 1 bowl champion. Other top records were by J. White Guyn, 17–7–1 for 1906–08; E.R. Sweetland, 23–5–0 for 1909–10 and 1912; Harry Gamage, 32–25–5 for 1927–33; and Blanton Collier, 41–36–3 for 1954–61.

MISCELLANEA

First game was victory over Transylvania in 1881 . . . highest score was 87–0 over Wilmington in 1914 . . . highest since W.W. II was 83–0 over North Dakota in 1950 . . . worst defeat was 82–0 by St. Louis in 1905 . . . worst since W.W. II was 45–0 by Tennessee in 1970 and by Alabama in 1980 . . . highest against Wildcats since W.W. II was 58–30 by Indiana in 1969 . . . longest winning streak of 12 in 1909–10 ended by St. Louis 9–0 . . . longest losing string of 8 in 1966–67 broken with 22–7 win over West Virginia . . . consensus All America players were Bob Gain, T, 1950; Babe Parilli, B, 1950–51; Lou Michaels, T, 1956–57; Sam Ball, T, 1965; and Art Still, DL, 1977 . . . Academic All America choices were Tom Ranieri, LB, 1974; Mark Keene, C, 1978; and Jim Kovach, LB, 1978 . . . Bob Gain, T, won Outland Trophy in 1950.

Long Beach, California State University (49ers; Brown & Gold) (PCAA)

NOTABLE TEAMS

1955—5–2–0. First varsity team lost only to Occidental 21–6 and Pomona 21–14. 1964—8–2–0. Dick Degan ran for 693 yards to lead 49ers to wins over all but San Diego St. and Cal St. L.A. (0–7). 1965—9–1–0. Don Reed's best team lost only to Cal St. L.A. 27–21 as Jack Reilly passed for 2,002 yards and 21 TDs and Shelly Novack caught 68 for 1,013 yards and 13 scores and 49ers scored 327. 1969—8–3–0. Scored 319 as Leon Burns ran for 1,659 yards and scored 164 points while Jeff Severson intercepted 15 passes; won 7 of last 8 in 1st year under Jim Strangeland. 1970—9–2–0. Got share of 1st PCAA title as Burns ran for 1,033 yards and Jim Kirby for 856 while Severson picked off 8 passes; won last 8 after losses to Pacific 9–6 and Hawaii 23–14, then tied Louisville 24–24 in Pasadena Bowl. 1975—9–2–0. Herb

Lusk ran for 1,596 yards and Mike Wills caught 39 passes for 701 yards; lost only to Southwestern Louisiana (22–17 in opener) and San Jose St. 1976— 8–3–0. Won 7 of first 8 as DL Kise Fiatoa anchored defense in Wayne Howard's last year. 1980—8–3–0. Kevin Starkey passed for 1,955 yards and 19 TDs and ran for 282 more; 49ers won last 7 to take 3rd PCAA title.

BOWL RECORD

Pasadena 0–0–1.

CONFERENCE TITLES

Pacific Coast Athletic Association 1970*, 1971, 1980.

TOP 10 AP & UPI RANKING

None.

MAJOR RIVALS

Long Beach St. has played at least 10 games with Cal Poly-SLO (12–6–0), Cal St. Fullerton (9–3–0), Cal St. L.A. (6–8–2), Cal St. Northridge (8–3–0), Fresno St. (14–12–0), Pacific (10–9–0), San Diego St. (9–13–0), San Francisco St. (3–8–0), San Jose St. (3–11–0) and UC Santa Barbara (11–5–0).

COACHES

Dean of Long Beach St. coaches was Don Reed with record of 57–47–2 for 1958–68. Second in wins was Dave Currey, 40–36–0 for 1977–83 with 1 conference title. Other winning records were by Mike DeLotto, 13–10–0 for 1955–57; Jim Strangeland, 31–24–2 for 1969–73 with 2 conference titles and 1 bowl team; and Wayne Howard, 23–10–0 for 1974–76.

MISCELLANEA

First game was 21–6 loss to Occidental in 1955 . . . first win was 28–12 over LaVerne same year . . . highest score was 65–0 over Cal Baptist in 1955 . . . worst defeat was 65–12 by Cal Poly-SLO in 1956 . . . longest winning streak of 10 in 1975–76 ended by San Jose St. 34–7 . . . longest winless string of 9 in 1973 broken with 35–10 win over Wichita St. . . . Long Beach St. has had no consensus All America players . . . LB Joe Donohue made Academic All America in 1983.

Louisiana State (Fighting Tigers; Purple & Gold) (SEC)

NOTABLE TEAMS

1896—6–0–0. Outscored foes 136–4. 1901—5–1–0. Lost to Auburn 28–0 but blanked others 167–0. 1902—6–1–0. Lost to Vanderbilt 27–5 but shut out others. 1907—7–3–0. Scored 266 and shut out 5. 1908—10–0–0. Outscored foes 442–11, shutting out 7, as Doc Fenton scored 125. 1909—6–2–0. Shut out 5; lost to Sewanee and to unbeaten Arkansas. 1913—6–1–2. Lost only to unbeaten Auburn 7–0 as L.H. Dupont scored 15 TDs. 1915—6–2–0. Shut out 5. 1916—7–1–2. Lost only to Sewanee 7–0. 1919—6–2–0. Shut out 5. 1921—6–1–1. Tied Alabama 7–7 and lost to Tulane 21–0. 1928—6–2–1. Lost to Arkansas and Alabama. 1933—7–0–3. Shut out 6 behind T Jack Torrance; tied Centenary, Vanderbilt and Tulane. 1934—7–2–2. Biff Jones' last team lost close ones to Tulane 13–12 and Tennessee 19–13. 1935—9–1–0. Bernie Moore's 1st team won Tigers' 1st SEC title as E Gaynell Tinsley became 1st LSU consensus All America; lost only to Rice 10–7 in opener, but lost to TCU in Sugar Bowl 3–2. 1936—9–0–1. Scored 281 and shut out 5 as Tinsley starred again and Tigers repeated as SEC champs; tied Texas 6–6 in 2nd game and lost to Santa Clara in Sugar Bowl 21–14. 1937—9–1–0. Shut out 6 behind T Eddie Gatto and lost only to Vanderbilt 7–6; lost to Santa Clara in Sugar Bowl 6–0. 1942—7–3–0. Alvin Dark ran and passed for 989 yards. 1943—5–3–0. Steve Van Buren scored 98 points to lead nation and ran for 847 yards; beat Texas A&M in Orange Bowl 19–14 after losing to Aggies 28–13 in regular season. 1945—7–2–0. Scored 245 but lost to unbeaten Alabama and to Mississippi St. 1946—9–1–0. Y.A. Tittle passed for 13 TDs as Tigers lost only to Georgia Tech 26–7; tied Arkansas in Cotton Bowl 0–0. 1949—8–2–0. Won last 6, but lost to unbeaten Oklahoma in Sugar Bowl 35–0. 1958—10–0–0. Outscored foes 275–53 behind backs Billy Cannon, Johnny Robinson and Warren Rabb and C Max Fugler; won national championship, then beat Clemson in Sugar Bowl 7–0. 1959—9–1–0. Heisman winner Cannon starred again as Tigers shut out 5 and lost only to Tennessee 14–13; lost Sugar Bowl 21–0 to Mississippi (beaten 7–3 in regular season). 1961—9–1–0. Paul Dietzel's last team lost only to Rice 16–3 in opener as G Roy Winston starred; beat Colorado in Orange Bowl 25–7. 1962—8–1–1. Charles McClendon's 1st team led nation in scoring defense and lost only to unbeaten Mississippi 15–7 and tied Rice 6–6 behind T Fred Miller and HB Billy Stovall; beat Texas in Cotton Bowl 13–0. 1963

—7–3–0. Lost only to Rice in first 6. 1964—7–2–1. Won 4 by TD or less as Doug Moreau led nation's kickers with 13 FGs; beat Syracuse in Sugar Bowl 13–10. 1965—7–3–0. Upset undefeated Arkansas in Cotton Bowl 14–7. 1967—6–3–1. No loss by more than 3 points; beat undefeated Wyoming in Sugar Bowl 20–13. 1968—7–3–0. Lost only to Miami (Fla.) in first 6; beat Florida St. in inaugural Peach Bowl 31–27. 1969—9–1–0. Led nation in rushing defense as Tommy Casanova starred at DB and George Bevan at LB; scored 349 but lost to Mississippi 26–23. 1970—9–2–0. Again led nation in rushing defense behind Casanova and LB Mike Anderson while losing only to Texas A&M 20–18 in opener and to Notre Dame 3–0; won SEC but lost to unbeaten national champion Nebraska in Orange Bowl 17–12. 1971 —8–3–0. Scored 320 behind QB Bert Jones and TB Art Cantrelle, with 2 of losses by TD or less; beat Iowa St. in Sun Bowl 33–15. 1972—9–1–1. Jones passed for 1,446 yards and 14 TDs as Tigers lost only to Alabama 35–21 and tied Florida 3–3; lost to Tennessee in Bluebonnet Bowl 24–17. 1973—9–2–0. Won first 9 behind TB Brad Davis and LB Warren Capone before losing to unbeaten national champion Alabama; lost to unbeaten Penn St. in Orange Bowl 16–9. 1977—8–3–0. Scored 375 as Charles Alexander ran for 1,686 yards; lost only to Alabama in last 6, but lost to Stanford in Sun Bowl 24–14. 1978—8–3–0. Alexander (1,172 yards) and QB David Woodley led attack; lost 2 by TD or less and lost to Missouri in Liberty Bowl 20–15. 1982—8–2–1. Scored 365 as Alan Risher passed for 1,834 yards and 17 TDs; lost close ones to Mississippi St. 27–24 and Tulane 31–28, then to Nebraska in Orange Bowl 21–20.

BOWL RECORD

Bluebonnet 0–2–0; Cotton 2–0–1; Liberty 0–1–0; Orange 2–3–0; Peach 1–0–0; Sugar 3–5–0; Sun 1–1–0; Tangerine 1–0–0.

CONFERENCE TITLES

Southern 1932. Southeastern 1935, 1936, 1958, 1961*, 1970.

TOP 10 AP & UPI RANKING

1936	2	1958	1–1	1964	7–7	1971	U–10
1937	8	1959	3–3	1965	8–U	1972	U–10
1946	8	1961	4–3	1969	10–7		
1949	9	1962	7–8	1970	7–6		

MAJOR RIVALS

LSU has played at least 15 games with Alabama (11–32–4), Arkansas (23–12–2), Auburn (14–9–1), Florida (16–12–2), Georgia (9–6–1), Georgia Tech (5–12–0), Kentucky (24–9–1), Louisiana Tech (15–1–0), Mississippi (39–29–4), Mississippi St. (45–29–3), Rice (35–13–5), Southwestern Louisiana (19–0–0), Tennessee (2–15–3), Texas (7–8–1), Texas A&M (22–14–3), Tulane (52–22–7) and Vanderbilt (13–6–1).

COACHES

Dean of LSU coaches was Charles McClendon with record of 137–59–7 for 1962–79, including 1 conference title and 13 bowl teams. He was national coach of the year in 1970. Bernie H. Moore was 83–39–6 for 1935–47 with 2 conference titles and 5 bowl teams. Paul Dietzel was 46–24–3 for 1955–61 with 1 conference title, 3 bowl teams and 1 unbeaten national champion. He was national coach of the year in 1958. Other top records were by Russ Cohen, 23–13–1 for 1928–31; and Lawrence M. (Biff) Jones, 20–5–6 for 1932–34 with 1 conference title and 1 unbeaten team.

MISCELLANEA

First game was 34–0 loss to Tulane in 1893 . . . 1st win was 36–0 over Natchez AC in 1894 . . . 1st win over college foe was 30–0 over Centenary in 1894 . . . highest score was 93–0 over Southwestern Louisiana in 1936 . . . highest since W.W. II was 77–0 over Rice in 1977 . . . worst defeat was 63–9 by Texas A&M in 1914 . . . worst since W.W. II was 46–0 by Tulane in 1948 . . . highest against Tigers since W.W. II was 55–31 by Mississippi in 1980 . . . longest winning streak of 19 in 1957–59 ended by Tennessee 14–13 . . . unbeaten string of 18 in 1933–34 ended by Tulane 13–12 . . . unbeaten string of 16 in 1961–62 ended by Mississippi 15–7 . . . winning streak of 15 in 1907–09 ended by Sewanee 15–6 . . . longest winless string of 7 in 1955–56 broken with 13–0 win over Oklahoma St. . . . LSU has had 10 consensus All America players since 1935 . . . multi-year selections were Gaynell Tinsley, E, 1935–36; Billy Cannon, B, 1958–59; Tom Casanova, DB, 1970–71; and Charles Alexander, RB, 1977–78 . . . others were Ken Kavanaugh, E, 1939; Sid Fournet, T, 1954; Roy Winston, G, 1961; Jerry Stovall, B, 1962; Mike Anderson, LB, 1970; and Bert Jones, QB, 1972 . . . Academic All America players were Mickey Mangham, E, 1959; Charles (Bo) Strange, C, 1960; Billy Booth, T, 1961; Jay Michaelson, K, 1971; Tyler

Lafauci, OG, and Joe Winkler, DB, 1973; Brad Davis, RB, 1974; and Robert Dugas, OT, 1977 . . . Billy Cannon, HB, won Heisman Trophy in 1959 . . . LSU ranks in top 20 in both total victories and all-time winning percentage.

Louisville (Cardinals; Cardinal Red & Black) (Independent)

NOTABLE TEAMS

1913—5–1–0. Lost finale to Kentucky 20–0, but blanked others 251–0. 1925—8–0–0. Tom King's 1st team blanked first 7 foes and beat Marshall 7–2 in finale. 1926—6–2–0. Scored 226 but lost to Xavier (O.) and Centre. 1946—6–2–0. Frank Camp's 1st team lost only to Western Kentucky 20–19 and Eastern Kentucky. 1947—7–0–1. Outscored foes 193–63; tie was with St. Joseph's (Ind.) 7–7. 1949—8–3–0. Scored 343; lost only to Southern Mississippi 26–21 in last 5. 1955—7–2–0. Scored 289 behind Lenny Lyles and won last 7. 1957—8–1–0. Scored 316 as Lyles ran for 1,207 yards and scored 21 TDs; lost only to Kent St. 13–7, but beat Drake in Sun Bowl 34–20. 1960—7–2–0. Gave up only 6 points in 4 October games. 1970—8–3–0. Won last 7 to take first Missouri Valley title; tied Long Beach St. in Pasadena Bowl 24–24. 1972—9–1–0. Scored 309 as Howard Stevens led nation in all-purpose running and John Madeya threw 16 TD passes; lost only to Tulsa 28–26 and shared MVC title.

BOWL RECORD

Independence 0–1–0; Pasadena 0–0–1; Sun 1–0–0.

CONFERENCE TITLES

Missouri Valley 1970, 1972*.

TOP 10 AP & UPI RANKING

None.

MAJOR RIVALS

Louisville has played at least 15 games with Centre (3–10–3), Cincinnati (8–18–1), Dayton (13–12–0), Drake (10–5–1), Eastern Kentucky (15–7–1),

Georgetown (Ky.) (7–10–0), Kent St. (8–9–0), Marshall (16–8–0), Memphis St. (7–14–0), North Texas St. (6–10–0), Transylvania (7–12–0), Tulsa (7–11–0), Western Kentucky (12–12–0) and Wichita St. (13–4–0).

COACHES

Dean of Louisville coaches was Frank Camp with record of 118–95–2 for 1946–68, including 1 bowl champion and 1 unbeaten team. Only other winning record for at least 5 years of coaching was by Tom King with 27–21–0 for 1925–30, including 1 unbeaten team.

MISCELLANEA

First game was 32–0 win over Transylvania in 1912 . . . highest score was 100–0 over Washington (Tenn.) in 1913 . . . highest since W.W. II was 72–0 over Wayne St. in 1955 . . . worst defeat was 105–0 by Murray St. in 1932 . . . worst since W.W. II was 59–0 by Florida St. in 1953 . . . highest against Cardinals since W.W. II was 69–19 by Memphis St. in 1969 . . . longest unbeaten string of 10 in 1925–26 ended by Xavier (O.) 20–7 . . . longest losing string of 24 in 1931–33 broken with 13–7 win over Eastern Kentucky . . . Louisville has had no consensus All America players and no Academic All America selections.

Maryland (Terrapins, Terps; Red & White, Black & Gold) (ACC)

NOTABLE TEAMS

1893—6–0–0. Outscored foes 104–16. 1896—6–2–2. Shut out 5; lost two 6–0 games. 1912—6–1–1. H.C. Byrd's 1st team lost only to St. John's 27–0. 1916—6–2–0. Lost close ones to Navy 14–7 and Haverford 7–6. 1918—4–1–1. Lost opener to American U. 13–6 and tied Johns Hopkins 0–0 in finale. 1920—7–2–0. Shut out 5, losing to Rutgers and Princeton. 1923—7–2–1. Again shut out 5; lost to Virginia Tech 16–7 and to unbeaten Yale 16–14. 1931—8–1–1. G Jess Krajcovic starred as Terps lost only to Vanderbilt 39–12 and tied Kentucky 6–6. 1934—7–3–0. Byrd's last team shut out 6 and lost none by more than 7 points. 1935—7–2–2. HB Bill Guckeyson and E Vic Willis starred as Terps lost only to North Carolina and Indiana. 1937—8–2–0. HB Jim Meade led team to Southern Conference title; lost close ones to Pennsylvania 28–21 and Penn State 21–14. 1942—7–2–0.

Tommy Mont passed for 1,076 yards and 12 TDs as Terps lost only to VMI and Duke. 1945—6–2–1. Bear Bryant's 1st college team scored in double figures in all, losing only to Virginia Tech and William & Mary. 1947—7–2–1. Jim Tatum's 1st team was sparked by Lu Gambino's 16 TDs and 96 points to lead nation in scoring; tied Georgia in Gator Bowl 20–20. 1949—8–1–0. Scored 246 behind FB Ed Modzelewski and lost only to Michigan St. 14–7; beat Missouri in Gator Bowl 20–7. 1950—7–2–1. Scored 274 as Bob Shemonski scored 16 TDs and 97 points. 1951—9–0–0. Outscored foes 353–62, leading nation in scoring average as Modzelewski ran for 834 yards and 11 TDs and G Bob Ward became 1st Maryland All America; upset unbeaten national champion Tennessee in Sugar Bowl 28–13. 1952—7–2–0. Jack Scarbath passed for 1,149 yards and Lloyd Colteryahn caught 32 for 593 yards as Terps won first 7, then lost to Mississippi 21–14 and Alabama. 1953—10–0–0. Outscored foes 298–31, shutting out 6 and leading nation in rushing defense and scoring defense; won national championship but lost to Oklahoma in Orange Bowl 7–0. 1954—7–2–1. Lost to unbeaten UCLA 12–7 and to Miami (Fla.) 9–7 before winning last 5 behind G Bob Pellegrini and HB Ronnie Walker. 1955—10–0–0. Tatum's last team outscored foes 211–57 as Ed Vereb scored 16 TDs and team led nation in rushing defense; lost to unbeaten national champion Oklahoma in Orange Bowl 20–6. 1961—7–3–0. Won 5 by less than TD as Gary Collins caught 30 passes. 1973—8–3–0. Jerry Claiborne's 2nd team scored 319 as Louis Carter ran for 801 yards and 14 TDs and DT Randy White led defense; lost to Georgia in Peach Bowl 17–16. 1974—8–3–0. Scored 313 as Bob Avellini passed for 1,648 yards; no loss by more than 7 points, including 7–3 defeat by Tennessee in Liberty Bowl. 1975—8–2–1. Larry Dick passed for 1,190 yards and Kim Hoover caught 38 for 532 yards as Terps won 2nd straight ACC title; beat Florida in Gator Bowl 13–0. 1976—11–0–0. Alvin Maddox, Steve Atkins and Tim Wilson each ran for more than 600 yards as Terps took ACC again; lost to Houston in Cotton Bowl 30–21. 1978—9–2–0. Atkins ran for 1,261 yards and 11 TDs and Dean Richards caught 35 passes for 575 yards; lost to Texas in Sun Bowl 42–0. 1980—8–3–0. Charles Wysocki ran for 1,359 yards and 11 TDs as team won 4 by less than TD and swept last 5; lost to Florida in Tangerine Bowl 35–20. 1982—8–3–0. Bobby Ross's 1st team scored 353 as Boomer Esiason passed for 2,302 yards and 18 TDs and Willie Joyner ran for 1,063 yards; lost inaugural Aloha Bowl to Washington 21–20. 1983—8–3–0. Esiason passed for 2,322 yards and 15 TDs, as Terps won ACC; lost to Tennessee in Florida Citrus Bowl 30–23.

BOWL RECORD

Aloha 0–1–0; Cotton 0–1–0; Florida Citrus 0–1–0; Gator 2–0–1; Hall of Fame 1–0–0; Liberty 0–1–0; Orange 0–2–0; Peach 0–1–0; Sugar 1–0–0; Sun 0–1–0; Tangerine 0–1–0.

CONFERENCE TITLES

Southern 1937, 1951*. Atlantic Coast 1953*, 1955*, 1974, 1975, 1976, 1983.

TOP 10 AP & UPI RANKING

1951	3–4	1955	3–3
1953	1–1	1976	8–U
1954	8–U		

MAJOR RIVALS

Maryland has played at least 15 games with Clemson (17–14–1), Duke (13–14–0), Florida (6–11–0), Gallaudet (9–6–1), Georgetown (6–9–0), Johns Hopkins (16–11–5), Navy (5–14–0), North Carolina (21–25–1), North Carolina St. (19–17–4), Penn St. (1–26–0), Richmond (11–5–2), St. John's College (18–11–0), South Carolina (17–11–0), Syracuse (13–13–2), Virginia (31–15–2), VMI (14–9–2), Virginia Tech (14–10–0), Wake Forest (23–8–1), Washington & Lee (13–5–2), Washington College (18–3–1) and West Virginia (9–10–2).

COACHES

Dean of Maryland coaches was H.C. Byrd with record of 121–86–17 for 1911–34. Jim Tatum compiled record of 73–15–4 for 1947–55 with 3 conference titles, 5 bowl teams, 3 teams unbeaten in regular season and 1 national champion. Tatum was national coach of the year in 1953. Jerry Claiborne was 77–37–3 for 1972–81 with 3 conference titles, 7 bowl teams and 1 team unbeaten in regular season. Tom Nugent was 36–34–0 for 1959–65; and Bobby Ross was 16–8–0 for 1982–83 with 1 conference title and 2 bowl teams.

MISCELLANEA

First game was 50–0 loss to St. John's in 1892 . . . first win was 36–0 over Eastern H.S. in 1893 . . . first win over college foe was 18–0 over Baltimore

City College in 1893 . . . highest score was 80–0 over Washington College in 1927 . . . highest since W.W. II was 74–13 over Missouri in 1954 . . . worst defeat was 76–0 by Navy in 1913 . . . worst since W.W. II was 48–0 by Penn State in 1969 . . . highest against Terps since W.W. II was 63–27 by Penn State in 1971 . . . longest unbeaten string of 22 in 1950–52 ended by Mississippi 21–14 . . . winning streaks of 15 in 1954–55 ended by Oklahoma 20–6 in Orange Bowl and in 1975–76 ended by Houston 30–21 in Cotton Bowl . . . longest losing string of 16 in 1966–68 broken with 33–24 win over North Carolina . . . consensus All America players were Bob Ward, G, 1951; Dick Modzelewski, T, and Jack Scarbath, B, 1952; Stan Jones, T, 1953; Bob Pellegrini, C, 1955; Gary Collins, E, 1961; Randy White, DL, 1974; Joe Campbell, DT, 1976; and Dale Castro, K, 1979 . . . Academic All America choices were Bernie Faloney, B, 1953; Kim Hoover, DE, 1975; and Joe Muffler, DL, 1978 . . . Outland Trophy winners were Dick Modzelewski, T, 1952; and Randy White, DE, 1974 . . . White also won the Lombardi Trophy in 1974.

Memphis State (Tigers; Blue & Gray) (Independent)

NOTABLE TEAMS

1927—6–2–1. Lost to Middle Tennessee and Southwestern (Tenn.). 1929 —8–0–2. Shut out 6, including 0–0 ties with Southeast Missouri St. and Delta St. 1933—7–1–1. Shut out 5; lost to Western Kentucky 19–0 and tied Arkansas St. 0–0. 1938—10–0–0. Outscored foes 281–35, shutting out 5. 1947—6–2–1. Ralph Hatley's 1st team shut out 5. 1949—9–1–0. Scored 385 and blanked 5, losing only to Mississippi 40–7 in opener. 1950—9–2–0. Scored 374 but lost to Mississippi and Vanderbilt. 1960—8–2–0. Scored 303 behind QB James Earl Wright; lost to Mississippi and Mississippi St. 1961 —8–2–0. Scored 332; lost successive games to Mississippi St. 23–16 and Furman 7–6. 1962—8–1–0. Scored 261 and lost only to unbeaten Mississippi 21–7 in 2nd game. 1963—9–0–1. Dave Casinelli ran for 1,016 yards and 14 TDs to lead nation in scoring and rushing; tie was with unbeaten Mississippi 0–0. 1966—7–2–0. Won 4 by TD or less. 1969—8–2–0. Danny Pierce passed for 1,049 yards to lead Tigers to 2nd straight Missouri Valley title; scored 328 and won last 7. 1973—8–3–0. Flanker Bobby Ward starred as Tigers scored in double figures in all; 2 of losses by less than TD.

BOWL RECORD

Pasadena 1–0–0.

CONFERENCE TITLES

Missouri Valley 1968, 1969, 1971.

TOP 10 AP & UPI RANKING

None.

MAJOR RIVALS

Tigers have played at least 15 games with Arkansas St. (14–18–3), Cincinnati (10–5–0), Louisville (14–7–0), Middle Tennessee St. (8–12–0), Mississippi (5–31–1), Mississippi St. (6–16–0), Murray St. (8–9–0), North Texas St. (15–4–0), Southern Mississippi (13–20–1), Tennessee Tech (8–8–3) and Union (10–11–0).

COACHES

Dean of Memphis St. coaches was Billy Murphy with record of 91–44–1 for 1958–71, including 3 conference titles, 1 bowl champion and 1 unbeaten team. Ralph Hatley was 59–43–5 for 1947–57 with 1 minor bowl champion. Second in tenure was Zach Curlin, 41–60–14 for 1924–36 with 1 unbeaten team.

MISCELLANEA

First game was 0–0 tie with Memphis University School in 1912 . . . first win was 13–6 over Bolton Agricultural College same year . . . highest score was 115–0 over Somerville H.S. in 1916 . . . highest since W.W. II was 76–7 over NATTC in 1950 . . . worst defeat was 92–0 by Mississippi in 1935 . . . worst since W.W. II was 58–0 by Texas A&M in 1978 . . . highest against Tigers since W.W. II was 66–17 by Florida St. in 1979 . . . longest unbeaten string of 17 in 1962–63 ended by Mississippi 30–0 in 1964 . . . longest losing string of 14 in 1936–37 broken with 46–0 win over Jacksonville (Ala.) . . . Memphis State has had no consensus All America players and no Academic All America choices.

Miami (Fla.) (Hurricanes; Orange, Green & White) (Independent)

NOTABLE TEAMS

1926—8-0-0. First year of competition saw only freshman games; outscored foes 122-13, blanking 6. 1933—5-0-2. Shut out 5, including 0-0 ties with Tampa and Stetson; lost to Duquesne 33-7 in Palm Festival game. 1934—5-2-1. Lost to Rollins 14-0 and Tampa 7-6; lost inaugural Orange Bowl to Bucknell 26-0. 1936—6-2-2. Shut out 5 as punt returner Eddie Dunn starred. 1938—8-2-0. Dunn ran for 683 yards and scored 14 TDs, again starring in punt returns. 1941—8-2-0. Shut out 5 but lost to Florida and Alabama. 1942—7-2-0. Lost only to North Carolina St. 2-0 in last 8. 1943—5-1-0. Lost only to Jacksonville NATTC 20-0. 1945—8-1-1. Lost only to Georgia 27-21 and tied South Carolina 13-13 as Harry Ghaul scored 13 TDs; beat Holy Cross in Orange Bowl 13-6. 1946—8-2-0. Ghaul averaged 42.1 yards per punt as team lost only to North Carolina and LSU. 1950—9-0-1. Scored in double figures in all behind B Frank Smith and T Al Carapella; tied Louisville 13-13 in mid-season and lost to unbeaten Clemson in Orange Bowl 15-14. 1951—7-3-0. Smith (with 764 rushing yards) and HB Jim Dooley led Hurricanes; beat Clemson in Gator Bowl 14-0. 1954—8-1-0. Scored 257 as E Frank McDonald starred; lost only to Auburn 14-13. 1956—8-1-1. Led nation in total defense and rushing defense and FB Don Bosseler ran for 723 yards as Hurricanes lost only to Pittsburgh 14-7 in finale. 1961—7-3-0. E Bill Miller caught 43 passes for 640 yards and became Hurricanes' 1st consensus All America choice; lost 2 by 3 points or less, and lost to Syracuse in Liberty Bowl 15-14. 1962—7-3-0. George Mira passed for 1,572 yards as team won 4 by 3 points or less; Andy Gustafson's 4th bowl team lost to Nebraska in Gotham Bowl 36-34. 1966—7-2-1. Swept final 7 after close losses to Florida St. 23-20 and LSU 10-8; beat Virginia Tech in Liberty Bowl 14-7. 1967—7-3-0. Ted Hendricks starred as DE as team lost only to Notre Dame 24-22 in last 8; lost to Colorado in Bluebonnet Bowl 31-21. 1980—8-3-0. Scored in double figures in all behind QB Jim Kelly as MG Jim Burt starred on defense; beat Virginia Tech in Peach Bowl 20-10. 1981—9-2-0. Won last 6 after close losses to Texas 14-7 and Mississippi St. 14-10; Kelly passed for 2,403 yards and Larry Brodsky caught 37 passes for 631 yards while Dan Miller kicked 18 FGs. 1983—10-1-0. Frosh QB Bernie Kosar passed for 2,329 yards and 15 TDs and team ranked 3rd in nation in scoring defense; lost only to Florida 28-3 in opener and upset unbeaten Nebraska 31–30 in Orange Bowl to win national championship.

BOWL RECORD

Bluebonnet 0–1–0; Gator 1–0–0; Gotham 0–1–0; Liberty 1–1–0; Orange 2–2–0; Peach 1–0–0.

CONFERENCE TITLES

None.

TOP 10 AP & UPI RANKING

1954	U–9	1981	8–U
1956	6–6	1983	1–1
1966	9–10		

MAJOR RIVALS

Miami has played at least 12 games with Alabama (2–13–0), Florida (21–24–0), Florida St. (15–12–0), Georgia (4–7–1), Houston (8–7–0), Notre Dame (3–13–1), Pittsburgh (7–8–1), Rollins (14–3–1), South Carolina (6–5–2), Tampa (6–5–2) and Tulane (6–5–1).

COACHES

Dean of Miami coaches was Andy Gustafson with record of 93–65–3 for 1948–63, including 4 bowl teams and 1 team unbeaten in regular season. Jack Harding was 54–32–3 for 1937–42 and 1945–47 with 1 Orange Bowl champion. Other top records were by Charlie Tate, 34–27–3 for 1964–70 with 2 bowl teams; and Howard Schnellenberger, 41–16–0 for 1979–83 with 2 bowl champions and 1 national title. He was coach of the year in 1983.

MISCELLANEA

First game was 7–0 win over Rollins in freshman competition in 1926 ... first varsity game was 39–3 win over Rollins in 1927 ... highest score was 75–7 over Fordham in 1954 ... worst defeat was 70–14 by Texas A&M in 1944 ... worst since W.W. II was 44–0 by Notre Dame in 1973 ... highest against Hurricanes since W.W. II was 56–16 by Syracuse in 1970 ... longest unbeaten string of 14 in 1955–56 ended by Pitt 14–7 ... longest winless string of 9 in 1963–64 broken with 10–7 win over Detroit ... consensus All America players were Bill Miller, E, 1961; Tom Beier, DB,

1966; Ted Hendricks, DE, 1967–68; Tony Cristiani, DL, 1973; Rubin Carter, MG, 1974; and Fred Marion, DB, 1981 . . . Fran Curci, B, was Academic All America in 1959.

Miami (Ohio) (Redskins; Red & White) (MAC)

NOTABLE TEAMS

1907—6–1–0. Lost to DePauw 17–6. 1908—7–0–0. Shut out 6 and outscored foes 109–10. 1913—6–2–0. Lost to Oberlin and Western Reserve. 1915—6–2–0. Lost to Indiana and Denison. 1916—7–0–1. George Little's 1st team outscored foes 239–12, shutting out 6, and won Ohio Conference title. 1917—6–0–2. Blanked foes 202–0 including 0–0 ties with Kentucky and Wooster. 1918—5–0–1. Outscored foes 195–13 to win 3rd straight Ohio title; tie was with Cincinnati 0–0 in finale. 1919—7–1–0. Lost only to Oberlin 13–0. 1921—8–0–0. Little's last team outscored foes 238–12, shutting out 6, and won last Ohio Conference title. 1927—8–1–0. Scored 255 and lost only to Wittenberg 23–0. 1928—6–2–0. Shut out 5. 1929—7–2–0. Shut out 6. 1932—7–1–0. Frank Wilton's 1st team won Buckeye Conference title, losing only to Illinois 20–7 in opener. 1933—7–2–0. Won last 5 after losses to Indiana 7–0 and Ohio U. 6–0. 1936—7–1–1. Won 4 by TD or less and took 3rd Buckeye title; lost to Ohio Wesleyan 13–0 and tied Cincinnati 0–0. 1943—7–2–1. Scored 294 but lost to Western Michigan and Arkansas A&M. 1944—8–1–0. Sid Gillman's 1st team lost only to DePauw 13–7 in finale. 1945—7–2–0. Shut out 5 but lost to Miami (Fla.) 27–13 and Purdue 21–7. 1946—7–3–0. Close losses to Purdue 13–7, Miami (Fla.) 20–17 and Cincinnati 13–7. 1947—8–0–1. Gillman's last team starred Paul Dietzel at C, Ara Parseghian at HB and Mel Olix at QB (1,081 yards passing); tied Xavier (0.) 6–6, then beat Texas Tech in Sun Bowl 13–12. 1948—7–1–1. Scored 249 as Olix threw 12 TD passes; won 1st Mid-American Conference title, losing only to Dayton 7–0 and tying Virginia 14–14. 1950—8–1–0. Scored 322 as John Pont starred at HB; lost only to Xavier (0.) 7–0 in 2nd game, and beat Arizona St. in Salad Bowl 34–21. 1951—7–3–0. Ara Parseghian's 1st team starred Pont at HB and Clive Rush at E (32 pass receptions). 1952—8–1–0. Scored 284 as Tom Pagna ran for 1,044 yards and Jim Root passed for 1,056; lost finale to Cincinnati 34–9. 1953—7–1–1. Scored 327 behind Pagna and QB Dick Hunter; lost only to Cincinnati 14–0 in finale. 1954—8–1–0. Scored 294 and won MAC title, losing only to Dayton 20–12. 1955—9–0–0. Parseghian's last team outscored foes 226–47 to take

4th MAC title. 1956—7-1-1. John Pont's 1st team lost only to George Washington 7-6 in opener and tied Bowling Green 7-7 as Bill Mallory starred at E. 1962—8-1-1. Pont's last team lost only to Ohio U. 12-6 and tied Bowling Green 24-24 as E Bob Jencks scored 84 points; lost to Houston in Tangerine Bowl 49-21. 1965—7-3-0. Bruce Matte ran and passed for 1,390 yards and Redskins won last 6 in Bo Schembechler's 3rd year. 1966 —9-1-0. John Erisman caught 41 passes for 600 yards and 9 TDs to lead team to 2nd straight MAC title; lost only to Bowling Green 17-14. 1968— 7-3-0. Schembechler's last team lost 2 by less than 3 points. 1969—7-3-0. Bill Mallory's 1st team lost none by more than 4 points as Jim Bengala passed for 1,276 yards and Mike Palija caught 43 for 567 yards. 1970—7-3-0. Lost 2 by 1 point each as Bengala (1,265 yards) and Palija (41 catches for 639 yards) teamed up again and Tim Fortney ran for 1,063 yards. 1971—7-3-0. Bob Hitchens ran for 1,157 yards. 1972—7-3-0. Hitchens ran for 1,370 yards and scored 90 points. 1973—10-0-0. Led nation in total defense and rushing defense in Mallory's last year; outscored foes 207-69 to win MAC and beat Florida in Tangerine Bowl 16-7. 1974—9-0-1. Dick Crum's 1st team scored 282 behind running of Rob Carpenter; tied Purdue 7-7 in 2nd game and beat Georgia in Tangerine Bowl 21-10. 1975—10-1-0. Carpenter ran for 1,022 yards as Redskins lost only to Michigan St. 14-13 and won 3rd straight MAC title; beat South Carolina in Tangerine Bowl 20-7. 1977 —10-1-0. Crum's last team won 5 by TD or less, losing only to South Carolina 42-19 in 2nd game; Larry Fortner passed for 1,473 yards and 15 TDs. 1978—8-2-1. Won last 7 as Mark Hunter ran for 1,046 yards. 1981 —8-2-1. Greg Jones ran for 1,134 yards as Redskins lost only to North Carolina and Toledo.

BOWL RECORD

Salad 1-0-0; Sun 1-0-0; Tangerine 3-1-0.

CONFERENCE TITLES

Ohio Conference 1916, 1917, 1918, 1921. Buckeye 1932, 1933, 1936. Mid-American 1948, 1950, 1954, 1955, 1957, 1958, 1965*, 1966*, 1973, 1974, 1975, 1977.

TOP 10 AP & UPI RANKING

1974	10-10

MAJOR RIVALS

Miami has played at least 15 games with Bowling Green (28–10–3), Cincinnati (48–34–6), Dayton (29–10–3), Denison (15–7–2), Kent St. (25–6–0), Marshall (28–4–1), Ohio U. (34–25–1), Ohio Wesleyan (17–15–1), Toledo (21–10–0), Western Michigan (33–8–0) and Wittenberg (12–9–1).

COACHES

Most victories at the "cradle of coaches" were compiled by Frank Wilton with record of 44–39–5 for 1932–41, including 3 conference titles. Best winning percentage for at least 5 years of coaching was by Ara Parseghian with 39–6–1 for 1951–55, including 2 conference titles and 1 unbeaten team. Other outstanding records were by George Little, 27–3–2 for 1916 and 1919–21 with 2 unbeaten teams; Chester Pittser, 41–25–2 for 1924–31; Sid Gillman, 31–6–1 for 1944–47 with an unbeaten bowl champion; John Pont, 43–22–2 for 1956–62 with 2 conference titles and a bowl team; Glenn E. (Bo) Schembechler, 40–17–3 for 1963–68 with 2 conference titles; Bill Mallory, 39–12–0 for 1969–73 with 1 conference title and an unbeaten bowl champion; and Dick Crum, 34–10–1 for 1974–77 with 3 conference titles, 2 bowl champions and an unbeaten team. Bo Schembechler ranks in top 15 in winning percentage.

MISCELLANEA

First game was 0–0 tie with Cincinnati in 1888 . . . first win was 34–0 over Cincinnati in 1889 . . . highest score was 91–0 over Earlham in 1917 . . . highest since W.W. II was 81–0 over Toledo in 1953 . . . worst defeat was 104–0 by Ohio Wesleyan in 1891 . . . worst since 1900 was 80–0 by Ohio St. in 1904 . . . worst since W.W. II was 49–7 by North Carolina in 1981. Tied for highest against Redskins since W.W. II was defeat 49–21 by Houston in Tangerine Bowl in 1962 . . . longest unbeaten string of 27 in 1915–19 ended by Oberlin 13–0 . . . unbeaten string of 24 in 1972–75 ended by Michigan St. 14–13 . . . longest winless string of 16 in 1939–40 broken with 53–0 win over Hanover in 1941 . . . Miami has had no consensus All America players . . . Andy Pederzolli, DB, was Academic All America in 1973 . . . Miami ranks in top 25 in both all-time wins and winning percentage.

Michigan (Wolverines; Maize & Blue) (Big 10)

NOTABLE TEAMS

1888—4–1–0. Outscored foes 126–14 in first 4 but lost finale to Chicago U. Club 26–4. 1890—4–1–0. Lost only to Cornell in finale 20–5. 1893—7–3–0. Scored 278 and won last 5. 1894—8–1–1. Lost only to Cornell 22–0. 1895 —8–1–0. Scored 261 and shut out 7, losing only to Harvard 4–0. 1896— 9–1–0. Shut out 8 but lost finale to Chicago 7–6. 1897—6–1–1. Shut out 5, losing only to Chicago 21–12. 1898—10–0–0. Outscored foes 205–28, shutting out 6, and won 1st Big 10 title as C William Cunningham was 1st All America. 1899—8–2–0. Shut out first 7 before losing to Pennsylvania 11–10. 1900—7–2–1. Shut out 6. 1901—10–0–0. Fielding H. Yost's 1st team blanked opponents 501–0 to earn national championship as E Neil Snow starred and Willie Heston scored 20 TDs; beat Stanford in inaugural Rose Bowl 49–0. 1902—11–0–0. "Point-a-minute" team outscored foes 644–12 and repeated as national champs as Heston scored 15 TDs. 1903—11–0–1. Scored 565 as HB Heston scored 16 TDs; scored on only by Minnesota in 6–6 tie. 1904—10–0–0. Yost's 4th straight unbeaten team outscored foes 567–22 and won 5th Big 10 title as Heston added 21 TDs to career total. 1905—12–1–0. Blanked 12 foes 495–0 before losing finale to unbeaten national champion Chicago 2–0. 1906—4–1–0. Lost finale to Pennsylvania 17–0 but won Big 10. 1907—5–1–0. Blanked foes 107–0 before losing finale to Penn 6–0. 1909—6–1–0. Lost only to Notre Dame 11–3 behind G Albert Benbrook. 1910—3–0–3. Benbrook and E Stanfield Wells led defense that gave up no more than 3 points in any game. 1911—5–1–2. Lost only to Cornell 6–0. 1912—5–2–0. Lost to Syracuse and Penn. 1913— 6–1–0. Lost only to unbeaten Michigan St. 12–7 behind HB James Craig and T Miller Pontius. 1916—7–2–0. Won first 7 before losing squeakers to Cornell 23–20 and Penn 10–7. 1917—8–2–0. Won first 8 behind FB Cedric Smith. 1918—5–0–0. Outscored foes 96–6 and won Big 10. 1920—5–2–0. Lost close ones to Illinois 7–6 and unbeaten Ohio State 14–7. 1921—5–1–1. Shut out 5, losing only to Ohio State 14–0. 1922—6–0–1. Outscored foes 183–13 behind HB Harry Kipke; tie was 0–0 with Vanderbilt. 1923— 8–0–0. Yost's 8th unbeaten team outscored foes 150–12 to take 2nd straight Big 10 title. 1924—6–2–0. Shut out 5 behind G E.R. Slaughter. 1925— 7–1–0. Lost to Northwestern 3–2 but outscored others 225–0 behind QB Benny Friedman (760 yards and 11 TDs passing) and E Bennie Oosterbaan. 1926—7–1–0. Yost's last team lost only to Navy 10–0 and won 11th Big 10 title behind Friedman and Oosterbaan. 1927—6–2–0. Shut out 5; 1 of losses was to national champion Illinois. 1930—8–0–1. Harry Kipke's 2nd team shut out 6 and won Big 10; tie was with Michigan St. 0–0. 1931—8–1–1. Shut out 8, including last 6; lost only to Ohio St. 20–7 and tied Michigan St. 0–0. 1932—8–0–0. Blanked 6 and won national championship behind QB Harry Newman, C Charles Bernard and E Tom Petoskey. 1933—7–0–1. Kipke's 2nd straight national champion shut out 5 and won 4th consecutive Big 10 title behind Bernard, Petoskey and T Francis Wistert; tie was with Minnesota 0–0. 1938—6–1–1. Fritz Crisler's 1st team lost only to Minnesota 7–6 behind G Ralph Heikkinen. 1939—6–2–0. Tom Harmon ran and passed for 1,372 yards and scored 14 TDs and 102 points. 1940—7–1–0. Shut out 5 and lost only to unbeaten national champion Minnesota 7–6 as triple threat Harmon led nation for 2nd straight season in both scoring (117 points) and all-purpose running (1,312 yards) and won Heisman Trophy. 1941—6–1–1. Lost only to unbeaten national champion Minnesota 7–0 and tied Ohio St. 20–20 as FB Bob Westfall ran for 688 yards. 1942—7–3–0. Lost only to Ohio St. in last 5 behind linemen Albert Wistert and Julius Franks. 1943—8–1–0. Scored 302 behind FB Bill Daley (817 yards) and won Big 10 while losing only to national champion Notre Dame 35–12. 1944—8–2–0. Lost to Indiana and unbeaten Ohio St. (18–14). 1945—7–3–0. Two of losses were to unbeaten teams, Indiana and national champion Army. 1946—6–2–1. Bob Chappuis ran and passed for 1,265 yards as Wolverines lost only to unbeaten Army 20–13 and to Illinois 13–9. 1947—9–0–0. Crisler's last team outscored foes 345–53 and led nation in total offense, passing and scoring average as Chappuis ran and passed for 1,625 yards and HB Chalmers Elliott scored 10 TDs; beat Southern California in Rose Bowl 49–0. 1948—9–0–0. Bennie Oosterbaan's 1st team outscored foes 252–44, shutting out 5 and leading nation in scoring defense; won national championship behind QB Pete Elliott, E Dick Rifenburg and T Alvin Wistert. 1949—6–2–1. Wistert starred again as Wolverines lost only to unbeaten Army 21–7 and to Northwestern 21–20 in successive games. 1950—5–3–1. HB Don Dufek and T Allen Wahl led team to 4th straight Big 10 title with wins in 5 of last 6 games; upset unbeaten California in Rose Bowl 14–6. 1955—7–2–0. Won first 6 as E Ron Kramer starred. 1956—7–2–0. Kramer starred again as Wolverines lost only to Michigan St. and Minnesota. 1964—8–1–0. Bob Timberlake ran and passed for 1,515 yards and kicked 23 extra points to lead team to Big 10 title; lost only to Purdue 21–20 and beat Oregon St. in Rose Bowl 34–7. 1968—8–2–0. Bump Elliott's last team lost opener to California and finale to unbeaten national champion Ohio St.; Ron Johnson ran for 1,391 yards and 19 TDs and Dennis

Brown ran and passed for 1,777 yards. 1969—8–2–0. Bo Schembechler's 1st team won last 5 to take Big 10 as Don Moorhead had 1,886 yards of total offense and Jim Mandich caught 50 passes for 676 yards; lost to Southern California in Rose Bowl 10–3. 1970—9–1–0. Scored 288 behind linemen Dan Dierdorf and Henry Hill but lost finale to unbeaten national champion Ohio St. 20–9. 1971—11–0–0. Outscored foes 409–70 and led nation in rushing defense and scoring defense behind HB Billy Taylor (1,297 yards rushing), LB Mike Taylor and G Reggie McKenzie; lost to Stanford in Rose Bowl 13–12. 1972—10–1–0. Gave up just 57 points and again led nation in scoring defense but lost finale to Ohio St. 14–11; T Paul Seymour starred on line. 1973—10–0–1. Scored 330 behind QB Dennis Franklin; tie was with Ohio St. 10–10 in finale. 1974—10–1–0. Scored 324 and won share of 4th straight Big 10 title while leading nation in scoring defense but lost finale to Ohio St. 12–10; Gordon Bell ran for 1,048 yards and 11 TDs. 1975— 8–1–2. Scored 318 as Bell ran for 1,388 yards and 14 TDs; lost finale to unbeaten Ohio St. 21–14 and lost to Oklahoma in Orange Bowl 14–6. 1976 —10–1–0. Scored 426 and shut out 5 while leading nation in total offense, rushing, scoring average and scoring defense as Rob Lytle ran for 1,469 yards and 16 TDs; lost only to Purdue 16–14, then to Southern California in Rose Bowl 14–6. 1977—10–1–0. Scored 333 behind linemen Walt Downing and Mark Donahue as Russell Davis ran for 1,092 yards and Rick Leach had 1,723 yards of total offense; lost to Minnesota 16–0 and to Washington in Rose Bowl 27–20. 1978—10–1–0. Scored 362 behind Leach's 1,894 yards of total offense; lost to Michigan St. 24–15 and to Southern California in Rose Bowl 17–10. 1979—8–3–0. Lost none by more than 3 points, including 17–15 loss to North Carolina in Gator Bowl. 1980— 9–2–0. Won last 8 to take 30th Big 10 title as Butch Woolfolk ran for 1,042 yards and Anthony Carter caught 51 passes for 818 yards and 14 TDs; beat Washington in Rose Bowl 23–6. 1982—8–3–0. Lawrence Ricks ran for 1,300 yards and Steve Smith passed for 1,681 yards and 14 TDs as Wolverines lost 2 by TD or less; lost to UCLA in Rose Bowl 24–14. 1983— 9–2–0. Scored 348 as Smith passed for 1,295 yards and 13 TDs and Bob Bergeron kicked 15 FGs and 30 extra points; Schembechler's 11th bowl team lost to Auburn in Sugar Bowl 9–7.

BOWL RECORD

Bluebonnet 1–0–0; Gator 0–1–0; Orange 0–1–0; Rose 5–6–0; Sugar 0–1–0.

CONFERENCE TITLES

Big 10 1898, 1901*, 1902, 1903*, 1904*, 1906*, 1918*, 1922*, 1923*, 1925, 1926*, 1930*, 1931*, 1932, 1933, 1943*, 1947, 1948, 1949*, 1950, 1964, 1969*, 1971, 1972*, 1973*, 1974*, 1976*, 1977*, 1978*, 1980, 1982.

TOP 10 AP & UPI RANKING

1940	3	1947	2	1970	9–7	1977	9–8
1941	5	1948	1	1971	6–4	1978	5–5
1942	9	1949	7	1972	6–6	1980	4–4
1943	3	1950	9–6	1973	6–6	1981	U–10
1944	8	1956	7–7	1974	3–5	1983	8–9
1945	6	1964	4–4	1975	8–8		
1946	6	1969	9–8	1976	3–3		

MAJOR RIVALS

Michigan has played at least 15 games with Albion (16–1–0), Case (26–0–1), Chicago (20–8–0), Cornell (6–12–0), Illinois (50–19–0), Indiana (32–8–0), Iowa (27–5–3), Michigan St. (50–21–5), Minnesota (49–22–3), Navy (12–5–1), Northwestern (39–11–2), Notre Dame (11–5–0), Ohio St. (44–31–5), Pennsylvania (11–8–2), Purdue (26–9–0) and Wisconsin (34–8–1).

COACHES

Dean of Michigan coaches was Fielding H. Yost with record of 165–29–10 for 1901–23 and 1925–26, including 10 conference titles, a Rose Bowl champion, 8 unbeaten teams and 2 national champions. He ranks in top 10 in both all-time victories and winning percentage. Glenn E. (Bo) Schembechler compiled a record of 140–31–3 for 1969–83 with 10 conference titles, 11 bowl teams and 2 teams unbeaten in regular season. He ranks in top 15 in winning percentage. Other outstanding records were by Harry G. Kipke, 46–26–4 for 1929–37 with 4 conference titles, 3 unbeaten teams and 2 national champions; H.O. (Fritz) Crisler, 71–16–3 for 1938–47 with 2 conference titles, 1 Rose Bowl champion and 1 unbeaten team; Bennie G. Oosterbaan, 63–33–4 for 1948–58 with 3 conference titles, 1 Rose Bowl champion and 1 unbeaten national champion; and Chalmers W. (Bump) Elliott, 51–42–2 for 1959–68 with 1 conference title and 1 Rose Bowl champion. National coach of the year awards went to Fritz Crisler, 1947; Bennie Oosterbaan, 1948; and Bo Schembechler, 1969.

MISCELLANEA

First game was win over Racine in 1879 . . . first win over college foe was 17–5 over Stevens Institute in 1883 . . . highest score was 130–0 over West Virginia in 1904 . . . highest since W.W. II was 70–14 over Navy in 1976 and 70–21 over Illinois in 1981 . . . biggest margin since W.W. II was 69–0 over Pittsburgh in 1947 and over Northwestern in 1975 . . . worst defeat was 56–0 by Cornell in 1889 . . . highest against Wolverines was 58–12 by Cornell in 1891 . . . highest since 1900 was 55–24 defeat by Northwestern in 1958 . . . worst defeat since 1900 was 40–0 by Minnesota in 1935 . . . worst since W.W. II was 50–14 by Ohio St. in 1968 . . . longest unbeaten string of 56 in 1901–05 broken by Chicago 2–0 . . . winning streak of 25 in 1946–49 ended by Army 21–7 . . . unbeaten string of 22 in 1931–33 ended by Michigan St. 16–0 in 1934 . . . unbeaten string of 21 in 1973–74 ended by Ohio St. 12–10 . . . longest losing string of 7 in 1936–37 broken with 7–6 win over Iowa . . . Michigan has had 44 consensus All America players since 1898 . . . multi-year choices were Willie Heston, B, 1903–04; Albert Benbrook, G, 1909–10; Bennie Oosterbaan, E, 1925–27; Benny Friedman, B, 1925–26; Tom Harmon, B, 1939–40; Alvin Wistert, T, 1948–49; Ron Kramer, E, 1955–56; Dave Brown, DB, 1973–74; Mark Donahue, G, 1976–77; and Anthony Carter, WR, 1981–82 . . . unanimous choices for 1 year were Harry Newman, B, 1932; Chuck Bernard, C, 1933; Ralph Heikkinen, G, 1938; Bill Daley, B, 1943; Bob Chappuis, B, 1947; Jack Clancy, E, 1966; Jim Mandich, E, 1969; and Mike Taylor, LB, 1971 . . . others selected since 1970 were Dan Dierdorf, T, 1970; Reggie McKenzie, G, 1971; Paul Seymour, T, and Randy Logan, DB, 1972; Dave Gallagher, DL, 1973; Rob Lytle, RB, 1976; Ron Simpkins, LB, 1979; and Ed Muransky, OL, and Kurt Becker, OL, 1981 . . . Academic All America selections were Dick Balzhiser, B, 1952; Jim Orwig, T, 1955 and 1957; Bob Timberlake, QB, 1964; Dave Fisher, FB, and Dick Vidmer, QB, 1966; Jim Mandich, E, 1969; Phil Seymour, DE, 1970; Bruce Elliott, DB, 1971; Bill Hart, OG, 1972; Kirk Lewis, OG, 1974; Dan Jilek, DE, 1975; Norm Betts, TE, 1981; Robert Thompson, LB, 1982; and Stefan Humphries, OG, 1982–83 . . . Tom Harmon, B, won Heisman Trophy in 1940 . . . Michigan ranks in top 5 in both all-time victories and winning percentage.

Michigan State (Spartans; Green & White) (Big 10)

NOTABLE TEAMS

1903—6-1-1. Chester Brewer's 1st team shut out 5, losing only to Notre Dame 12-0. 1904—8-1-0. Outscored foes 380-16, shutting out 6 and losing only to Albion 4-0. 1905—9-2-0. Shut out 8 but lost to Notre Dame and Northwestern. 1906—7-2-2. Shut out 7; lost close ones to Notre Dame 5-0 and Olivet 8-6. 1908—6-0-2. Shut out first 5, including 0-0 ties with Michigan and DePaul. 1909—8-1-0. Lost only to Notre Dame 17-0; outscored others 233-0. 1910—6-1-0. Brewer's last team for 7 years shut out 5, losing only to Michigan 6-3. 1911—5-1-0. John Macklin's 1st team lost only to Michigan 15-3. 1912—7-1-0. Scored 297, losing only to Michigan 55-7. 1913—7-0-0. Outscored foes 180-28, beating Michigan for first time 12-7. 1914—5-2-0. Lost to Michigan and Nebraska. 1915—5-1-0. Macklin's last team scored 258 as B Jerry DaPrato became Spartans' 1st consensus All America; lost only to Oregon St. 20-0. 1930—5-1-2. Shut out 5, losing only to Georgetown 14-13. 1932—7-1-0. Scored 220, losing only to unbeaten national champion Michigan 26-0. 1934—8-1-0. Charles Bachman's 2nd team won 3 by TD or less; lost only to Syracuse 10-0. 1935—6-2-0. G Sidney Wagner starred as Spartans lost only to Boston College and Marquette. 1936—6-1-2. Shut out 5, losing only to Marquette 13-7. 1937—8-1-0. Won 4 by TD or less and lost only to Manhattan 3-0; lost to Auburn in Orange Bowl 6-0. 1944—6-1-0. Led nation in pass defense while losing only to Missouri 13-7. 1947—7-2-0. Biggie Munn's 1st team lost only to Kentucky 7-6 after opening game 55-0 pasting by unbeaten Michigan. 1948—6-2-2. Unbeaten in last 7 after losses to unbeaten national champion Michigan (13-7) and Notre Dame; Lynn Chandnois scored 12 TDs. 1950—8-1-0. Scored 243 as Sonny Grandelius ran for 1,023 yards and 12 TDs; lost only to Maryland 34-7. 1951—9-0-0. Scored 270 behind T Don Coleman, E Bob Carey and QB Al Dorow; won 4 by TD or less. 1952—9-0-0. Scored 312 behind G Frank Kush and C Dick Tamburo and led nation in rushing defense on way to national championship. 1953—8-1-0. Munn's last team shared Big 10 title in 1st year in league, losing only to Purdue 6-0; beat UCLA in Rose Bowl 28-20. 1955—8-1-0. Duffy Daugherty's 2nd team lost only to Michigan 14-7 behind QB Earl Morrall and T Norman Masters; beat UCLA in Rose Bowl 17-14. 1956—7-2-0. Lost close ones to Illinois 20-13 and Minnesota 14-13. 1957—8-1-0. Scored 264 behind C Dan Currie and HB Walt Kowalczyk (9 TDs); lost only to Purdue 20-13. 1960—6-2-1.

Lost only to Ohio St. in last 6. 1961—7–2–0. Lost successive games to Minnesota and Purdue (7–6). 1963—6–2–1. Lost to Southern California (13–10) and Illinois. 1965—10–0–0. Led nation in rushing defense and scoring defense behind DE Bubba Smith and DB George Webster and scored in double figures in all behind QB Steve Juday and HB Clint Jones (12 TDs); won share of national title despite 14–12 Rose Bowl loss to UCLA team beaten 13–3 in season opener. 1966—9–0–1. Daugherty's 2nd straight unbeaten team scored 293 as Gene Washington caught 27 passes for 677 yards and 7 TDs with Smith and Webster again sparking defense; tie was with unbeaten Notre Dame 10–10. 1978—8–3–0. Scored 411 as Ed Smith passed for 2,226 yards and 20 TDs and Kirk Gibson caught 42 for 806 yards; won last 7 to gain share of Big 10 title.

BOWL RECORD

Orange 0–1–0; Rose 2–1–0.

CONFERENCE TITLES

Big 10 1953*, 1965, 1966, 1978*.

TOP 10 AP & UPI RANKING

1950	8–9	1953	3–3	1957	3–3	1965	2–1
1951	2–2	1955	2–2	1961	8–9	1966	2–2
1952	1–1	1956	9–10	1963	9–10		

MAJOR RIVALS

Spartans have played at least 15 games with Albion (11–4–3), Alma (22–4–4), Illinois (11–11–1), Indiana (23–9–2), Iowa (10–10–1), Kalamazoo (9–8–0), Marquette (18–6–1), Michigan (21–50–5), Minnesota (13–11–0), Northwestern (20–8–0), Notre Dame (17–31–1), Ohio St. (8–14–0), Olivet (18–4–1), Purdue (18–18–2) and Wisconsin (15–11–0).

COACHES

Dean of Michigan St. coaches was Hugh (Duffy) Daugherty with record of 109–69–5 for 1954–72, including 2 conference titles, 2 bowl teams, 2 teams unbeaten in regular season and 1 national champion. He was national coach of the year in 1955 and 1965. Clarence (Biggie) Munn was 54–9–2 for 1947–53 with 1 conference title, 1 Rose Bowl champion, 2 perfect records and 1 national champion. He was national coach of the year in 1952. Other outstanding records were by Chester L. Brewer, 58–23–7 for 1903–10, 1917 and 1919 with 1 unbeaten team; John F. Macklin, 29–5–0 for 1911–15 with 1 perfect record; James H. Crowley, 22–8–3 for 1929–32; Charles W. Bachman, 70–34–10 for 1933–46 with 1 bowl team; and Darryl D. Rogers, 24–18–2 for 1976–79 with 1 conference title.

MISCELLANEA

First game was 10–0 win over Lansing H.S. in 1896 . . . 1st win over college foe was 26–6 over Olivet in 1897 . . . highest score was 109–0 over Olivet in 1920 . . . highest since W.W. II was 75–0 over Arizona in 1949 . . . worst defeat was 119–0 by Michigan in 1902 . . . worst since W.W. II was 55–0 by Michigan in 1947 . . . highest against Spartans since W.W. II was 56–14 by UCLA in 1974 . . . longest winning streak of 28 in 1950–53 ended by Purdue 6–0 . . . winning streak of 15 in 1912–14 ended by Michigan 3–0 . . . longest winless string of 11 in 1916–17 broken with 21–6 win over Albion in 1918 . . . Michigan State has had 17 consensus All America players since 1915 . . . multi-year choices were Bubba Smith, DE, and George Webster, DB, 1965–66 . . . unanimous choices for single year were Don Coleman, T, 1951; and Brad VanPelt, DB, 1972 . . . others since 1960 were George Saimes, B, 1962; Sherman Lewis, B, 1963; and Clint Jones, B, 1966 . . . Academic All America selections were John Wilson, HB, 1952; Don Dohoney, E, 1953; Buck Nystrom, G, 1955; Branche Martin, HB, 1957; Don Bierowicz, DT, and Don Japinga, DB, 1965; Pat Gallinagh, DT, 1966; Al Brenner, E and S, 1968; Ron Saul, OG, and Rich Saul, DE, 1969; John Shinsky, DT, 1973; and Alan Davis, DB, 1979 . . . Ed Bagdon, G, won Outland Trophy in 1949 . . . Spartans rank in top 20 in all-time winning percentage.

Minnesota (Golden Gophers; Maroon & Gold) (Big 10)

NOTABLE TEAMS

1890—5–1–1. Scored 208; tied Ex-Collegiates 0–0 and lost to Ex-Collegian 14–11. 1892—5–0–0. Scored 120, double figures in all. 1893—6–0–0. Outscored foes 148–32. 1895—7–3–0. Shut out 5; lost only to Grinnell 6–4 in last 6 games. 1896—8–2–0. Shut out 6; lost first 2 to Wisconsin 6–0 and Michigan 6–4. 1900—10–0–2. Dr. Henry Williams' 1st team shut out 9 and won Gophers' 1st Big 10 title. 1901—9–1–0. Lost opener to unbeaten Wisconsin 18–0 but shut out others 183–0. 1902—9–2–0. Scored 335 and shut out 8, losing only to unbeaten teams, national champion Michigan and Nebraska (6–0). 1903—13–0–1. Scored 618 and shut out 12 as T Fred Schacht became 1st consensus All America; tie was with unbeaten Michigan 6–6 in 3rd game. 1904—13–0–0. Outscored foes 725–12, blanking all but Nebraska (16–12), and won share of 3rd Big 10 title. 1905—10–1–0. Outscored foes 466–22, shutting out 9; lost opener to Wisconsin 16–12. 1906 —4–1–0. Lost only to Carlisle Indians 17–0 while winning Big 10. 1909— 6–1–0. Lost only to Michigan 15–6 in finale as Johnny McGovern starred at QB. 1910—6–1–0. Lost finale to Michigan 6–0 but blanked others 179–0. 1911—6–0–1. Yielded just 15 points in winning 3rd straight Big 10 title; tie was with Wisconsin 6–6. 1913—5–2–0. Lost close ones to unbeaten teams, Nebraska 7–0 and Chicago 13–7. 1914—6–1–0. Lost only to unbeaten Illinois 21–6. 1915—6–0–1. Williams' 5th unbeaten team starred Bert Baston at E; tie with Illinois 6–6. 1916—6–1–0. Scored 348 as Baston starred again along with QB Shorty Long; lost only to Illinois 14–9. 1917 —4–1–0. Lost only to Wisconsin 10–7. 1923—5–1–1. Lost only to unbeaten Michigan 10–0 and tied Wisconsin 0–0 as Earl Martineau starred at HB. 1927—6–0–2. Ties with Indiana 14–14 and Notre Dame 7–7. 1928—6– 2–0. Lost close ones to Iowa 7–6 and Northwestern 10–9. 1929—6–2–0. Dr. Clarence Spears' last team won last 5 behind T Bronko Nagurski; losses were to Iowa 9–7 and Michigan 7–6. 1931—7–3–0. Biggie Munn starred at G as Gophers lost only to Stanford in last 6. 1933—4–0–4. Bernie Bierman's 2nd team had 6 games decided by TD or less. 1934—8–0–0. Outscored foes 270–38 behind HB Pug Lund, G Bill Bevan and E Butch Larson and won 1st national championship. 1935—8–0–0. Bierman's 3rd straight unbeaten team outscored foes 194–46 behind linemen Bud Wilkinson and Dick Smith. 1936—7–1–0. Shut out 5 behind T Ed Widseth and won national champion- ship despite 6–0 loss to Northwestern in mid-season. 1937—6–2–0. Lost close ones to Nebraska 14–9 and Notre Dame 7–6 but won 11th Big 10 title. 1938—6–2–0. Lost to Northwestern 6–3 and Notre Dame, but repeated as conference champs. 1940—8–0–0. Won 5 by TD or less behind T Urban Odson and HB George Franck and won national title. 1941—8–0–0. Bier- man's 5th unbeaten team outscored foes 186–38 behind Heisman winner Bruce Smith at HB and Dick Wildung at T and retained national title. 1948 —7–2–0. Lost only to Northwestern 19–16 and to unbeaten national cham- pion Michigan as T Leo Nomellini and E Bud Grant starred. 1949—7–2–0. Lost close ones to Michigan 14–7 and Purdue 13–7 in successive games as C Clayton Tonnemaker starred along with Nomellini and Grant. 1954—

7–2–0. Murray Warmath's 1st team lost only to Michigan and Wisconsin as Bob McNamara ran for 708 yards. 1956—6–1–2. Won 4 by TD or less and lost only to Iowa 7–0. 1960—8–1–0. Outscored foes 221–71, losing only to Purdue 23–14 and winning share of 1st Big 10 title in 19 years behind linemen Tom Brown and Greg Larson; lost to Washington in Rose Bowl 17–7. 1961—7–2–0. Lost only to Missouri 6–0 in opener and Wisconsin 23–21 in finale behind QB Sandy Stephens and T Bobby Bell; beat UCLA in Rose Bowl 21–3. 1962—6–2–1. Shut out 5 as Bell starred again. 1967—8–2–0. Won 4 by TD or less and won share of Big 10 title.

BOWL RECORD

Hall of Fame 0–1–0; Rose 1–1–0.

CONFERENCE TITLES

Big 10 1900*, 1903*, 1904*, 1906*, 1909, 1910*, 1911, 1915*, 1934, 1935*, 1937, 1938, 1940, 1941, 1960*, 1967*.

TOP 10 AP & UPI RANKING

1936	1	1941	1	1961	6–6
1937	5	1949	8	1962	10–10
1938	10	1956	U–9		
1940	1	1960	1–1		

MAJOR RIVALS

Minnesota has played at least 15 games with Chicago (13–5–1), Grinnell (12–2–2), Illinois (24–19–2), Indiana (27–15–3), Iowa (51–24–2), Michigan (22–49–3), Michigan St. (11–13–0), Nebraska (29–17–2), North Dakota (18–0–0), Northwestern (39–22–4), Ohio St. (6–21–0), Purdue (22–17–3), Washington (10–7–0) and Wisconsin (49–36–8).

COACHES

Dean of Minnesota coaches was Dr. Henry L. Williams with record of 136–33–8 for 1900–21, including 8 conference titles and 5 unbeaten teams. He ranks in the top 15 in all-time winning percentage. Bernie Bierman was 93–35–6 for 1932–41 and 1945–50 with 6 conference titles, 5 unbeaten teams and 4 national champions. Other outstanding records were by Dr. Clarence Spears, 28–9–2 for 1925–29 with 1 unbeaten team; and Murray Warmath, 86–77–7 for 1954–71 with 2 conference titles and 2 Rose Bowl teams. Warmath was national coach of the year in 1960.

MISCELLANEA

First game was 4–0 win over Hamline in 1882 . . . highest score was 146–0 over Grinnell in 1904 . . . highest since W.W. II was 57–3 over Ohio U. in 1982 . . . worst defeat was 84–13 by Nebraska in 1983 . . . longest unbeaten string of 28 in 1933–36 ended by Northwestern 6–0 . . . unbeaten string of 27 in 1903–04 ended by Wisconsin 16–12 in 1905 . . . unbeaten string of 18 in 1899–1900 ended by Wisconsin 18–0 in 1901 . . . winning streak of 18 in 1939–42 ended by Iowa Seahawks 7–6 . . . longest losing string of 10 in 1957–58 broken with 39–12 win over Michigan St. . . . Minnesota has had 25 consensus All America players since 1903 . . . multi-year choices were Herb Joesting, B, 1926–27; Ed Widseth, T, 1935–36; Dick Wildung, T, 1941–42; and Leo Nomellini, T, 1948–49 . . . unanimous single-year selections were Clayton Tonnemaker, C, 1949; Paul Giel, B, 1953; Tom Brown, G, 1960; and Bobby Bell, T, 1962 . . . other choices since W.W. II were Sandy Stephens, B, 1961; Carl Eller, T, 1963; and Aaron Brown, DE, 1965 . . . Academic All America selections were Bob Hobart, T, 1956; Frank Brixius, T, 1960; Bob Stein, DE, 1968; and Barry Mayer, RB, 1970 . . . Bruce Smith, HB, won Heisman Trophy in 1941 . . . Outland Trophy winners were Tom Brown, G, 1960; and Bobby Bell, T, 1962 . . . Minnesota ranks in top 20 both in all-time total victories and winning percentage.

Mississippi (Rebels; Cardinal Red & Navy Blue) (SEC)

NOTABLE TEAMS

1893—4–1–0. First varsity team lost only to Southern A.C. 24–0. 1894— 6–1–0. Lost only to Vanderbilt (40–0). 1910—7–1–0. Shut out 7, losing only to Vanderbilt 9–2. 1935—9–2–0. Shut out 6 behind T Bill Richardson; lost to Catholic U. in Orange Bowl 20–19. 1938—9–2–0. Harry J. Mehre's 1st team lost only to Vanderbilt and Tennessee as HB Parker Hall led nation in scoring and all-purpose running. 1939—7–2–0. QB Bill Schneller and TB Junie Hovious led attack. 1940—9–2–0. FB Merle Hapes had 1,081 yards of total offense and Hovious had 1,031 as Rebels lost only to Arkansas 21–20 and Mississippi St. 1941—6–2–1. Lost to Georgetown in opener and to Mississippi St. (6–0) in finale as Hovious starred again. 1947—8–2–0. John Vaught's 1st team saw Charley Conerly (1st Mississippi consensus All America) lead nation in passing with 1,367 yards and 18 TDs and Barney Poole led nation in pass receiving with 52 catches for 511 yards and 8 TDs; lost close ones to Vanderbilt 10–6 and Arkansas 19–14 but won 1st SEC title and beat TCU in Delta Bowl 13–9. 1948—8–1–0. Poole starred again as Rebels lost only to Tulane 20–7. 1952—8–0–2. Kline Gilbert starred at T as Rebels won 4 by TD or less; tied Kentucky and Vanderbilt, then lost to unbeaten Georgia Tech in Sugar Bowl 24–7. 1953—7–2–1. Lost only to Auburn and Maryland as G Crawford Mims starred. 1954—9–1–0. Scored 283 and led nation in total defense as T Rex Reed Boggan starred; won SEC, losing only to outsider Arkansas 6–0, but lost to Navy in Sugar Bowl 21–0. 1955— 9–1–0. Lost only to Kentucky 21–14 in 2nd game as QB Eagle Day and FB Paige Cothren led attack; beat TCU in Cotton Bowl 14–13. 1956—7–3–0. Cothren and T Billy Yelverton led Rebels to 207–82 edge over foes. 1957 —8–1–1. G Jackie Simpson led team to wins over all but Arkansas (12–6 loss) and Mississippi St. (7–7); beat Texas in Sugar Bowl 39–7. 1958—8–2–0. QB Bobby Franklin ran and passed for 960 yards and 16 TDs as Rebels lost only to unbeaten national champion LSU and to Tennessee (18–16); beat Florida in Gator Bowl 7–3. 1959—9–1–0. Outscored foes 329–21, shutting out 7 and leading nation in scoring defense, behind FB Charles Flowers (11 TDs) and G Marvin Terrell; avenged 7–3 loss to LSU by whipping Tigers in Sugar Bowl 21–0. 1960—9–0–1. Scored 266 behind QB Jake Gibbs (ran and passed for 1,216 yards and 17 TDs); tied 6–6 by LSU but beat Rice in Sugar Bowl 14–6 and gained share of national championship. 1961—9–1–0. Scored 326 (led nation in total offense) and shut out 5 behind FB Billy Ray Adams (10 TDs) but lost to LSU 10–7; lost to Texas in Cotton Bowl 12–7. 1962—9–0–0. Outscored foes 230–40 and led nation in total defense behind T Jim Dunaway and QB Glynn Griffing; beat Arkansas in Sugar Bowl 17–13. 1963—7–0–2. Led nation in rushing defense and scoring defense as C Kenny Dill and T Whaley Hall starred; tied Memphis St. 0–0 in opener and Missis- sippi St. 10–10 in finale, then lost to Alabama in Sugar Bowl 12–7. 1966— 8–2–0. Shut out 5 but lost successive games to unbeaten Alabama 17–7 and to Georgia 9–3; lost to Texas in Bluebonnet Bowl 19–0. 1969—7–3–0. Scored 307 as QB Archie Manning ran and passed for 2,264 yards and 23 TDs; 2 of losses by single point and beat Arkansas in Sugar Bowl 27–22. 1970—7–3–0. Vaught's last full-year team scored 285 as Manning had 1,594 yards of total offense (throwing for 14 TDs and scoring 6); lost to Auburn in Gator Bowl 35–28. 1971—9–2–0. Scored 322 as TB Greg Ainsworth scored 11 TDs; beat Georgia Tech in Peach Bowl 41–18.

BOWL RECORD

Bluebonnet 0–2–0; Cotton 1–1–0; Delta 1–0–0; Gator 1–1–0; Independence 0–1–0; Liberty 2–0–0; Orange 0–1–0; Peach 1–0–0; Sugar 5–3–0; Sun 0–1–0.

CONFERENCE TITLES

Southeastern 1947, 1954, 1955, 1960, 1962, 1963.

TOP 10 AP & UPI RANKING

1952	7–7	1959	2–2	1963	7–7
1954	6–6	1960	2–3	1969	8–U
1955	9–10	1961	5–5		
1957	7–8	1962	3–3		

MAJOR RIVALS

Rebels have played at least 15 games with Alabama (5–30–2), Arkansas (16–14–0), Florida (8–6–1), Georgia (7–14–1), Houston (15–3–0), Kentucky (19–10–1), LSU (29–39–4), Memphis St. (31–5–1), Mississippi St. (45–29–6), Sewanee (6–8–1), Southern Mississippi (18–5–0), Southwestern (Tenn.) (20–1–2), Tennessee (18–31–1), Tulane (28–27–0), Union (14–0–1) and Vanderbilt (28–28–2).

COACHES

Dean of Mississippi coaches was John H. Vaught with record of 190–61–12 for 1947–70 and part of 1973, with 6 conference titles, 18 bowl teams (10 winners), 4 teams unbeaten in regular season and 1 national champion. He ranks in top 15 in all-time coaching victories. Harry J. Mehre was 39–26–1 for 1938–45. Other top records were by Dr. N.P. Stauffer, 17–7–2 for 1909–11; and Billy R. Kinard, 16–9–0 for 1971–73 with 1 bowl champion.

MISCELLANEA

First game was 56–0 win over Southwest Baptist University (later Union University) in 1893 . . . highest score was 114–0 over Southwest Baptist in 1904 . . . highest since W.W. II was 69–7 over Southern Mississippi in 1969 . . . worst defeat was 91–0 by Vanderbilt in 1915 . . . worst since W.W. II was 49–0 by Georgia in 1974 . . . highest against Rebels since W.W. II was 61–17 by LSU in 1970 . . . longest unbeaten string of 21 in 1959–61 ended by LSU 10–7 . . . unbeaten string of 19 in 1962–63 ended by Alabama 12–7 in Sugar Bowl . . . longest winless string of 11 in 1916–17 broken with 21–0 win over Mississippi College . . . consensus All America players were Charley Conerly, B, 1947; Crawford Mims, G, 1953; Charlie Flowers, B, 1959; Jake Gibbs, B, 1960; Jim Dunaway, T, 1962; and Jim Miller, P, 1979 . . . Academic All America choices were Harold Easterwood, C, 1954; Robert Khayat, T, and Flowers, B, 1959; Doug Elmore, B, 1961; Stan Hindman, G, 1965; Steve Hindman, HB, 1968; Julius Fagan, K, 1969; Greg Markow, DE, 1974; Robert Fabris, E, and George Plasketes, DE, 1977; and Ken Toler, WR, 1980.

Mississippi State (Bulldogs; Maroon & White) (SEC)

NOTABLE TEAMS

1903—3-0-2. Shut out 4; tied Mississippi and Tulane. 1910—7-2-0. Shut out 7 but lost to Auburn and Mississippi. 1911—7-2-1. Shut out 6, losing close ones to Auburn 11–5 and Tulane 5–4. 1913—6-1-1. W.D. Chadwick's last team lost only to unbeaten Auburn (34–0) and tied LSU 0–0. 1914— 6-2-0. Shut out 6. 1917—6-1-0. Lost only to Auburn 13–6. 1919—6-2-0. Won 6 straight before losing to Auburn 7–0 and Alabama 14–6. 1935— 8-3-0. Ralph Sasse's 1st team shut out 5 as Ike Pickle starred in backfield. 1936—7-2-1. Shut out 7 behind T Alex Lott and E Chuck Gelatka; lost to Duquesne in Orange Bowl 13–12. 1939—8-2-0. Allyn McKeen's 1st team shut out 6 behind E Buddy Elrod and C Shag Goolsby; lost 7–0 games to Auburn and Alabama. 1940—9-0-1. Elrod was MVP in SEC as Bulldogs won over all but Auburn (7–7 in 3rd game); beat Georgetown in Orange Bowl 14–7. 1941—8-1-1. T Bill Arnold and B Blondy Black led team to 1st SEC title despite 0–0 tie with LSU; lost only to unbeaten Duquesne 16–0. 1942—8-2-0. Won last 7 after losses to Alabama and LSU as Black starred again. 1944—6-2-0. Won 6 straight behind B Shorty McWilliams (14 TDs) before losing to Alabama and Mississippi. 1946—8-2-0. Scored 271 as McWilliams starred again; shut out 5. 1947—7-3-0. McWilliams ran and passed for 848 yards and 9 TDs and handled punting and punt returns. 1957 —6-2-1. B Billy Stacy sparked team; lost only to Tennessee 14–9 and unbeaten national champion Auburn 15–7. 1963—6-2-2. Lost close ones to Memphis St. 17–10 and Alabama 20–19 as linemen Pat Watson and Tommy Neville starred; beat North Carolina St. in Liberty Bowl 16–12. 1974—

8–3–0. Bob Tyler's 2nd team scored 301 behind Walter Packer (994 yards rushing and 1,201 all-purpose) and DL Jimmy Webb became 1st consensus All America; beat North Carolina in Sun Bowl 26–24. **1976—9-2-0.** Lost only to Florida and Alabama but had to forfeit all games for 0–11–0 season because of NCAA recruiting violations. **1980—9-2-0.** Emory Bellard's 2nd team won 5 by TD or less as Mardye McDole had 978 yards and 7 TDs in all-purpose running; lost to Nebraska in Sun Bowl 31–17.

BOWL RECORD

Hall of Fame 1–0–0; Liberty 1–0–0; Orange 1–1–0; Sun 1–1–0.

CONFERENCE TITLES

Southeastern 1941.

TOP 10 AP & UPI RANKING

1940	9

MAJOR RIVALS

Mississippi St. has played at least 15 games with Alabama (11–54–3), Auburn (16–39–2), Florida (14–22–2), Georgia (5–10–0), Howard (Samford) (16–1–1), Kentucky (5–10–0), LSU (29–45–3), Memphis St. (15–7–0), Millsaps (14–2–1), Mississippi (29–45–6), Mississippi College (16–3–0), Southern Mississippi (8–11–1), Tennessee (13–19–1) and Tulane (19–22–2).

COACHES

Dean of Bulldog coaches was Allyn McKeen with record of 65–19–3 for 1939–48, including 1 conference title and 1 unbeaten Orange Bowl champion. W.D. Chadwick was 29–12–2 for 1909–13. Other top records were by Ralph Sasse, 20–10–2 for 1935–37 with 1 bowl team; Bob Tyler, 39–25–3 for 1973–78 with 1 bowl champion (record was 21–44–2 after forfeits); and Emory Bellard, 28–29–0 for 1979–83 with 2 bowl teams.

MISCELLANEA

First game was 21–0 loss to Southern Baptist U. in 1895 . . . first win was 17–0 over Mississippi in 1901 . . . highest score was 82–0 over Howard in 1910 . . . highest since W.W. II was 69–0 over Murray St. in 1946 . . . worst defeat was 74–0 by Houston in 1969 . . . longest unbeaten string of 21 in

1939–41 ended by Duquesne 16–0 . . . longest losing string of 27 (17 by forfeit) in 1975–77 broken with 28–0 win over West Texas St. in 1978 . . . winless string of 17 in 1967–68 broken with 17–14 win over Richmond in 1969 . . . only consensus All America player was Jimmy Webb, DL, 1974 . . . Academic All America choices were Jackie Parker, B, 1953; Ron Bennett, E, 1956; Frank Dowsing, DB, 1972; Webb, DE, 1973; and Will Coltharp, DE, 1976.

Missouri (Tigers; Old Gold & Black) (Big 8)

NOTABLE TEAMS

1895—7–1–0. Lost mid-season game to Nebraska 12–10. 1899—9–2–0. Shut out 8, including first 7; lost to Drake and Kansas. 1907—7–2–0. Scored 278. 1908—6–2–0. Lost to Iowa St. and Kansas. 1909—7–0–1. Won first Missouri Valley title; tie was 6–6 with Iowa St. 1913—7–1–0. Lost only to Illinois 24–7. 1916—6–1–1. Shut out 6, losing only to Kansas St. 7–6 and tying Iowa St. 0–0. 1919—5–1–2. Won MVC, losing only to Nebraska 12–5. 1920—7–1–0. Lost only to Oklahoma 28–7. 1921—6–2–0. Lost close ones to Kansas St. 7–5 and Kansas 15–9. 1924—7–2–0. Gwinn Henry's 2nd team shut out 6 and won MVC. 1925—6–1–1. Repeated as conference champs behind T Ed Lindenmeyer, losing only to Kansas 10–7 in finale. 1926—5–1–2. Lost only to Oklahoma 10–7. 1927—7–2–0. Won 5th and last MVC title. 1936—6–2–1. Won 3 by TD margin. 1939—8–1–0. Won first Big 6 title as Paul Christman ran and passed for 1,252 yards; lost only to Ohio St. 19–0 in 2nd game and to Georgia Tech in Orange Bowl 21–7. 1941—8–1–0. Led nation in rushing as Bob Steuber ran for 855 yards and C Darold Jenkins became Tigers' first consensus All America; lost opener to Ohio St. 12–7 and lost to Fordham in Sugar Bowl 2–0. 1942—8–3–1. Steuber led nation in scoring with 121 points (18 TDs and 13 extra points), running for 1,098 yards. 1945—6–3–0. Won 4th Big 6 title, losing only to Michigan St. 14–7 in last 7; lost to Texas in Cotton Bowl 40–27. 1948—8–2–0. Scored 308 behind QB Hal Entsminger; lost to unbeaten Clemson in Gator Bowl 24–23. 1949—7–3–0. HB Richard Braznell ran for 766 yards and Eugene Ackerman caught 42 passes for 621 yards; lost 2 by single point with other losses to unbeaten Oklahoma and to Maryland in Gator Bowl 20–7. 1960 —9–1–0. Dan Devine's 3rd team lost only to Kansas in finale 23–7 (but later won that by forfeit for 10–0–0 record) as Danny LaRose starred at E; beat Navy in Orange Bowl 21–14. 1961—7–2–1. Lost only to Colorado 7–6 and

Oklahoma 7–0 in successive games. 1962—7–1–2. John Roland ran for 830 yards and 13 TDs as Tigers lost only to Oklahoma 13–0; beat Georgia Tech in Bluebonnet Bowl 14–10. 1963—7–3–0. Won 3 of 4 decided by TD or less. 1965—7–2–1. Charlie Brown ran for 937 yards and Gary Lane scored 9 TDs as Tigers lost only to Kentucky 7–0 in opener and to unbeaten Nebraska 16–14; beat Florida in Sugar Bowl 20–18. 1967—7–3–0. Won 3 of 4 decided by TD or less behind T Russ Washington. 1968—7–3–0. Roger Wehrli sparked defense as Tigers won 7 straight in mid-season; beat Alabama in Gator Bowl 35–10. 1969—9–1–0. Scored 362 as Joe Moore ran for 1,312 yards and Terry McMillan passed for 1,963; lost only to Colorado 31–24 and to unbeaten Penn St. in Orange Bowl 10–3. 1980—8–3–0. Scored 307 as Phil Bradley passed for 1,632 yards and Ron Fellows caught 33 for 586 yards; lost to Purdue in Liberty Bowl 28–25.

BOWL RECORD

Bluebonnet 1–0–0; Cotton 0–1–0; Fiesta 0–1–0; Gator 1–2–0; Hall of Fame 1–0–0; Holiday 0–1–0; Liberty 1–1–0; Los Angeles Christmas Festival 0–1–0; Orange 1–3–0; Sugar 1–1–0; Sun 1–0–0; Tangerine 1–0–0.

CONFERENCE TITLES

Missouri Valley 1909, 1919, 1924, 1925, 1927. Big 6 1939, 1941, 1942, 1945. Big 8 1960, 1969*.

TOP 10 AP & UPI RANKING

1939	6	1965	6–6
1941	7	1968	9–U
1960	5–4	1969	6–6

MAJOR RIVALS

Missouri has played at least 15 games with Colorado (32–13–3), Drake (14–4–0), Iowa St. (46–22–8), Kansas (43–40–9), Kansas St. (48–16–5), Nebraska (32–42–3), Oklahoma (22–47–5), Oklahoma St. (20–10–0), St. Louis (10–10–1), SMU (7–13–1), and Washington (Mo.) (25–11–2).

COACHES

Dean of Missouri coaches was Don Faurot with record of 101–79–10 for 1935–42 and 1946–56, including 3 conference titles and 4 bowl teams. Dan Devine was 93–37–7 for 1958–70 with 2 conference titles and 6 bowl teams.

Other top records were by Gwinn Henry, 40–28–9 for 1923–31 with 3 conference titles and 1 post-season team; and Warren Powers, 43–26–2 for 1978–83 with 5 bowl teams (3 winners).

MISCELLANEA

First game was 22–6 win over Picked Team in 1890 . . . first win over college foe was 36–6 over Washburn in 1891 . . . highest score was 90–0 over Engineers in 1890 . . . highest since 1900 was 70–6 over Tarkio in 1907 . . . highest since W.W. II was 69–21 over Kansas in 1969 . . . biggest margin of victory since 1900 was 69–0 over Drury in 1913 . . . biggest since W.W. II was 57–0 over Colorado in 1962 . . . worst defeat was 65–0 by Texas in 1932 . . . worst since W.W. II was 74–13 by Maryland in 1954 . . . biggest margin of defeat since W.W. II was 62–0 by Nebraska in 1972 . . . longest unbeaten string of 11 in 1909–10 ended by Iowa St. 6–5 . . . longest winless string of 17 in 1933–34 broken with 39–0 win over William Jewell in 1935 . . . consensus All America players were Darold Jenkins, C, 1941; Danny LaRose, E, 1960; Johnny Roland, DB, 1965; Roger Wehrli, DB, 1968; and Kellen Winslow, TE, 1978 . . . Academic All America choices were Tom Hertz, G, 1962; Dan Schuppan, DE, and Bill Powell, DT, 1966; Carl Garber, MG, 1968; John Weisenfels, LB, 1970; Greg Hill, K, 1972; and Van Darkow, LB, 1981.

Navy (Midshipmen; Navy Blue & Gold) (Independent)

NOTABLE TEAMS

1889—4–1–1. Tied Dickinson 0–0 and lost to Lehigh 26–6 in successive games. 1890—5–1–1. Won first Army-Navy game 24–0; lost only to Lehigh 24–4. 1891—5–2–0. Won first 5. 1892—5–2–0. Won last 5. 1894—4–1–2. Lost only to unbeaten Pennsylvania 12–0. 1895—5–2–0. Blanked first 5 but lost last 2 to Orange A.C. 10–6 and Lehigh 6–4. 1897—8–1–0. Blanked 7, losing only to Princeton 28–0 in opener. 1898—6–1–1. Lost to Princeton 30–0 and tied Lehigh 6–6. 1904—7–2–1. Shut out 6. 1905—10–1–1. Shut out 8, losing only to Swarthmore 6–5 and tying Army 6–6. 1906—8–2–2. Shut out 9, losing close ones to Princeton and Penn St. by 5–0 scores. 1907 —9–2–1. Shut out 8 as E Bill Dague became Navy's first consensus All America. 1908—9–2–1. Shut out 7 as QB Ed Lange and T Percy Northcroft starred. 1910—8–0–1. Scored only 99 but blanked all foes, including 0–0 tie with Rutgers. 1911—6–0–3. Doug Howard's 1st team shut out 7, including 3 0–0 ties. 1913—7–1–1. Shut out 7, including 0–0 tie with Pittsburgh in opener, and lost only to Army 22–9 in finale. 1917—7–1–0. Outscored foes 443–23 as Ernest Von Heimberg starred at E and Bill Ingram scored 21 TDs; lost to West Virginia 7–0 in 2nd game in coach Gil Dobie's 1st defeat in more than 11 years of college coaching. 1918—4–1–0. Scored 283 but lost finale to Great Lakes 7–6. 1919—6–1–0. Scored 298 and shut out 5, losing only to Georgetown 6–0. 1920—6–2–0. Bob Folwell's 1st team lost only to North Carolina St. 14–7 and Princeton 14–0. 1921—6–1–0. Lost only to Penn State 13–7 and shut out others. 1922—5–2–0. Lost close ones to Penn 13–7 and Army 17–14 as Wendell Taylor starred at E. 1923— 5–1–2. Lost only to Penn St. 21–3; made service academy's 1st trip to a bowl, tying Washington 14–14 in Rose. 1926—9–0–1. Bill Ingram's 1st team scored in double figures in all behind HB Tom Hamilton and T Frank Wickhorst; tie was with Army 21–21 in finale played in Chicago. 1929— 6–2–2. Lost only to unbeaten national champion Notre Dame 14–7 and to Penn 7–2. 1934—8–1–0. Won 3 by less than TD behind HB Buzz Borries and T Slade Cutter; lost only to Pitt 31–7. 1940—6–2–1. Led nation in total defense but lost successive games to Penn and Notre Dame (13–7). 1941 —7–1–1. Shut out 5, including 0–0 tie with Harvard; lost only to Notre Dame 20–13. 1943—8–1–0. Linemen George Brown and Don Whitmire starred as Midshipmen lost only to national champion Notre Dame 33–6. 1945—7–1–1. C Dick Scott and E Dick Duden led team to wins over all but Notre Dame (6–6) and unbeaten national champion Army (32–13 loss in finale). 1952—6–2–1. Eddie Erdelatz's 3rd team, with Steve Eisenhauer at G, lost only to Maryland and Notre Dame. 1954—7–2–0. Scored 304 as Ronnie Beagle starred at E; lost close ones to Pitt 21–19 and Notre Dame 6–0, but beat Mississippi in Sugar Bowl 21–0. 1955—6–2–1. Led nation in passing as George Welsh led in total offense (1,348 yards) and passing (1,319 yards and 8 TDs) and Beagle again starred at E. 1956—6–1–2. Lost only to Tulane 21–6 in 3rd game. 1957—8–1–1. Lost only to North Carolina 13–7 and tied Duke 6–6 behind T Bob Reifsnyder and QB Tom Forrestal; beat Rice in Cotton Bowl 20–7. 1960—9–1–0. Heisman winner Joe Bellino scored 18 TDs and passed for 2 more as Middies lost only to Duke 19–10; lost to Missouri in Orange Bowl 21–14. 1961—7–3–0. Greg Mather led nation in kicking with 11 FGs in 15 attempts and also starred at E. 1963— 9–1–0. Scored 314 behind Heisman winner Roger Staubach (1,892 yards of total offense) while losing only to SMU 32–28; won 5th Lambert Trophy but lost to unbeaten national champion Texas in Cotton Bowl 28–6. 1978—

8–3–0. Won first 7; beat Brigham Young in inaugural Holiday Bowl 23–16. 1980—8–3–0. Eddie Meyers ran for 957 yards and Steve Fehr kicked 17 FGs as Midshipmen lost 2 by 3 points or less; lost to Houston in Garden State Bowl 35–0.

BOWL RECORD

Cotton 1–1–0; Garden State 0–1–0; Holiday 1–0–0; Liberty 0–1–0; Orange 0–1–0; Rose 0–0–1; Sugar 1–0–0.

CONFERENCE TITLES

None. Won Lambert Trophy in 1943, 1954, 1957, 1960*, 1963.

TOP 10 AP & UPI RANKING

1941	10	1945	3	1960	4–6
1943	4	1954	5–5	1963	2–2
1944	4	1957	5–6		

MAJOR RIVALS

Navy has played at least 15 games with Air Force (8–8–0), Army (40–37–7), Boston College (9–10–0), Columbia (13–9–1), Dickinson (10–1–4), Duke (14–9–5), Georgetown (13–4–2), Georgia Tech (8–13–0), Lehigh (11–5–2), Maryland (14–5–1), Michigan (5–12–1), Notre Dame (9–47–1), Pennsylvania (20–21–4), Penn State (17–18–2), Pittsburgh (11–16–2), Princeton (10–11–6), St. John's College (18–3–0), Syracuse (8–13–0), Virginia (25–5–0) and William & Mary (35–4–1).

COACHES

Most victories compiled by George Welsh with record of 55–46–1 for 1973–81, including 3 bowl teams. Eddie Erdelatz was 50–26–8 for 1950–58 with 2 Lambert Trophy winners and 2 bowl champions. Wayne Hardin was 38–22–2 for 1959–64 with 2 Lambert Trophy winners and 2 bowl teams. Other outstanding records included Doug Howard, 25–7–4 for 1911–14 with 1 unbeaten team; Bob Folwell, 24–12–2 for 1920–24 with 1 bowl team; and Bill Ingram, 32–13–4 for 1926–30 with 1 unbeaten team.

MISCELLANEA

First game was 0–0 tie with Baltimore A.C. in 1879 . . . first win was 8–0 over Johns Hopkins in 1882 . . . highest score was 127–0 over Ursinus in

1918 . . . highest since W.W. II was 65–7 over Princeton in 1953 . . . worst defeat was 70–14 by Michigan in 1976 . . . longest unbeaten string of 22 in 1909–12 ended by Lehigh 14–0 . . . longest winless string of 15 in 1947–49 broken with 28–7 win over Princeton . . . Navy has had 20 consensus All America players since 1907 . . . multi-year choices were Don Whitmire, T, 1943–44; and Ron Beagle, E, 1954–55 . . . unanimous choices for 1 year were Frank Wickhorst, T, 1926; Joe Bellino, B, 1960; Roger Staubach, B, 1963; and Chet Moeller, DB, 1975 . . . most recent selection was Napoleon McCallum, RB, 1983 . . . Academic All America selections were Steve Eisenhauer, G, 1953; Tom Forrestal, QB, 1957; Joe Tranchini, B, 1958; Dan Pike, RB, 1969; and Ted Dumbauld, LB, 1980 . . . Heisman Trophy winners were Joe Bellino, HB, 1960; and Roger Staubach, QB, 1963 . . . Navy ranks in top 20 in total all-time victories.

Nebraska (Cornhuskers; Scarlet & Cream) (Big 8)

NOTABLE TEAMS

1894—6–2–0. Lost only to Missouri 18–14 and Doane. 1897—5–1–0. Shut out 4, losing only to Iowa St. 10–0. 1900—7–1–1. Blanked 8 straight before losing finale to Minnesota 20–12. 1901—7–2–0. Lost to Minnesota and to unbeaten Wisconsin. 1902—10–0–0. Blanked foes 187–0. 1903—11–0–0. Walter C. Booth's 2nd straight unbeaten team outscored foes 292–16, shutting out 8. 1904—9–3–0. Scored 310 and shut out 7; 2 losses by TD or less. 1905—9–2–0. Booth's last team scored 316 but lost to Michigan and Minnesota. 1907—8–2–0. Scored 323 and won 1st Missouri Valley Conference title. 1908—7–2–1. Ernest Kroger starred in backfield as Huskers lost only to unbeaten Kansas and to Carlisle Indians. 1910—7–1–0. Scored 260 and shut out 6 to take MVC; lost to Minnesota 27–0. 1911—5–1–2. Jumbo Stiehm's 1st team scored 281 and shut out 5, losing only to Minnesota 21–3. 1912—7–1–0. Again lost only to Minnesota (13–0). 1913—8–0–0. Won 5th MVC title, outscoring foes 138–28 and beating Minnesota 7–0. 1914—7–0–1. T Vic Halligan and B Guy Chamberlin led team to wins over all but South Dakota (0–0). 1915—8–0–0. Stiehm's last team scored 282 and shut out 5 as Chamberlin became 1st consensus All America at E. 1916—6–2–0. Won 7th straight MVC title. 1917—5–2–0. Won MVC again, losing only to outsiders Michigan and Syracuse (10–9). 1921—7–1–0. Scored 283 and shut out 5, losing only to Notre Dame 7–0. 1922—7–1–0. Scored 276 and lost only to Syracuse 9–6; won 2nd straight MVC title. 1926—6–2–0. Lost close ones to Missouri 14–7 and Washington 10–6, but won 13th and last MVC title. 1927—6–2–0. Lost to Missouri 7–6 and Pittsburgh 21–13. 1928— 7–1–1. Won 1st Big 6 title behind G Dan McMullen, shutting out 5 and losing only to Army 13–3. 1931—8–2–0. Dana Bible's 3rd team won his 2nd Big 6 title. 1932—7–1–1. Won 5 by TD or less, losing only to Minnesota 7–6, behind C Lawrence Ely. 1933—8–1–0. Shut out 6 and won 3rd straight Big 6 title behind FB George Sauer; lost only to Pittsburgh 6–0. 1935— 6–2–1. Lost close ones to Missouri 12–7 and Pitt 6–0 but won Big 6. 1936 —7–2–0. Bible's last team shut out 5 and won conference behind FB Sam Francis. 1937—6–1–2. L. McC. Jones' 1st team shut out 5 and lost only to national champion Pittsburgh 13–7 behind linemen Fred Shirey and Charles Brock. 1939—7–1–1. Won 5 by TD or less and lost only to Missouri 27–13. 1940—8–1–0. Lost opener to unbeaten national champion Minnesota 13–7 but swept to 9th Big 6 title behind linemen Warren Alfson and Forrest Behm; lost to unbeaten Stanford in Rose Bowl 21–13. 1950—6–2–1. Scored 267 as Bobby Reynolds led nation with 157 points (22 TDs and 25 extra points); one of losses was to unbeaten national champion Oklahoma. 1954 —6–4–0. Bob Smith led running attack; team got to Orange Bowl as Big 7 runner-up, but lost to Duke there 34–7. 1962—8–2–0. Bob Devaney's 1st team lost only to Missouri and Oklahoma; beat Miami (Fla.) in Gotham Bowl 36–34. 1963—9–1–0. Led nation in rushing behind G Bob Brown and lost only to Air Force 17–13; beat Auburn in Orange Bowl 13–7. 1964—9–1–0. Won 2nd straight Big 8 title despite 17–7 loss to Oklahoma in finale; lost to unbeaten national champion Arkansas in Cotton Bowl 10–7. 1965—10–0–0. Scored 321 and led nation in rushing behind FB Frank Solich as DT Walt Barnes led defense; lost to national champion Alabama in Orange Bowl 39–28. 1966—9–1–0. Won 4th straight Big 8 title behind OG LaVerne Allers, MG Wayne Meylan and DB Larry Wachholtz; lost to Oklahoma 10–9 in finale and to unbeaten Alabama in Sugar Bowl 34–7. 1969—8–2–0. Won last 6 to gain share of conference title; beat Georgia in Sun Bowl 45–6. 1970 —10–0–1. Scored 409 as Johnny Rodgers caught 35 passes and Guy Ingles caught 34; tied Southern California 21–21 in 2nd game but beat LSU in Orange Bowl 17–12 to earn share of national title. 1971—12–0–0. Scored 469 as Jeff Kinney ran for 1,037 yards, Jerry Tagge passed for 2,019 yards and 17 TDs and Johnny Rodgers caught 53 passes for 872 yards and 11 TDs while MG Rich Glover and DE Willie Harper sparked defense; whipped unbeaten Alabama 38–6 in Orange Bowl to clinch national championship. 1972—8–2–1. Devaney's last team scored 461 as Heisman winner Rodgers caught 55 passes for 942 yards and Glover and Harper again starred on defense; lost close ones to UCLA 20–17 in opener and to Oklahoma 17–14 in finale, but whipped Notre Dame 40–6 in Orange Bowl. 1973—8–2–1.

Tom Osborne's 1st team led nation in pass defense; beat Texas in Cotton Bowl 19–3. 1974—8–3–0. Scored 360 behind C Rik Bonness and T Marvin Crenshaw as QB David Humm passed for 1,526 yards and 12 TDs; beat Florida in Sugar Bowl 13–10. 1975—10–1–0. Scored 353 behind Bonness and FB Tony Davis and lost only to national champion Oklahoma in finale 35–10; lost to unbeaten Arizona State in Fiesta Bowl 17–14. 1976—8–3–1. Scored 389 as Vince Ferragamo passed for 2,071 yards and 20 TDs; beat Texas Tech in Bluebonnet Bowl 27–24. 1977—8–3–0. Scored 294 behind C Tom Davis as I.M. Hipp ran for 1,301 yards; beat North Carolina in Liberty Bowl 21–17. 1978—9–2–0. Scored 420 and led nation in total offense as Tom Sorley passed for 1,571 yards and Rick Berns scored 10 TDs; lost Orange Bowl 31–24 to Oklahoma team beaten 17–14 in regular season. 1979—10–1–0. Scored 366 as Jarvis Redwine ran for 1,042 yards and lost only to Oklahoma 17–14 in finale; lost to Houston in Cotton Bowl 17–14. 1980—9–2–0. Scored 435 and led nation in rushing behind G Randy Schleusener as Redwine ran for 1,119 yards and Roger Craig scored 15 TDs; lost close ones to Florida St. 18–14 and Oklahoma 21–17 but beat Mississippi St. in Sun Bowl 31–17. 1981—9–2–0. Scored 349 and led nation in pass defense as Craig ran for 1,060 yards; won last 8 after losses to Iowa 10–7 and Penn St. 30–24; lost to unbeaten national champion Clemson in Orange Bowl 22–15. 1982—11–1–0. Scored 493 and led nation in total offense, rushing and scoring average (41.1) behind C Dave Rimington (2-time Outland Trophy winner) and RB Mike Rozier (1,689 yards and 15 TDs); lost only to national champion Penn St. 27–24 but beat LSU in Orange Bowl 21–20. 1983—12–0–0. Scored 624 and led nation in rushing and scoring average (52) as Heisman winner Rozier led nation's rushers and scorers with 2,148 yards and 29 TDs behind line led by Outland winner Dean Steinkuhler; won 3rd straight Big 8 title but lost to national champion Miami (Fla.) 31–30 in Orange Bowl.

BOWL RECORD

Bluebonnet 1–0–0; Cotton 1–2–0; Fiesta 0–1–0; Gotham 1–0–0; Liberty 1–0–0; Orange 5–5–0; Rose 0–1–0; Sugar 1–1–0; Sun 2–0–0.

CONFERENCE TITLES

Missouri Valley 1907, 1910, 1911, 1912, 1913, 1914, 1915, 1916, 1917, 1921, 1922, 1923, 1926. Big 6 1928, 1929, 1931, 1932, 1933, 1935, 1936, 1937, 1940. Big 8 1963, 1964, 1965, 1966, 1969*, 1970, 1971, 1972, 1975*, 1978*, 1981, 1982, 1983.

TOP 10 AP & UPI RANKING

1936	9	1966	6–7	1974	9–8	1979	9–7
1940	8	1970	1–3	1975	9–9	1980	7–7
1963	6–5	1971	1–1	1976	9–7	1981	U–9
1964	6–6	1972	4–9	1977	U–10	1982	3–3
1965	5–3	1973	7–U	1978	8–8	1983	2–2

MAJOR RIVALS

Nebraska has played at least 15 games with Colorado (30–11–1), Doane (16–2–0), Indiana (7–9–3), Iowa (24–12–3), Iowa St. (63–13–2), Kansas (66–21–3), Kansas St. (56–10–2), Minnesota (17–29–2), Missouri (42–32–3), Oklahoma (27–34–3), Oklahoma St. (21–2–1), Pittsburgh (4–15–3) and South Dakota (14–1–2).

COACHES

Tied for longest tenure were Bob Devaney and Tom Osborne, both of whom rank in top 15 in career winning percentage. Devaney was 101–20–2 for 1962–72, including 8 conference titles, 9 bowl teams (6 winners), 3 teams unbeaten in regular season and 2 national champions. He was national coach of the year in 1971. Osborne was 108–25–2 for 1973–83 with 5 conference titles and 11 bowl teams (6 winners). Other outstanding records include W.C. Booth, 52–8–1 for 1900–05 with 2 unbeaten teams; E.O. Stiehm, 35–2–3 for 1911–15 with 5 conference titles and 3 unbeaten teams; Dana X. Bible, 50–15–7 for 1929–36 with 6 conference titles; and L.McC. Jones, 28–14–4 for 1937–41 with 2 conference titles and a Rose Bowl team. Bible ranks in top 10 in all-time victories.

MISCELLANEA

First game was 10–0 win over Omaha YMCA in 1890 . . . 1st win over college foe was 18–0 over Doane in February 1891 . . . highest score was 119–0 over Haskell in 1910 . . . highest since W.W. II was 84–13 over Minnesota in 1983 . . . worst defeat was 61–7 by Minnesota in 1945 . . . worst since W.W. II was 55–7 by Oklahoma in 1954 and 54–6 by same foe in 1956 . . . longest unbeaten string of 34 in 1912–16 ended by Kansas 7–3 . . . unbeaten string of 32 in 1969–71 ended by UCLA 20–17 in 1972 . . . winning streak of 27 in 1901–04 ended by Colorado 6–0 . . . longest losing string of 7 in 1957 broken with 14–7 win over Penn St. in 1958 . . . Nebraska has had 27 consensus All America players since 1915 . . . multi-year choices were Ed Weir, T, 1924–25; Wayne Meylan, MG, 1966–67; Johnny Rodgers, FL, 1971–72; Willie Harper, DE, 1971–72; Dave Rimington, C, 1981–82; and Mike Rozier, RB, 1982–83 . . . unanimous choices for 1 year were Bob Brown, G, 1963; Larry Kramer, T, 1964; Rich Glover, MG, 1972; John Dutton, DL, 1973; Rik Bonness, C, 1975; Junior Miller, TE, 1979; and Irving Fryar, WR, 1983 . . . other recent picks were Marvin Crenshaw, OT, 1974; Dave Butterfield, DB, 1976; Kelvin Clark, OT, 1978; Randy Schleusener, OL, and Jarvis Redwine, RB, 1980; and Dean Steinkuhler, OG, 1983 . . . Academic All America choices were James Huge, E, 1962; Dennis Claridge, B, 1963; Marv Mueller, DB, 1966; Randy Reeves, DB, 1969; Larry Jacobson, DT, and Jeff Kinney, HB, 1971; Frosty Anderson, E, 1973; Rik Bonness, C, and Tom Heiser, RB, 1975; Vince Ferragamo, QB, 1976; Ted Harvey, RB, 1976–77; George Andrews, DL, and James Pillen, DB, 1978; Kelly Saalfeld, C, and Rod Horn, DL, 1979; Randy Schleusener, OG, 1979–80; Jeff Finn, TE, 1980; Randy Theiss, OT, and Ric Lindquist, DB, 1981; Dave Rimington, C, 1981–82; and Rob Stuckey, DL, and Scott Strasburger, DL, 1983 . . . Heisman Trophy winners were Johnny Rodgers, FL, 1972; and Mike Rozier, RB, 1983 . . . Outland Trophy winners were Larry Jacobson, DT, 1971; Rich Glover, MG, 1972; Dave Rimington, C, 1981–82; and Dean Steinkuhler, OG, 1983 . . . Steinkuhler also won Lombardi award in 1983 . . . Nebraska is in top 15 in all-time winning percentage and in total victories.

Nevada–Las Vegas (Rebels; Scarlet & Gray) (PCAA)

NOTABLE TEAMS

1968—8–1–0. Scored 266 and lost only to Cal Lutheran 17–13 in finale in 1st varsity season as Bill Casey passed for 1,423 yards and Mark Larson caught 27. **1973**—8–3–0. Ron Meyer's 1st team scored 304 and had 2 losses by less than TD as Mike Thomas ran for 1,741 yards and scored 21 TDs. **1974**—11–0–0. Scored 398 as Thomas ran for 1,408 yards and scored 19 TDs; beat Alcorn St. 35–22 and lost to Delaware 49–11 in NCAA playoffs. **1976**—9–2–0. Tony Knap's 1st team scored 325 as Glenn Carano passed for 2,024 yards, Mike Haverty caught 51 for 738 yards and Raymond Strong ran for 907 and scored 10 TDs; lost to Akron 27–6 in NCAA playoffs. **1977** —9–2–0. Scored 300 behind Greg Van Ness (1,736 yards passing), Brian Harris (45 receptions for 663 yards) and Strong (843 yards rushing); lost to

Boise St. and San Diego St. 1979—9–1–2. Scored 370 as Michael Morton ran for 881 yards and scored 11 TDs, Sam King passed for 1,594 yards and Sam Greene caught 40 for 821 yards and 9 scores; lost only to Texas-El Paso 17–15 in 3rd game.

BOWL RECORD

None.

CONFERENCE TITLES

None.

TOP 10 AP & UP RANKING

None.

MAJOR RIVALS

UNLV has played at least 6 games with Boise St. (3–3–0), Cal St. Fullerton (7–1–0), Hawaii (3–6–0), Nevada-Reno (8–4–0), Northern Arizona (4–2–0), Santa Clara (4–2–0) and Weber St. (4–2–0).

COACHES

Tony Knap was dean of UNLV coaches with record of 47–20–2 for 1976–81. Ron Meyer was 27–8–0 for 1973–75 and Bill Ireland was 26–23–1 for 1968–72.

MISCELLANEA

First game was 27–20 win over St. Mary's in 1968 . . . highest score was 72–7 over New Mexico in 1980 . . . biggest margin of victory was 69–0 over Cal Tech in 1968 . . . worst defeat was 51–7 by Miami (Fla.) in 1972 . . . highest against Rebels was 69–28 by Utah in 1981 . . . longest winning streak of 12 in 1974 ended by Delaware 49–11 in NCAA playoffs . . . longest losing string of 8 in 1972 broken with 38–6 win over St. College of Arkansas in 1973 . . . UNLV has had no consensus All America players and no Academic All America choices.

New Mexico (Lobos; Cherry & Silver) (WAC)

NOTABLE TEAMS

1905—5-1-1. Shut out 5; tied Menaul H.S. 5-5 in opener and lost finale to New Mexico St. 40-0. 1908—5-1-0. Lost finale to Arizona 10-5. 1919—3-0-2. Had scoreless ties with Colorado Mines and New Mexico Military. 1924—5-1-0. Yielded just 12 points; lost to New Mexico St. 6-0. 1927—8-0-1. Outscored foes 215-28; tie was 6-6 with Texas-El Paso. 1934—8-1-0. Scored 251 behind E Ralph Bowyer and B Abdon Paiz; lost only to Arizona 14-6. 1938—8-2-0. Won Border Conference behind G John Martel and HB William Dwyer but lost to Texas-El Paso 7-6 and to unbeaten Texas Tech; lost to Utah in Sun Bowl 26-0. 1939—8-2-0. Lost to Texas Tech and Arizona St. as Jack Henley starred at E. 1945—5-1-1. Won first 5 before losing to Utah 21-20 and tying Texas Tech 6-6. 1952—7-2-0. Shut out 5 behind DT Jack Barger and DL Don Papin; lost close ones to Brigham Young 14-10 and Arizona 13-7. 1958—7-3-0. HB Don Perkins ran and passed for 782 yards and E Don Black caught 9 TD passes. 1959—7-3-0. Perkins averaged 34.7 yards on 15 kickoff returns and scored 12 TDs; lost 2 by less than TD. 1962—7-2-1. Bill Weeks' 3rd team led nation in pass defense and won 1st WAC title as Bobby Santiago ran for 806 yards and scored 11 TDs. 1964—9-2-0. Won last 6 and took 3rd straight WAC title as QB Stan Quintana ran and passed for 1,249 yards. 1970—7-3-0. Scored 291 as QB Rocky Long ran and passed for 1,323 yards and FB Sam Scarber ran for 961 and 13 TDs. 1982—10-1-0. Scored 374 as David Osborn passed for 1,607 yards and 15 TDs and ran for 539 yards and 7 TDs; lost only to Brigham Young 40-12.

BOWL RECORD

Aviation 1-0-0; Harbor 0-0-1; Sun 1-2-0.

CONFERENCE TITLES

Border 1938*. Western Athletic 1962, 1963, 1964*.

TOP 10 AP & UPI RANKING

None.

MAJOR RIVALS

Lobos have played at least 15 games with Albuquerque Indian School (14–4–1), Arizona (18–39–3), Arizona St. (5–22–1), Brigham Young (11–21–1), Colorado St. (17–16–0), Denver (9–9–0), New Mexico St. (46–23–5), New Mexico Military (11–7–3), Northern Arizona (19–3–0), Texas Tech (4–22–2), Texas-El Paso (31–21–3), Utah (8–15–2) and Wyoming (20–20–0).

COACHES

Dean of New Mexico coaches was Roy W. Johnson with record of 41–32–6 for 1920–30, including 1 unbeaten team. Ted Shipkey was 30–17–2 for 1937–41 with 1 conference title and 1 bowl team. Bill Weeks was 40–41–1 for 1960–67 with 3 conference titles and 1 bowl team.

MISCELLANEA

First game was 5–0 loss to Albuquerque H.S. in 1892 . . . 1st win was 4–0 over same team in 1893 . . . 1st win over college foe was 25–5 over New Mexico St. in 1893 . . . highest score was 108–0 over Northern Arizona in 1916 . . . highest since W.W. II was 78–0 over Northern Arizona in 1950 . . . worst defeat was 110–3 by New Mexico St. in 1917 . . . worst since W.W. II was 72–7 by Nevada-Las Vegas in 1980 . . . highest against Lobos since W.W. II was 75–12 by Texas-El Paso in 1967 . . . longest unbeaten string of 11 in 1903–05 ended by New Mexico St. 40–0 . . . longest losing string of 21 in 1967–69 broken with 16–7 win over Kansas . . . New Mexico has had no consensus All America players . . . Academic All America choices were Bob Johnson, S, 1975; and Robert Rumbaugh, LB, 1977–78.

New Mexico State (Aggies; Crimson & White) (PCAA)

NOTABLE TEAMS

1905—5–0–1. Blanked opponents 128–0; tied El Paso H.S. 0–0. 1911—7–0–0. Scored 192 and shut out all but New Mexico (10–6) in Arthur Badenoch's 2nd year. 1912—5–1–0. Outscored first 5 foes 256–7 but lost finale to New Mexico Military 10–0. 1913—7–0–1. Badenoch's last team gave up just 24 points; tie was 0–0 with El Paso H.S. 1915—5–2–0. Lost

opener to El Paso H.S. 6–3 and finale to New Mexico 13–0. 1920—5–1–1.
Lost only to New Mexico 41–0. 1922—6–2–0. Lost successive games to St.
Mary's Indian School and Arizona. 1923—9–0–0. Robert Brown's 1st team
outscored foes 218–17, shutting out 5. 1924—7–3–0. No loss by more than
7 points. 1935—7–1–1. Backs Lauro Apodaca and Lem Pratt led team to
wins over all but Arizona (9–6 loss) and Western New Mexico (0–0); tied
Hardin-Simmons in Sun Bowl 14–14. 1937—7–2–0. Shut out 5 behind T Joe
Yurcic. 1938—7–2–0. Won share of Border Conference title, losing only to
Arkansas St. 12–6 and New Mexico 6–2 behind Yurcic and QB Eddie Miller.
1959—7–3–0. Lost no game by more than 5 points as Pervis Atkins led
nation in rushing (971 yards), scoring (107 points) and all-purpose running
(1,800 yards); beat North Texas St. in Sun Bowl 28–8. 1960—10–0–0. Led
nation in total offense and scoring (394 points) as Bob Gaiters led nation in
rushing (1,338 yards) and scoring (145 points) and Atkins led in all-purpose
running (1,613 yards); beat Utah St. in Sun Bowl 20–13. 1965—8–2–0. Jim
Bohl ran for 1,191 yards, Hartwell Menefee caught 40 passes for 577 yards
and Jim Miller intercepted 8 passes. 1966—7–3–0. Bohl ran for 1,148 yards,
Sal Olivas passed for 1,154 yards and 17 TDs and Abelardo Alba picked off
8 enemy passes. 1967—7–2–1. Olivas led nation in total offense (2,184
yards), Doug Dalton ran for 1,123 yards and scored 14 TDs, and Howard
Taylor caught 49 passes for 639 yards and 6 TDs in Warren Woodson's last
year.

BOWL RECORD

Sun 2–0–1.

CONFERENCE TITLES

Border 1938*, 1960. Missouri Valley 1976*, 1978.

TOP 10 AP & UPI RANKING

None.

MAJOR RIVALS

Aggies have played at least 15 games with Arizona (5–29–1), Arizona St.
(6–20–1), Hardin-Simmons (5–9–1), New Mexico (24–45–14), New Mexico Military (15–12–3), North Texas St. (8–14–2), Northern Arizona (17–
7–1), Texas-Arlington (12–6–0), Texas-El Paso (26–35–2), Tulsa (2–13–0),
West Texas St. (11–24–2) and Wichita St. (15–7–1).

COACHES

Most wins were by Warren B. Woodson with record of 63–37–3 for 1958–67, including 1 conference title, 2 Sun Bowl champions and 1 unbeaten team. Gerald H. Hines was 55–36–10 for 1929–39 with 1 bowl team. Other top records were by John O. Miller, 18–4–5 for 1899 and 1901–07 with 1 unbeaten team; Arthur H. Badenoch, 22–3–1 for 1910–13 with 2 unbeaten teams; and Robert R. Brown, 21–6–1 for 1923–25 with 1 unbeaten team.

MISCELLANEA

First game was 10–0 win over Las Cruces in 1893 . . . 1st win over college foe was 39–0 over New Mexico Tech in 1905 . . . highest score was 116–0 over Ft. Bliss, Texas, in 1912 . . . highest since W.W. II was 90–0 over Northern Arizona in 1967 . . . worst defeat was 92–7 by Texas-El Paso in 1948 . . . longest winning streak of 16 in 1959–61 ended by New Mexico 41–7 . . . longest losing string of 14 in 1954–55 broken with 19–7 win over Corpus Christi U. . . . New Mexico St. has had no consensus All America players . . . Academic All America choices were Jim Bohl, HB, 1966; and Ralph Jackson, OG, 1974–75.

North Carolina (Tar Heels; Carolina Blue & White) (ACC)

NOTABLE TEAMS

1892—5–1–0. Lost 2nd game to Virginia 30–18 but blanked other foes 178–0. 1895—7–1–1. Shut out 6; tied Sewanee 0–0 and lost finale to Virginia 6–0. 1897—7–3–0. Shut out 6 in W.A. Reynolds' 1st year. 1898—9–0–0. Outscored foes 201–8, shutting out 7. 1901—7–2–0. Blanked first 7 before losses to Virginia and Clemson. 1902—5–1–3. Shut out 6, losing only to Georgetown 12–5. 1909—5–2–0. Lost to VMI 3–0 and Virginia Tech. 1911—6–1–1. Shut out 6, including 0–0 tie with Virginia Tech; lost finale to Virginia 28–0. 1914—10–1–0. Scored 359 and shut out 5, losing only to Virginia 20–3 in finale. 1922—9–1–0. Bill Fetzer's 2nd team lost only to Yale 18–0 in 2nd game. 1925—7–1–1. Shut out 6 after losing opener to Wake Forest 6–0; tied Virginia 3–3 in finale. 1929—9–1–0. Scored 346 and lost only to Georgia 19–12. 1934—7–1–1. Carl Snavely's 1st team lost only to Tennessee 19–7 and tied North Carolina St. 7–7. 1935—8–1–0. Shut out

6 and lost only to Duke 25–0 as Don Jackson ran and passed for 1,205 yards and 15 TDs. 1936—8–2–0. Ray Wolf's 1st team lost only to Tulane and Duke. 1937—7–1–1. Lost only to Fordham 14–0 as E Andy Bershak became 1st Tar Heel consensus All America. 1938—6–2–1. Shut out 6, losing only to Tulane 17–14 and unbeaten, unscored-on Duke 14–0. 1939—8–1–1. Lost only to Duke 13–3 as Jim Lalanne ran and passed for 15 TDs and George Stirnweiss had 779 yards in all-purpose running. 1946—8–1–1. Freshman Charlie Justice ran and passed for 1,217 yards and 13 TDs as Tar Heels lost only to Tennessee 20–14; won Southern Conference but lost to unbeaten Georgia in Sugar Bowl 20–10. 1947—8–2–0. Won last 7 as Justice ran, passed, returned punts and kickoffs and punted. 1948—9–0–1. Justice (with 1,620 yards and 23 TDs running and passing and a 44-yard punting average), T Len Szafaryn and E Art Weiner (31 catches for 481 yards and 6 scores) led team to wins over all but William & Mary (7–7); lost to Oklahoma in Sugar Bowl 14–6. 1949—7–3–0. Weiner led nation in pass receiving (52 catches for 762 yards and 7 TDs) and Justice ran and passed for 1,108 yards and 14 TDs as team won 4 by TD or less and won Southern Conference; lost to Rice in Cotton Bowl 27–13. 1963—8–2–0. Bob Lacey caught 48 passes and FB Ken Willard and C Chris Hanburger also starred; won 1st ACC title and beat Air Force in Gator Bowl 35–0. 1970—8–3–0. Scored 346 as Don McCauley scored 21 TDs and led nation in all-purpose running (2,021 yards); lost to unbeaten Arizona St. in Peach Bowl 48–26. 1971—9–2–0. Lewis Jolley ran for 712 yards and caught 23 passes for 367 more and John Bunting starred at LB; won ACC but lost to Georgia in Gator Bowl 7–3. 1972—10–1–0. Scored in double figures in all behind G Ron Rusnak and Lou Angelo intercepted 8 passes as Tar Heels lost only to Ohio State 29–14; beat Texas Tech in Sun Bowl 32–28. 1976—9–2–0. Mike Voight ran for 1,407 yards and 18 TDs to lead attack; lost to Kentucky in Peach Bowl 21–0. 1977—8–2–1. Bill Dooley's last team was unbeaten in last 7 behind DT Dee Hardison and running of freshman Amos Lawrence (1,211 yards); led nation in scoring defense and won ACC but lost to Nebraska in Liberty Bowl 21–17. 1980—10–1–0. Dick Crum's 3rd team lost only to Oklahoma 41–7 as Lawrence led offense with 1,118 yards rushing and LB Lawrence Taylor starred on defense; beat Texas in Bluebonnet Bowl 16–7. 1981—9–2–0. Scored 344 and lost only to South Carolina and unbeaten national champion Clemson; beat Arkansas in Gator Bowl 31–27. 1983—8–3–0. Scored 334 as Ethan Horton ran for 1,107 yards and Tyrone Anthony for 1,063 while Scott Stankavage passed for 1,721 yards and 16 TDs; lost to Florida State in Peach Bowl 28–3.

BOWL RECORD

Bluebonnet 1–0–0; Cotton 0–1–0; Gator 3–1–0; Liberty 0–1–0; Peach 0–3–0; Sugar 0–2–0; Sun 2–1–0.

CONFERENCE TITLES

Southern 1946, 1949. Atlantic Coast 1963*, 1971, 1972, 1977, 1980.

TOP 10 AP & UPI RANKING

1946	9	1980	10–9
1947	9	1981	9–8
1948	3		

MAJOR RIVALS

Tar Heels have played at least 15 games with Clemson (12–19–1), Davidson (31–4–4), Duke (36–30–4), Georgia (12–16–2), Georgia Tech (7–10–2), Maryland (25–21–1), North Carolina St. (49–18–6), Notre Dame (1–15–0), South Carolina (33–13–4), Tennessee (10–20–1), Virginia (51–34–3), VMI (14–6–1), Virginia Tech (8–11–6) and Wake Forest (53–25–2).

COACHES

Dean of Tar Heel coaches was Bill Dooley with record of 69–53–2 for 1967–77, including 3 conference titles and 6 bowl teams. Carl Snavely was 59–35–5 for 1934–35 and 1945–52 with 2 conference titles, 3 bowl teams and 1 team unbeaten in regular season. Other top records were by T.C. Trenchard, 26–9–2 for 1895 and 1913–15; W.A. Reynolds, 27–7–4 for 1897–1900 with 1 unbeaten team; Bob and Bill Fetzer, 30–12–4 for 1921–25; Ray Wolf, 38–17–3 for 1936–41; and Dick Crum, 50–20–1 for 1978–83 with 1 conference title and 5 bowl teams (4 winners).

MISCELLANEA

First game was 6–4 loss to Wake Forest in 1888 . . . 1st win was 33–0 over Wake Forest in 1889 . . . highest score was 65–0 over Virginia Medical in 1914 and over Wake Forest in 1928 . . . highest since W.W. II was 62–13 over VMI in 1970 and 62–8 over Army in 1982 . . . biggest margin since W.W. II was 56–0 over East Carolina in 1981 . . . worst defeat was 66–0 by Virginia in 1912 . . . worst since W.W. II was 52–2 by Florida in 1969 . . . highest against Tar Heels since W.W. II was 54–32 by Clemson in 1974 . . . longest unbeaten string of 17 in 1947–48 ended by Oklahoma 14–6 in

Sugar Bowl . . . longest losing string of 12 in 1966–67 broken with 14–0 win over Maryland . . . consensus All America players were Andy Bershak, E, 1937; Charlie Justice, B, 1948; Don McCauley, B, 1970; Ron Rusnak, G, 1972; Ken Huff, G, 1974; Dee Hardison, DL, 1977; Lawrence Taylor, LB, 1980; and William Fuller, DL, 1983 . . . Ken Willard, B, was Academic All America in 1964.

North Carolina State (Wolfpack; Red & White) (ACC)

NOTABLE TEAMS

1905—4-1-1. Shut out 5, losing only to Virginia 10–0 and tying North Carolina 0–0. **1907—6-0-1.** Tie was with North Carolina All-Stars 5–5. **1908—6-1-0.** Shut out 5, losing only to Virginia 6–0. **1909—6-1-0.** Eddie Green's 1st team shut out 5, losing only to Virginia Tech 18–5 in finale. **1910 —4-0-2.** Ties were with Georgetown 0–0 in opener and Villanova 6–6 in finale. **1913—6-1-0.** Green's last team lost only to VMI 14–7. **1917— 6-2-1.** QB Dick Gurley and T John Ripple led team. **1919—7-2-0.** Shut out 5. **1920—7-3-0.** Scored 284 and won 4 of last 5. **1927—9-1-0.** HB Jack McDowall led team to wins over all but Furman (20–0 loss in 2nd game). **1932—6-1-2.** Shut out 5, losing only to North Carolina 13–0. **1944— 7-2-0.** TB Howard Turner led Wolfpack to wins over all but Clemson (13–7) and Wake Forest. **1946—8-2-0.** Turner starred again as team lost only to Virginia Tech 14–6 and Vanderbilt 7–0; lost to Oklahoma in Gator Bowl 34–13. **1957—7-1-2.** HB Dick Christy scored 83 points to lead Wolfpack to 1st ACC title; won 4 by TD or less and lost only to William & Mary 7–6. **1963—8-2-0.** Got share of ACC title behind QB Jim Rossi and linemen Bill Sullivan and Bert Wilder; lost to Mississippi St. in Liberty Bowl 16–12. **1967—8-2-0.** Won first 8 before losing to Penn St. 13–8 and Clemson 14–6 as Gerald Warren led nation's kickers with 17 FGs and DT Dennis Byrd (1st Wolfpack consensus All America) and DB Fred Combs starred on defense; beat Georgia in Liberty Bowl 14–7. **1973—8-3-0.** Lou Holtz's 2nd team scored 365 behind G Bill Yoest and B Willie Burden (1,014 yards rushing); won ACC and beat Kansas in Liberty Bowl 31–18. **1974—9-2-0.** FB Stan Fritts ran for 1,169 yards and Roland Hooks for 850 while Dave Buckey passed for 1,481; tied Houston in Bluebonnet Bowl 31–31. **1978—8-3-0.** C Jim Ritcher and RB Ted Brown (1,350 yards rushing) led attack; beat Pittsburgh in Tangerine Bowl 30–17.

BOWL RECORD

Bluebonnet 0–0–1; Gator 0–1–0; Liberty 2–1–0; Peach 2–1–0; Tangerine 1–0–0.

CONFERENCE TITLES

Atlantic Coast 1957, 1963*, 1964, 1965*, 1968, 1973, 1979.

TOP 10 AP & UPI RANKING

1974   U–9

MAJOR RIVALS

North Carolina St. has played at least 15 games with Clemson (18–33–1), Davidson (30–9–6), Duke (19–36–4), Maryland (17–19–4), North Carolina (18–49–6), Penn St. (2–17–0), Richmond (17–1–1), South Carolina (19–23–4), Virginia (25–7–1), VMI (7–11–1), Virginia Tech (16–20–3), Wake Forest (44–27–6), Washington & Lee (5–11–1) and William & Mary (10–8–0).

COACHES

Dean of Wolfpack coaches was Earle Edwards with record of 77–88–8 for 1954–70, including 5 conference titles and 2 bowl teams. Lou Holtz was 33–12–3 for 1972–75 with 1 conference title and 4 bowl teams. Other outstanding records were by Eddie Green, 25–8–2 for 1909–13 with 1 unbeaten team; and Bo Rein, 27–18–1 for 1976–79 with 1 conference title and 2 bowl champions.

MISCELLANEA

First game 14–6 win over Raleigh Academy in 1892 . . . 1st win over college foe was 40–0 over Richmond in 1895 . . . highest score was 100–0 over Hampton Road in 1919 . . . highest since W.W. II was 57–8 over East Carolina in 1973 . . . worst defeat was 128–0 by Georgia Tech in 1918 . . . worst since W.W. II was 61–0 by West Virginia in 1953 . . . State has won 9 straight 3 times, latest in 1973–74 ended by North Carolina 33–14 . . . longest losing string of 10 in 1953–54 broken with 26–0 win over William & Mary . . . consensus All America players were Dennis Byrd, DT, 1967; Bill Yoest, G, 1973; Ted Brown, RB, 1978; and Jim Ritcher, C,

1978–79 ... Academic All America choices were Roman Gabriel, QB, 1960; Joseph Scarpati, HB, 1963; Steve Warren, OT, 1967; Craig John, OG, 1971; Stan Fritts, RB, 1973; Justus Everett, C, 1973–74; and Calvin Warren, P, 1980.

Northwestern (Wildcats; Purple & White) (Big 10)

NOTABLE TEAMS

1896—6–1–2. Lost only to Chicago 18–6. 1901—8–2–1. Shut out 5, losing only to unbeaten national champion Michigan and to Minnesota. 1903— 9–2–3. Shut out 8 and won share of Big 10 title in Walter McCornack's 1st year. 1904—8–2–0. Shut out 7, losing only to Chicago and unbeaten Minnesota. 1905—8–2–1. Lost to unbeaten national champion Chicago and to Minnesota in McCornack's last season. 1916—6–1–0. Lost only to unbeaten Ohio State 23–3 in finale. 1917—5–2–0. Lost successive games to Ohio St. and Chicago. 1926—7–1–0. Outscored foes 179–22 behind HB Ralph (Moon) Baker (1st Wildcat consensus All America) and T Bob Johnson to take share of Big 10 title; lost only to Notre Dame 6–0. 1930—7–1–0. Outscored first 7 foes 182–22 but lost finale to unbeaten national champion Notre Dame 14–0; won share of Big 10 behind FB Reb Russell and E Frank Baker. 1931—7–1–1. Repeated as Big 10 champs behind HB Pug Rentner and tackles Dallas Marvil and Jack Riley; tied Notre Dame 0–0 and lost finale to Purdue 7–0. 1936—7–1–0. Pappy Waldorf's 2nd team won Big 10 title, losing only to Notre Dame 26–6 in finale. 1940—6–2–0. Lost close ones to unbeaten national champion Minnesota 13–12 and to Michigan 20–13 as T Alf Bauman starred. 1943—6–2–0. Otto Graham ran and passed for 730 yards and scored 61 points as Wildcats lost only to Michigan and to national champion Notre Dame. 1948—7–2–0. Art Murakowski ran for 622 yards behind C Alex Sarkisian as Wildcats lost only to unbeaten teams, national champion Michigan and Notre Dame (12–7); upset unbeaten California in Rose Bowl 20–14. 1962—7–2–0. Tom Myers passed for 1,537 yards and Paul Flatley caught 45 for 626 yards as Wildcats won 6 straight before losing to Wisconsin and Michigan St.

BOWL RECORD

Rose 1–0–0.

CONFERENCE TITLES

Big 10 1903*, 1926*, 1930*, 1931*, 1936.

TOP 10 AP & UPI RANKING

1948   7

MAJOR RIVALS

Northwestern has played at least 15 games with Beloit (12–3–4), Chicago (8–26–3), Illinois (33–40–5), Indiana (33–22–1), Iowa (14–30–3), Lake Forest (17–4–3), Michigan (11–39–2), Michigan St. (8–20–0), Minnesota (22–39–4), Notre Dame (7–34–2), Ohio St. (13–41–1), Purdue (19–33–1), and Wisconsin (22–44–5).

COACHES

Dean of Northwestern coaches was Lynn (Pappy) Waldorf with record of 49–45–7 for 1935–46, including 1 conference title. He was national coach of the year in 1935. Dick Hanley was 36–26–4 for 1927–34 with 2 conference titles. Second to Waldorf in tenure was Bob Voights with a record of 33–39–1 for 1947–54 with 1 Rose Bowl champion. Other top records were by Walter McCornack, 25–6–4 for 1903–05; C.M. Hollister, 25–16–4 for 1899–1902; Glenn Thistlethwaite, 21–17–1 for 1922–26; and Ara Parseghian, 36–35–1 for 1956–63. Alex Agase was national coach of the year in 1970.

MISCELLANEA

First game was loss to Lake Forest in 1882 . . . 1st win was over same team same year . . . highest score was 97–0 over Oshkosh Normal in 1904 . . . highest since W.W. II was 55–24 over Michigan in 1958 . . . biggest margin since W.W. II was 48–0 over Syracuse in 1948 and over Illinois in 1970 . . . worst defeat was 76–0 by Chicago in 1899 . . . worst since 1900 was 78–6 by Iowa in 1913 . . . worst since W.W. II was 69–0 by Michigan in 1975 . . . highest against Wildcats since W.W. II was 70–6 by Ohio St. in 1981 . . . longest unbeaten string of 11 in 1935–36 ended by Notre Dame 26–6 . . . longest losing string of 34 (NCAA record) in 1979–82 broken with 31–6 win over Northern Illinois . . . consensus All America players were Ralph Baker, B, 1926; Frank Baker, E, 1930; Jack Riley, T, Dallas Marvil, T, and Pug Rentner, B, 1931; Steve Reid, G, 1936; Alf Bauman, T, 1940; Max

Morris, E, 1945; Ron Burton, B, 1959; and Jack Cvercko, G, 1962 . . . Academic All America choices were Al Viola, G, 1956; Andy Cvercko, T, 1958; Larry Onesti, C, 1961; Paul Flatley, B, 1962; George Burman, E, 1963; Joe Zigulich, OG, 1970; Rob Dean, E, 1976; and Jim Ford, OT, 1980.

Notre Dame (Fighting Irish; Gold & Blue) (Independent)

NOTABLE TEAMS

1893—4–1–0. Lost finale to Chicago 8–0. 1897—4–1–1. Tied Rush Medical 0–0 in opener and lost to Chicago 34–5. 1901—8–1–1. Shut out 6, losing only to Northwestern 2–0. 1902—6–2–1. Lost to unbeaten national champion Michigan 23–0 and to Knox (12–5). 1903—8–0–1. Blanked foes 292–0, tying Northwestern 0–0. 1906—6–1–0. Lost to Indiana 12–0 but blanked others 107–0. 1907—6–0–1. Tie was 0–0 with Indiana. 1908—8–1–0. Scored 326 and shut out 6, losing only to Michigan 12–6. 1909—7–0–1. Scored 236 and shut out 6, including 0–0 tie with Marquette in finale. 1910—4–1–1. Lost to Michigan St. 17–0 and tied Marquette 5–5. 1911—6–0–2. Outscored foes 222–9; ties were 0–0 with Pittsburgh and Marquette. 1912—7–0–0. Outscored foes 389–27, beating Pitt 3–0 and Marquette 69–0. 1913—7–0–0. Jesse Harper's 1st team outscored foes 268–41, including famous 35–13 upset of Army at West Point behind Gus Dorais' passing; Dorais was 1st Irish All America. 1914—6–2–0. Scored 287, losing only to Yale and unbeaten national champion Army (20–7). 1915—7–1–0. Scored 230 and shut out 5, losing only to unbeaten Nebraska 20–19. 1916—8–1–0. Lost to unbeaten Army 30–10 but blanked others 283–0. 1917—6–1–1. Harper's last team shut out 6, including 0–0 tie with Wisconsin; lost only to Nebraska 7–0. 1919—9–0–0. Knute Rockne's 2nd team outscored foes 229–47 as George Gipp ran for 729 yards and passed for 727 more. 1920—9–0–0. Outscored foes 251–44 as Gipp ran for 827 yards, passed for 709 and kicked 9 FGs. 1921—10–1–0. Outscored foes 375–41 behind G Hunk Anderson, E Eddie Anderson (26 receptions for 394 yards) and TB John Mohardt (ran and passed for 1,776 yards and 21 TDs); lost only to unbeaten Iowa 10–7 in 3rd game. 1922—8–1–1. Shut out 6, including 0–0 tie with Army, and lost only to Nebraska 14–6 in finale. 1923—9–1–0. Scored 275 as Don Miller (698 yards rushing) and Red Maher each scored 10 TDs; lost only to Nebraska 14–7. 1924—9–0–0. Outscored foes 258–44 behind C Adam Walsh and the Four Horsemen (Miller ran for 763 yards, Harry

Stuhldreher passed for 471, Jim Crowley ran and passed for 975, kicked 17 extra points and scored 9 TDs, and Elmer Layden starred at FB); won 1st national championship and beat Stanford 27–10 in Rose Bowl. 1925—7–2–1. Lost to Army and Nebraska. 1926—9–1–0. Shut out 7 as C Art Boeringer starred; lost only to Carnegie Tech 19–0 in big upset. 1927—7–1–1. Christie Flanagan ran for 731 yards behind G John Smith; tied Minnesota 7–7 and lost to Army 18–0 in successive games. 1929—9–0–0. QB Frank Carideo and G Jack Cannon led team to national championship; won 4 by TD or less. 1930—10–0–0. Rockne's last team won his 3rd national title while scoring 265 and upsetting Southern California 27–0 in finale; Carideo again directed attack as Marchy Schwartz ran for 927 yards and passed for 319. 1931—6–2–1. Shut out 6 before losing to national champion USC (16–14) and Army in last 2. 1932—7–2–0. Scored 255 and shut out 6 behind T Joe Kurth; 1 of losses was to unbeaten USC. 1935—7–1–1. Elmer Layden's 2nd team lost only to Northwestern 14–7 and tied Army 6–6 in successive games; won 3 by TD or less, including famous 18–13 upset of Ohio St. in last-quarter rally. 1936—6–2–1. Lost to Pitt and Navy. 1937—6–2–1. Won 5 by TD or less; lost to Carnegie Tech 9–7 and to national champion Pitt 21–6. 1938—8–1–0. T Joe Beinor led team to wins over all but Southern California (13–0 in finale). 1939—7–2–0. Won 6 by TD or less, losing only to Iowa 7–6 and USC 20–12. 1940—7–2–0. Layden's last team won 4 by TD or less, losing to Iowa and Northwestern. 1941—8–0–1. Frank Leahy's 1st team won last 3 by TD or less after 0–0 tie with Army; Angelo Bertelli passed for 1,027 yards. 1942—7–2–2. Bertelli passed for 1,039 yards and 10 TDs and intercepted 8 passes, and Bob Dove starred at E as Irish lost only to Georgia Tech and Michigan. 1943—9–1–0. Led nation in total offense and rushing while scoring 340 and winning national championship despite 19–14 loss to Great Lakes in finale; Creighton Miller led nation in rushing with 911 yards and intercepted 6 passes while Bertelli became Notre Dame's first Heisman Trophy winner. 1944—8–2–0. Bob Kelly ran for 681 yards, caught 18 passes for 283 more and scored 13 TDs as Irish lost only to Navy and undefeated national champion Army. 1945—7–2–1. Lost to unbeaten national champion Army and to Great Lakes. 1946—8–0–1. Outscored foes 271–24 and led nation in total offense, rushing, total defense and scoring defense behind QB Johnny Lujack and T George (Moose) Connor; won national championship despite 0–0 tie with unbeaten defending champions, Army. 1947—9–0–0. Outscored foes 291–52 and retained national title behind Heisman winner Lujack, Connor, G Bill Fischer and HB Terry Brennan (11 TDs). 1948—9–0–1. Scored 320 behind Fischer and FB Emil Sitko (742 yards rushing and 9 TDs); tie was with Southern California 14–14 in finale. 1949—10–0–0.

Scored 360 and led nation in total offense as QB Bob Williams passed for 1,347 yards and 16 TDs, Heisman winner Leon Hart caught 19 for 5 TDs and Sitko ran for 712 yards and 9 TDs; T Jim Martin led line as Irish won 4th national title for Leahy. 1951—7–2–1. Jim Mutscheller finished fine career at E as Irish lost only to SMU 27–20 and unbeaten Michigan St. 1952 —7–2–1. John Lattner ran for 732 yards and intercepted 4 passes as Irish lost only to Pitt 22–19 and unbeaten national champion Michigan St. 21–3. 1953 —9–0–1. Leahy's last team and 6th unbeaten one scored 317 behind T Art Hunter, Heisman winner Lattner and Neil Worden (859 yards rushing and 11 TDs); tie was with Iowa 14–14. 1954—9–1–0. Ralph Guglielmi passed for 1,162 yards and intercepted 5 passes to lead team to wins over all but Purdue (27–14 in 2nd game). 1955—8–2–0. Paul Hornung passed for 743 yards and 9 TDs and intercepted 5 passes. 1957—7–3–0. Won 3 by TD or less as G Al Ecuyer starred. 1964—9–1–0. Ara Parseghian's 1st team scored 287 as John Huarte passed for 2,062 yards and 16 TDs (and won Heisman) and Jack Snow caught 60 passes for 1,114 yards and 9 TDs while Tony Carey led nation with 8 interceptions; lost only to Southern California 20–17 in finale. 1965—7–2–1. Scored 270 behind G Dick Arrington as DB Nick Rassas (6 interceptions) sparked defense; lost only to Purdue 25–21 and unbeaten national champion Michigan St. 12–3. 1966—9–0–1. Outscored foes 362–38, leading nation in scoring average and shutting out 6, and won national championship despite 10–10 tie with unbeaten Michigan St.; G Tom Regner and E Jim Seymour (48 catches for 862 yards and 8 TDs) led offense and LB Jim Lynch, DE Alan Page and DB Tom Schoen (7 interceptions) led defense. 1967—8–2–0. Scored 337 and Schoen and DE Kevin Hardy led defense; won last 6 after losses to Purdue 28–21 and national champion USC. 1968—7–2–1. Scored 376 behind T George Kunz, QB Terry Hanratty, Seymour (53 catches for 736 yards) and Bob Gladieux (713 yards rushing and 14 TDs). 1969—8–1–1. Scored 334 as Joe Theismann passed for 1,531 yards and 13 TDs and DT Mike McCoy led defense; lost only to Purdue 28–14 in 2nd game, but lost to unbeaten national champion Texas in Cotton Bowl 21–17. 1970—9–1–0. Scored 330 behind G Larry DiNardo, Theismann (2,429 yards and 16 TDs passing) and Tom Gatewood (77 pass receptions for 1,123 yards and 7 TDs); lost only to USC 38–28 in finale, but upset unbeaten Texas in Cotton Bowl 24–11. 1971—8–2–0. DE Walt Patulski and DB Clarence Ellis led defense and Gatewood again starred on offense. 1972 —8–2–0. DT Greg Marx led defense and Mike Townsend led nation with 10 interceptions while QB Tom Clements directed offense to 283 points; lost only to Missouri 30–26 and to unbeaten national champion USC, then to Nebraska in Orange Bowl 40–6. 1973—10–0–0. Outscored foes 358–66 as

TE Dave Casper starred on offense and DB Townsend on defense; beat undefeated Alabama 24–23 in Sugar Bowl to earn national championship. 1974—9–2–0. Parseghian's last team led nation in total defense and rushing defense behind DT Mike Fanning and LB Greg Collins while offense was led by QB Clements, E Pete Demmerle (43 catches for 667 yards and 6 TDs) and B Wayne Bullock (855 yards rushing and 12 TDs); beat undefeated Alabama in Orange Bowl 13–11. 1975—8–3–0. Dan Devine's 1st team had 2 losses by TD or less as Steve Niehaus starred at T. 1976—8–3–0. Al Hunter ran for 1,058 yards and 13 TDs and DE Ross Browner led defense; beat Penn St. in Gator Bowl 20–9. 1977—10–1–0. Scored 382 as Jerome Heavens ran for 994 yards and Ken MacAfee caught 54 passes for 797 yards and 6 TDs, while defense was led by Browner and DB Luther Bradley; lost only to Mississippi 20–13 in 2nd game, and upset unbeaten Texas in Cotton Bowl 38–10 to win national championship. 1978—8–3–0. Vagas Ferguson ran for 1,192 yards and Joe Montana passed for 2,010 behind C Dave Huffman and LB Bob Golic led defense; won 8 straight before losing finale to national champion Southern California 27–25, but beat Houston in Cotton Bowl 35–34 on last play of game. 1980—9–1–1. Devine's last team lost only to USC 20–3 in finale behind C John Scully and LB Bob Crable; lost to unbeaten national champion Georgia in Sugar Bowl 17–10.

BOWL RECORD

Cotton 3–1–0; Gator 1–0–0; Liberty 1–0–0; Orange 1–1–0; Rose 1–0–0; Sugar 1–1–0.

CONFERENCE TITLES

None.

TOP 10 AP & UPI RANKING

1936	8	1946	1	1957	10–9	1973	1–4
1937	9	1947	1	1964	3–3	1974	6–4
1938	5	1948	2	1965	9–8	1977	1–1
1941	3	1949	1	1966	1–1	1978	7–6
1942	6	1952	3–3	1967	5–4	1980	9–10
1943	1	1953	2–2	1968	5–8		
1944	9	1954	4–4	1969	5–9		
1945	9	1955	8–9	1970	2–5		

MAJOR RIVALS

Notre Dame has played at least 15 games with Army (33–8–4), Carnegie Tech (15–4–0), Georgia Tech (25–4–1), Indiana (22–5–1), Iowa (13–8–3), Miami (Fla.) (13–3–1), Michigan (5–11–0), Michigan St. (31–17–1), Navy (47–9–1), North Carolina (15–1–0), Northwestern (34–7–2), Pittsburgh (32–14–1), Purdue (34–19–2), Southern California (28–23–4) and Wisconsin (8–6–2).

COACHES

Dean of Notre Dame coaches was legendary Knute Rockne with record of 105–12–5 for 1918–30, including 1 Rose Bowl champion, 5 unbeaten teams and 3 national champions. Frank Leahy was 87–11–9 for 1941–43 and 1946–53 with 6 unbeaten teams and 4 national champions. Rockne and Leahy rank 1–2 in all-time winning percentage. Leahy was national coach of the year in 1941, as was Ara Parseghian in 1964. Parseghian was 95–17–4 for 1964–74 with 5 bowl teams, 2 unbeaten teams and 3 national champions. Other top records were by Jesse C. Harper, 34–5–1 for 1913–17 with 1 unbeaten team; Elmer Layden, 47–13–3 for 1934–40; Terry Brennan, 32–18–0 for 1954–58; and Dan Devine, 53–16–1 for 1975–80 with 4 bowl teams (3 winners) and 1 national champion.

MISCELLANEA

First game was 8–0 loss to Michigan in 1887 . . . 1st win was 20–0 over Harvard School of Chicago in 1888 . . . 1st win over college foe was 9–0 over Northwestern in 1889 . . . highest score was 142–0 over American Medical in 33-minute game in 1905 . . . highest since W.W. II was 69–13 over Pitt in 1965 and 69–14 over Georgia Tech in 1977 . . . biggest margin of victory since W.W. II was 64–0 over Duke in 1966 . . . worst defeat was 59–0 by Army in 1944 . . . worst since W.W. II were 40–0 by Oklahoma and 48–8 by Iowa, both in 1956 . . . highest against Irish since W.W. II was 55–24 by Southern California in 1974 . . . longest unbeaten string of 39 in 1946–50 ended by Purdue 28–14 . . . unbeaten string of 27 in 1910–14 ended by Yale 28–0 . . . unbeaten string of 26 in 1929–31 ended by Southern California 16–14 . . . winning streak of 20 in 1919–21 ended by Iowa 10–7 . . . longest losing string of 8 in 1960 broken with 17–0 win over Southern California . . . Notre Dame has had 67 consensus All America players since 1913 . . . multi-year choices were Frank Carideo, B, 1929–30; Marchy

Schwartz, B, 1930–31; Bob Dove, E, 1941–42; George Connor, T, 1946–47; John Lujack, B, 1946–47; Bill Fischer, G, 1947–48; Leon Hart, E, 1948–49; Emil Sitko, B, 1948–49; Johnny Lattner, B, 1952–53; Ken Mac-Afee, E, 1976–77; Ross Browner, DE, 1976–77; and Bob Crable, LB, 1980–81 . . . single-year unanimous choices were Joe Kurth, T, 1932; Ed Beinor, T, 1938; Ralph Guglielmi, B, 1954; Dick Arrington, G, 1965; Nick Eddy, B, and Jim Lynch, LB, 1966; Mike McCoy, DT, 1969; Walt Patulski, DE, 1971; Greg Marx, DT, 1972; Steve Niehaus, DT, 1975; Bob Golic, LB, 1978; and John Scully, C, 1980 . . . others since 1970 were Tom Gatewood, E, and Larry DiNardo, G, 1970; Clarence Ellis, DB, 1971; Dave Casper, TE, and Mike Townsend, DB, 1973; Pete Demmerle, WR, and Gerry DiNardo, G, 1974; Luther Bradley, DB, 1977; Dave Huffman, C, 1978; and Vagas Ferguson, RB, 1979 . . . Academic All America selections were Joe Heap, B, 1952–54; Don Schaefer, B, 1955; Bob Wetoska, E, 1958; Bob Lehmann, G, 1963; Tom Regner, OG, and Jim Lynch, LB, 1966; Jim Smithberger, DB, 1967; George Kunz, OT, 1968; Jim Reilly, OT, 1969; Larry DiNardo, OG, and Joe Theismann, QB, 1970; Tom Gatewood, E, 1970–71; Greg Mark, OT, 1971–72; Mike Creaney, E, 1972; David Casper, E, Robert Thomas, K, and Gary Potempa, LB, 1973; Pete Demmerle, E, and Reggie Barnett, DB, 1974; Ken MacAfee, E, and Dave Vinson, OG, 1977; Joe Restic, S, 1977, and DB, 1978; Tom Gibbons, DB, and Bob Burger, OG, 1980; and John Krimm, DB, 1981 . . . Heisman Trophy winners were Angelo Bertelli, QB, 1943; John Lujack, QB, 1947; Leon Hart, E, 1949; John Lattner, HB, 1953; Paul Hornung, QB, 1956; and John Huarte, QB, 1964 . . . Outland Trophy winners were George Connor, T, 1946 (first award); Bill Fischer, G, 1948; and Ross Browner, DE, 1976 . . . Lombardi Award winners were Walt Patulski, DE, 1971; and Ross Browner, DE, 1977 . . . Notre Dame has highest winning percentage in college football history and ranks in top 5 in all-time total victories.

Ohio State (Buckeyes; Scarlet & Gray) (Big 10)

NOTABLE TEAMS

1892—5–2–0. Scored 260; lost to Oberlin and Western Reserve. 1899—9–0–1. Blanked 9 foes 179–0 and tied Case 5–5 in 3rd game. 1900—8–1–1. Shut out 7; lost to Ohio Medical 11–6 and tied Michigan 0–0 in successive late-season games. 1902—6–2–2. Lost to unbeaten national champion Michigan and to Case. 1903—8–3–0. Lost only to Case in first 7. 1905—8–2–2.

Shut out 8; lost to Michigan and Indiana. 1906—8–1–0. A. E. Herrnstein's 1st team shut out 7 and lost to Michigan 6–0 in 4th game. 1907—7–2–1. Shut out 6. 1909—7–3–0. Herrnstein's last team shut out 6. 1910—6–1–3. Shut out 6; lost to Case 14–10. 1914—5–2–0. John W. Wilce's 2nd team lost only to unbeaten Illinois and to Wisconsin (7–6). 1915—5–1–1. Lost only to Wisconsin 21–0. 1916—7–0–0. Outscored foes 258–29 and won 1st Big 10 title behind B Charles Harley (1st Buckeye consensus All America) and T Robert Karch. 1917—8–0–1. Outscored foes 292–6 behind Harley and E Charles Bolen and repeated as Big 10 champs; tie was 0–0 with Auburn. 1919—6–1–0. Shut out 5 as Harley made All America for 3rd time; lost only to Illinois 9–7 in finale. 1920—7–0–0. Outscored foes 150–20 behind G Iolas Huffman and B Gaylord Stinchcomb; won Big 10 but lost to unbeaten national champion California in Rose Bowl 28–0. 1921—5–2–0. Huffman starred at T as Buckeyes shut out 5; lost only to Oberlin 7–6 and Illinois 7–0. 1926—7–1–0. Lost only to Michigan 17–16. 1933—7–1–0. Shut out 5 and lost only to national champion Michigan 13–0 in Sam Willaman's last year. 1934—7–1–0. Francis A. Schmidt's 1st team scored 267 behind linemen Regis Monahan and Merle Wendt; lost only to Illinois 14–13 in 2nd game. 1935—7–1–0. Scored 237 as Wendt starred again along with C Gomer Jones; lost only to Notre Dame 18–13 and got share of Big 10 title. 1937 —6–2–0. Shut out 6. 1939—6–2–0. E Esco Sarkkinen led team to Big 10 title; shut out 5 and lost only to unbeaten Cornell 23–14 and Michigan 21–14. 1941—6–1–1. Paul E. Brown's 1st team won 4 by TD or less, losing only to Northwestern 14–7 and tying Michigan 20–20. 1942—9–1–0. Scored 337 behind E Robert Shaw and T Charles Csuri and won Big 10 and 1st national championship despite 17–7 loss to Wisconsin. 1944—9–0–0. Scored 287 as Heisman winner Les Horvath ran for 924 yards and 12 TDs and passed for 344 yards behind G Bill Hackett and E Jack Dugger; won Big 10 under Carroll Widdoes. 1945—7–2–0. Ollie Cline ran for 936 yards behind G Warren Amling. 1949—6–1–2. Wes Fesler's 3rd team won Big 10, losing only to Minnesota 27–0; upset unbeaten California in Rose Bowl 17–14. 1954—9–0–0. Woody Hayes' 1st unbeaten team won Big 10 and share of national championship behind Howard (Hopalong) Cassady (701 yards rushing and 13 pass receptions for 148 yards) and E Dean Dugger; beat Southern California in Rose Bowl 20–7. 1955—7–2–0. Cassady ran for 958 yards and 14 TDs and won Heisman; team won Big 10 with 5 straight wins after losses to Stanford 6–0 and Duke 20–14. 1957—8–1–0. Scored 257 as Don Clark ran for 737 yards; lost only to TCU 18–14 in opener and won Big 10, then beat Oregon in Rose Bowl 10–7. 1958—6–1–2. Won 4 by TD or less as Bob White ran for 859 yards and 12 TDs; lost only to Northwestern

21–0. 1960—7–2–0. Bob Ferguson ran for 853 yards and 13 TDs as Buckeyes lost only to Purdue 24–21 and Iowa. 1961—8–0–1. Won Big 10 and share of national title as Ferguson ran for 938 yards and 11 TDs; tie was with TCU 7–7 in opener. 1964—7–2–0. LB Dwight Kelley and DB Arnold Chonko sparked defense as Buckeyes lost only to Penn St. and Michigan. 1965—7–2–0. Won 4 by TD or less behind Kelley and T Doug Van Horn; swept last 5 after losses to North Carolina and unbeaten national champion Michigan St. 1968—9–0–0. Scored 296 behind T Dave Foley and B Jim Otis (985 yards rushing and 17 TDs) to win Big 10; beat Southern California in Rose Bowl 27–16 to clinch national championship. 1969—8–1–0. Scored 383 behind Otis (1,027 yards and 15 TDs) and QB Rex Kern (1,585 yards of total offense) as MG Jim Stillwagon and DB Jack Tatum led defense; upset by Michigan 24–12 in finale but still got share of Big 10. 1970—9–0–0. Hayes' 4th unbeaten team was led by Stillwagon, Tatum and DB Mike Sensibaugh (national interception leader with 8) on defense and Kern and John Brockington (1,142 yards rushing and 17 TDs) on offense; won share of national title despite 27–17 loss to Stanford in Rose Bowl. 1972—9–1–0. Harold Henson led nation in scoring with 20 TDs for 120 points behind T John Hicks while LB Randy Gradishar led defense as Buckeyes won 16th Big 10 title despite 19–12 loss to Michigan St.; lost to unbeaten national champion Southern California in Rose Bowl 42–17. 1973—9–0–1. Outscored foes 371–43 and led nation in scoring defense as Hicks and Gradishar starred again and soph Archie Griffin ran for 1,577 yards; tied Michigan 10–10 in finale, then beat USC in Rose Bowl 42–21. 1974—10–1–0. Scored 420 behind T Kurt Schumacher, C Steve Meyers and Heisman winner Griffin (1,695 yards rushing and 12 TDs) while DB Neal Colzie sparked defense; lost only to Michigan St. 16–13, but lost to national champion Southern California in Rose Bowl 18–17. 1975—11–0–0. Hayes' 6th unbeaten team scored 374 to lead nation as Pete Johnson topped individual scorers with 26 TDs for 156 points and Griffin ran for 1,450 yards and won Heisman again behind G Ted Smith while DB Tim Fox led defense; lost Rose Bowl 23–10 to UCLA team beaten 41–20 in 4th game. 1976—8–2–1. Jeff Logan ran for 1,248 yards behind T Chris Ward while DE Bob Brudzinski and P Tom Skladany also starred; beat Colorado in Orange Bowl 27–10. 1977—9–2–0. Scored 337 behind Ward, G Aaron Brown and Ron Springs (1,166 yards rushing) as LB Tom Cousineau and DB Ray Griffin led defense; lost only to Oklahoma 29–28 and Michigan 14–6, then to Alabama in Sugar Bowl 35–6. 1979—11–0–0. Earle Bruce's 1st team scored 374 behind G Ken Fritz and QB Art Schlichter (2,246 yards of total offense); lost to Southern California in Rose Bowl 17–16. 1980—9–2–0. Scored 368 as Calvin Murray ran for 1,267 yards, Schlichter had 2,255 yards of total offense and Doug Donley caught 43 passes for 887 yards and 7 TDs; lost to Penn St. in Fiesta Bowl 31–19. 1981—8–3–0. Scored 356 as Schlichter passed for 2,392 yards and 15 TDs and Tim Spencer ran for 1,121 yards and 12 TDs; beat Navy in Liberty Bowl 31–28. 1982—8–3–0. Lost 2 by TD or less and swept last 6 as Spencer ran for 1,371 yards and 12 TDs and LB Marcus Marek starred on defense; beat Brigham Young in Holiday Bowl 47–17. 1983—8–3–0. Scored 382 as Keith Byars ran for 1,126 yards and 19 TDs and Mike Tomczak passed for 1,716 yards; beat Pittsburgh in Fiesta Bowl 28–23.

BOWL RECORD:

Fiesta 1–1–0; Gator 0–1–0; Holiday 1–0–0; Liberty 1–0–0; Orange 1–0–0; Rose 5–6–0; Sugar 0–1–0.

CONFERENCE TITLES

Big 10 1916, 1917, 1920, 1935*, 1939, 1942, 1944, 1949*, 1954, 1955, 1957, 1961, 1968, 1969*, 1970, 1972*, 1973*, 1974*, 1975, 1976*, 1977*, 1979, 1981*.

TOP 10 AP & UPI RANKING

1942	1	1957	2–1	1969	4–5	1976	6–5
1944	2	1958	8–7	1970	5–2	1979	4–4
1949	6	1960	8–8	1972	9–3	1983	9–8
1950	U–10	1961	2–2	1973	2–3		
1954	1–2	1964	9–9	1974	4–3		
1955	6–5	1968	1–1	1975	4–4		

MAJOR RIVALS

Ohio St. has played at least 15 games with Case (11–10–2), Denison (14–1–2), Illinois (48–20–4), Indiana (47–10–4), Iowa (29–11–2), Kenyon (17–6–0), Michigan (31–44–5), Michigan St. (14–8–0), Minnesota (21–6–0), Northwestern (41–13–1), Oberlin (13–9–3), Ohio Wesleyan (26–2–1), Otterbein (13–2–3), Pittsburgh (13–4–1), Purdue (22–8–2), Southern California (9–8–1), Wisconsin (40–9–4) and Wittenberg (12–3–0).

COACHES

Dean of Ohio St. coaches was Woodrow W. (Woody) Hayes with record of 205–61–10 for 1951–78, including 13 conference titles, 11 bowl teams, 6 teams unbeaten in regular season and 5 national champions. He ranks 4th in all-time coaching victories with 238. John W. Wilce was 78–33–9 for 1913–28 with 3 conference titles, 1 Rose Bowl team and 3 teams unbeaten in regular season. Other outstanding records for at least 4 years were A.E. Herrnstein, 28–10–1 for 1906–09; Sam S. Willaman, 26–10–5 for 1929–33; Francis A. Schmidt, 39–16–1 for 1934–40 with 2 conference titles; Wesley E. Fesler, 21–13–3 for 1947–50 with 1 conference title and 1 Rose Bowl champion; and Earle Bruce, 47–13–0 for 1979–83 with 2 conference titles, 5 bowl teams and 1 team unbeaten in regular season. National coach of the year award went to Carroll Widdoes, 1944; Woody Hayes, 1957, 1968 and 1975; and Earle Bruce, 1979.

MISCELLANEA

First game was 20–14 win over Ohio Wesleyan in 1890 . . . highest score was 128–0 over Oberlin in 1916 . . . highest since W.W. II was 83–21 over Iowa in 1950 . . . biggest margin since W.W. II was 63–0 over Northwestern in 1980 . . . worst defeat was 86–0 by Michigan in 1902 . . . worst since W.W. II was 58–6 by Michigan in 1946 . . . longest winning streak of 22 in 1967–69 ended by Michigan 24–12 . . . unbeaten string of 21 in 1915–18 ended by Michigan 14–0 . . . unbeaten string of 19 in 1973–74 ended by Michigan St. 16–13 . . . unbeaten string of 18 in 1898–1900 ended by Ohio Medical 11–6 . . . longest losing string was 5 twice in the 1890s . . . Ohio St. has had 32 consensus All America players since 1916 . . . multi-year choices were Charles Harley, B, 1916–17, 1919; Iolas Huffman, G, 1920, and T, 1921; Wes Fesler, E, 1928–30; Warren Amling, G, 1945, and T, 1946; Howard Cassady, B, 1954–55; Bob Ferguson, B, 1960–61; Jim Stillwagon, MG, and Jack Tatum, DB, 1969–70; Randy Gradishar, LB, 1972–73; Archie Griffin, B, 1974–75; Chris Ward, T, 1976–77; and Tom Cousineau, LB, 1977–78 . . . single-year unanimous choices were Les Horvath, B, 1944; Vic Janowicz, B, 1950; Jim Parker, G, 1956; Dave Foley, T, 1968; and John Hicks, OT, 1973 . . . other selections since 1970 were Kurt Schumacher, OT, and Steve Myers, C, 1974; Ted Smith, G, and Tim Fox, DB, 1975; Bob Brudzinski, DE, 1976; Ken Fritz, G, 1979; and Marcus Marek, LB, 1982 . . . Academic All America choices were John Borton, B, 1952; Dick Hilinski, T, 1954; Bob White, B, 1958; Tom Perdue, E, 1961; Bill Ridder, MG, 1965; Dave Foley, OT, 1966 and 1968; Mark Stier, LB, 1968; Bill Urbanik, DT, 1969; Rick Simon, OG, 1971; Randy Gradishar, LB, 1973; Brian Baschnagel, RB, 1974–75; Bill Lukens, OG, and Pete Johnson, RB, 1976; Jeff Logan, RB, 1977; Marcus Marek, LB, 1980; Joseph Smith, OT, 1982; and John Frank, TE, 1982–83 . . . Heisman Trophy winners were Les Horvath, QB, 1944; Vic Janowicz, HB, 1950; Howard Cassady, HB, 1955; and Archie Griffin, RB, 1974–75 . . . Outland Trophy winners were Jim Parker, G, 1956; Jim

Stillwagon, MG, 1970; and John Hicks, OT, 1973 . . . Lombardi Trophy winners were Stillwagon, 1970 (first award); and Hicks, 1973 . . . Ohio St. ranks in top 10 in both all-time total victories and winning percentage.

Oklahoma (Sooners; Crimson & Cream) (Big 8)

NOTABLE TEAMS

1900—3-1-1. Lost opener to unbeaten Texas 28-2 but gave up no more points. 1905—7-2-0. Bennie Owen's 1st team shut out 6. 1908—8-1-1. Outscored foes 272-35, losing only to unbeaten Kansas 11-0. 1911—8-0-0. Outscored opponents 282-15. 1913—6-2-0. Scored 323 behind FB Claude Reeds but lost to Missouri 20-17 and Texas 14-6. 1914—9-1-1. Scored 440, losing only to unbeaten Texas 32-7 and tying Kansas 16-16 in successive games. 1915—10-0-0. Scored 370 and won share of Southwest Conference title behind FB Forest Geyer. 1918—6-0-0. Scored 278 and shut out all but Phillips U. (13-7). 1920—6-0-1. Owen's 4th unbeaten team won Missouri Valley Conference led by T Roy Smoot and HB Phil White; tie was with Kansas St. 7-7. 1938—10-0-0. Shut out 8 and led nation in rushing defense while winning first Big 6 title as E Waddy Young became Sooners' 1st consensus All America; lost to unbeaten Tennessee in Orange Bowl 17-0. 1939—6-2-1. Unbeaten in first 7 behind T Gilford Duggan and E Frank Ivy; lost to Missouri 7-6 and Nebraska 13-7. 1943—7-2-0. Won last 5 to take Big 6 title. 1946—7-3-0. Scored 275 and led nation in rushing defense behind guards Buddy Burris and Plato Andros; won share of Big 6 and beat North Carolina St. in Gator Bowl 34-13. 1947—7-2-1. Bud Wilkinson's 1st team won last 5 to share Big 6 title as Burris starred again. 1948—9-1-0. Scored 336 as QB Jack Mitchell directed attack behind Burris; lost only to Santa Clara 20-17 in opener and beat North Carolina in Sugar Bowl 14-6. 1949—10-0-0. QB Darrell Royal directed attack as George Thomas topped nation with 117 of team's 364 points behind linemen Wade Walker and Stan West; led nation in rushing defense and beat LSU 35-0 in Sugar Bowl. 1950—10-0-0. Scored 345 as Claude Arnold ran and passed for 1,339 yards and 17 TDs behind T Jim Weatherall, and Leon Heath starred at FB; won 1st national championship despite 13-7 loss to Kentucky in Sugar Bowl. 1951—8-2-0. Scored 321 and won 6th straight conference title behind Weatherall and C Tom Catlin; lost only to Texas A&M 14-7 and Texas 9-7. 1952—8-1-1. Led nation with 407 points behind Heisman winner Billy Vessels (nation's all-purpose running leader with 1,512 yards and

18 TDs), FB Buck McPhail (1,018 yards rushing), QB Eddie Crowder and Catlin; lost only to Notre Dame 27–21 and tied Colorado 21–21. **1953—8–1–1.** Led nation in rushing behind G J.D. Roberts, losing only to Notre Dame 28–21 in opener; upset unbeaten national champion Maryland in Orange Bowl 7–0. **1954—10–0–0.** Scored 304 behind C Kurt Burris and E Max Boydston and won 9th straight conference title. **1955—10–0–0.** Scored 365 and led nation in total offense, rushing and scoring average behind G Bo Bolinger and HB Tommy McDonald; shut out 5 and beat undefeated Maryland 20–6 in Orange Bowl to win national championship. **1956—10–0–0.** Again led nation in total offense, rushing and scoring average (46.6) as Clendon Thomas led nation's scorers with 18 TDs and McDonald scored 17 behind C Jerry Tubbs and G Bill Krisher; shut out 6 and retained national title. **1957—9–1–0.** Scored 285 and lost only to Notre Dame 7–0 as Thomas and Krisher starred again; won 12th straight conference title and beat Duke in Orange Bowl 48–21. **1958—9–1–0.** Led nation in scoring defense and lost only to Texas 15–14 as C Bob Harrison starred; beat Syracuse in Orange Bowl 21–6. **1959—7–3–0.** Lost only to Nebraska 25–21 in last 7 and won 14th consecutive conference title. **1962—8–2–0.** Won last 7 to take Big 8 title after successive losses to Notre Dame 13–7 and Texas 9–6; lost to Alabama in Orange Bowl 17–0. **1963—8–2–0.** Wilkinson's last team lost only to unbeaten national champion Texas and to Nebraska as FB Jim Grisham and T Ralph Neely starred. **1967—9–1–0.** Chuck Fairbanks' 1st team led nation in scoring defense behind MG Granville Liggins and Steve Barrett's 7 interceptions; lost only to Texas 9–7 and beat Tennessee in Orange Bowl 26–24. **1968—7–3–0.** Scored 316 as Bob Warmack ran and passed for 1,814 yards and 15 TDs and Steve Owens ran for 1,536 yards and 21 TDs; got share of Big 8 but lost to SMU in Bluebonnet Bowl 28–27. **1971—10–1–0.** Scored 494 and led nation in total offense, rushing and scoring average behind QB Jack Mildren (2,018 yards of total offense and 27 TDs running and passing), Greg Pruitt (1,665 yards rushing and 17 TDs) and C Tom Brahaney; lost only to Nebraska 35–31 but beat Auburn in Sugar Bowl 40–22. **1972—10–1–0.** Fairbanks' last team again led nation in rushing behind Brahaney and Pruitt as LB Rod Shoate led defense; scored 371 and lost only to Colorado 20–14, then beat Penn St. in Sugar Bowl 14–0 but later forfeits dropped season record to 7–4–0. **1973—10–0–1.** Barry Switzer's 1st team scored 400 as Steve Davis ran and passed for 1,821 yards and 27 TDs, Joe Washington ran for 1,173 yards and Waymon Clark ran for 1,014; Shoate and MG Lucious Selmon sparked defense as Sooners beat all but Southern California (7–7 in 2nd game). **1974—11–0–0.** Scored 473 and led nation in total offense, rushing and scoring average behind Davis (1,260

yards and 20 TDs in total offense), Washington (1,321 yards rushing) and G John Roush on offense with Shoate sparking defense; won national title. 1975—10–1–0. Scored 330 but featured defense led by DT Lee Roy Selmon, MG Dewey Selmon and DE Jimbo Elrod; lost only to Kansas 23–3 but beat Michigan in Orange Bowl 14–6 to retain national title. 1976— 8–2–1. Won share of 4th straight Big 8 title, then beat Wyoming in Fiesta Bowl 41–7. 1977—10–1–0. Led nation in rushing while scoring 405 points behind QB Thomas Lott (1,074 yards total offense) as Zac Henderson intercepted 7 passes on defense; lost only to unbeaten Texas 13–6 and to Arkansas in Orange Bowl 31–6. 1978—10–1–0. Scored 409 and led nation in rushing and scoring average as Billy Sims topped nation in rushing (1,762 yards) and scoring (20 TDs) to win Heisman behind G Greg Roberts; lost only to Nebraska 17–14 and got revenge in Orange Bowl 31–24. 1979—10–1–0. Scored 382 as Sims again led nation with 132 points (22 TDs and 1,506 yards rushing) and LB George Cumby led defense; lost only to Texas 16–7 and beat undefeated Florida St. in Orange Bowl 24–7. 1980—9–2–0. Scored 378 behind OL Louis Oubre and QB J. C. Watts (1,568 yards and 18 TDs in total offense); won last 7 to take 8th straight Big 8 title, then beat Florida St. in Orange Bowl 18–17. 1982—8–3–0. Freshman Marcus Dupree ran for 905 yards and 12 TDs and DL Rick Bryan led defense as Sooners lost only to Nebraska 28–24 in last 8; lost to Arizona St. in Fiesta Bowl 32–21.

BOWL RECORD

Bluebonnet 0–1–1; Fiesta 1–1–0; Gator 1–1–0; Orange 9–3–0; Sugar 4–1–0; Sun 1–0–0.

CONFERENCE TITLES

Southwest 1915*, 1918*. Missouri Valley 1920. Big 6 1938, 1943, 1944, 1946*, 1947*. Big 7 1948, 1949, 1950, 1951, 1952, 1953, 1954, 1955, 1956, 1957. Big 8 1958, 1959, 1962, 1967, 1968*, 1973, 1974, 1975*, 1976*, 1977, 1978*, 1979, 1980.

TOP 10 AP & UPI RANKING

1938	4	1954	3–3	1967	3–3	1976	5–6
1948	5	1955	1–1	1968	U–10	1977	7–6
1949	2	1956	1–1	1971	2–3	1978	3–3
1950	1–1	1957	4–4	1972	2–2	1979	3–3
1951	10–U	1958	5–5	1973	3–2	1980	3–3
1952	4–4	1962	8–7	1974	1–U		
1953	4–5	1963	10–8	1975	1–1		

MAJOR RIVALS

Oklahoma has played at least 15 games with Colorado (29–8–1), Iowa St. (50–4–2), Kansas (53–22–6), Kansas St. (54–11–4), Missouri (46–23–5), Nebraska (34–27–3), Oklahoma St. (60–12–6), Texas (28–47–3), and Tulsa (8–6–1).

COACHES

Dean of Oklahoma coaches was Bud Wilkinson with record of 145–29–4 for 1947–63, including 14 conference titles, 8 bowl teams (6 winners), 5 teams unbeaten in regular season and 3 national champions. He took national coach of the year award in 1949. Bennie Owen was 122–54–16 for 1905–26 with 3 conference titles and 4 unbeaten teams. Barry Switzer was 106–21–3 for 1973–83 with 8 conference titles, 8 bowl teams (6 winners), 2 unbeaten teams and 2 national champions. Switzer ranks in top 5 and Wilkinson in top 10 in all-time winning percentage. Others with outstanding records include Tom Stidham, 27–8–3 for 1937–40 with 1 conference title and 1 Orange Bowl team unbeaten in regular season; Dewey Luster, 27–18–3 for 1941–45 with 2 conference titles; and Chuck Fairbanks, 52–15–1 for 1967–72 with 2 conference titles and 5 bowl teams.

MISCELLANEA

First game was 34–0 loss to Oklahoma City in 1895 . . . 1st win was 12–0 over Norman H.S. in 1896 . . . 1st win over college foe was 16–0 over Oklahoma City in 1897 . . . highest score was 179–0 over Kingfisher College in 1917 . . . highest since W.W. II was 82–42 over Colorado in 1980 . . . biggest margin of victory since W.W. II was 72–3 over Utah St. in 1974 . . . worst defeat was 47–0 by Oklahoma St. in 1945 . . . worst since W.W. II was 38–0 by Notre Dame in 1966 . . . highest score against Sooners ever was 59–21 by Kansas St. in 1969 . . . longest winning streak of 47 (NCAA record) in 1953–57 ended by Notre Dame 7–0 . . . longest unbeaten string of 48 ended in same game . . . unbeaten string of 37 in 1972–75 ended by Kansas 23–3 . . . winning streak of 31 in 1948–50 ended by Kentucky 13–7 in Sugar Bowl . . . longest losing string of 5 in 1961 broken with 17–6 win over Kansas St. . . . Oklahoma has had 36 consensus All America players since 1938 . . . multi-year choices were Jim Weatherall, T, 1950–51; Greg Pruitt, B, 1971–72; Tom Brahaney, C, 1971–72; Rod Shoate, LB, 1973–74; Billy Sims, RB, 1978–79; and Rick Bryan, DL, 1982–83 . . . single-year unanimous choices were Jerry Tubbs, C, 1956; Granville Liggins, MG, 1967; Steve Owens, B, 1969; Lucious Selmon, DL, 1973; Joe Washington, RB, 1974; Leroy Selmon, DT, 1975; Mike Vaughan, OT, 1976; Zac Henderson, DB, 1977; Greg Roberts, G, 1978; and George Cumby, LB, 1979 . . . other selections since 1970 were John Roush, G, 1974; Dewey Selmon, MG, and Jimbo Elrod, DE, 1975; Louis Oubre, OL, 1980; and Terry Crouch, OL, 1981 . . . Academic All America choices were Tom Catlin, C, and Carl Allison, E, 1952; Jerry Tubbs, C, 1956; Doyle Jennings, T, 1957; Ross Coyle, E, 1958; Wayne Lee, C, 1962; Newt Burton, G, 1963–64; Ron Shotts, HB, 1966–67; Eddie Hinton, DB, 1968; Joe Wylie, RB, 1970, 1972; Jack Mildren, QB, 1971; Randy Hughes, S, 1974; Leroy Selmon, DT, and Dewey Selmon, LB, 1975; and Jay Jimerson, DB, 1980 . . . Heisman Trophy winners were Billy Vessels, HB, 1952; Steve Owens, HB, 1969; and Billy Sims, HB, 1978 . . . Outland Trophy winners were Jim Weatherall, T, 1951; J.D. Roberts, G, 1953; Leroy Selmon, DT, 1975; and Greg Roberts, G, 1978 . . . Leroy Selmon won Lombardi Award in 1975 . . . Oklahoma ranks in top 10 in all-time winning percentage and in top 15 in total victories.

Oklahoma State (Cowboys; Orange & Black) (Big 8)

NOTABLE TEAMS

1911—5–2–0. Scored 256, losing only to Kansas St. and unbeaten Oklahoma. 1912—6–2–0. Scored 272 and won first 5 before losing to Oklahoma. 1914—6–2–1. Paul Davis' last team scored 327 and shut out 5. 1924— 6–1–2. Shut out 6, losing only to TCU 17–10. 1930—7–2–1. Pappy Waldorf's 2nd team shut out 5 and won 1st Missouri Valley Conference title; lost only to Oklahoma City 6–0 and Haskell 13–12. 1931—8–2–1. Shut out 5 and got share of conference title again. 1932—9–1–2. Shut out 5 and lost only to Jefferson 12–6 while taking 3rd straight MVC title. 1933—6–2–1. Waldorf's last team was unbeaten in last 6 after losses to Colorado 6–0 and Oklahoma City 19–13; won 4th straight MVC title. 1944—7–1–0. HB Bob Fenimore led nation in total offense (1,758 yards) as Cowboys lost only to Navy Zoomers 15–0; beat TCU in Cotton Bowl 34–0. 1945—8–0–0. Fenimore led nation in total offense (1,641 yards), rushing (1,048 yards) and all-purpose running (1,577 yards) to become first OSU consensus All America as team scored 252 points; beat St. Mary's in Sugar Bowl 33–13. 1953 —7–3–0. Won 4 by TD or less to take 8th and last MVC title; Earl Lunsford ran for 748 yards. 1958—7–3–0. Lost no game by more than 8 points as Jim Wood starred at E; beat Florida St. in Bluegrass Bowl 15–6. 1976—8–3–0. Terry Miller ran for 1,714 yards and 23 TDs and Charlie Weatherbie had 1,197 yards of total offense behind C Derrel Gofourth as Cowboys got share of Big 8 title for first time; beat Brigham Young in Tangerine Bowl 49–21.

BOWL RECORD

Bluebonnet 1–0–0; Bluegrass 1–0–0; Cotton 1–0–0; Delta 0–1–0; Fiesta 1–0–0; Independence 0–1–0; Sugar 1–0–0; Tangerine 1–0–0.

CONFERENCE TITLES

Missouri Valley 1930*, 1931*, 1932, 1933, 1944, 1945, 1948, 1953*. Big 8 1976*.

TOP 10 AP & UPI RANKING

1945	5

MAJOR RIVALS

Cowboys have played at least 15 games with Arkansas (15–30–1), Central St. (Okla.) (14–5–2), Colorado (11–14–1), Creighton (10–7–1), Houston (7–7–1), Iowa St. (14–10–1), Kansas (17–22–3), Kansas St. (26–12–0), Missouri (10–20–0), Nebraska (2–21–1), Oklahoma (12–60–6), Oklahoma City (6–9–2), TCU (10–6–2), Texas Tech (7–11–3), Tulsa (26–22–5) and Wichita St. (20–5–1).

COACHES

Dean of Oklahoma St. coaches was Jim Lookabaugh with record of 58–41–6 for 1939–49, including 3 conference titles, 3 bowl teams and 1 unbeaten team. Lynn (Pappy) Waldorf was 34–10–7 for 1929–33 with 4 conference titles. Other top records were by Paul J. Davis, 29–16–1 for 1909–14; Jim Stanley, 35–31–2 for 1973–78 with 1 conference title and 2 bowl champions; and Jimmy Johnson, 29–25–3 for 1978–83 with 2 bowl teams.

MISCELLANEA

First game was 12–0 loss to Kingfisher in 1901 . . . 1st win was 17–0 over Northwestern (Okla.) same year . . . highest score was 134–0 over Phillips in 1914 . . . highest since W.W. II was 70–7 over Southern Illinois in 1973

. . . worst defeat was 75–0 by Oklahoma in 1904 . . . worst since W.W. II was 73–12 by Oklahoma in 1946 . . . longest unbeaten string of 14 in 1944–46 ended by Texas 54–6 . . . longest winless string of 11 in 1903–05 broken with 5–0 win over Central State and in 1919–20 broken with 53–0 win over Southwestern (Okla.) in 1921 . . . consensus All America players were Bob Fenimore, B, 1945; John Ward, T, 1969; Derrel Gofourth, C, 1976; and Terry Miller, RB, 1977 . . . Academic All America choices were Dale Meinert, G, 1954; Tom Wolfe, OT, 1972 and 1974; Doug Tarrant, LB, 1973; and Joe Avanzini, DE, 1977.

Oregon (Ducks; Lemon Yellow & Emerald Green) (Pacific-10)

NOTABLE TEAMS

1906—5–0–1. Yielded just 10 points; tie was with O.A.C. 0–0. 1907— 5–1–0. Lost opener to O.A.C. 4–0 but outscored others 100–10. 1908— 5–2–0. Lost successive games to Whitworth and Washington. 1910—4–1–0. Outscored first 4 foes 172–6 but lost finale to Multnomah A.C. 5–0. 1915 —7–2–0. Shut out 5 in a row in mid-season. 1916—6–0–1. Scored 230 behind QB Shy Huntington and shut out 5 to gain share of 1st Pacific Coast Conference title despite 0–0 tie with Washington; beat Pennsylvania in Rose Bowl 14–0. 1919—5–1–0. Beat all but Washington St. (7–0) behind QB Bill Steers and G Ken Bartlett; won share of PCC but lost to Harvard in Rose Bowl 7–6. 1921—5–1–3. Lost only to unbeaten California 39–0. 1922— 6–1–1. Shut out 5 behind linemen Carl Vonder Ahe and Tiny Shields; lost only to Multnomah A.C. 20–0 and tied Washington 3–3. 1928—9–2–0. Won last 5 behind HB John Kitzmiller. 1929—7–3–0. Lost only to Stanford in first 8. 1930—7–2–0. Won first 7 behind Kitzmiller before losing to Oregon St. and St. Mary's (7–6). 1931—6–2–2. Shut out 5 as George Christenson starred at T; lost only to national champion Southern California and St. Mary's. 1933—9–1–0. Won 4 by TD or less and shut out 5 behind HB Mike Mikulak; lost to USC 26–0 but gained share of PCC title. 1947— 7–3–0. Won last 6 behind QB Norm Van Brocklin, HB Jake Leicht and C Brad Ecklund. 1948—9–1–0. Won 4 by TD or less and lost only to unbeaten national champion Michigan 14–0 as Van Brocklin passed for 1,010 yards and Ecklund starred again; won share of PCC title but lost to SMU in Cotton Bowl 21–13. 1957—7–3–0. HB Jim Shanley and G Harry Mondale led team to share of PCC title; lost no game by more than 7, including 10–7 loss to unbeaten national champion Ohio St. in Rose Bowl. 1959—8–2–0. Lost only to Washington 13–12 and Oregon St. 15–7 as C Bob Peterson and HB Willie West starred. 1960—7–2–1. QB Dave Grosz led team to wins over all but Michigan and Washington (7–6); lost to Penn St. in Liberty Bowl 41–12. 1963—7–3–0. Scored 274 behind HB Mel Renfro and QB Bob Berry (1,675 yards passing); lost 2 by TD but beat SMU in Sun Bowl 21–14. 1964 —7–2–1. Berry passed for 1,478 yards behind C Dave Tobey and G Mark Richards as Ducks won 5 by 8 points or less; lost only to Stanford 10–8 and Oregon St. 7–6.

BOWL RECORD

Cotton 0–1–0; Liberty 0–1–0; Rose 1–2–0; Sun 1–0–0.

CONFERENCE TITLES

Pacific Coast 1916*, 1919*, 1933*, 1948*, 1957*.

TOP 10 AP & UPI RANKING

1948	9

MAJOR RIVALS

Oregon has played at least 15 games with California (18–30–2), Idaho (48–3–4), Multnomah A.C. (11–19–4), Oregon St. (40–37–10), Pacific (15–1–2), San Jose St. (9–6–0), Southern California (9–24–2), Stanford (16–33–1), UCLA (13–29–0), Utah (14–5–0), Washington (26–46–5), Washington St. (27–28–7) and Willamette (22–1–1).

COACHES

Dean of Oregon coaches was Len Casanova with record of 82–73–8 for 1951–66, including 1 conference title and 3 bowl teams. Hugo Bezdek was 30–10–4 for 1906 and 1913–17 with 1 conference title, 1 Rose Bowl champion and 2 unbeaten teams. Other top records were by Shy Huntington, 26–12–6 for 1918–23 with 1 conference title and 1 Rose Bowl team; and Prink Callison, 33–23–2 for 1932–37 with 1 conference title. Jim Aiken was 21–20–0 for 1947–50 with 1 conference title and 1 bowl team.

MISCELLANEA

First game was 44–2 win over Albany College in 1894 . . . highest score was

115–0 over Puget Sound in 1910 . . . highest since W.W. II was 58–14 over Idaho in 1969 and 58–0 over Washington in 1973 . . . worst defeat was 66–0 by Washington in 1974 . . . highest against Ducks was 71–7 by Texas in 1941 . . . highest against Oregon since W.W. II was 68–3 by Oklahoma in 1972 . . . longest unbeaten string of 16 in 1915–17 ended by Washington St. 26–3 . . . longest losing string of 14 in 1974–75 broken with 18–7 win over Utah . . . Oregon's only consensus All America player was Mel Renfro, HB, in 1962 . . . Academic All America selections were Steve Barnett, OT, 1962; and Tim Casey, LB, 1965.

Oregon State (Beavers; Orange & Black) (Pacific-10)

NOTABLE TEAMS

1893—4–1–0. First varsity team lost only to Portland U. 26–12. 1902—4–1–1. Lost to Washington 16–5 but shut out others, including 0–0 tie with Oregon. 1906—4–1–2. Lost to Willamette 4–0 but shut out others. 1907—6–0–0. Blanked opponents 137–0. 1911—5–2–0. Lost to Alumni 3–2 and unbeaten Washington 34–0. 1914—7–0–2. Shut out 6; tied Washington 0–0 and Oregon 3–3. 1925—7–2–0. Paul Schissler's 2nd team scored 268, losing only to Stanford and Southern California. 1926—7–1–0. Scored 221 and shut out 5 as Percy Locey starred at T; lost only to USC 17–7. 1930—7–3–0. Shut out 6; lost 2 by TD. 1933—6–2–2. Lon Stiner's 1st team shut out 6 as T Ade Schwammel and HB Red Franklin starred. 1939—9–1–1. Won 4 by TD or less behind G Prescott Hutchins and E Joe Wendlick; lost only to USC 19–7 and tied UCLA 13–13. 1941—7–2–0. Won last 5 after losses to USC 13–7 and Washington St. 7–0 as linemen Vic Sears and Leonard Younce and FB Jim Kisselburgh led Beavers to 1st Pacific Coast Conference title; beat Duke 20–16 in Rose Bowl transplanted to Durham, N.C., because of W.W. II. 1946—7–1–1. Lost opener to unbeaten UCLA 50–7 but C Bill Gray and HB Bob Stevens led team to wins over all others except Stanford (0–0). 1949—7–3–0. HB Ken Carpenter ran for 689 yards; lost only to Stanford in last 7. 1956—7–2–1. Tommy Prothro's 2nd team was unbeaten in last 7 and won PCC behind T John Witte, Beaver's 1st consensus All America; lost Rose Bowl 35–19 to Iowa team that beat OSU 14–13 in regular season. 1957—8–2–0. Got share of PCC title despite successive losses to UCLA and Washington as FB Nub Beamer ran for 760 yards. 1962—8–2–0. Heisman winner Terry Baker led nation in total offense (2,276 yards) and Vern Burke led nation's pass receivers (69 catches for 1,007 yards and 10 TDs); won last 6, then beat Villanova in Liberty Bowl 6–0. 1964—8–2–0. Prothro's last team won 5 by TD or less to earn share of Pacific 8 title as Jack O'Billovich starred at LB and Rich Koeper at T; lost to Michigan in Rose Bowl 34–7. 1966— 7–3–0. Dee Andros' 2nd team won last 6; FB Pete Pifer ran for 1,088 yards. 1967—7–2–1. Won 5 by 8 points or less behind linemen Jon Sandstrom and Jess Lewis as FB Bill Enyart ran for 851 yards. 1968—7–3–0. Scored 285 behind C John Didion as Enyart ran for 1,304 yards; lost no game by more than 4 points.

BOWL RECORD

Liberty 1–0–0; Rose 1–2–0.

CONFERENCE TITLES

Pacific Coast 1941, 1956, 1957*. Pacific 8 1964*.

TOP 10 AP & UPI RANKING

1956	10–U
1964	8–8
1967	7–8

MAJOR RIVALS

Beavers have played at least 15 games with California (15–25–0), Idaho (33–6–0), Montana (21–2–1), Multnomah A.C. (7–11–4), Oregon (37–40–10), Southern California (7–41–4), Stanford (15–34–2), UCLA (9–23–4), Washington (25–41–4), Washington St. (36–33–3) and Willamette (21–2–0).

COACHES

Dean of Oregon St. coaches was Lon Stiner with record of 74–49–17 for 1933–42 and 1945–48, including 1 conference title and 1 Rose Bowl champion. Tommy Prothro was 63–37–2 for 1955–64 with 3 conference titles and 3 bowl teams. Paul J. Schissler was 48–30–2 for 1924–32. Dee Andros was 2nd in tenure with record of 51–64–1 for 1965–75.

MISCELLANEA

First game was 62–0 win over Albany College in 1893 . . . highest score was 76–0 over Willamette in 1931 . . . highest since W.W. II was 66–18 over Idaho in 1959 . . . biggest margin since W.W. II was 59–0 over Hawaii in 1976 . . . worst defeat was 61–0 by UCLA in 1954 . . . highest against Beavers was 63–9 by Stanford in 1981 . . . longest unbeaten string of 15 in 1913–15 ended by Washington St. 29–0 . . . longest losing string of 14 in 1979–80 broken with 31–28 win over Fresno St. in 1981 . . . consensus All America players were John Witte, T, 1956; Ted Bates, T, 1958; Terry Baker, QB, 1962; Vern Burke, E, 1963; and John Didion, C, 1968 . . . Baker won Heisman Trophy in 1962 . . . Academic All America players were Baker, B, 1962; and Bill Enyart, FB, 1967–68.

Pacific (Tigers; Orange & Black) (PCAA)

NOTABLE TEAMS

1922—6–1–0. Shut out 5 but lost finale to Fresno St. 12–7. 1923—7–0–0. Outscored foes 171–12, shutting out 5. 1925—5–2–0. Won 4 by TD or less. 1928—5–2–0. Won first 5 behind G Al Keystone and HB Jim Countryman. 1938—7–3–0. Won last 6 and took Far Western Conference title as 9 players won all-conference spots. 1943—7–2–0. Won 3 by TD or less under fabled coach Amos Alonzo Stagg as RB John Podesto and T Art McCaffray starred; lost only to Southern California 6–0 and March Field 19–10. 1947—8–1–0. Larry Siemering's 1st team scored 312 as QB Eddie LeBaron passed for 1,073 yards and 16 TDs and Bruce Orvis ran for 976 yards; lost only to Santa Clara 21–20 and won 2 bowl games, beating Utah St. 35–21 in Grape Bowl and Wichita St. 26–14 in Raisin Bowl. 1948—7–1–1. Scored 321 behind LeBaron (1,006 yards passing) and HB Don Brown (12 TDs), losing only to San Jose St. 14–7; tied Hardin-Simmons in Raisin Bowl 35–35. 1949— 11–0–0. Outscored foes 575–66 as LeBaron passed for 1,282 yards and 12 TDs, John Rohde caught 25 passes for 483 yards and 7 TDs and Eddie Macon scored 10 TDs. 1969—7–3–0. Doug Scovil's last team scored in double figures in all as Mickey Ackley passed for 1,244 yards and Jack Morrison caught 31 for 506 yards. 1972—8–3–0. Mitchell True ran for 1,164 yards and 10 TDs; lost only to San Diego St. in last 9. 1973—7–2–1. Scored 279 behind G Willie Viney and RB Willard Harrell (1,319 yards and

14 TDs rushing and national all-purpose running leader with 1,777 yards; MG Larry Bailey led defense.

BOWL RECORD

Grape 1–0–1; Raisin 1–0–0; Sun 1–1–0.

CONFERENCE TITLES

Far Western 1936, 1938, 1940, 1941, 1942. California Collegiate 1947.

TOP 10 AP & UPI RANKING

1949	10

MAJOR RIVALS

Pacific has played at least 15 games with Chico St. (19–1–0), Fresno St. (24–33–2), Hawaii (15–7–0), Idaho (11–9–1), Long Beach St. (9–10–0), Nevada-Reno (9–10–1), San Diego St. (7–14–0), San Jose St. (21–31–4), UC Davis (17–6–2) and Utah St. (5–11–0).

COACHES

Dean of Pacific coaches was Amos Alonzo Stagg with record of 59–77–7 for 1933–46, including 5 conference titles. Stagg, who ranks 2nd in all-time coaching victories with 314, was national coach of the year in 1943. Larry Siemering was 35–5–3 for 1947–50 with 1 conference title, 2 bowl teams (1 played in 2 bowls) and 1 undefeated team. Other top records were by Erwin (Swede) Righter, 54–34–4 for 1921–32 with 1 unbeaten team; Jack (Moose) Myers, 39–33–5 for 1953–60; and Doug Scovil, 21–19–0 for 1966–69.

MISCELLANEA

First game was 79–0 defeat by California freshmen in 1919 . . . 1st win was 20–0 over Navy-Mare Island same year . . . 1st win over college foe was 35–0 over Fresno St. in 1921 . . . highest score was 88–0 over Cal Poly-SLO in 1949 . . . worst defeat was 132–0 by Nevada-Reno in 1919 . . . worst since W.W. II was 64–6 by Idaho in 1963 . . . highest against Tigers since W.W. II was 70–19 by New Mexico St. in 1961 . . . longest unbeaten string of 17 in 1948–50 ended by LSU 19–0 . . . longest losing string of 11 in 1964–65 broken with 21–0 win over Hawaii . . . Pacific has had no consensus All

America players . . . Bruce Filarsky was Academic All America as OG, 1978, and DL, 1979.

Pennsylvania (Quakers, Red and Blue; Red & Blue) (Ivy)

NOTABLE TEAMS

1883—6-2-1. Lost only to Harvard and Princeton. 1884—5-1-1. Lost only to Princeton 31-0. 1890—11-3-0. Lost to Princeton twice and to Yale. 1891—11-2-0. Lost only to Princeton and unbeaten national champion Yale as C John Adams became Penn's 1st All America. 1892—15-1-0. George Woodruff's 1st team shut out 11 and lost only to unbeaten national champion Yale (28-0) as B Harry Thayer starred. 1893—12-3-0. Scored 484 and shut out 9; 1 of losses was to unbeaten national champion Princeton. 1894— 12-0-0. Outscored foes 366-20, shutting out 9 as 4 players made All America. 1895—14-0-0. Outscored foes 478-24, shutting out 10, and won 1st national championship behind B George Brooke, E Charles Gelbert, C Alfred Bull and G Charles Wharton. 1896—14-1-0. Shut out 11 and lost only to Lafayette 6-4 as Gelbert and Wharton starred again. 1897—15-0-0. Outscored foes 443-20, shutting out 12, and won 2nd national title under Woodruff as B John Minds, G T. Truxtun Hare and T John Outland starred. 1898—12-1-0. Scored 416 and shut out first 9, losing only to unbeaten national champion Harvard 10-0 as Hare and Outland starred again. 1900 —12-1-0. Shut out 7 and lost only to Harvard 17-5 as Hare made All America for 4th time. 1903—9-3-0. Carl Williams' 2nd team shut out 8. 1904—12-0-0. Shut out all but Swarthmore (6-4 in 2nd game) and won national championship behind backs Andy Smith and Vincent Stevenson. 1905—12-0-1. Shut out 7 as T Otis Lamson and C Robert Torrey starred; tie was 6-6 with Lafayette. 1907—11-1-0. Williams' last team shut out 8 behind linemen August Ziegler and Dexter Draper; lost only to Carlisle Indians 26-6. 1908—11-0-1. Shut out 7 and won national title despite 6-6 tie with Carlisle in Sol Metzger's only year as coach; B William Hollenback and E Hunter Scarlett starred. 1909—7-1-2. Andy Smith's 1st team lost only to Michigan 12-6. 1910—9-1-1. Shut out 7 behind C Ernest Cozens and B LeRoy Mercer; lost only to Ursinus 8-5 in opener and tied Michigan 0-0. 1916—7-2-1. Unbeaten in last 5 after losses to Swarthmore 6-0 and unbeaten national champion Pittsburgh; lost to Oregon in Rose Bowl 14-0. 1917—9-2-0. Shut out 7, including last 6, while losing only to unbeaten teams (national champion Georgia Tech and Pitt). 1919—6–2–1. Shut out 5 as E Henry Miller starred. 1924—9–1–1. Louis Young's 2nd team shut out 7 and lost only to California 14–0 in finale behind T Edward McGinley. 1925 —7–2–0. Shut out 5 as George Thayer starred at E. 1926—7–1–1. Shut out 6, losing only to Illinois 3–0 and tying Cornell 10–10. 1928—8–1–0. Scored 269 behind B Paul Scull and shut out 6, losing only to Navy 6–0. 1929— 7–2–0. Young's last team won 4 by TD or less, losing only to California 12–7 and Penn St. 19–7. 1932—6–2–0. Lost successive games to Pitt and Ohio St. 1936—7–1–0. Lost only to Yale 7–0 in 2nd game. 1940—6–1–1. Red Munger's 3rd team scored 247 behind C Raymond Frick and B Francis X. Reagan, losing only to Michigan 14–0 and tying Harvard 10–10. 1941— 7–1–0. Lost only to Navy 13–6 and won informal Ivy title for 11th time. 1943—6–2–1. Scored 248 behind B Robert Odell but lost successive games to Navy and North Carolina (9–6). 1945—6–2–0. Scored 237 behind T George Savitsky, losing only to Navy 14–7 and unbeaten national champion Army. 1946—6–2–0. Scored 265 as Savitsky starred again; lost to Princeton 17–14 and unbeaten Army. 1947—7–0–1. Outscored foes 219–35 behind Savitsky, C Chuck Bednarik and B Anthony Minisi; tie was with Army 7–7. 1959—7–1–1. Steve Sebo's last team won formal Ivy title for 1st time, losing only to Harvard 12–0 and tying Navy 22–22; stars included E Barney Berlinger, G John Marchiano and B Fred Doelling. 1968—7–2–0. Won 5 by TD or less as Gerry Santini ran for 880 yards. 1974—6–2–1. Marty Vaughn passed for 1,503 yards and Bob Bucola caught 39 as Penn lost only to Harvard and Yale. 1982—7–3–0. Won 4 by 8 points or less and earned share of Ivy title.

BOWL RECORD

Rose 0–1–0.

CONFERENCE TITLES

Ivy (informal) 1904, 1905*, 1907, 1909, 1910, 1917, 1918, 1924, 1925*, 1940, 1941, 1946*, 1947, 1952. Ivy (formal) 1959, 1982*, 1983*.

TOP 10 AP & UPI RANKING

1936	10
1945	8
1947	7

MAJOR RIVALS

Penn has played at least 15 games with Army (4–11–2), Brown (38–12–2), Bucknell (16–2–0), Carlisle (13–6–2), Columbia (45–17–1), Cornell (50–35–5), Dartmouth (23–26–2), Franklin & Marshall (34–1–0), Gettysburg (18–0–1), Harvard (17–35–2), Lafayette (51–16–4), Lehigh (42–8–0), Michigan (8–11–2), Navy (21–20–4), Penn St. (25–18–4), Princeton (20–54–1), Rutgers (10–6–0), Swarthmore (30–4–1), Virginia (15–1–0) and Yale (14–36–1).

COACHES

Dean of Penn coaches was George Woodruff with record of 124–15–2 for 1892–1901, including 3 perfect records and 2 national championships. He ranks 3rd in all-time winning percentage. George A. Munger was 82–42–10 for 1938–53 with 5 informal Ivy titles and 1 unbeaten team. Carl S. Williams was 60–10–4 for 1902–07 with 3 informal Ivy titles and 2 unbeaten teams. Other top records included E.O. Wagenhurst, 38–18–0 for 1888–91; Andrew Smith, 30–10–3 for 1909–12 with 2 informal Ivy titles; Robert F. Folwell, 27–10–2 for 1916–19 with 2 informal Ivy titles; and Louis A. Young, 49–15–2 for 1923–29 with 2 informal Ivy titles.

MISCELLANEA

First game was 6 goals to 0 loss to Princeton in 1876 . . . 1st win was 4 goals to 0 over All Philadelphia same year . . . 1st win over college foe was shutout of Swarthmore in 1878 . . . highest score was 96–6 over Vineland College in 1886 . . . highest since 1900 was 89–0 over Delaware in 1919 and again in 1921 . . . highest since W.W. II was 66–0 over Lafayette in 1946 . . . worst defeat was 96–0 by Princeton in 1887 . . . worst since 1900 was 61–0 by Army in 1945 . . . worst since W.W. II was 58–0 by Lehigh in 1981 . . . highest against Red and Blue since 1900 was 62–7 by Army in 1944 . . . longest winning streak of 34 in 1894–96 ended by Lafayette 6–4 . . . winning streak of 31 in 1896–98 ended by Harvard 10–0 . . . unbeaten string of 30 in 1903–06 ended by Swarthmore 4–0 . . . unbeaten string of 24 in 1907–09 ended by Michigan 12–6 . . . longest winless string of 23 in 1953–56 broken with 14–7 win over Dartmouth . . . winless string of 17 in 1978–80 broken with 24–13 win over Columbia . . . Penn has had 32 consensus All America players since 1891 . . . multi-year choices were Charles Gelbert, E, 1894–96; George Brooke, B, 1894–95; Charles Wharton, G, 1895–96; John Outland,

T, 1897, and B, 1898; T. Truxtun Hare, G, 1897–1900; Pete Overfield, C, 1898–99; August Ziegler, G, 1906–07; William Hollenback, B, 1906, 1908; E. Leroy Mercer, B, 1910, 1912; Henry Miller, E, 1917, 1919; and Chuck Bednarik, C, 1947–48 . . . Penn has had no Academic All America choices . . . Penn ranks in top 10 in all-time total victories.

Penn State (Nittany Lions; Blue & White) (Independent)

NOTABLE TEAMS

1891—6–2–0. Lost only to Lehigh and Bucknell. 1892—5–1–0. Lost opener to Penn 20–0, but shut out others. 1893—4–1–0. Lost to Penn 18–6. 1894 —6–0–1. Outscored foes 179–18; tie was with Navy 6–6. 1902—7–3–0. Shut out 7. 1905—8–3–0. Shut out 8 in 2nd year under Tom Fennell. 1906 —8–1–1. Lost to Yale 10–0 but shut out others, including 0–0 tie with Gettysburg, as C W.T. Dunn became Nittany Lions' 1st consensus All America. 1909—5–0–2. Bill Hollenback's 1st team shut out 5 but tied Carlisle Indians 8–8 and Penn 3–3. 1911—8–0–1. Shut out 7, including 0–0 tie with Navy; beat Penn for 1st time, 22–6. 1912—8–0–0. Outscored foes 285–6 (Cornell scored in 29–6 game). 1915—7–2–0. Lost to Harvard and unbeaten Pittsburgh. 1916—8–2–0. Scored 348 but lost to Penn and unbeaten national champion Pitt. 1919—7–1–0. Hugo Bezdek's 2nd team shut out 5 as Bob Higgins starred at E; lost only to Dartmouth 19–13. 1920—7–0–2. Won first 7 before ties with Lehigh 7–7 and Pitt 0–0 behind HB Charley Way. 1921—8–0–2. HB Glenn Killinger led Lions to wins over all but Harvard (21–21) and Pitt (0–0). 1922—6–3–1. Shut out 5 but lost 2 of last 3, then lost to Southern California in Rose Bowl 14–3. 1923—6–2–1. Shut out 5 as G Joe Bedenk and HB Harry Wilson starred. 1927—6–2–1. Lost only to Bucknell and Pitt. 1939—5–1–2. Lost only to unbeaten Cornell (47–0). 1940—6–1–1. Shut out 5 behind C Leon Gajecki; lost only to Pitt 20–7 in finale and tied Syracuse 13–13. 1941—7–2–0. Won last 6. 1942—6–1–1. Won 4 by TD or less and lost only to West Virginia 24–0. 1946—6–2–0. Lost close ones to Michigan St. 19–16 and Pitt 14–7. 1947—9–0–0. Outscored foes 319–27, shutting out 6 and leading nation in total defense, rushing defense (yielding only an NCAA record 17 yards a game) and scoring defense behind T Negley Norton and G Steve Suhey; won 1st Lambert Trophy and tied unbeaten SMU in Cotton Bowl 13–13. 1948— 7–1–1. Bob Higgins' last team lost only to Pitt 7–0 and tied Michigan St.

14–14 as Sam Tamburo starred at E. 1952—7–2–1. Rip Engle's 3rd team lost only to unbeaten national champion Michigan St. and Syracuse. 1954—7–2–0. Lenny Moore ran for 1,082 yards and 12 TDs as Lions lost only to West Virginia 19–14 and TCU 20–7 in successive games. 1956—6–2–1. Lost close ones to Army 14–7 and Syracuse 13–9 as Sam Valentine starred at G. 1959—8–2–0. QB Rich Lucas ran and passed for 1,238 yards and intercepted 5 passes to lead team to wins over all but undefeated national champion Syracuse 20–18 and Pitt 22–7; beat Alabama in inaugural Liberty Bowl 7–0. 1961—7–3–0. Galen Hall ran and passed for 1,013 yards and Bob Mitinger starred at E as Lions lost only to Maryland 21–17 in last 6 and won Lambert; beat Georgia Tech in Gator Bowl 30–15. 1962—9–1–0. HB Roger Kochman had 1,056 yards in all-purpose running and Dave Robinson starred on defense at E as Lions lost only to Army 9–6; lost to Florida in Gator Bowl 17–7. 1963—7–3–0. Lost no game by more than 9 points as Pete Liske passed for 1,117 yards. 1967—8–2–0. Joe Paterno's 2nd team scored 282 and won last 7 after losses to Navy 23–22 and UCLA 17–15 as Tom Sherman passed for 1,616 yards and 13 TDs and Jack Curry caught 41 for 681 yards; won 5th Lambert and tied Florida St. 17–17 in Gator Bowl. 1968—10–0–0. Scored 339 as Charlie Pittman ran for 950 yards and 14 TDs, Ted Kwalick caught 31 passes and Dennis Onkotz starred as LB and punt returner; beat Kansas in Orange Bowl 15–14. 1969—10–0–0. Scored 312 behind Pittman while Onkotz, DT Mike Reid and S Neal Smith (10 interceptions) sparked defense; beat Missouri in Orange Bowl 10–3. 1970—7–3–0. Scored 300 and won last 5 as Jack Ham starred on defense. 1971—10–1–0. Scored 454 behind T Dave Joyner and HB Lydell Mitchell (1,754 yards and 29 TDs in all-purpose running); lost to Tennessee 31–11 in finale but beat Texas in Cotton Bowl 30–6. 1972—10–1–0. Scored 358 behind HB John Cappelletti (1,117 yards and 12 TDs rushing) and QB John Hufnagel (2,039 yards and 15 TDs passing) while DE Bruce Bannon and LB John Skorupan led defense; lost opener to Tennessee 28–21 and lost to Oklahoma in Sugar Bowl 14–0. 1973—11–0–0. Paterno's 3rd unbeaten team scored 436 behind Heisman winner Cappelletti (1,522 yards rushing and 17 TDs) and Tom Shuman (1,375 yards passing and 13 TDs) while DT Randy Crowder and LB Ed O'Neil led defense; beat LSU in Orange Bowl 16–9. 1974—9–2–0. Lost close ones to Navy 7–6 and North Carolina St. 12–7 as DT Mike Hartenstine starred; beat Baylor in Cotton Bowl 41–20. 1975—9–2–0. Chris Bahr kicked 18 FGs and Greg Buttle starred at LB and Tom Rafferty at OG as Lions won 4 by TD or less and won 5th straight Lambert; lost to Alabama in Sugar Bowl 13–6. 1977—10–1–0. Scored 348 behind T Keith Dorney and QB Chuck Fusina (2,221 yards and 15 TDs passing) as Randy Sidler starred at MG; lost to Kentucky 24–20 but beat Arizona St. in Fiesta Bowl 42–30. **1978—** 11–0–0. Scored 326 and led nation in total defense and rushing defense as Matt Bahr led nation in FGs with 22 and Pete Harris led in interceptions with 10; Dorney, Fusina, DT Bruce Clark and DT Matt Millen also starred, but Lions lost to national champion Alabama in Sugar Bowl 14–7. **1980—9–2–0.** Curt Warner ran for 922 yards behind offensive linemen Bill Dugan and Sean Farrell as Lions lost only to Nebraska 21–7 and Pitt 14–9; beat Ohio St. in Fiesta Bowl 31–7. **1981—9–2–0.** Scored 345 as Warner ran for 1,044 yards and Todd Blackledge passed for 1,557 and 12 TDs; beat Southern California in Fiesta Bowl 26–10. **1982—10–1–0.** Scored 368 behind Blackledge (2,218 yards and 22 TDs passing) and Warner (1,041 yards rushing) but lost mid-season game to Alabama 42–21; beat undefeated Georgia in Sugar Bowl 27–23 to earn national championship.

BOWL RECORD

Aloha 1–0–0; Cotton 2–0–1; Fiesta 3–0–0; Gator 1–2–1; Liberty 3–0–0; Orange 3–0–0; Rose 0–1–0; Sugar 1–3–0.

CONFERENCE TITLES

None. Won Lambert Trophy in 1947, 1961, 1962, 1964, 1967, 1968, 1969, 1971, 1972, 1973, 1974, 1975, 1977, 1978, 1981, 1982.

TOP 10 AP & UPI RANKING

1947	4	1968	2–3	1973	5–5	1978	4–4
1959	U–10	1969	2–2	1974	7–7	1980	8–8
1962	9–9	1971	5–U	1975	10–10	1981	3–3
1967	10–U	1972	10–8	1977	5–4	1982	1–1

MAJOR RIVALS

Penn St. has played at least 15 games with Army (13–10–2), Bucknell (28–10–0), Dickinson (11–5–1), Gettysburg (27–0–1), Lafayette (10–5–1), Lebanon Valley (20–0–0), Lehigh (16–6–1), Maryland (26–1–0), Navy (18–17–2), Pennsylvania (18–25–4), Pittsburgh (41–38–4), Syracuse (35–21–5), Temple (18–3–1) and West Virginia (41–7–2).

COACHES

Joe Paterno has been Penn St.'s most successful coach with record of 171–38–2 for 1966–83, including 12 Lambert Trophy winners, 16 bowl teams

(11 winners), 4 teams unbeaten in regular season and 1 national champion. He ranks in top 10 in all-time winning percentage, and was national coach of the year in 1968, 1978 and 1982. Charles A. (Rip) Engle was 104–48–4 for 1950–65 with 3 Lambert Trophy winners and 4 bowl teams (3 winners). Bob Higgins, dean of Penn St. coaches, was 91–57–10 for 1930–48 with 1 unbeaten Cotton Bowl team. Other top records were by Tom Fennell, 33–17–1 for 1904–08; Bill Hollenback, 28–9–4 for 1909 and 1911–14 with 3 unbeaten teams; and Hugo Bezdek, 65–30–11 for 1918–29 with 1 Rose Bowl team and 2 unbeaten teams.

MISCELLANEA

First game was 54–0 win over Bucknell in 1887 . . . highest score was 109–7 over Lebanon Valley in 1921 . . . highest since W.W. II was 75–0 over Fordham in 1947 . . . worst defeat was 106–0 by Lehigh in 1889 . . . worst since 1900 was 47–0 by Cornell in 1939 . . . worst since W.W. II was 49–11 by UCLA in 1966 and 44–6 by Nebraska in 1983 . . . highest against Nittany Lions since 1900 was 55–14 by Navy in 1944 . . . longest unbeaten string of 31 in 1967–70 ended by Colorado 41–13 . . . unbeaten string of 30 in 1919–22 ended by Navy 14–0 . . . unbeaten strings of 19 in 1911–13 ended by Washington & Jefferson 17–0 and in 1977–78 ended by Alabama 14–7 in Sugar Bowl . . . longest losing string of 7 in 1931 broken with 31–0 win over Lehigh . . . Penn St. has had 21 consensus All America players since 1906 . . . multi-year choices were Dennis Onkotz, LB, 1968–69; and Bruce Clark, DL, 1978–79 . . . unanimous single-year choices were Ted Kwalick, E, 1968; Mike Reid, DT, 1969; John Cappelletti, B, 1973; Keith Dorney, OT, and Chuck Fusina, QB, 1978; and Sean Farrell, OL, 1981 . . . others since 1970 were Jack Ham, LB, 1970; Dave Joyner, T, 1971; Bruce Bannon, DE, and John Skorupan, LB, 1972; Mike Hartenstine, DL, 1974; and Greg Buttle, LB, 1975 . . . Academic All America choices were Joe Bellas, T, 1965; John Runnells, LB, 1965–66; Rich Buzin, OT, 1967; Charlie Pittman, HB, and Dennis Onkotz, LB, 1969; Dave Joyner, OT, 1971; Bruce Bannon, DE, 1972; Mark Markovich, OG, 1973; Chuck Benjamin, DT, 1976; Keith Dorney, OT, 1978; Todd Blackledge, QB, Scott Radecic, LB, 1982; and Harry Hamilton, DB, 1982, and LB, 1983 . . . John Cappelletti, HB, won Heisman Trophy in 1973 . . . Mike Reid, DT, won Outland Trophy in 1969 . . . Bruce Clark, DT, won Lombardi Trophy in 1978 . . . Penn St. ranks in top 15 in all-time winning percentage and in top 10 in total victories.

Pittsburgh (Panthers; Blue & Gold) (Independent)

NOTABLE TEAMS

1901—7–2–1. Lost opener to Penn St. and finale to Allegheny. 1904—10–0–0. Scored 406 and blanked all but Penn St. (22–5). 1905—10–2–0. Scored 405 and shut out 10 but lost to Cornell and Penn St. 1907—9–1–0. Shut out 8, losing only to Cornell 18–5. 1908—8–3–0. Joseph Thompson's 1st team shut out 7. 1909—6–2–1. Shut out 5 but lost close ones to Notre Dame 6–0 and Penn St. 5–0. 1910—9–0–0. Blanked foes 282–0, scoring in double figures in all. 1913—6–2–1. Lost to Bucknell and Washington & Jefferson. 1914—8–1–0. Won 3 by TD or less but lost to Washington & Jefferson 13–10. 1915—8–0–0. Pop Warner's 1st Panther team scored 247 and shut out 6 behind C Robert Peck (Pitt's 1st consensus All America). 1916—8–0–0. Outscored foes 255–25 and won 1st national championship behind Peck and E James Herron. 1917—9–0–0. Scored 230 and shut out 6 behind guards Jock Sutherland and Dale Seis and FB George McLaren. 1918—4–0–0. Outscored foes 131–6 in schedule curtailed by W.W. I and won national title behind McLaren, HB Tom Davies and T Leonard Hilty. 1919—6–2–1. Lost to Syracuse and Penn St. for Warner's 1st defeats at Pitt. 1920—6–0–2. Won 3 by TD or less behind C Herb Stein and Davies; ties were with Syracuse 7–7 and Penn 0–0. 1922—8–2–0. Shut out 5 but lost successive close games to Lafayette 7–0 and West Virginia 9–6. 1925—8–1–0. Jock Sutherland's 2nd team shut out 6 and lost only to Lafayette 20–9 in 2nd game. 1927—8–0–1. Outscored foes 283–20, shutting out 7, behind T Bill Kern and B Gibby Welch; lost to Stanford in Rose Bowl 7–6. 1928—6–2–1. Shut out 7 behind T Mike Getto but lost close ones to West Virginia 9–6 and Carnegie Tech 6–0. 1929—9–0–0. Outscored foes 277–43 behind G Ray Montgomery and E Joe Donchess as HB Toby Uansa ran for 964 yards; lost to Southern California in Rose Bowl 47–14. 1930—6–2–1. Shut out 5, losing only to unbeaten national champion Notre Dame and Ohio St. 1931—8–1–0. Outscored foes 280–37 behind T Jess Quatse; lost only to Notre Dame 25–12. 1932—9–0–1. Sutherland's 3rd unbeaten team shut out 8 and won 4 by TD or less behind E Joe Skladany and HB Warren Heller; tied Ohio St. 0–0 in mid-season and lost to unbeaten Southern California in Rose Bowl 35–0. 1933—8–1–0. Shut out 7 as Skladany starred again; lost only to Minnesota 7–3. 1934—8–1–0. Lost only to unbeaten national champion Minnesota 13–7 as Chuck Hartwig starred at G. 1935—7–1–2. Shut out 6 and lost only to Notre Dame 9–6. 1936—7–1–1. Scored 224 as Marshall

Goldberg ran for 886 yards while losing only to Duquesne 7–0 and tying Fordham 0–0; beat Washington in Rose Bowl 21–0. 1937—9–0–1. Shut out 6, including 0–0 tie with Fordham, and won national championship behind Goldberg and T Tony Matisi. 1938—8–2–0. Sutherland's last team lost only to Carnegie Tech 20–10 and unbeaten, unscored-on Duke 7–0 as Goldberg starred again. 1955—7–3–0. John Michelosen's 1st team won 5 of last 6 to win Lambert Trophy and get to Sugar Bowl, but lost to Georgia Tech 7–0 there. 1956—7–2–1. Won 4 by TD or less as E Joe Walton starred; lost to Georgia Tech in Gator Bowl 21–14. 1963—9–1–0. HB Paul Martha led team to wins over all but Navy (24–12). 1976—11–0–0. John Majors' last team scored 354 as Heisman winner Tony Dorsett led nation in rushing (1,948 yards) and scoring (134 points) and MG Al Romano led defense; beat Georgia in Sugar Bowl 27–3 to wrap up national championship. 1977— 8–2–1. Jackie Sherrill's 1st team scored 394 as Elliott Walker ran for 1,025 yards and Matt Cavanaugh passed for 1,844; lost opener to Notre Dame's national champions and finale to Penn St. 15–13, but beat Clemson in Gator Bowl 34–3. 1978—8–3–0. No loss by more than 10 as Hugh Green led defense; lost to North Carolina St. in Tangerine Bowl 30–17. 1979—10– 1–0. Won 3 by TD or less and lost only to North Carolina 17–7 in 2nd game behind QB Dan Marino and DE Green; beat Arizona in Fiesta Bowl 16–10. 1980—10–1–0. Led nation in total defense and rushing defense behind Green and LB Sal Sunseri as T Mark May and Marino led offense; lost only to Florida St. 36–22, but beat South Carolina in Gator Bowl 37–9. 1981— 10–1–0. Sherrill's last team scored 361 behind Marino (2,615 yards and 34 TDs passing) and again led nation in total defense and rushing defense behind Sunseri; lost finale to Penn St. 48–14, but beat Georgia in Sugar Bowl 24–20. 1982—9–2–0. Marino passed for 2,251 yards and Bryan Thomas caught 49 as T Jimbo Covert also starred on offense; lost to unbeaten SMU in Cotton Bowl 7–3. 1983—8–2–1. Lost successive early-season games to Maryland 13–7 and West Virginia 24–21 but won 4 by TD or less behind OT Bill Fralic; lost to Ohio St. in Fiesta Bowl 28–23.

BOWL RECORD

Cotton 0–1–0; Fiesta 1–2–0; Gator 2–1–0; Rose 1–3–0; Sugar 2–1–0; Sun 1–0–0; Tangerine 0–1–0.

CONFERENCE TITLES

None. Won Lambert Trophy in 1955, 1976, 1979, 1980.

TOP 10 AP & UPI RANKING

1936	3	1976	1–1	1981	4–2
1937	1	1977	8–7	1982	10–9
1938	8	1979	7–6		
1963	4–3	1980	2–2		

MAJOR RIVALS

Pitt has played at least 15 games with Army (19–6–2), Carnegie Tech (24–5–1), Duke (9–8–0), Geneva (16–6–0), Miami (Fla.) (8–7–1), Navy (16–11–2), Nebraska (15–4–3), Notre Dame (14–32–1), Ohio St. (4–13–1), Penn St. (38–41–4), Syracuse (24–13–2), Washington & Jefferson (18–13–2), Westminster (15–0–2) and West Virginia (52–23–1).

COACHES

Dean of Pitt coaches was Dr. John B. (Jock) Sutherland with record of 111–20–12 for 1924–38, including 4 Rose Bowl teams, 4 teams unbeaten in regular season and 1 national champion. He ranks in top 10 in all-time winning percentage. Glenn S. (Pop) Warner was 59–11–4 for 1915–23 with 4 unbeaten teams and 2 national champions. He ranks 3rd in all-time coaching victories. Jackie Sherrill was 50–9–1 for 1977–81 with 2 Lambert Trophy winners and 5 bowl teams (4 winners). Other top records were by Joseph H. Thompson, 30–14–2 for 1908–12 with 1 perfect record; John P. Michelosen, 56–49–7 for 1955–65 with 1 Lambert Trophy and 2 bowl teams; John Majors, who was national coach of the year in 1973 and 1976, 33–13–1 for 1973–76 with 1 Lambert Trophy, 3 bowl teams (2 winners) and an unbeaten national champion; and Foge Fazio, 17–6–1 for 1982–83 with 2 bowl teams.

MISCELLANEA

First game was 38–0 loss to Allegheny A.A. in 1890 . . . 1st win was 10–4 over Geneva same year . . . highest score was 96–0 over Dickinson in 1914 . . . highest since W. W. II was 76–0 over Temple in 1977 . . . worst defeat was 69–0 by Michigan in 1947 . . . high score was matched by Army 69–7 in 1944 and by Notre Dame 69–13 in 1965 . . . longest winning streak of 33 in 1914–19 ended by Syracuse 24–3 . . . unbeaten string of 22 in 1936–38 ended by Carnegie Tech 20–10 . . . winning streak of 17 in 1980–81 ended by Penn St. 48–14 . . . longest losing string of 10 in 1950–51 broken with 32–12 win over West Virginia and in 1971–72 broken with 35–20 win over

Boston College . . . Pitt has had 34 consensus All America players since 1915
. . . multi-year choices were Robert Peck, C, 1915–16; Herb Stein, C,
1920–21; Joe Skladany, E, 1932–33; Marshall Goldberg, B, 1937–38; and
Hugh Green, DL, 1978–80 . . . unanimous single-year selections were Gibby
Welch, B, 1927; Joe Donchess, E, 1929; Warren Heller, B, 1932; Joe
Walton, E, 1956; Mike Ditka, E, 1960; Tony Dorsett, B, 1976; Mark May,
OL, 1980; and Bill Fralic, OT, 1983 . . . other choices since 1960 were Paul
Martha, B, 1963; Al Romano, MG, 1976; Tom Brzoza, C, Randy Holloway,
DL, and Bob Jury, DB, 1977; Sal Sunseri, LB, 1981; and Jimbo Covert, OT,
1982 . . . Academic All America choices were Dick Deitrick, T, 1952; Lou
Palatella, T, 1954; Joe Walton, E, 1956; John Guzik, G, 1958; Jeff Delaney,
LB, 1976; Greg Meisner, LB, 1980; Rob Fada, OG, 1981–82; and J.C.
Pelusi, DL, 1982 . . . Tony Dorsett, HB, won Heisman Trophy in 1976
. . . Mark May, OT, won Outland Trophy in 1980 . . . Hugh Green, DE,
won Lombardi Award in 1980 . . . Pitt ranks in top 20 in total victories and
in top 25 in all-time winning percentage.

Princeton (Tigers; Orange & Black) (Ivy)

NOTABLE TEAMS

1878—6–0–0. Shut out 5. 1879—4–0–1. Tie was 0–0 with Yale in finale.
1880—4–0–1. Again tied Yale 0–0 in finale. 1881—7–0–2. Won first 7
before 0–0 ties with Harvard and Yale. 1882—7–2–0. Lost to Harvard and
unbeaten Yale. 1883—7–1–0. Lost only to unbeaten Yale 6–0 in finale. 1884
—9–0–1. Outscored foes 404–13; tie was 0–0 with Yale in finale. 1885—
9–0–0. Outscored foes 539–25. 1886—7–0–1. Outscored foes 320–27 but
tied Yale 0–0 in finale. 1887—7–2–0. Won 7 straight before losing to
Harvard and unbeaten Yale. 1888—11–1–0. Outscored foes 609–16 but lost
finale to unbeaten Yale 10–0. 1889—10–0–0. Won 1st national championship, outscoring foes 484–29 as backs Edgar Allan Poe, Roscoe Channing
and Knowlton Ames made 1st All America team along with linemen Hector
Cowan and William George. 1890—11–1–1. Scored 478 and shut out 9
behind B Sheppard Homans but lost finale to Yale 32–0. 1891—12–1–0.
Shut out 12 as Homans starred again, but lost finale to unbeaten national
champion Yale 19–0. 1892—12–2–0. Outscored foes 433–18 but lost to
Penn 6–4 and unbeaten national champion Yale 12–0. 1893—11–0–0. Shut
out 8 and won national title behind backs Philip King and Franklin Morse
and linemen Langdon Lea, Arthur Wheeler and Thomas Trenchard. 1894—

8–2–0. Lea and Wheeler starred again as Tigers lost only to unbeaten teams Penn and national champion Yale. 1895—10–1–1. Shut out 9 behind Lea and G Dudley Riggs, losing only to Yale 20–10 in finale. 1896—10–0–1. Won national title despite 0–0 tie with Lafayette in 2nd game; outscored foes 299–12 behind backs Addision Kelly and John Baird. 1897—10–1–0. Blanked first 10 foes 339–0 as Kelly starred again, but lost finale to Yale 6–0. 1898—11–0–1. Shut out 11 behind T Arthur Hillebrand; tie was 5–5 with Army. 1899—12–1–0. Shut out 10 behind Hillebrand and E Arthur Poe, losing only to Cornell 5–0. 1900—8–3–0. Won first 8, shutting out 6. 1901 —9–1–1. Won first 9, shutting out 8, before tying Army 6–6 and losing to Yale 12–0. 1902—8–1–0. Shut out 7 but again lost finale to Yale 12–5. 1903 —11–0–0. Scored 259 and shut out all but Yale (11–6) and won national championship behind B Dana Kafer and linemen John DeWitt and Howard Henry. 1904—8–2–0. Lost only to Navy (10–9) and Yale. 1905—8–2–0. Lost to Dartmouth (6–0) and unbeaten Yale. 1906—9–0–1. William Roper's 1st team outscored foes 205–9 and won national championship despite 0–0 tie with Yale in finale; B Edward Dillon and T James Cooney led team. 1907 —7–2–0. Scored 282 but lost close ones to Cornell 6–5 and national champion Yale 12–10. 1909—6–2–1. Won 3 by 3 points or less, losing only to Lafayette 6–0 and unbeaten national champion Yale. 1910—7–1–0. Shut out first 7 but lost finale to Yale 5–3. 1911—8–0–2. Shut out 7 and won 6th national championship despite ties with Lehigh 6–6 and Navy 0–0; led by linemen Sanford White, Edward Hart and Joseph Duff. 1912—7–1–1. Scored 322 behind G John Logan, losing only to unbeaten national champion Harvard 16–6 and tying Yale 6–6. 1915—6–2–0. Won first 6, then lost to Harvard 10–6 and Yale 13–7. 1916—6–2–0. Shut out 5 but again lost last 2 to Harvard 3–0 and Yale 10–0. 1920—6–0–1. Outscored foes 144–23 behind B Don Lourie and T Stan Keck; tie was with Harvard 14–14. 1922 —8–0–0. Shut out 5 and won 4 by TD or less behind T Herb Treat. 1925 —5–1–1. B Jake Slagle and C Ed McMillan led team to wins over all but Navy (10–10) and Colgate (9–0 loss). 1926—5–1–1. Tied Washington & Lee 7–7 and lost only to Navy 27–13. 1927—6–1–0. B Mike Miles led Tigers to wins over all but Yale (14–6 loss in finale). 1928—5–1–2. Roper's last team lost only to Navy 9–0 in finale. 1933—9–0–0. Outscored foes 217–8, shutting out first 7, in Fritz Crisler's 2nd year. 1934—7–1–0. Outscored foes 280–38 and lost only to Yale 7–0 behind C Edward Kalbaugh. 1935—9–0–0. Outscored foes 256–32 as G John Weller starred. 1939— 7–1–0. Won 4 by TD or less, losing only to Cornell 20–7 in 2nd game. 1950 —9–0–0. Scored 349 to lead nation and won Lambert Trophy behind T Hollie Donan and B Dick Kazmaier (1,372 yards total offense). 1951—

9–0–0. Charlie Caldwell's 2nd straight Lambert winner scored 310 behind Heisman winner Kazmaier (1,827 yards of total offense to lead nation) and E Frank McPhee. 1952—8–1–0. Scored 297 and shut out 5, losing only to Pennsylvania 13–7 as McPhee starred again. 1955—7–2–0. Lost only to Colgate and Harvard (7–6), winning informal Ivy title for 8th time in 20th century. 1956—7–2–0. Caldwell's last team scored 237 and won first 7. 1957 —7–2–0. Richard Colman's 1st team lost close ones to Colgate 12–10 and Yale 20–13 but won 1st formal Ivy title. 1960—7–2–0. Hugh Scott ran for 760 yards and passed for 367 more as Tigers lost only to Rutgers 13–8 in opener and to unbeaten Yale. 1963—7–2–0. Cosmo Iacavazzi led nation in scoring with 14 TDs as Tigers got share of Ivy title. 1964—9–0–0. Iacavazzi (909 yards rushing and 10 TDs) and G Stas Maliszewski led Tigers to 3rd Ivy title; outscored foes 216–53, shutting out 4 straight in mid-season. 1965 —8–1–0. Scored 281 behind Maliszewski, Ron Landeck (1,949 yards and 24 TDs running and passing) and Charley Gogolak (led nation with 16 FGs and 33–33 extra points); lost only to Dartmouth 28–14 in finale. 1966—7–2–0. Won 5 by TD or less and took share of Ivy title.

BOWL RECORD

None.

CONFERENCE TITLES

Ivy (informal) 1903, 1906, 1911, 1933, 1935, 1950, 1951, 1955. Ivy (formal) 1957, 1963*, 1964, 1966*, 1969*.

TOP 10 AP & UPI RANKING

1950	6–8
1951	6–6

MAJOR RIVALS

Princeton has played at least 15 games with Brown (36–14–0), Colgate (19–14–1), Columbia (44–8–1), Cornell (41–23–2), Dartmouth (29–31–3), Harvard (43–27–6), Lafayette (27–2–3), Lehigh (33–2–2), Navy (18–11–6), Pennsylvania (54–20–1), Rutgers (53–17–1), Stevens Tech (23–0–0) and Yale (38–58–10).

COACHES

Dean of Princeton coaches was William W. Roper with record of 89–28–16 for 1906–08, 1910–11 and 1919–30, including 2 informal Ivy titles, 4 unbeaten teams and 2 national champions. Charles W. Caldwell Jr. was 70–30–3 for 1945–56 with 3 informal Ivy titles and 2 unbeaten Lambert Trophy winners. He was national coach of the year in 1950. Other outstanding records were by Richard W. Colman Jr., 75–33–0 for 1957–68 with 4 Ivy titles and 1 unbeaten team; and Herbert O. (Fritz) Crisler, 35–9–5 for 1932–37 with 2 informal Ivy titles and 2 unbeaten teams. He ranks in top 20 in all-time winning percentage.

MISCELLANEA

First game was 6 goals to 4 goals loss to Rutgers in nation's 1st intercollegiate game in 1869 . . . 1st win was 8 goals to 0 win over Rutgers in rematch same year . . . highest score was 140–0 over Lafayette in 1884 . . . highest since 1900 was 75–0 over Amherst in 1934 . . . highest since W.W. II was 66–0 over Williams in 1950 . . . worst defeat was 65–7 by Navy in 1953 . . . longest unbeaten string of 34 in 1884–87 ended by Harvard 12–0 . . . winning streak of 24 in 1949–52 ended by Penn 13–7 . . . winning streak of 18 in 1893–94 ended by Penn 12–0 . . . longest losing string of 8 in 1976–77 broken with 28–7 win over Columbia . . . Princeton has had 49 consensus All America players since 1889 . . . multi-year choices were Jesse Riggs, G, and Sheppard Homans, B, 1890–91; Philip King, B, 1891–93; Arthur Wheeler, G, 1892–94; Langdon Lea, T, 1893–95; Addison Kelly, B, 1896–97; Arthur Hillebrand, T, 1898–99; John DeWitt, G, 1902–03; James Cooney, T, 1904, 1906; James McCormick, B, 1905, 1907; L. Casper Wister, E, 1906–07; Harold Ballin, T, 1913–14; and Stan Keck, T, 1920, and G, 1921 . . . choices since W.W. II were Dick Kazmaier, B, 1951; Frank McPhee, E, 1952; and Stas Maliszewski, G, 1965 . . . Academic All America choices were Dick Sandler, DT, 1968; Kevin Fox, OG, 1976; and Kevin Guthrie, WR, 1982–83 . . . Kazmaier, HB, won Heisman Trophy in 1951 . . . Princeton ranks in top 5 in total victories and in top 10 in all-time winning percentage.

Purdue (Boilermakers; Old Gold & Black) (Big 10)

NOTABLE TEAMS

1892—8–0–0. Outscored foes 320–24. 1894—9–1–0. Blanked 6, losing only to Minnesota 24–0, and won 4th straight Indiana Association title. 1902 —7–2–1. Shut out 7, but lost successive games to Chicago and Illinois. 1904 —9–3–0. Blanked 7 and won last 5. 1905—6–1–1. Shut out 6, losing only to unbeaten national champion Chicago 19–0 and tying Indiana 11–11. 1913 —4–1–2. Lost only to unbeaten Chicago 6–0. 1914—5–2–0. Lost successive games to Wisconsin and Chicago. 1924—5–2–0. James Phelan's 3rd team lost only to Ohio State 7–0 and Chicago. 1927—6–2–0. Lost close ones to Chicago 7–6 and Wisconsin 12–6. 1929—8–0–0. Outscored foes 187–44 and won Big 10 title in Phelan's last year as T Elmer Sleight and HB Ralph Welch became Purdue's 1st consensus All America players. 1930—6–2–0. Noble Kizer's 1st team lost close ones to Michigan 14–13 and Indiana 7–6. 1931—9–1–0. Shut out 6 behind E Paul Moss and earned share of Big 10 title; lost only to Wisconsin 21–14. 1932—7–0–1. Moss and FB Roy Horstmann starred as Boilermakers beat all but Northwestern (7–7). 1933— 6–1–1. Lost only to Iowa 14–6 and tied Minnesota 7–7 as Duane Purvis starred at HB. 1938—5–1–2. Lost only to Minnesota 7–0 as Cecil Isbell starred at HB. 1943—9–0–0. Outscored foes 214–55 and won share of Big 10 title behind G Alex Agase and FB Tony Butkovich. 1945—7–3–0. Won 7 of first 8 as T Tom Hughes starred. 1958—6–1–2. Jack Mollenkopf's 3rd team lost only to Wisconsin 31–6. 1965—7–2–1. QB Bob Griese passed for 1,719 yards and 11 TDs and Bob Hadrick caught 47 passes for 562 yards as Purdue lost only to unbeaten national champion Michigan St. 14–10 and Illinois. 1966—8–2–0. Scored 283 behind Griese (1,749 yards and 12 TDs passing) and SE Jim Beirne (64 receptions for 768 yards and 8 TDs), losing only to unbeaten national co-champions Notre Dame and Michigan St.; beat Southern California in Rose Bowl 14–13. 1967—8–2–0. Scored 291 behind national scoring leader Leroy Keyes (114 points and 986 yards rushing) and soph QB Mike Phipps (1,800 yards and 11 TDs passing); lost close ones to Oregon St. 22–14 and Indiana 19–14 but earned share of Big 10 title. 1968 —8–2–0. Again scored 291 behind Keyes (1,003 yards rushing) and Phipps as MG Chuck Kyle led defense; lost to unbeaten national champion Ohio St. and Minnesota. 1969—8–2–0. Mollenkopf's last team scored 354 behind Phipps (2,527 yards and 23 TDs passing) and Ashley Bell (49 receptions for 669 yards and 11 TDs) as DB Tim Foley starred on defense (5 interceptions); lost to Michigan and Ohio St. **1978—8-2-1.** Jim Young's 2nd team lost only to Notre Dame and Michigan as John Macon ran for 913 yards, Mark Herrmann passed for 1,904 yards and 14 TDs and Scott Sovereen kicked 15 FGs; beat Georgia Tech in Peach Bowl 41-21. **1979—9-2-0.** Herrmann passed for 2,377 yards and 16 TDs as team scored in double figures in all; beat Tennessee in Bluebonnet Bowl 27-22. **1980—8-3-0.** Scored 300 behind Herrmann (3,212 yards and 23 TDs passing) and TE Dave Young (70 receptions for 959 yards and 9 TDs); won 8 of last 9, then beat Missouri in Liberty Bowl 28-25.

BOWL RECORD

Bluebonnet 1-0-0; Liberty 1-0-0; Peach 1-0-0; Rose 1-0-0.

CONFERENCE TITLES

Indiana Association 1891, 1892, 1893, 1894. Big 10 1918*, 1929, 1931*, 1943*, 1952*, 1967*.

TOP 10 AP & UPI RANKING

1943	5	1968	10–U
1966	7–6	1979	10–10
1967	9–9		

MAJOR RIVALS

Purdue has played at least 15 games with Chicago (14–27–1), DePauw (26–1–0), Illinois (28–31–6), Indiana (53–27–6), Iowa (40–18–2), Michigan (9–26–0), Michigan St. (18–18–2), Minnesota (17–22–3), Northwestern (33–19–1), Notre Dame (19–34–2), Ohio St. (8–22–2), Wabash (19–8–2) and Wisconsin (22–30–7).

COACHES

Dean of Purdue coaches was Jack Mollenkopf with record of 84–39–9 for 1956–69, including 1 Big 10 title and 1 Rose Bowl champion. Noble Kizer was 42–13–3 for 1930–36 with 1 Big 10 title and 1 unbeaten team. Jim Young was 38–19–1 for 1977–81 with 3 bowl champions. James Phelan was 35–22–5 for 1922–29 with 1 Big 10 title and 1 unbeaten team.

MISCELLANEA

First game was 48–6 loss to Butler in 1887 . . . 1st win was 34–10 over DePauw in 1889 . . . highest score was 96–0 over Butler in 1893 . . . highest since 1900 was 91–0 over Rose Poly in 1912 . . . highest since W.W. II was 62–7 over Boston University in 1947 . . . worst defeat was 56–0 by Chicago in 1907 and by Iowa in 1922 . . . worst since W.W. II was 51–0 by Michigan in 1974 . . . highest against Boilermakers since W.W. II was 52–21 by Michigan in 1982 and 52–6 by Notre Dame in 1983 . . . longest unbeaten string of 20 in 1931–33 ended by Iowa 14–6 . . . winning string of 16 in 1891–93 ended by Michigan 46–8 . . . longest losing string of 11 in 1906–08 broken with 40–0 win over Earlham . . . Purdue has had 15 consensus All America players since 1929 . . . only multi-year choice was Leroy Keyes, B, 1967–68 . . . unanimous choices for single year were Paul Moss, E, 1932; Mike Phipps, QB, 1969; and Dave Young, TE, and Mark Herrmann, QB, 1980 . . . others since 1965 were Bob Griese, QB, 1965; Chuck Kyle, MG, 1968; and Otis Armstrong, B, and Dave Butz, DT, 1972 . . . Academic All America selections were Len Dawson, B, 1956; Jerry Beabout, T, 1960; Sal Ciampi, G, 1965; Jim Beirne, E, and Lance Olssen, DT, 1967; Tim Foley, DB, 1968–69; Mike Phipps, QB, and Bill Yanchar, DT, 1969; Bob Hoftiezer, DE, 1973; Ken Loushin, DL, 1979; and Tim Seneff, DB, 1980–81.

Rice (Owls; Blue & Gray) (Southwest)

NOTABLE TEAMS

1916—6–1–2. Scored 346, losing only to Texas 16–2 in opener. 1917— 7–1–0. Scored 230 and lost only to unbeaten Texas A&M 10–0 in finale. 1919—8–1–0. Shut out 5 as E Shirley Brick led team to wins over all but Texas (32–7). 1932—7–3–0. Lost only to Texas in first 7. 1934—9–1–1. Jimmy Kitts' 1st team shut out 6 and won 1st Southwest Conference title behind HB Bill Wallace and T Ralph Miller; lost only to TCU 7–2 and tied LSU 9–9. 1935—8–3–0. Wallace and FB John McCauley starred as Owls lost only to unbeaten SMU in first 9. 1937—5–3–2. Lost only to TCU 7–2 in last 8 and won Southwest Conference; upset unbeaten Colorado in Cotton Bowl 28–14. 1940—7–3–0. Won 5 of first 6 behind linemen Moose Hartman and Ken Whitlow in Jess Neely's 1st year. 1942—7–2–1. Unbeaten in last 6 as G Weldon Humble starred. 1946—8–2–0. Earned share of Southwest Conference title behind Humble (Owl's 1st consensus All America) and B Carl

Russ; lost only to LSU 7–6 and Arkansas 7–0, and beat Tennessee in Orange Bowl 8–0. 1949—9-1-0. Lost only to LSU 14–7 in 2nd game and won Southwest title behind E Froggie Williams and C Joe Watson: beat North Carolina in Cotton Bowl 27–13. 1953—8-2-0. Scored 267 behind linemen Richard Chapman and John Hudson and FB Kosse Johnson (944 yards rushing and 10 TDs) and took SWC title; lost close ones to SMU 12–7 and Kentucky 19–13 but beat Alabama in Cotton Bowl 28–6. 1954—7-3-0. HB Dick Moegle ran for 905 yards and 12 TDs behind G Kenny Paul; won 5 of last 6. 1957—7-3-0. Won 4 by TD or less and took SWC title behind QB King Hill (1,244 yards of total offense) and E Buddy Dial; lost to Navy in Cotton Bowl 20–7. 1960—7-3-0. Lost no game by more than 5 points as G Rufus King and E Johnny Burrell starred; lost to national champion Mississippi in Sugar Bowl 14–6. 1961—7-3-0. Won 4 of last 5 behind Burrell and B Roland Jackson, but lost to Kansas in Bluebonnet Bowl 33–7.

BOWL RECORD

Bluebonnet 0–1–0; Cotton 3–1–0; Orange 1–0–0; Sugar 0–1–0.

CONFERENCE TITLES

Southwest 1934, 1937, 1946*, 1949, 1953*, 1957.

TOP 10 AP & UPI RANKING

1946	10
1949	5
1953	6–6
1957	8–7

MAJOR RIVALS

Rice has played at least 15 games with Arkansas (28–28–3), Baylor (27–35–2), LSU (13–35–5), Sam Houston St. (14–1–0), SMU (24–38–1), Southwestern (16–5–0), Texas (20–49–1), Texas A&M (27–38–3), TCU (26–33–3), Texas Tech (16–17–1) and Tulane (10–8–1).

COACHES

Dean of Rice coaches was Jess Neely with record of 144–124–10 for 1940–66, including 4 conference titles and 6 bowl teams. He ranks 5th in all-time total victories. Jimmy Kitts was 33–29–4 for 1934–39 with 2 conference titles and 1 Cotton Bowl champion.

MISCELLANEA

First game was 7–0 win over Houston H.S. in 1912 . . . 1st win over college foe was 20–6 over Sam Houston same year . . . highest score was 146–3 over SMU in 1916 . . . highest since W.W. II was 55–0 over New Mexico in 1949 and over VMI in 1969 . . . worst defeat was 81–0 by Austin in 1912 . . . worst since W.W. II was 77–0 by LSU in 1977 . . . longest unbeaten string of 15 in 1916–17 ended by Texas A&M 10–0 . . . longest losing string of 14 in 1977–78 broken with 21–14 win over TCU . . . consensus All America players were Weldon Humble, G, 1946; James Williams, E, 1949; Dicky Moegle, B, 1954; Buddy Dial, E, 1958; and Tommy Kramer, QB, 1976 . . . Academic All America selections were Richard Chapman, G, 1952–53; Dicky Moegle, B, 1954; Steve Bradshaw, DL, 1969; Lamont Jefferson, LB, 1979; and Brian Patterson, DB, 1983.

Rutgers (Scarlet Knights, Scarlet; Scarlet) (Independent)

NOTABLE TEAMS

1915—7–1–0. Outscored foes 351–33, losing only to Princeton 10–0 in 2nd game, as Elmer Bracher ran for 1,021 yards. 1917—7–1–1. Scored 295 and shut out 6 as E Paul Robeson became Scarlet Knights' first consensus All America; lost only to Syracuse 14–10 and tied West Virginia 7–7. 1918—5–2–0. Won first 5 as Robeson starred again. 1923—7–1–1. Foster Sanford's last team shut out 6 and lost only to West Virginia 27–7. 1924—7–1–1. Scored 249 but tied Lehigh 13–13 and lost finale to Bucknell 12–7. 1938—7–1–0. Harvey Harman's 1st team shut out 5, losing only to New York University 25–6. 1939—7–1–1. Won all but Richmond (6–6) and Brown (13–0 loss in finale). 1941—7–2–0. Harman's last team till after W.W. II lost only to Syracuse and Lafayette. 1945—5–2–0. Harry Rockafeller's last team lost only to Swarthmore (13–6 in opener) and Princeton. 1946—7–2–0. Harman resumed coaching and saw team win last 5 after losses to Columbia 13–7 and Princeton 14–7. 1947—8–1–0. Scored 262 and lost only to Columbia 40–28 in opener. 1948—7–2–0. B Frank Burns led team to wins over all but Columbia and Brown. 1958—8–1–0. Scored 301 and led nation in scoring average as Bill Austin ran for 747 yards and Bob Simms caught 33 passes for 9 TDs; lost only to Quantico Marines 13–12. 1960—8–1–0. John

Bateman's 1st team lost only to Villanova 14–12. 1961—9–0–0. Scored in double figures in all behind C Alex Kroll as Sam Mudie scored 10 TDs; beat Princeton 16–13 in opener in only close game. 1968—8–2–0. Scored 276 as Bryant Mitchell ran for 1,204 yards and John Pollock intercepted 9 passes. 1975—9–2–0. Frank Burn's 3rd team scored 347 as Curt Edwards ran for 1,157 yards; won last 7. 1976—11–0–0. Scored 287 and led nation in total defense, rushing defense and scoring defense; Bert Kosup passed for 1,445 yards. 1977—8–3–0. Won 8 of last 9. 1978—9–2–0. Lost only to unbeaten Penn St. 26–10 in opener and to Colgate 14–9 in finale as Kennan Startzell kicked 14 FGs; lost to Arizona St. in Garden State Bowl 34–18. 1979—8–3–0. Scored in double figures in all as Ed McMichael passed for 1,529 yards and Startzell kicked 13 FGs; won 5 of last 6.

BOWL RECORD

Garden State 0–1–0.

CONFERENCE TITLES

Middle 3 1947. Middle Atlantic 1958, 1960, 1961.

TOP 10 AP & UPI RANKING

None.

MAJOR RIVALS

Rutgers has played at least 15 games with Army (5–12–0), Bucknell (12–4–0), Colgate (21–15–0), Columbia (23–21–5), Connecticut (16–5–0), Delaware (15–13–3), Haverford (5–9–3), Holy Cross (8–11–0), Lafayette (41–30–1), Lehigh (43–30–1), New York University (23–18–2), Pennsylvania (6–9–0), Princeton (17–53–1), Stevens Tech (30–11–5) and Ursinus (9–8–0).

COACHES

Frank R. Burns leads Rutgers coaches in victories with record of 78–43–1 for 1973–83, including 1 bowl team and 1 perfect record. Harvey J. Harman had longest tenure with record of 74–44–2 for 1938–41 and 1946–55, including 1 conference title. John F. Bateman was 73–51–0 for 1960–72 with 2 conference titles and 1 perfect record. Other top records were by G. Foster Sanford, 56–32–5 for 1913–23; Harry J. Rockafeller, 33–26–1 for 1927–30 and 1942–45; and John R. Stiegman, 22–15–0 for 1956–59 with 1 conference title.

MISCELLANEA

First game was 6–4 win over Princeton in 1st intercollegiate football game in 1869 . . . highest score was 96–0 over RPI in 1915 . . . highest since W.W. II was 79–6 over King's Point in 1949 . . . worst defeat was 98–0 by Yale in 1883 . . . worst since 1900 was 56–0 by Lafayette in 1927 . . . worst since W.W. II was 48–0 by Boston College in 1956 . . . highest against Scarlet Knights since 1900 was 61–19 by Princeton in 1952 . . . longest winning streak of 18 in 1975–76 ended by Penn St. 45–7 in 1977 . . . longest losing string of 14 in 1900–02 broken with 10–0 with over Stevens Tech . . . consensus All America players were Paul Robeson, E, 1917–18; and Alex Kroll, C, 1961 . . . Rutgers has had no Academic All America choices.

San Diego State (Aztecs; Scarlet & Black) (WAC)

NOTABLE TEAMS

1923—8–2–0. C.E. Peterson's 3rd team won last 7 after losses to Occidental and UCLA. **1924—7–1–2.** Lost only to Fresno St. 7–0 in finale. **1936—6–1–1.** Leo Calland's 2nd team lost only to San Diego Marines 14–0 and tied New Mexico St. 7–7. **1937—7–1–0.** Shut out 7 but lost to Redlands 10–9. **1947—7–2–1.** Bill Schutte's 1st team was unbeaten in last 7, but lost to Hardin-Simmons in Harbor Bowl 53–0. **1951—10–0–1.** Scored 385, including 34–13 win over Hawaii in Pineapple Bowl, and won 2nd straight California Collegiate title as Jesse Thompson passed for 1,304 yards and 13 TDs and Ed Ricketts intercepted 12 passes; tie was with Arizona St. 27–27. **1961—7–2–1.** Don Coryell's 1st team lost only to Long Beach St. 17–15 and Fresno St. **1962—8–2–0.** Scored 294 as Kern Carson ran for 796 yards and scored 12 TDs. **1963—7–2–0.** Scored 317 as Carson scored 12 TDs again and Rod Dowhower passed for 1,136 yards. **1964—8–2–0.** Outscored foes 423–71 behind Dowhower (1,728 yards and 22 TDs passing) and Jim Allison (1,186 yards and 16 TDs rushing), but lost close ones to Cal St.-L.A. 7–0 and San Jose St. 20–15. **1965—8–2–0.** Scored 353 as Don Horn passed for 1,688 yards and 21 TDs, Gary Garrison scored 14 TDs and caught 70 passes for 916 yards, and Nate Johns ran for 921 yards. **1966—10–0–0.** Scored 289 as Horn passed for 2,234 yards and 18 TDs, Craig Scoggins caught 81 for 1,212 yards and 8 scores, and DE Leo Carroll stood out on defense; beat

Montana St. in Camellia Bowl 28–7. 1967—9–1–0. Scored 292 as Haven Moses caught 54 passes for 958 yards; won 6th and last California Collegiate title, then beat San Francisco St. in Camellia Bowl 27–6. 1968—9–0–1. Scored 377 behind Dennis Shaw (2,139 yards and 19 TDs passing) and Tom Nettles (62 receptions for 1,227 yards and 14 TDs) as DE Fred Dryer led defense; tie was with Tennessee St. 13–13. 1969—10–0–0. Coryell's 3rd unbeaten team scored 464 and led nation in total offense, passing and scoring average as Shaw led nation in total offense (3,197 yards) and passed for 39 TDs and Tim Delaney caught 85 passes for 1,259 yards and 14 TDs; won 1st PCAA title and beat Boston U. in Pasadena Bowl 28–7. 1970—9–2–0. Scored 364 behind Brian Sipe (2,618 yards and 23 TDs passing) and Delaney (62 receptions for 794 yards); won 9 straight before losses to Long Beach St. and Iowa St. 1972—10–1–0. Coryell's last team featured Isaac Curtis (44 receptions for 832 yards) and DB Joe Lavender; lost only to Houston (49–14) and won 3rd PCAA title. 1973—9–1–1. Claude Gilbert's 1st team scored 321 and led nation in passing behind Jesse Freitas (nation's leading passer with 2,993 yards and 21 TDs and total offense leader with 2,901 yards); lost only to Houston 14–9 and tied San Jose St. 27–27. 1974 —8–2–1. Won 5th PCAA title in 6 years as Dwight McDonald led nation's pass receivers with 86 catches for 1,157 yards; lost close ones to Arizona 17–10 and North Texas St. 14–9. 1975—8–3–0. Scored 320 and led nation in passing behind Craig Penrose (nation's passing leader with 2,660 yards and 15 TDs) and Duke Fergerson (57 receptions for 886 yards). 1976— 10–1–0. Won 5 by TD or less as David Turner ran for 982 yards and LB Travis Hitt sparked defense; lost only to Brigham Young 8–0. 1977—10– 1–0. Scored 349 as Turner ran for 1,252 yards and 13 TDs, Joe Davis passed for 2,360 yards and 24 TDs and Dennis Pearson caught 49 for 864 yards; lost only to Fresno St. 34–14. 1979—8–3–0. Tony Allen ran for 1,094 yards and 10 TDs and DB Terrell Ward sparked defense; 1 of losses was to unbeaten Brigham Young.

BOWL RECORD

Harbor 0–1–0; Pasadena 1–0–0.

CONFERENCE TITLES

California Collegiate A.A. 1950, 1951, 1962, 1963*, 1966, 1967. Pacific Coast Athletic Association 1969, 1970*, 1972, 1973, 1974.

TOP 10 AP & UPI RANKING

None.

MAJOR RIVALS

Aztecs have played at least 15 games with Cal Poly-SLO (13–9–0), Cal St.-Fresno (22–16–4), Cal St.-Long Beach (13–9–0), Cal St.-Los Angeles (11–5–1), LaVerne (10–2–3), Occidental (11–7–1), Pacific (14–7–0), Pomona (10–7–1), Redlands (17–7–2), San Jose St. (11–16–2), UC Santa Barbara (26–8–1) and Whittier (12–10–2).

COACHES

Dean of San Diego St. coaches was Don Coryell with record of 104–19–2 for 1961–72, including 7 conference titles, 3 bowl teams (2 minor) and 3 unbeaten teams. Claude Gilbert was 61–26–2 for 1973–80 with 2 conference titles. Other top records were by C.E. Peterson, 45–31–4 for 1921–29; Leo Calland, 34–22–4 for 1935–41; and Bill Schutte, 48–36–4 for 1947–55 with 2 conference titles, 1 bowl team and 1 unbeaten team.

MISCELLANEA

First game was 6–0 win over Army-Navy Academy in 1921 . . . 1st win over college foe was 38–13 over Santa Barbara St. in 1923 . . . highest score was 72–0 over Santa Barbara in 1953 . . . worst defeat was 66–0 by Fresno St. in 1942 and by Arizona St. in 1957 . . . highest score against Aztecs was 68–17 by Pacific in 1958 . . . longest unbeaten string of 31 in 1967–70 ended by Cal St.-Long Beach 27–11 . . . winning string of 25 in 1965–67 ended by Utah St. 31–25 . . . unbeaten string of 16 in 1923–24 ended by Fresno St. 7–0 . . . longest winless strings of 10 in 1942–45 broken with 7–0 win over Fresno St. and in 1959–60 broken with 27–20 win over Pepperdine . . . San Diego St. has had no consensus All America players and no Academic All America choices.

San Jose State (Spartans; Royal Blue, Gold & White) (PCAA)

NOTABLE TEAMS

1898—5–0–1. Tie was with San Jose H.S. 6–6. 1932—7–0–2. Dudley De-Groot's 1st team shut out 5, including 0–0 ties with Fresno St. and Nevada-Reno. 1937—11–2–1. Lost only to unbeaten Santa Clara and to San Diego St. 7–6. 1938—11–1–0. Scored 322 and shut out 6 as Dave Titchenal intercepted 6 passes; lost only to Hawaii 13–12 in finale. 1939—13–0–0. De-Groot's last team scored 324 and shut out 8 as Leroy Zimmerman intercepted 8 passes and returned 3 for TDs and Aubrey Minter intercepted 6. 1940—11–1–0. Lost opener to Texas A&I 10–0 but yielded only 52 points thereafter as Minter starred in kickoff returns. 1942—7–2–0. Lost close ones to San Francisco 20–13 and Fresno St. 6–0. 1946—8–1–1. Bill Hubbard's 1st team lost only to unbeaten Hardin-Simmons 34–7 in 2nd game as Spartans returned to football after 3-year W.W. II layoff; beat Utah St. in Raisin Bowl 20–0. 1947—9–3–0. Scored 327 and lost only to Fresno St. 21–20 in last 5; Billy Parton and Babe Nomura starred as punt returners. 1948—9–3–0. Scored 373, with Harry Russell intercepting 7 passes and Al Cementina 6; lost only to St. Mary's 19–14 in last 10. 1954—7–3–0. Won 3 by TD or less. 1974—8–3–1. Darryl Rogers' 2nd team scored in double figures in all as Craig Kimball passed for 2,401 yards and 23 TDs and Ron Ploger kicked 12 FGs and 35 extra points. 1975—9–2–0. DT Kim Bokamper and LB Carl Ekern led defense while Rick Kane ran for 1,144 yards and Roger Profitt passed and ran for 1,861 to lead team to 1st PCAA title; Lou Rodriguez kicked 16 FGs and DB Gerald Small intercepted 7 passes, returning 2 for TDs. 1981—9–2–0. Jack Elway's 3rd team scored 355 behind HB Gerald Willhite (1,193 yards rushing and 14 TDs), QB Steve Clarkson (3,373 yards and 28 TDs passing) and WR Tim Kearse (71 receptions for 946 yards) and won 4th PCAA title; lost to Toledo 27–25 in inaugural California Bowl. 1982—8–3–0. Scored 331 and won 3 by less than TD as Clarkson passed for 2,485 yards and 20 TDs and Kearse caught 51 for 799 yards.

BOWL RECORD

California 0–1–0; Pasadena 0–1–0; Raisin 2–0–0.

CONFERENCE TITLES

Pacific Coast Athletic Association 1975, 1976, 1978*, 1981.

TOP 10 AP & UPI RANKING

None.

MAJOR RIVALS

Spartans have played at least 15 games with Arizona St. (11–15–0), California (3–19–0), Fresno St. (27–21–3), Hawaii (11–6–0), Idaho (8–6–1), Oregon (6–9–0), Pacific (31–21–4), San Diego St. (16–10–2), Santa Clara (12–4–2), Stanford (7–32–1) and Utah St. (8–9–0).

COACHES

Dudley S. DeGroot leads Spartan coaches with record of 59–19–8 for 1932–39, including 2 unbeaten teams. Wilbur V. (Bill) Hubbard was 36–11–1 for 1946–49 with 2 bowl champions. Other top records were by Darryl Rogers, 22–9–3 for 1973–75 with 1 conference title; Lynn Stiles, 22–16–0 for 1976–78 with 2 conference titles; and Jack Elway, 35–20–1 for 1979–83 with 1 conference title and 1 bowl team.

MISCELLANEA

First game was 0–0 tie with Pacific in 1895 . . . 1st win was 18–0 over Pacific in 1898 . . . highest score was 103–0 over University of Mexico in 1949 . . . worst defeat was 79–0 by Stanford freshmen in 1923 . . . worst since W.W. II was 66–0 by Arizona St. in 1968 . . . highest against Spartans since W.W. II was 68–20 by Stanford in 1968 . . . longest unbeaten string of 18 in 1940–41 ended by Nevada-Reno 20–19 . . . longest losing string of 10 in 1922–23 broken with 13–0 win over Hollister J.C. in 1924 . . . San Jose St. has had no consensus All America players . . . Jim Toews, OG, was Academic All America in 1975.

South Carolina (Fighting Gamecocks; Garnet & Black) (Independent)

NOTABLE TEAMS

1902—6–1–0. Shut out 5, losing only to Furman 10–0. 1903—8–2–0. Shut out 7, losing to North Carolina and North Carolina St. (6–5). 1921—5–1–2. Sol Metzger's 2nd team lost only to Furman 7–0, yielding no more than 7 in any game. 1924—7–3–0. Metzger's last team shut out 5; won 6 of first 7. 1925—7–3–0. Lost close games to North Carolina 7–0, Virginia Tech 6–0 and Furman 2–0. 1928—6–2–2. Billy Laval's 1st team shut out 6 but lost to Clemson and North Carolina St. 1943—5–2–0. Lost only to 176th Infantry 13–7 and North Carolina. 1947—6–2–1. Rex Enright's 2nd post-war team blanked last 4 foes after losses to Maryland and Mississippi. 1953—7–3–0. Johnny Gramling passed for 1,045 yards behind C Leon Cunningham and G Frank Mincevich. 1956—7–3–0. Warren Giese's 1st team lost no game by more than 8 points behind T Sam DeLuca and backs King Dixon and Alex Hawkins.1958—7–3–0. Hawkins and FB John Saunders led team to 5 wins in last 6 games. 1969—7–3–0. Won 4 by 8 points or less behind QB Tommy Suggs, FB Warren Muir (917 yards rushing) and DT Jimmy Poston; won only ACC title but lost to West Virginia in Peach Bowl 14–3. 1979—8–3–0. Won 5 by TD or less as George Rogers ran for 1,548 yards; lost to Missouri in Hall of Fame Bowl 24–14. 1980—8–3–0. Scored 339 behind Rogers (who led nation's rushers with 1,781 yards and won Heisman) and Eddie Leopard (11 FGs and 42 extra points); lost to Pittsburgh in Gator Bowl 37–9.

BOWL RECORD

Gator 0–2–0; Hall of Fame 0–1–0; Peach 0–1–0; Tangerine 0–1–0.

CONFERENCE TITLES

Atlantic Coast 1969.

TOP 10 AP & UPI RANKING

None.

MAJOR RIVALS

Gamecocks have played at least 15 games with The Citadel (37–6–3), Clemson (30–48–3), Davidson (6–13–0), Duke (13–24–2), Erskine (15–1–0), Furman (27–17–1), Georgia (6–30–2), Georgia Tech (7–10–0), Maryland (11–17–0), North Carolina (13–33–4), North Carolina St. (22–20–4), Presbyterian (12–3–0), Virginia (19–10–1), Wake Forest (32–20–2) and Wofford (15–4–0).

COACHES

Dean of South Carolina coaches was Rex Enright with record of 64–69–7 for 1938–42 and 1946–55. Most successful was Jim Carlen, 45–36–1 for 1975–81 with 3 bowl teams. Paul Dietzel was 42–53–1 for 1966–74 with 1 conference title and 1 bowl team. Other top records were by N.B. Edgerton, 19–13–3 for 1912–15; Sol Metzger, 26–18–2 for 1920–24; Billy Laval, 39–26–6 for 1928–34; and Warren Giese, 28–21–1 for 1956–60.

MISCELLANEA

First game was 40–0 loss to Georgia in 1894 . . . 1st win was 14–10 over Furman in 1895 . . . highest score was 89–0 over Welsh Neck in 1903 . . . highest since W.W. II was 73–0 over Wichita St. in 1980 . . . worst defeat was 63–0 by Navy in 1920 . . . worst since W.W. II was 42–0 by LSU in 1961 . . . highest against Gamecocks since W.W. II was 56–35 by North Carolina St. in 1973 and 56–26 by Florida St. in 1982 . . . longest unbeaten string of 10 in 1914–15 broken by Virginia 13–0 . . . longest winless string of 15 in 1963–64 broken with 17–14 win over The Citadel . . . only consensus All America choice was George Rogers, RB, 1980 . . . Rogers, HB, also won Heisman Trophy in 1980 . . . South Carolina has had no Academic All America choices.

Southern California (Trojans; Cardinal & Gold) (Pacific-10)

NOTABLE TEAMS

1897—5–1–0. Lost only to San Diego YMCA 18–0; blanked others 100–0. 1898—5–1–1. Both 0–0 tie and 6–0 loss were to Los Angeles H.S. 1904— 6–1–0. Lost only to Sherman Inst. 17–0. 1907—5–1–0. Lost finale to Los

Angeles H.S. 16–6. 1910—7–0–1. Dean Cromwell's 2nd team outscored foes 189–24; tie was with Pomona 9–9 in finale. 1919—4–1–0. Gloomy Gus Henderson's 1st team lost only to California 14–13. 1920—6–0–0. Outscored foes 170–21. 1921—10–1–0. Scored 362 and shut out 8, losing only to unbeaten California 38–7. 1922—10–1–0. Shut out 7, losing only to unbeaten California 12–0; beat Penn St. in Rose Bowl 14–3. 1923—6–2–0. Lost to Washington and California. 1924—9–2–0. Henderson's last team lost only to California 7–0 and St. Mary's 14–10 in successive games. 1925— 11–2–0. Howard Jones' 1st team scored 456 and shut out 7 behind G Brice Taylor; lost only to Stanford 13–9 and Washington St. 17–12. 1926—8–2–0. Scored 317 as Mort Kaer ran for 852 yards and became Trojans' 1st consensus All America; lost pair of 13–12 games to unbeaten national champion Stanford and to Notre Dame (in 1st meeting). 1927—8–1–1. Scored 287 behind T Jess Hibbs as Morley Drury ran for 1,163 yards; tied Stanford 13–13 and lost only to Notre Dame 7–6, but earned share of 1st Pacific Coast Conference title. 1928—9–0–1. Outscored foes 267–59 behind Hibbs and beat Notre Dame for 1st time (27–14); won 1st national championship despite 0–0 tie with California. 1929—9–2–0. Scored 445 as Russ Saunders ran for 972 yards; 1 of losses was to unbeaten national champion Notre Dame, but beat undefeated Pittsburgh in Rose Bowl 47–14. 1930—8–2–0. Scored 382 as Orv Mohler ran for 983 yards; lost only to unbeaten teams Washington St. 7–6 and national champion Notre Dame (27–0). 1931— 9–1–0. Scored 342 and shut out 6 behind G Johnny Baker and B Gus Shaver (936 yards rushing); lost only to St. Mary's 13–7 in opener but beat undefeated Tulane in Rose Bowl 21–12 and won national title. 1932—9–0–0. Yielded only 13 points and shut out 7 behind T Ernie Smith; beat Pittsburgh in Rose Bowl 35–0. 1933—10–1–1. Shut out 8 and Cotton Warburton ran for 885 yards and 12 TDs behind G Aaron Rosenberg; lost only to Stanford 13–7 and tied Oregon St. 0–0. 1938—8–2–0. Grenny Lansdell ran and passed for 920 yards behind G Harry Smith as Trojans got share of PCC title; upset unbeaten, unscored-on Duke in Rose Bowl 7–3. 1939—7–0–2. Jones' 3rd unbeaten team and 7th PCC champion again starred Smith and Lansdell (1,221 yards of total offense); tied Oregon 7–7 in opener and UCLA 0–0 in finale, but beat undefeated, unscored-on Tennessee in Rose Bowl 14–0. 1943—7–2–0. Jeff Cravath's 2nd team shut out first 6 and won PCC; beat Washington in Rose Bowl 29–0. 1944—7–0–2. Won last 6 after ties with UCLA 13–13 and California 6–6; beat Tennessee in Rose Bowl 25–0. 1945 —7–3–0. Won 3rd straight PCC title but lost to unbeaten Alabama 34–14 for 1st Rose Bowl loss in 9 appearances. 1947—7–1–1. Lost only to unbeaten national champion Notre Dame in finale (38–7), then lost to unbeaten

Michigan in Rose Bowl 49–0. 1952—9–1–0. Jesse Hill's 2nd team led nation in scoring defense behind DB Jim Sears, who also had 1,030 yards of total offense; lost only to Notre Dame 9–0 in finale, then beat Wisconsin in Rose Bowl 7–0. 1954—8–3–0. Won 8 of first 9; lost to unbeaten national champion Ohio St. in Rose Bowl 20–7. 1956—8–2–0. Hill's last team lost only to Stanford 27–19 and Oregon 7–0. 1959—8–2–0. Won first 8 behind T Ron Mix and McKeever twins Mike (G) and Marlin (E). 1962—10–0–0. John McKay's 3rd team was led by QB Pete Beathard (1,238 yards of total offense), Hal Bedsole (33 receptions for 827 yards and 11 TDs) and LB Damon Bame; beat Wisconsin in Rose Bowl 42–37 and won national title. 1963—7–3–0. Bame starred again along with Mike Garrett (833 yards rushing) and Beathard (1,036 yards total offense). 1964—7–3–0. Garrett ran for 948 yards and 10 TDs and Craig Fertig passed for 1,671 yards. 1965— 7–2–1. Scored 262 as Garrett led nation's rushers (1,440 yards) and scored 16 TDs to win Heisman; lost only to unbeaten Notre Dame and to UCLA (20–16). 1966—7–3–0. Troy Winslow teamed with Ron Drake (52 receptions for 607 yards) to lead team to 4th AAWU title; lost to Purdue in Rose Bowl 14–13. 1967—9–1–0. O.J. Simpson led nation in rushing (1,415 yards) and all-purpose running (1,700 yards) behind T Ron Yary and defense was led by DE Tim Rossovich and LB Adrian Young as Trojans lost only to Oregon St. 3–0; beat Indiana in Rose Bowl 14–3 and won national championship. 1968—9–0–1. Simpson again led nation in rushing (1,709 yards) and all-purpose running (1,966 yards) and scored 23 TDs to win Heisman; tied Notre Dame in finale 21–21, then lost to unbeaten national champion Ohio St. in Rose Bowl 27–16. 1969—9–0–1. Clarence Davis ran for 1,351 yards behind T Sid Smith and DT Al Cowlings sparked defense as Trojans beat all but Notre Dame (14–14) and won 2nd straight Pac-8 title; beat Michigan in Rose Bowl 10–3. 1972—11–0–0. McKay's 4th unbeaten team scored 425 behind Anthony Davis (1,191 yards rushing and 19 TDs), QB Mike Rae (2,001 yards total offense) and TE Charles Young; beat Ohio St. in Rose Bowl 42–17 to clinch national title. 1973—9–1–1. Davis (1,112 yards rushing and 15 TDs), Pat Haden (1,832 yards passing) and WR Lynn Swann (42 catches for 714 yards) led offense as Trojans lost only to unbeaten national champion Notre Dame 23–14 and tied Oklahoma 7–7; lost to Ohio St. in Rose Bowl 42–21. 1974—9–1–1. Scored 345 as Davis ran for 1,421 yards and scored 18 TDs while LB Richard Wood sparked defense; lost opener to Arkansas 22–7 and tied California 15–15, but beat Ohio St. in Rose Bowl 18–17 to gain share of national title. 1976—10–1–0. John Robinson's 1st team scored 372 as Ricky Bell ran for 1,433 yards and 14 TDs and Vince Evans ran and passed for 1,526 yards; lost only to Missouri 46–25 in opener, and beat Michigan in Rose Bowl 14–6. **1978—11–1–0.** Charles White led nation in all-purpose running (2,096 yards) and scored 14 TDs behind G Pat Howell and Paul McDonald passed for 19 TDs as Trojans lost only to Arizona St. 20–7; beat Michigan in Rose Bowl 17–10 to earn share of national championship. **1979—10–0–1.** White led nation in rushing (1,803 yards) and all-purpose running (1,941 yards) and won Heisman behind G Brad Budde as McDonald passed for 2,223 yards and 18 TDs; had mid-season 21–21 tie with Stanford but beat undefeated Ohio St. in Rose Bowl 17–16. **1980—8–2–1.** Marcus Allen led nation in all-purpose running (1,794 yards) and DB Ronnie Lott led in interceptions with 8; lost successive late-season games to Washington 20–10 and UCLA 20–17. **1981—9–2–0.** Allen won Heisman, leading nation in rushing (2,342 yards), all-purpose running (2,559 yards) and scoring (23 TDs) as Trojans lost only to Arizona 13–10 and Washington 13–3; lost to Penn St. in Fiesta Bowl 26–10. **1982 —8–3–0.** Robinson's last team scored 302 as Jeff Simmons caught 56 passes for 973 yards and Don Mosebar and Bruce Matthews starred on line; MG George Achica led defense as Trojans lost no game by more than 8 points.

BOWL RECORD

Bluebonnet 1–0–0; Fiesta 0–1–0; Liberty 1–0–0; Los Angeles Christmas Festival 1–0–0; Rose 17–6–0.

CONFERENCE TITLES

Pacific Coast 1927*, 1928, 1929, 1931, 1932, 1938*, 1939*, 1943, 1944, 1945, 1947, 1952. AAWU 1959*, 1962, 1964*, 1966, 1967. Pacific 8 1968, 1969, 1972, 1973, 1974, 1976. Pacific 10 1978, 1979.

TOP 10 AP & UPI RANKING

1938	7	1962	1–1	1969	3–4	1978	2–1
1939	3	1964	10–10	1972	1–1	1979	2–2
1944	7	1965	10–9	1973	8–7		
1947	8	1967	1–1	1974	2–1		
1952	5–4	1968	4–2	1976	2–2		

MAJOR RIVALS

Trojans have played at least 15 games with California (44–23–4), Notre Dame (23–28–4), Occidental (16–5–2), Ohio St. (8–9–1), Oregon (25–9–2), Oregon St. (41–7–4), Pomona (13–4–4), Stanford (41–18–3), UCLA (30–17–6), Washington (34–19–3) and Washington St. (37–4–4).

COACHES

John McKay tops USC coaches in wins with record of 127–40–8 for 1960–75, including 9 conference titles, 9 bowl teams (6 winners), 4 teams unbeaten in regular season and 4 national champions. He was national coach of the year in 1962 and 1972. Howard H. Jones was 121–36–13 for 1925–40, including 7 conference titles, 5 Rose Bowl champions, 3 unbeaten teams and 2 national champions. He ranks in top 15 in total coaching wins. John Robinson was 67–14–2 for 1976–82 with 3 conference titles, 5 bowl teams (4 winners), 1 unbeaten team and 1 national champion. Other top records were by Dean B. Cromwell, 21–8–6 for 1909–10 and 1916–18 with 1 unbeaten team; Elmer C. (Gloomy Gus) Henderson, 45–7–0 for 1919–24 with 1 Rose Bowl champion and 1 unbeaten team; Newell J. (Jeff) Cravath, 54–28–8 for 1942–50 with 4 conference titles, 4 Rose Bowl teams and 1 unbeaten team; and Jesse T. Hill, 45–17–1 for 1951–56 with 1 conference title and 2 Rose Bowl teams.

MISCELLANEA

First game was 16–0 win over Alliance A.C. in 1888 . . . 1st win over college foe was 40–0 over Loyola in 1889 . . . highest score was 80–0 over Pomona in 1925 . . . highest since W.W. II was 70–33 over Washington St. in 1970 . . . biggest margin of victory since W.W. II was 56–0 over Oregon St. in 1976 . . . worst defeat was 51–0 by Notre Dame in 1966 . . . longest unbeaten string of 28 in 1978–80 ended by Washington 20–10 . . . unbeaten string of 27 in 1931–33 ended by Stanford 13–7 . . . unbeaten string of 23 in 1971–73 ended by Notre Dame 23–14 . . . unbeaten string of 18 in 1974–75 ended by California 28–14 . . . unbeaten string of 17 in 1938–40 ended by Stanford 21–7 . . . longest winless string of 8 in 1941–42 broken with 26–12 win over Washington St. . . . USC has had 44 consensus All America players since 1926 . . . multi-year choices were Ron Yary, T, 1966–67; O.J. Simpson, B, 1967–68; Richard Wood, LB, 1973–74; Ricky Bell, RB, 1975–76; Dennis Thurman, DB, 1976–77; and Charles White, RB, 1978–79 . . . unanimous choices for single year were Ernie Smith, T, 1932; Cotton Warburton, B, 1933; Harry Smith, G, 1939; Mike Garrett, B, 1965; Charles Young, TE, 1972; Anthony Davis, RB, 1974; Pat Howell, G, 1978; Brad Budde, G, 1979; Ronnie Lott, DB, 1980; Marcus Allen, RB, 1981; and Don Mosebar, OT, 1982 . . . others named since 1970 were Charlie Weaver, DE, 1970; Lynn Swann, WR, Booker Brown, OT, and Artimus Parker, DB, 1973; Gary Jeter, DT, 1976; Keith Van Horne, OL, 1980; Roy Foster, OL, 1981; Bruce

Matthews, OG, and George Achica, MG, 1982; and Tony Slaton, C, 1983 . . . Academic All America choices were Dick Nunis, DB, 1952; Mike McKeever, G, 1959–60; Marlin McKeever, E, 1960; Charles Arrobio, T, 1965; Steve Sogge, QB, 1967–68; Harry Khasigian, OG, 1969; Pat Haden, QB, 1973–74; Rich Dimler, DL, 1978; and Paul McDonald, QB, Keith Van Horne, OT, and Brad Budde, OG, 1979 . . . Heisman Trophy winners were Mike Garrett, HB, 1965; O.J. Simpson, HB, 1968; Charles White, HB, 1979; and Marcus Allen, HB, 1981 . . . Ron Yary, T, won Outland Trophy in 1967 . . . Brad Budde, OG, won Lombardi Trophy in 1979 . . . USC ranks in top 10 in all-time winning percentage and in top 15 in total victories.

Southern Methodist (Mustangs; Red & Blue) (Southwest)

NOTABLE TEAMS

1923—9-0-0. Outscored foes 207–9, shutting out 7 and winning 1st Southwest Conference title behind E Jim Stewart and B Logan Stollenwerck. 1924 —5-0-4. Won 4 by TD or less as E Gene Bedford, C Buddy King and B Smack Reisor starred; lost to West Virginia Wesleyan in Dixie Classic 9–7. 1926—8-0-1. Ray Morrison's 3rd unbeaten team scored 229 and won SWC behind B Gerald Mann; tie was with Missouri 7–7. 1927—7-2-0. Scored 267 as Mann starred again along with Redman Hume (17 TDs and 109 points). 1929—6-0-4. Shut out 5 behind T Marion Hammon and G Choc Sanders. 1931—9-1-1. Won SWC title behind Hammon and B Weldon Mason; tied TCU 0–0 and lost only to St. Mary's 7–2 in finale. 1934—8-2-2. Morrison's last team shut out 6 as T Clyde Carter and B Bobby Wilson starred; lost to Rice 9–0 and Baylor 13–6. 1935—12-0-0. Matty Bell's 1st team outscored foes 288–32 as Wilson scored 13 TDs and became SMU's 1st consensus All America along with G J.C. Wetsel; lost to Stanford in Rose Bowl 7–0. 1940—8-1-1. Won 4 by TD or less as B Preston Johnston starred; tied Pittsburgh 7–7 and lost only to Texas A&M 19–7, but got share of SWC title. 1947—9-0-1. Won 5 by 10 points or less and won SWC behind Doak Walker (684 yards rushing, 18–22 extra points, and 11 TDs, including 2 on kickoff returns and 1 on punt return), G Earl Cook and Paul Page (7 interceptions); tied TCU in finale 19–19 and tied unbeaten Penn St. in Cotton Bowl 13–13. 1948—8-1-1. Walker won Heisman Trophy, running for 532 yards and 11 TDs (plus kicking 17–22 extra points and averaging 42.1 yards on 35 punts) and Gil Johnson passed for 1,026 yards as Mustangs lost only to

Missouri 20–14 and tied TCU 7–7; beat Oregon in Cotton Bowl 21–13. 1966—8–2–0. Won 4 by TD or less and won SWC title; lost to Georgia in Cotton Bowl 24–9. 1968—7–3–0. Chuck Hixson led nation's passers with 3,103 yards and 21 TDs and Jerry Levias caught 80 for 1,131 yards and 8 TDs as SMU scored 283; beat Oklahoma in Bluebonnet Bowl 28–27. 1980 —8–3–0. Eric Dickerson ran for 928 yards and DB John Simmons intercepted 7 passes (returning 2 for TDs); lost to Brigham Young in Holiday Bowl 46–45. 1981—10–1–0. Ron Meyer's last team scored 365 as Dickerson ran for 1,428 yards and 19 TDs and Russell Carter intercepted 7 passes to spark defense; lost only to Texas 9–7 and won SWC title. 1982—10–0–1. Bobby Collins' 1st team scored 347 as Dickerson ran for 1,617 yards and 17 TDs and Craig James ran for 938 yards; tied Arkansas 17–17 in finale, then beat Pittsburgh in Cotton Bowl 7–3. 1983—10–1–0. Ranked 2nd in nation in total defense as Carter starred again, while Reggie Dupard ran for 1,249 yards; lost only to Texas 15–12 but lost to Alabama in Sun Bowl 28–7.

BOWL RECORD

Bluebonnet 1–0–0; Cotton 2–1–1; Dixie Classic 0–1–0; El Paso Charity 1–0–0; Holiday 0–1–0; Rose 0–1–0; Sun 0–2–0.

CONFERENCE TITLES

Southwest 1923, 1926, 1931, 1935, 1940*, 1947, 1948, 1966, 1981, 1982.

TOP 10 AP & UPI RANKING

1947	3	1981	5–U
1948	10	1982	2–2
1966	10–9		

MAJOR RIVALS

SMU has played at least 15 games with Arkansas (26–28–5), Baylor (34–25–7), Missouri (13–7–1), North Texas St. (24–2–1), Rice (38–24–1), Texas (21–38–4), Texas A&M (28–32–6), TCU (31–28–7) and Texas Tech (13–18–0).

COACHES

Dean of SMU coaches was Ray Morrison with record of 84–44–22 for 1915–16 and 1922–34, including 3 conference titles, 2 bowl teams and 4 unbeaten teams. Matty Bell was 79–40–8 for 1935–41 and 1945–49 with 4 conference titles, 3 bowl teams and 2 unbeaten teams. Ron Meyer was 34–32–1 for 1976–81 with 1 conference title and 1 bowl team. Hayden Fry was 3rd in tenure with record of 49–66–1 for 1962–72, including 1 conference title and 3 bowl teams. Bobby Collins was 21–2–1 for 1982–83 with 1 conference title and 2 bowl teams.

MISCELLANEA

First game was 43–0 defeat by TCU in 1915 . . . 1st win was 13–2 over Hendrix same year . . . highest score was 70–0 over Daniel Baker in 1920 . . . highest since W.W. II was 59–27 over Grambling in 1981 . . . biggest margin of victory since W.W. II was 58–0 over Rice in 1978 . . . worst defeat was 146–3 by Rice in 1916 . . . worst since W.W. II was 56–3 by Alabama in 1976 . . . longest unbeaten string of 19 in 1922–24 ended by West Virginia Wesleyan 9–7 in Dixie Classic . . . unbeaten string of 15 in 1946–48 ended by Missouri 20–14 . . . longest winless string of 13 in 1915–16 broken with 20–7 win over Meridian in 1917 . . . consensus All America players were J.C. Wetsel, G, and Bobby Wilson, B, 1935; Doak Walker, B, 1947–49; Kyle Rote, B, 1950; Dick Hightower, C, 1951; John LaGrone, MG, 1966; Jerry Levias, E, 1968; Robert Popelka, DB, 1972; Louie Kelcher, G, 1974; Emanuel Tolbert, WR, 1978; John Simmons, DB, 1980; Eric Dickerson, RB, 1982; and Russell Carter, DB, 1983 . . . Academic All America choices were Dave Powell, E, 1952; Darrell Lafitte, G, 1953; Raymond Berry, E, 1954; David Hawk, G, 1955; Tom Koenig, G, 1957–58; Raymond Schoenke, T, 1962; John LaGrone, MG, 1966; Lynn Thornhill, OG, and Jerry Levias, E, 1968; Cleve Whitener, LB, 1972; and Brian O'Meara, OT, 1983 . . . Doak Walker, HB, won Heisman Trophy in 1948.

Southern Mississippi (Golden Eagles; Black & Gold) (Independent)

NOTABLE TEAMS

1919—4–1–2. Lost only once after 2-year layoff during W.W. I. 1936—7–2–1. Pooley Hubert's last team. 1937—7–3–0. Reed Green's 1st team shut out 7 and lost none by more than 8 points. 1938—7–2–0. Shut out 6 but lost to Mississippi and Northwestern Louisiana (6–0).1941—9–0–1. Outscored foes 246–40, but tied Southwestern Louisiana 0–0. 1946—7–3–0. Shut out 5 and lost 2 by 1 point each. 1947—7–3–0. Lost only to Mississippi St. 14–7 in last 5 games. 1948—7–3–0. Green's last team lost only to Alabama in last 7. 1949—7–3–0. Pie Vann's 1st team scored 299. 1952— 10–1–0. Lost opener to Alabama 20–6 but scored 402 for season; lost to Pacific in Sun Bowl 26–7. 1953—9–1–0. Shut out 5 and lost only to Memphis St. 27–13; lost to Texas-El Paso in Sun Bowl 37–14. 1955—9–1–0. Scored 277 and lost only to UT-Chattanooga 10–0. 1956—7–1–1. Won first 7 before losing to Florida St. 20–19 and tying Alabama 13–13; lost to West Texas St. in Tangerine Bowl 20–13. 1957—8–2–0. Shut out 7 but lost to Houston and Alabama; lost to East Texas St. in Tangerine Bowl 10–9. 1958 —9–0–0. Outscored foes 210–55, shutting out 5. 1961—8–2–0. Lost only to Memphis St. and North Carolina St. (7–6). 1962—9–1–0. Scored 265, losing only to Memphis St. 8–6. 1965—7–2–0. Led nation in total defense and won 3 by less than TD, losing only to Mississippi St. and William & Mary (3–0). 1980—8–3–0. Sammy Winder ran for 996 yards and led nation in scoring with 20 TDs and Reggie Collier ran and passed for 1,732 yards; beat McNeese St. in Independence Bowl 16–14. 1981—9–1–1. Collier ran and passed for 2,009 yards and 18 TDs to lead Golden Eagles past all but Alabama (13–13) and Louisville (13–10 loss); lost to Missouri in Tangerine Bowl 19–17.

BOWL RECORD

Independence 1–0–0; Sun 0–2–0; Tangerine 0–3–0.

CONFERENCE TITLES

Gulf States 1950, 1951.

TOP 10 AP & UPI RANKING

None.

MAJOR RIVALS

Golden Eagles have played at least 15 games with Alabama (3–18–2), Florida St. (7–9–1), Louisiana College (12–3–0), Louisiana Tech (25–12–0), Memphis St. (20–13–1), Mississippi (5–18–0), Mississippi St. (11–8–1), Northwestern Louisiana (9–10–0), Richmond (14–2–0), Southeastern Louisiana (17–3–0), Southwestern Louisiana (26–7–1) and Spring Hill (7–9–1).

COACHES

Dean of Southern Mississippi coaches was Thad (Pie) Vann with record of 139–59–2 for 1949–68, including 2 conference titles, 4 bowl teams and 1 unbeaten team. Reed Green was 59–20–4 for 1937–42 and 1946–48 with 2 unbeaten teams. Other outstanding records were by Pooley Hubert, 24–19–5 for 1932–36; and Bobby Collins, 48–30–2 for 1975–81 with 2 bowl teams.

MISCELLANEA

Won first 2 games against non-collegiate opposition in 1912 . . . highest score since 1937 was 76–0 over Northwestern Louisiana in 1951 . . . worst defeat was 71–7 by Kentucky in 1949 . . . longest unbeaten string of 19 in 1940–46 ended by Auburn 13–12 . . . longest losing string of 9 in 1976 broken with 14–12 win over Memphis St. . . . Southern Mississippi has had no consensus All-America players and no Academic All America selections.

Southwestern Louisiana (Ragin' Cajuns; Vermilion & White) (Independent)

NOTABLE TEAMS

1908—6–0–0. Outscored foes 93–16, shutting out last 4. 1910—6–2–1. Shut out 7 but lost to Louisiana Tech and LSU's "B" team. 1916—7–1–0. T.R. Mobley's 1st team shut out 6 and lost only to LSU 24–0 in opener. 1917 —8–2–0. Scored 338 and shut out 8, losing only to LSU and Spring Hill. 1918—4–1–0. Lost only to Tulane (74–0). 1921—9–2–0. Shut out 6, losing only to Rice and Louisiana Tech. 1923—7–3–0. Won 7 straight after losing first 2. 1925—7–2–0. Chris Cagle scored 108 points to lead Bulldogs to wins over all but LSU and Sam Houston St. (7–2); won last 5. 1938—8–2–1. Johnny Cain's 2nd team shut out 6, losing only to Southern Mississippi and LSU in successive games. 1941—6–2–1. Shut out 5 but lost to Alabama and Louisiana Tech. 1943—5–0–1. Beat all but Arkansas A&M (20–20) under wartime coach Louis Whitman; beat A&M 24–7 in rematch in Oil Bowl on New Year's Day. 1947—6–2–0. George Mitchell's 1st team lost only to Southern Mississippi and Louisiana Tech. 1965—7–3–0. Won 4 of 6 decided by 8 points or less as Edward Pratt intercepted 9 passes; got share of 2nd Gulf States Conference title. 1968—8–2–0. Won 5 by TD or less as Jim Barton scored 13 TDs and Mike McDonald intercepted 8 passes; won Gulf States title. 1970—9-2-0. McDonald picked off 9 passes and Roland Henry ran for 627 yards and 9 TDs as Cajuns lost only to Southern Mississippi 16-14 and Tampa; won 4th and last Gulf States title, but lost to Tennessee St. in Grantland Rice Bowl 26-25. 1976—9-2-0. (7-4-0 by forfeit). Got share of Southland Conference title as Roy Henry passed for 1,709 yards and 18 TDs, Dave Oliver caught 59 for 876 yards and 10 scores, and Ron Irving intercepted 8 passes; lost only to Northwestern Louisiana 7-3 and McNeese St. 20-19 but later forfeited wins over Fresno St. and Cincinnati.

BOWL RECORD

None.

CONFERENCE TITLES

Gulf States 1952*, 1965*, 1968, 1970. Southland 1976*.

TOP 10 AP & UPI RANKING

None.

MAJOR RIVALS

Southwestern Louisiana has played at least 15 games with Arkansas St. (7-10-1), Lamar (15-10-0), Louisiana College (38-16-3), Louisiana St. (0-19-0), Louisiana Tech (28-34-5), McNeese St. (14-17-2), Northeast Louisiana (13-13-0), Northwestern Louisiana (34-33-3), Southern Mississippi (7-26-1), Spring Hill (7-11-0) and Stephen F. Austin (16-2-1).

COACHES

Dean of Southwestern Louisiana coaches was Russ Faulkinberry, 66-62-2 for 1961-73 with 3 conference titles. T. Ray Mobley was 57-49-6 for 1916, 1919 and 1921-30. Other top records were by Clement McNaspy, 26-13-4 for 1909-11, 1913 and 1918; Johnny Cain, 33-19-5 for 1937-41 and 1946; George Mitchell, 18-8-1 for 1947-49; and Raymond Didier, 29-27-2 for 1951-56 with 1 conference title.

MISCELLANEA

First game was 11-10 win over St. Martinville in 1908 . . . 1st win over college varsity foe was 18-0 over Louisiana College in 1910 . . . highest score was 65–14 over Corpus Christi in 1956 . . . biggest margin of victory was 64–0 over Alabama St. in 1946 . . . worst defeat was 96–0 by Tulane in 1912 . . . worst since W.W. II was 54–0 by Alabama in 1946 . . . longest winning streaks of 8 in 1916–17 ended by LSU 20–6 and in 1976 ended by Northwestern Louisiana 7–3 . . . longest losing string of 15 in 1973–74 broken with 21–20 win over UT-Chattanooga . . . Southwestern Louisiana has had no consensus All America players and no Academic All America choices.

Stanford (Cardinal; Cardinal & White) (Pacific-10)

NOTABLE TEAMS

1893—8–0–1. Outscored foes 284–17, shutting out 7; tie was with California 6–6. 1895—4–0–1. Gave up just 2 points before 6–6 tie with California in finale. 1897—4–1–0. Lost only to Reliance Club 10–0. 1900—7–2–1. Fielding Yost's only Stanford team shut out 8, losing only to Alumni 14–0 and Nevada-Reno 6–0. 1902—6–1–0. Lost only to unbeaten California 16–0. 1903—8–0–3. Shut out all but California (6–6). 1904—7–2–1. Shut out 8 and lost to 2 club teams by 5–0 scores. 1905—8–0–0. Outscored foes 138–13 in last year of varsity football preceding 12 years of rugby play. 1923—7–2–0. Outscored foes 284–46, losing only to Southern California 14–7 and California 9–0. 1924—7–0–1. Pop Warner's 1st Stanford team included school's 1st consensus All America player, E Jim Lawson; team won 1st Pacific Coast Conference title despite 20–20 tie with California in finale, but lost to unbeaten national champion Notre Dame in Rose Bowl 27–10. 1925—7–2–0. Ernie Nevers ran for 710 yards to lead team past all but Olympic Club and Washington. 1926—10–0–0. Outscored foes 261–66 and won 1st national championship as Ted Shipkey starred at E; tied unbeaten Alabama in Rose Bowl 7–7. 1927—7–2–1. Lost only to St. Mary's and Santa Clara (13–6); won PCC and beat undefeated Pittsburgh in Rose Bowl 7–6. 1928—8–3–1. Lost 2 by TD margins and other 10–0 to national champion USC as guards Seraphim Post and Don Robesky starred. 1929—9–2–0. Outscored foes 288–53 as Phil Moffatt intercepted 8 passes and starred on punt returns; lost only to USC 7–0 and Santa Clara 13–7. 1930—9–1–1. Shut out 6 as Moffatt picked off 9 passes, again starred on punt returns and scored 10 TDs; tied Minnesota 0–0 and lost only to USC 41–12. 1931—7–2–2. Shut out 6 but lost to national champion USC and California. 1933—8–1–1. C.E. Thornhill's 1st team won 5 by TD or less behind G Bill Corbus, losing only to Washington 6–0 and tying Northwestern 0–0; lost to Columbia in Rose

Bowl 7–0. 1934—9–0–1. Outscored foes 211–14, shutting out 8, and won 2nd straight PCC title behind T Bob Reynolds, E Monk Moscrip and FB Bobby Grayson (10 TDs); tied Santa Clara 7–7 and lost to unbeaten Alabama in Rose Bowl 29–13. 1935—7–1–0. Grayson and Moscrip starred again as Indians (as they were known then) shut out 6 and lost only to UCLA 7–6; beat undefeated SMU in Rose Bowl 7–0. 1940—9–0–0. Clark Shaughnessy's 1st team swept schedule under direction of QB Frankie Albert; won 7th PCC title and beat Nebraska in Rose Bowl 21–13. 1951—9–1–0. Chuck Taylor's 1st team won 4 by TD margin and took PCC behind E Bill McColl and QB Gary Kerkorian; lost finale to California 20–7 and lost to Illinois in Rose Bowl 40–7. 1969—7–2–1. Scored 349 as Jim Plunkett passed for 2,673 yards and 20 TDs and LB Don Parrish led defense; lost successive early season games to Purdue 36–35 and USC 26–24. 1970—8–3–0. Scored 316 behind Heisman winner Plunkett (2,715 yards and 18 TDs passing) and won PAC-8 title; upset unbeaten national champion Ohio St. in Rose Bowl 27–17. 1971—8–3–0. John Ralston's last team lost no game by more than 6 and won PAC-8 again behind Don Bunce (2,265 yards passing) and defensive stars LB Jeff Siemon and DB Benny Barnes (7 interceptions); upset undefeated Michigan in Rose Bowl 13–12. 1977—8–3–0. Won 4 by TD or less as Guy Benjamin led nation's passers with 2,521 yards and 19 TDs, Darrin Nelson ran for 1,069 yards and James Lofton caught 53 passes for 931 yards and 12 TDs; beat LSU in Sun Bowl 24–14.

BOWL RECORD

Bluebonnet 1–0–0; Rose 5–5–1; Sun 1–0–0.

CONFERENCE TITLES

Pacific Coast 1924, 1926, 1927*, 1933*, 1934, 1935*, 1940, 1951. Pacific 8 1970, 1971.

TOP 10 AP & UPI RANKING

1940	2
1951	7–7
1970	8–10
1971	10–U

MAJOR RIVALS

Stanford has played at least 15 games with California (40–36–10), Nevada-Reno (16–1–2), Oregon (33–16–1), Oregon St. (34–15–2), San Jose St. (32–7–1), Santa Clara (22–11–2), Southern California (21–40–3), UCLA (22–29–3), Washington (31–24–4) and Washington St. (20–16–1).

COACHES

Topping Stanford coaches in wins was Glenn (Pop) Warner with record of 71–17–8 for 1924–32, including 3 conference titles, 3 Rose Bowl teams, 2 teams unbeaten in regular season and 1 national champion. He ranks in top 5 in total victories. John Ralston was 55–36–3 for 1963–71 with 2 conference titles and 2 Rose Bowl champions. Other top records were by C.E. Thornhill, 35–25–7 for 1933–39 with 3 conference titles, 3 Rose Bowl teams and 1 team unbeaten in regular season; Charles A. Taylor, 40–29–2 for 1951–57 with 1 conference title and 1 Rose Bowl team; and Jack Christiansen, 30–22–3 for 1972–76. National coach of the year awards went to Clark Shaughnessy in 1940 and Chuck Taylor in 1951.

MISCELLANEA

First game was 10–6 win over Hopkins Academy in 1891 . . . 1st win over college opponent was 14–10 over California same year . . . highest score was 82–0 over Mare Island in 1923 and over UCLA in 1925 . . . highest since W.W. II was 74–20 over Hawaii in 1949 . . . biggest margin of victory since W.W. II was 63–0 over Idaho in 1949 . . . worst defeat was 80–0 by Mare Island in 1918 . . . worst since W.W. II was 72–0 by UCLA in 1954 . . . longest unbeaten string of 15 in 1925–27 ended by St. Mary's 16–0 . . . longest losing string of 19 in 1959–60 broken with 9–7 win over Tulane in 1961 . . . Stanford has had 18 consensus All America players since 1924 . . . multi-year choices were Bill Corbus, G, 1932–33; Bobby Grayson, B, 1934–35; Frank Albert, B, 1940–41; Bill McColl, E, 1950–51; and Ken Margerum, WR, 1979–80 . . . others selected since W.W. II were John Brodie, B, 1956; Jim Plunkett, B, 1970; Jeff Siemon, LB, 1971; Pat Donovan, DL, 1974; Guy Benjamin, QB, 1977; and John Elway, QB, 1982 . . . Academic All America choices were John Sande, C, and Terry Ewing, DB, 1970; Don Stevenson, RB, 1975–76; Guy Benjamin, QB, 1977; Vince Mulroy, WR, and Jim Stephens, OG, 1978; Pat Bowe, TE, Milt McCool, LB, and Joe St. Geme, DB, 1979; Darrin Nelson, RB, 1981; and John Bergren,

DL, 1981–83 . . . Jim Plunkett, QB, won Heisman Trophy in 1970 . . . Stanford ranks in top 20 in all-time winning percentage.

Syracuse (Orangemen; Orange) (Independent)

NOTABLE TEAMS

1890—8–3–0. Two of losses were to Union. 1895—6–2–2. Shut out 6. 1898 —8–2–1. Unbeaten in last 8 after 2 losses to Cornell. 1900—7–2–1. Won last 6. 1901—7–1–0. Shut out 5, losing only to Lafayette 5–0. 1902—6–2–1. Shut out first 5 but lost to Yale and Army. 1905—8–3–0. Shut out 6, losing only to unbeaten Yale in first 7. 1915—9–1–2. Outscored foes 331–16 behind guards Harold White and Chris Schlachter; shut out 9 and lost only to Princeton 3–0. 1917—8–1–1. Lost only to unbeaten Pittsburgh 28–0 as Alfred Cobb starred at T. 1918—5–1–0. Lost to unbeaten Michigan 15–0 but outscored others 141–6 behind linemen Joe Alexander and Louis Usher. 1919—8–3–0. Frank O'Neill's last team won 8 out of first 9 as Alexander starred again. 1920—6–2–1. John F. Meehan's 1st team shut out 5, losing only to Holy Cross 3–0 and Maryland 10–7. 1921—7–2–0. Shut out 6 but lost to Washington & Jefferson and Pitt. 1922—6–1–2. Shut out 5, losing only to Pitt 21–14. 1923—8–1–0. Outscored foes 237–19, shutting out 7 and losing only to Colgate 16–7. 1924—8–2–1. Meehan's last team lost only to West Virginia Wesleyan 7–3 and Southern California. 1925—8–1–1. Shut out first 7 before tying Ohio Wesleyan 3–3 and losing to Colgate 19–6. 1926 —7–2–1. Vic Hanson starred at E as Orange shut out 5 and lost only to Army 27–21 and Georgetown 13–7. 1931—7–1–1. Won first 7 before losing to Colgate 21–7 and tying Columbia 0–0 in Vic Hanson's 2nd year as coach. 1934—6–2–0. Won first 6 behind T James Steen before losing to Colgate and Columbia. 1935—6–1–1. Again won first 6, then lost to Colgate 27–0 and tied Maryland 0–0. 1952—7–2–0. Lost only to Bolling Field 13–12 in opener and to unbeaten national champion Michigan St. (48–7); won Lambert Trophy but lost to Alabama 61–6 in Orange Bowl. 1956—7–1–0. Jim Brown ran for 986 yards and 13 TDs as Orange beat all but Pitt (14–7 loss in 2nd game); lost to TCU in Cotton Bowl 28–27. 1958—8–1–0. Scored 264 behind QB Chuck Zimmerman and T Ron Luciano while losing only to Holy Cross 14–13 in 2nd game; lost to Oklahoma in Orange Bowl 21–6. 1959— 10–0–0. Outscored foes 390–59, leading nation in total offense, rushing offense, scoring average, total defense and rushing defense behind linemen Roger Davis and Robert Yates, E Fred Mautino and soph B Ernie Davis (10

TDs); beat Texas in Cotton Bowl 23–14 to nail down national championship. 1960—7–2–0. Davis ran for 877 yards and 10 TDs as Orange beat all but Pitt and Army (9–6). 1961—7–3–0. Davis won Heisman Trophy, running for 823 yards and 15 TDs and catching 16 passes for 157 yards as Orange lost only 1 by more than 2 points; beat Miami (Fla.) in Liberty Bowl 15–14. 1963—8–2–0. Lost only to Kansas 10–0 and Pitt 35–27. 1964—7–3–0. Led nation in rushing behind C Pat Killorin and FB Jim Nance (951 yards rushing and 13 TDs); 2 of losses by TD or less and lost to LSU in Sugar Bowl 13–10. 1965—7–3–0. Floyd Little led nation in all-purpose running with 1,990 yards and scored 14 TDs behind Killorin and DB Charley Brown sparked defense. 1966—8–2–0. Larry Csonka ran for 1,012 yards as Orange won last 8 after losses to Baylor and UCLA and won 4th Lambert under Ben Schwartzwalder; lost to Tennessee in Gator Bowl 18–12. 1967—8–2–0. Won 4 by TD or less as Csonka ran for 1,127 yards and Tom Coughlin caught 26 passes; lost only to Navy and Penn St.

BOWL RECORD

Cotton 1–1–0; Gator 0–1–0; Independence 1–0–0; Liberty 1–0–0; Orange 0–2–0; Sugar 0–1–0.

CONFERENCE TITLES

None. Won Lambert Trophy in 1952, 1956, 1959 and 1966.

TOP 10 AP & UPI RANKING

1956	8–8
1958	9–10
1959	1–1

MAJOR RIVALS

Syracuse has played at least 15 games with Army (7–9–0), Boston College (14–10–0), Boston U. (12–3–1), Brown (9–3–3), Clarkson (15–0–0), Colgate (28–31–5), Columbia (11–9–4), Cornell (11–23–0), Hobart (25–0–0), Holy Cross (23–5–0), Maryland (13–13–2), Navy (13–8–0), Penn St. (21–35–5), Pittsburgh (13–24–2), Rochester (21–3–1), Syracuse A.A. (11–7–1), Temple (8–8–1) and West Virginia (19–12–0).

COACHES

Dean of Syracuse coaches was Floyd (Ben) Schwartzwalder with record of 153–91–3 for 1949–73, including 4 Lambert Trophy winners, 7 bowl teams and 1 unbeaten national champion. He ranks in top 20 in total coaching victories, and was national coach of the year in 1959. Frank J. O'Neill was 52–19–6 for 1906–07, 1913–15 and 1917–19. Other top records were by John F. Meehan, 35–8–4 for 1920–24; and Victor A. Hanson, 33–21–5 for 1930–36.

MISCELLANEA

First game was 36–0 loss to Rochester in 1889 . . . 1st win was 4–0 over Rochester in 1890 . . . highest score was 144–0 over Manhattan in 1904 . . . highest since W.W. II was 71–0 over Colgate in 1959 . . . worst defeat was 71–0 by Union in 1891 . . . worst since 1900 was 62–0 by Princeton in 1912 . . . worst since W.W. II was 63–7 by Nebraska in 1983 . . . longest winning string of 15 in 1959–60 ended by Pitt 10–0 . . . longest winless string of 13 in 1891–93 broken with 16–14 win over Hamilton . . . losing string of 9 in 1948–49 broken with 20–13 win over Lafayette and in 1972–73 broken with 5–3 win over Holy Cross . . . consensus All America players were Frank Horr, T, 1908; Harold White, E, 1915; Alfred Cobb, T, 1917; Lou Usher, T, 1918; Joe Alexander, G, 1918–19; Pete McRae, E, 1923; Vic Hanson, E, 1926; Jim Brown, B, 1956; Roger Davis, G, 1959; Ernie Davis, B, 1960–61; and Larry Csonka, B, 1967 . . . Academic All America choices were Fred Mautino, E, 1960; Howard Goodman, LB, 1971, and Tony Romano, LB, 1983 . . . Ernie Davis, HB, won Heisman Trophy in 1961 . . . Syracuse ranks in top 25 in all-time victories.

Temple (Owls; Cherry & White) (Independent)

NOTABLE TEAMS

1894—4–1–0. First varsity team lost only to Ursinus 16–0. 1903—4–1–0. Lost to Trenton T.C. 6–0. 1907—4–0–2. Tied St. Joseph's 5–5 and Philadelphia College of Pharmacy 12–12. 1911—6–1–0. Lost to Penn Military 30–0 in 3rd game. 1915—3–1–1. Lost opener to Schuylkill 21–0 and tied Philadelphia Normal 0–0. 1927—7–1–0. Henry Miller's 3rd team scored 351 and shut out 6, losing only to Dartmouth (47–7). 1928—7–1–2. Shut out 7, losing only to Schuylkill 10–7. 1930—7–3–0. Lost only to Villanova 8–7 in first 8 games. 1931—8–1–1. Shut out 5, losing only to Carnegie Tech 19–13 and tying Bucknell 0–0. 1932—5–1–2. Miller's last team lost only to Villanova 7–0 in finale. 1934—7–0–2. Pop Warner's 2nd Temple team outscored foes 206–37, tying Indiana 6–6 and Bucknell 0–0; lost to Tulane in Sugar Bowl 20–14. 1935—7–3–0. Lost all 3 by TD or less. 1941—7–2–0. Lost only to Boston College and Michigan St. 1945—7–1–0. Lost to Penn St. 27–0, but outscored others 198–24. 1964—7–2–0. Scored 247 but lost to Connecticut and Bucknell (31–28). 1967—7–2–0. Won 4 by TD or less but lost to Buffalo and Dayton. 1970—7–3–0. Wayne Hardin's 1st team won 3 of 5 decided by TD or less. 1971—6–2–1. Scored 248 as Nick Mike-Mayer led nation in FGs with 12; lost only to Boston College and West Virginia. 1973—9–1–0. Scored 353 as Tom Sloan ran for 1,036 yards; lost only to Boston College (45–0 in 2nd game). 1974—8–2–0. Steve Joachim led nation in total offense (2,227 yards) and passing efficiency (1,950 yards and 20 TDs) and Henry Hynoski ran for 1,006 yards as Owls scored 335 and lost only to Cincinnati 22–20 and Pitt. 1979—9–2–0. Scored 371 as Mark Bright ran for 1,036 yards and Gerald Lucear caught 45 passes for 964 yards and 13 TDs; lost only to Pitt 10–9 and Penn St. 22–7, and beat California in Garden State Bowl 28–17.

BOWL RECORD

Garden State 1–0–0; Sugar 0–1–0.

CONFERENCE TITLES

Mid-Atlantic 1967.

TOP 10 AP & UPI RANKING

None.

MAJOR RIVALS

Temple has played at least 15 games with Boston College (3–11–2), Boston U. (8–9–1), Bucknell (16–20–8), Delaware (14–20–0), Holy Cross (9–12–2), Penn St. (3–18–1), Syracuse (8–8–1), Villanova (12–13–2) and West Virginia (10–11–0).

COACHES

Dean of Temple coaches was Wayne Hardin with record of 80–52–3 for 1970–82, including 1 bowl champion. Henry J. Miller was 50–15–8 for 1925–32. Other top records were by Glenn (Pop) Warner, 31–18–9 for 1933–38 with 1 bowl team and 1 team unbeaten in regular season; and George Makris, 45–44–4 for 1960–69 with 1 conference title.

MISCELLANEA

First game was 14–6 win over Philadelphia Dental College in 1894 . . . highest score was 110–0 over Blue Ridge in 1927 . . . highest since W.W. II was 82–28 over Bucknell in 1966 . . . biggest margin of victory since W.W. II was 56–0 over Holy Cross in 1974 . . . worst defeat was 96–0 by Franklin & Marshall in 1899 . . . worst since 1900 was 76–0 by Pitt in 1977 . . . longest winning streak of 14 in 1973–74 ended by Cincinnati 22–20 . . . longest losing string of 21 in 1957–59 broken with 26–13 win over Kings Point in 1960 . . . Temple has had no consensus All America players and no Academic All America choices.

Tennessee (Volunteers, Vols; Orange & White) (SEC)

NOTABLE TEAMS

1897—4–1–0. Lost to North Carolina 16–0; shut out others. 1899—5–2–0. Shut out last 4 after successive losses to Virginia Tech and unbeaten Sewanee. 1902—6–2–0. Lost only to Vanderbilt and Clemson as B Nash Buckingham starred. 1907—7–2–1. Shut out 6, losing only to Georgia Tech 6–4 and Alabama 5–0. 1908—7–2–0. B Walker Leach and G N.W. Dougherty led Vols to wins over all but Vanderbilt and Alabama (5–0 loss). 1914—9–0–0. Outscored foes 374–37 and won Southern Intercollegiate A.A. title behind linemen Farmer Kelly and Mush Kerr and B Russ Lindsay. 1916—8–0–1. Shut out 6, including 0–0 tie with Kentucky in finale, behind E Graham Vowell and B Buck Hatcher. 1920—7–2–0. Shut out 6 as Hatcher starred at T. 1921—6–2–1. M.B. Banks' 1st team shut out 6 and lost only to Dartmouth and Vanderbilt. 1922—8–2–0. Roe Campbell scored 10 TDs to lead Vols to wins over all but Georgia (7–3 loss) and Vanderbilt. 1926—8–1–0. Bob Neyland's 1st team shut out 6 and lost only to Vanderbilt 20–3 behind

G John Barnhill. 1927—8–0–1. Scored 245 and shut out 6 as Barnhill and B Dick Dodson starred; tie was with Vanderbilt 7–7. 1928—9–0–1. Won 4 by TD or less behind B Gene McEver (13 TDs); tie was 0–0 with Kentucky. 1929—9–0–1. Neyland's 3rd straight unbeaten team outscored foes 330–13, shutting out 8, as McEver scored 21 TDs and became Vols' 1st consensus All America; tie was with Kentucky 6–6. 1930—9–1–0. Shut out 7 and lost only to unbeaten Alabama 18–6 behind QB Bobby Dodd and G Harry Thayer. 1931—8–0–1. Shut out 6 as Herman Hickman starred at G and McEver returned for sr. year and scored 10 TDs; tied Kentucky 6–6 in finale, then beat New York U. 13–0 in New York City Charity game. 1932— 9–0–1. Neyland's 5th unbeaten team shut out 6 and won Southern Conference title behind B Beattie Feathers and E Van Rayburn; tie was with Vanderbilt 0–0. 1933—7–3–0. Feathers ran for 663 yards and scored 13 TDs as Vols lost no game by more than 8 points. 1934—8–2–0. Murray Warmath starred at G as Vols lost only to unbeaten Alabama 13–6 and to Fordham 13–12. 1936—6–2–2. Phil Dickens starred in backfield as team was unbeaten in last 7. 1938—10–0–0. Outscored foes 276–16, shutting out 7 and winning 1st SEC title behind E Bowden Wyatt, HB George Cafego and G Bob Suffridge; beat undefeated Oklahoma in Orange Bowl 17–0. 1939—10–0–0. Blanked foes 212–0 to lead nation in scoring defense as Cafego and Suffridge starred again along with G Ed Molinski; lost to Southern California in Rose Bowl 14–0. 1940—10–0–0. Neyland's 8th unbeaten team outscored foes 319–26, shutting out 8 to again lead in scoring defense and winning 3rd straight SEC title behind Suffridge and Molinski; lost to unbeaten Boston College in Sugar Bowl 19–13. 1941—8–2–0. With Neyland in military service, John Barnhill coached team to 6 straight wins after early losses to unbeaten Duke and Alabama. 1942—8–1–1. Again won last 6 after 0–0 tie with South Carolina and 8–0 loss to Alabama; beat undefeated Tulsa in Sugar Bowl 14–7. 1944—7–0–1. Beat all but Alabama (0–0) following year's layoff caused by W.W. II; lost to Southern California in Rose Bowl 25–0. 1945— 8–1–0. Barnhill's last team scored 238 and lost only to unbeaten Alabama 25–7. 1946—9–1–0. Won 6 by TD or less and lost only to Wake Forest 19–6 in Neyland's 1st post-war season; T Dick Huffman led team to share of SEC title, but Vols lost to Rice in Orange Bowl 8–0. 1949—7–2–1. Lost only to Duke and Georgia Tech as J.W. Sherrill intercepted 12 passes. 1950— 10–1–0. Scored 315 and led nation in pass defense as Bert Rechichar picked off 7 passes and Gordon Polofsky 6; lost only to Mississippi St. 7–0 in 2nd game and beat Texas in Cotton Bowl 20–14. 1951—10–0–0. Scored 373 and shut out 5 to win national championship behind linemen Ted Daffer and Bill Pearman and HB Hank Lauricella (881 yards rushing); Harold Payne scored

14 TDs and Andy Kozar 11 during season, but Vols lost to Maryland in Sugar Bowl 28–13. 1952—8–1–1. Neyland's last team led nation in total defense behind G John Michels and T Doug Atkins, losing only to Duke 7–0 in 2nd game and tying Kentucky 14–14; lost to Texas in Cotton Bowl 16–0. 1956—10–0–0. Bowden Wyatt's 2nd team outscored foes 268–75 behind HB Johnny Majors; won SEC but lost to Baylor in Sugar Bowl 13–7. 1957 —7–3–0. Two of losses by TD margin; beat Texas A&M in Gator Bowl 3–0. 1960—6–2–2. Lost successive games to Georgia Tech and Mississippi. 1965 —7–1–2. Doug Dickey's 2nd team lost only to Mississippi 14–13 as Frank Emanuel starred at LB; beat Tulsa in Bluebonnet Bowl 27–6. 1966—7–3–0. No loss by more than 7 points as LB Paul Naumoff led defense, Ron Widby averaged nearly 44 yards a punt, Dewey Warren passed for 1,716 yards and 18 TDs and Johnny Mills caught 48 passes for 725 yards; beat Syracuse in Gator Bowl 18–12. 1967—9–1–0. Won SEC behind C Bob Johnson, WR Richmond Flowers (41 receptions for 585 yards), Walter Chadwick (11 TDs) and Mike Jones (7 interceptions); lost only to UCLA 20–16 in opener, then to Oklahoma in Orange Bowl 26–24. 1968—8–1–1. Lost only to Auburn 28–14 and tied Georgia 17–17 behind G Charles Rosenfelder, LB Steve Kiner and DB Bill Young (9 interceptions); lost to Texas in Cotton Bowl 36–13. 1969—9–1–0. Doug Dickey's last team scored 315 and won SEC behind Kiner, G Chip Kell, Curt Watson (807 yards rushing), Gary Kreis (38 receptions for 609 yards) and Tim Priest (7 interceptions); lost only to Mississippi (38–0), then to Florida in Gator Bowl 14–13. 1970— 10–1–0. Bill Battle's 1st team scored 336 behind Kell, Watson, Bobby Scott (1,697 yards passing) and George Hunt (10 FGs and 42–43 extra points) while Priest intercepted 9 passes; lost only to Auburn 36–23 and beat Air Force in Sugar Bowl 34–13. 1971—9–2–0. Won last 6 behind B Bobby Majors and LB Jackie Walker after losses to Auburn 10–9 and unbeaten Alabama; beat Arkansas in Liberty Bowl 14–13. 1972—9–2–0. Haskel Stanback ran for 890 yards and 13 TDs, Ricky Townsend kicked 12 FGs and 31–31 extra points, and Conrad Graham intercepted 7 passes as Vols lost only to Auburn 10–6 and Alabama 17–10; beat LSU in Bluebonnet Bowl 24–17. 1973—8–3–0. Won 5 by TD or less as Stanback and Jimmy Wade paced running attack; lost to Texas Tech in Gator Bowl 28–19. 1983— 8–3–0. Johnnie Jones ran for 1,116 yards and DL Reggie White anchored defense as Vols lost only to Mississippi 13–10 in last 8; beat Maryland in Florida Citrus Bowl 30–23.

BOWL RECORD

Bluebonnet 2–1–0; Cotton 1–2–0; Florida Citrus 1–0–0; Garden State 1–0–0; Gator 2–2–0; Liberty 2–0–0; New York Charity 1–0–0; Orange 1–2–0; Peach 0–1–0; Rose 0–2–0; Sugar 2–3–0.

CONFERENCE TITLES

Southern Intercollegiate A.A. 1914. Southern 1932. Southeastern 1938, 1939*, 1940, 1946*, 1951*, 1956, 1967, 1969.

TOP 10 AP & UPI RANKING

1938	2	1946	7	1956	2–2	1970	4–4
1939	2	1950	4–3	1965	7–7	1971	9–9
1940	4	1951	1–1	1967	2–2	1972	8–U
1942	7	1952	8–8	1968	U–7		

MAJOR RIVALS

Vols have played at least 15 games with Alabama (25–34–7), Auburn (15–19–1), Clemson (11–5–2), Duke (11–12–2), Florida (13–4–0), Georgia (8–9–2), Georgia Tech (22–16–1), Kentucky (48–22–9), LSU (15–2–3), Maryville (25–1–1), Mississippi (31–18–1), Mississippi St. (19–13–1), North Carolina (20–10–1), Sewanee (12–10–0), Tennessee-Chattanooga (36–2–2) and Vanderbilt (46–26–5).

COACHES

Dean of Tennessee coaches was Robert R. Neyland with record of 173–31–12 for 1926–34, 1936–40 and 1946–52, including 6 conference titles, 8 bowl teams, 9 teams unbeaten in regular season and 1 national champion. He ranks in top 20 in total coaching victories and in top 10 in all-time winning percentage. Bill Battle was 59–22–2 for 1970–76 with 5 bowl teams (4 winners). Other top records were by Z.G. Clevenger, 26–15–2 for 1911–15 with 1 perfect record; M.B. Banks, 27–15–3 for 1921–25; John Barnhill, 32–5–2 for 1941–42 and 1944–45 with 2 bowl teams and 1 team unbeaten in regular season; Bowden Wyatt, national coach of the year in 1956, was 49–29–4 for 1955–62 with 1 SEC title, 2 bowl teams and 1 team unbeaten in regular season; Doug Dickey, 46–15–4 for 1964–69 with 2 SEC titles and 5 bowl teams; and Johnny Majors, 44–35–2 for 1977–83 with 4 bowl teams.

MISCELLANEA

First game was 24–0 loss to Sewanee in 1891 . . . 1st win was 25–0 over Maryville in 1892 . . . highest score was 104–0 over American U. in 1905 . . . highest since W.W. II was 68–0 over Tennessee Tech in 1951 . . . worst defeat was 70–0 by Duke in 1893 . . . worst since 1900 was 51–0 by Alabama in 1906 and by Vanderbilt in 1909 . . . Vanderbilt also won 51–7 in 1923 . . . worst defeat since W.W. II was 44–0 by Georgia in 1981 . . . Mississippi won 44–20 in 1979 . . . longest unbeaten string of 33 in 1926–30 ended by Alabama 18–6 . . . unbeaten string of 28 in 1930–33 ended by Duke 10–2 . . . winning streak of 23 in 1937–39 ended by Southern California 14–0 in Rose Bowl . . . winning streak of 20 in 1950–51 ended by Maryland 28–13 in Sugar Bowl . . . longest losing string of 7 in 1892–93 broken with 32–0 win over Maryville . . . Tennessee has had 20 consensus All America players since 1929 . . . multi-year choices were Steve Kiner, LB, 1968–69; Chip Kell, G, 1969–70; and Larry Sievers, E, 1975–76 . . . unanimous single-year choices were Bob Suffridge, G, 1940; Hank Lauricella, B, 1951; John Majors, B, 1956; Bob Johnson, C, 1967; Charles Rosenfelder, G, 1968; Bobby Majors, DB, 1971; and Reggie White, DL, 1983 . . . others since W.W. II were Dick Huffman, T, 1946; Frank Emanuel, LB, 1965; Paul Naumoff, LB, 1966; and Roland James, DB, 1979 . . . Academic All America choices were Charles Radar, T, 1956; Bill Johnson, G, 1957; Mack Gentry, DT, 1965; Bob Johnson, C, 1967; Tim Priest, DB, 1970; Timothy Irwin, T, 1980; and Mike Terry, DL, 1982 . . . Steve DeLong, T, won Outland Trophy in 1964 . . . Tennessee ranks in top 15 in all-time winning percentage and in total victories.

Texas (Longhorns; Orange & White) (Southwest)

NOTABLE TEAMS

1894—6–1–0. Outscored first 6 foes 191–0 but lost finale to Missouri 28–0. 1895—5–0–0. Blanked opponents 96–0. 1897—6–2–0. Won last 5. 1898— 5–1–0. Lost only to Sewanee 4–0 and blanked others 136–0. 1899—6–2–0. Shut out 5, losing only to unbeaten Sewanee and to Vanderbilt 6–0. 1900 —6–0–0. Outscored foes 113–13. 1901—8–2–1. Shut out 7. 1903—5–1–2. Lost only to Haskell 6–0. 1904—6–2–0. Scored 219 but lost to Haskell 4–0 and Chicago. 1906—9–1–0. Shut out 7, losing only to Vanderbilt (45–0). 1907—6–1–1. Tied Texas A&M 0–0 in opener and lost only to Missouri 5–4.

1910—6–2–0. Lost close ones to Texas A&M 14–8 and Oklahoma 3–0. 1911 —5–2–0. Dave Allerdice's 1st team lost only to Sewanee 6–5 and unbeaten Oklahoma 6–3. 1912—7–1–0. Scored 201, losing only to Oklahoma 21–6. 1913—7–1–0. Scored 250 but lost finale to unbeaten Notre Dame 30–7. 1914—8–0–0. Outscored foes 358–21, shutting out 5 as Len Barrell scored 121 points on 14 TDs, a FG and 34 extra points. 1916—7–2–0. Lost successive mid-season games to Baylor 7–3 and Missouri 3–0, but won 1st Southwest Conference title. 1918—9–0–0. Outscored foes 194–14, shutting out 6 and winning SWC. 1920—9–0–0. Outscored foes 282–13, shutting out 6 and winning 3rd conference title. 1921—6–1–1. Outscored foes 268–27, blanking 6; lost only to Vanderbilt 20–0 and tied Texas A&M 0–0. 1922— 7–2–0. Ivan Robertson kicked 9 FGs and scored 3 TDs as Longhorns lost only to Vanderbilt and Texas A&M (14–7). 1923—8–0–1. E.J. Stewart's 1st team outscored foes 241–21, shutting out 7; tie was with Baylor 7–7. 1925 —6–2–1. Shut out 5 but again lost to Vanderbilt and Texas A&M. 1927— 6–2–1. Lost to SMU and Texas A&M in Clyde Littlefield's 1st year. 1928— 7–2–0. Shut out 5 and lost only to Vanderbilt 13–12 and SMU 6–2 as Rufus King led team to SWC title. 1930—8–1–1. Shut out 7 and won SWC, losing only to Rice 6–0 and tying Centenary 0–0. 1932—8–2–0. Bohn Hilliard scored 12 TDs to lead Longhorns to wins over all but Centenary (13–6 loss) and TCU. 1934—7–2–1. Hilliard starred again as team lost only to Centenary and Rice. 1940—8–2–0. Pete Layden ran and passed for 1,077 yards and handled the punting as Texas beat all but Rice and SMU. 1941—8–1–1. Outscored foes 338–55 behind Jack Crain (11 TDs, a FG and 23 extra points), Layden, E Mal Kutner and G Chal Daniel; led nation in scoring but tied Baylor 7–7 and lost to TCU 14–7 in successive games. 1942—8–2–0. Led nation in total defense and Roy Dale McKay ran and passed for 1,193 yards and punted 42 times for a 39-yard average as Longhorns lost only to Northwestern 3–0 and TCU 13–7; won SWC and beat Georgia Tech 14–7 in 1st Cotton Bowl appearance. 1943—7–1–0. Ralph Ellsworth ran for 507 yards and Joe Parker starred at E as Texas lost only to Southwestern 14–7 in 2nd game; tied Randolph Field in Cotton Bowl 7–7. 1945—9–1–0. Won 3rd conference title in 4 years as Hub Bechtol caught 25 passes and became Longhorns' 1st consensus All America player; lost only to Rice 7–6 in midseason, and beat Missouri in Cotton Bowl 40–27. 1946—8–2–0. Dana Bible's last team scored 290 as Bobby Layne ran and passed for 1,460 yards and Bechtol starred again; lost to Rice 18–13 and TCU 14–0. 1947—9–1–0. Blair Cherry's 1st team scored 265 as Layne passed for 965 yards and Byron Gillory scored 8 TDs; lost only to unbeaten SMU 14–13 and beat Alabama in Sugar Bowl 27–7. 1948—6–3–1. Ray Borneman ran for 700 yards to lead

Longhorns to Orange Bowl despite losses to North Carolina, Oklahoma and SMU; lost to Georgia in bowl 41–28. 1950—9–1–0. Cherry's last team won SWC behind G Bud McFadin, Byron Townsend (841 yards rushing and 14 TDs) and Ben Proctor (24 pass catches for 453 yards); lost only to unbeaten national champion Oklahoma 14–13, then to Tennessee in Cotton Bowl 20–14. 1951—7–3–0. Ed Price's 1st team won 3 by TD or less as Gib Dawson ran for 671 yards and 9 TDs. 1952—8–2–0. Scored 262 behind G Harley Sewell and backs Billy Quinn (13 TDs) and James (T) Jones (1,018 yards passing); lost to Notre Dame and Oklahoma in early games, but won SWC and beat Tennessee in Cotton Bowl 16–0. 1953—7–3–0. E Carlton Massey starred as Longhorns won 5 of last 6 to gain share of SWC title. 1957 —6–3–1. Darrell Royal's 1st team lost only to SMU 19–12 in last 6, but lost to Mississippi in Sugar Bowl 39–7. 1958—7–3–0. Won 5 by less than TD. 1959—9–1–0. Won 4 by TD or less and got share of SWC, losing only to TCU 14–9; lost to unbeaten national champion Syracuse in Cotton Bowl 23–14. 1960—7–3–0. Lost no game by more than 7; tied Alabama in Bluebonnet Bowl 3–3. 1961—9–1–0. Scored 291 behind T Don Talbert and B Jimmy Saxton (846 yards rushing), losing only to TCU 6–0; got share of SWC and beat Mississippi in Cotton Bowl 12–7. 1962—9–0–1. Won 3 by TD or less and tied Rice 14–14 as Johnny Treadwell starred at G; lost to LSU in Cotton Bowl 13–0. 1963—10–0–0. Scored 215 and won 5 by TD or less behind T Scott Appleton and B Tommy Ford (738 yards rushing); won 3rd straight SWC title, then beat Navy in Cotton Bowl 28–6 to win 1st national championship. 1964—9–1–0. Ernie Koy (as runner and punter) and Tommy Nobis (on defense) led team to wins over all but unbeaten national champion Arkansas (14–13 loss); beat Alabama in Orange Bowl 21–17. 1968—8–1–1. Scored 343 behind Chris Gilbert (1,132 yards rushing and 13 TDs), James Street (1,099 yards passing) and Charles Speyrer (26 receptions for 449 yards), losing only to Texas Tech 31–22 in 2nd game after tying Houston 20–20 in opener; beat Tennessee in Cotton Bowl 36–13. 1969—10–0–0. Scored 414 and led nation in rushing behind tackles Bob McKay and Bobby Wuensch, B Jim Bertelsen (740 yards rushing and 13 TDs) and Speyrer (30 receptions for 492 yards); beat Notre Dame in Cotton Bowl 21–17 to wrap up national championship. 1970—10–0–0. Royal's 4th unbeaten team scored 412 to lead nation and again led in rushing behind Wuensch and Steve Worster (898 yards rushing and 14 TDs) while DE Bill Atessis led defense; lost to Notre Dame in Cotton Bowl 24–11 but still got share of national title. 1971—8–2–0. Scored 275 and won 4th straight SWC title behind T Jerry Sisemore, Bertelsen (879 yards rushing) and QB Donnie Wigginton (14 TDs); won last 5 but lost to Penn St. in Cotton Bowl 30–6. 1972—9–1–0.

Roosevelt Leaks ran for 1,099 yards and Alan Lowry ran for 11 TD's behind Sisemore as Longhorns lost only to Oklahoma 27–0; beat Alabama in Cotton Bowl 17–13. **1973—8-2-0.** Scored 364 and won 6th straight SWC title behind C Bill Wyman and Leaks (1,415 yards rushing and 14 TDs); won last 6 but lost to Nebraska in Cotton Bowl 19–3. **1974—8-3-0.** Again scored 364 as freshman Earl Campbell ran for 928 yards and Doug English and Bob Simmons starred at T; lost to Auburn in Gator Bowl 27–3. **1975—9-2-0.** Scored 363 behind Simmons, Campbell (1,118 yards rushing and 13 TDs) and Alfred Jackson (32 pass receptions for 596 yards), losing only to national champion Oklahoma and Texas A&M; beat Colorado in Bluebonnet Bowl 38–21. **1977—11-0-0.** Earl Campbell led nation in rushing (1,744 yards), scoring (19 TDs) and all-purpose running (1,855 yards) and won Heisman while DT Brad Shearer led defense; Fred Akers' 1st team scored 431 but lost to national champion Notre Dame in Cotton Bowl 38–10. **1978—8-3-0.** Johnny (Lam) Jones caught 25 passes for 446 yards, Russell Erxleben kicked 13 FGs and 24 extra points, and DT Steve McMichael and DB Johnnie Johnson sparked defense; beat Maryland in Sun Bowl 42–0. **1979—9-2-0.** A.J. (Jam) Jones ran for 918 yards, "Lam" Jones caught 36 passes for 535 yards and Johnson and McMichael again led defense as Longhorns lost only to Arkansas 17–14 and Texas A&M 13–7; lost to Washington in Sun Bowl 14–7. **1981—9-1-1.** "Jam" Jones ran for 834 yards behind T Terry Tausch, while DT Kenneth Sims led defense as Longhorns lost only to Arkansas (42–11) and tied Houston 14–14; beat Alabama in Cotton Bowl 14–12. **1982—9-2-0.** Darryl Clark ran for 1,049 yards and Texas won last 6 after losses to Oklahoma 28–22 and unbeaten SMU; lost to North Carolina in Sun Bowl 26–10. **1983—11-0-0.** Led nation in total defense behind DB Jerry Gray and LB Jeff Leiding while lineman Doug Dawson led offense; lost to Georgia in Cotton Bowl 10–9.

BOWL RECORD

Bluebonnet 2–1–1; Cotton 9–8–1; Gator 0–1–0; Orange 2–0–0; Sugar 1–1–0; Sun 1–2–0.

CONFERENCE TITLES

Southwest 1916, 1918*, 1920, 1928, 1930, 1942, 1943, 1945, 1950, 1952, 1953*, 1959*, 1961*, 1962, 1963, 1968*, 1969, 1970, 1971, 1972, 1973, 1975*, 1977, 1983.

TOP 10 AP & UPI RANKING

1941	4	1959	4–4	1969	1–1	1978	9–9
1945	10	1961	3–4	1970	3–1	1981	2–4
1947	5	1962	4–4	1972	3–5	1983	5–5
1950	3–2	1963	1–1	1973	U–8		
1952	10–U	1964	5–5	1975	6–7		
1953	U–8	1968	3–5	1977	4–5		

MAJOR RIVALS

Texas has played at least 15 games with Arkansas (49–16–0), Baylor (54–15–4), LSU (8–7–1), Oklahoma (47–28–3), Rice (49–20–1), SMU (38–21–4), Southwestern (20–2–0), Texas A&M (63–22–5), TCU (48–19–1), Texas Tech (27–6–0) and Tulane (15–1–1).

COACHES

Dean of Texas coaches was Darrell Royal with record of 167–47–5 for 1957–76, including 11 conference titles, 16 bowl teams, 4 teams unbeaten in regular season and 3 national champions. He was national coach of the year in 1961, 1963 and 1970. He ranks in top 15 in total coaching victories. Fred Akers was 66–17–1 for 1977–83 with 2 conference titles, 7 bowl teams and 2 teams unbeaten in regular season. Dana X. Bible was 63–31–3 for 1937–46 with 3 conference titles and 3 Cotton Bowl teams. Other top records were by Dave Allerdice, 33–7–0 for 1911–15 with 1 unbeaten team; E.J. Stewart, 24–9–3 for 1923–26 with 1 unbeaten team; Clyde Littlefield, 44–18–6 for 1927–33 with 2 conference titles; Blair Cherry, 32–10–1 for 1947–50 with 1 conference title and 3 bowl teams; and Ed Price, 33–27–1 for 1951–56 with 2 conference titles and 1 Cotton Bowl champion.

MISCELLANEA

First game was 18–16 win over Dallas in 1893 . . . 1st win over college foe was 38–0 over Texas A&M in 1894 . . . highest score was 92–0 over Daniel Baker in 1915 . . . highest since W.W. II was 81–16 over TCU in 1974 . . . biggest margin since W.W. II was 76–0 over Colorado in 1946 . . . worst defeat was 68–0 by Chicago in 1904 . . . worst since W.W. II was 46–0 by TCU in 1956 . . . highest against Texas since W.W. II was 52–13 by Oklahoma in 1973 . . . longest winning streak of 30 in 1968–70 ended by Notre Dame 24–11 in Cotton Bowl . . . winning streak of 15 in 1963–64 ended by Arkansas 14–13 . . . longest losing string of 10 in 1937–38 broken with

7–6 win over Texas A&M . . . Texas has had 26 consensus All America players since 1945 . . . multi-year choices were Hubert Bechtol, E, 1945–46; Jerry Sisemore, T, 1971–72; Johnnie Johnson, DB, 1978–79; and Kenneth Sims, DL, 1980–81 . . . others selected unanimously for single years were Bud McFadin, G, 1950; Jimmy Saxton, B, 1961; John Treadwell, G, 1962; Scott Appleton, T, 1963; Bill Wyman, C, 1973; Earl Campbell, RB, and Brad Shearer, DL, 1977; and Steve McMichael, DL, 1979 . . . other choices since 1970 were Bobby Wuensch, T, Steve Worster, B, and Bill Atessis, DE, 1970; Roosevelt Leaks, B, 1973; Bob Simmons, T, 1975; Terry Tausch, OL, 1981; and Doug Dawson, OL, Jeff Leiding, LB, and Jerry Gray, DB, 1983 . . . Academic All America selections were Maurice Doke, G, 1959; Johnny Treadwell, G, 1961–62; Pat Culpepper, B, 1962; Duke Carlisle, B, 1963; Gene Bledsoe, OT, 1966; Mike Perrin, DE, 1967; Corby Robertson, LB, 1967–68; Scott Henderson, LB, 1968–70; Bill Zapalac, DE, 1969–70; Steve Oxley, OT, and Mike Bayer, DB, 1972; Tommy Keel, S, 1972–73; and Doug Dawson, OG, 1983 . . . Earl Campbell, HB, won Heisman Trophy in 1977 . . . Outland Trophy winners were Scott Appleton, T, 1963; Tommy Nobis, LB, 1965; and Brad Shearer, DT, 1977 . . . Kenneth Sims, DT, won Lombardi Trophy in 1981 . . . Texas ranks in top 5 in all-time winning percentage and top 10 in total victories.

Texas A&M (Aggies; Maroon & White) (Southwest)

NOTABLE TEAMS

1902—7–0–2. Shut out 7, including 0–0 ties with Trinity and Texas; beat Texas 11–0 in return match for 1st win over Longhorns. 1905—7–2–0. Won first 6. 1906—6–1–0. Outscored first 6 foes 170–18 but lost finale to Texas 24–0. 1907—6–1–1. Tied Texas 0–0 in 2nd game and lost finale to Longhorns 11–6. 1909—7–0–1. Charles Moran's 1st team shut out 6; tie was with TCU 0–0. 1910—8–1–0. Shut out 5, losing only to Arkansas 5–0. 1911— 6–1–0. Shut out 5, losing only to Texas 6–0. 1912—8–1–0. Outscored foes 366–26, shutting out 6 and losing only to Kansas St. 13–10. 1914—6–1–1. Moran's last team lost only to Haskell 10–0. 1915—6–2–0. Won first 5 but lost 7–0 games to Rice and Mississippi St. 1917—8–0–0. Dana Bible's 1st team blanked foes 270–0 and won 1st Southwest Conference title behind linemen Ox Ford and E.S. Wilson and backs Rip Collins and Jack Mahan. 1918—6–1–0. Lost only to unbeaten Texas 7–0. 1919—10–0–0. Blanked foes 275–0 and won SWC as Wilson and Mahan starred again along with linemen W.E. Murrah and C.R. Drake and HB R.G. Higginbotham. 1920 —6–1–1. Outscored foes 229–7, tying LSU 0–0 and losing finale to unbeaten Texas 7–3. 1921—5–1–2. Lost only to LSU 6–0 and won 3rd SWC title behind Murrah, E T.F. Wilson and B Sam Sanders; beat undefeated Centre in Dixie Classic 22–14. 1924—7–2–1. Shut out 6, losing only to Baylor 15–7 and Texas 7–0. 1925—7–1–1. Shut out 5 and won SWC behind backs Joel Hunt and W.W. Wilson and linemen L.G. Dietrich and Barlow Irvin; lost only to TCU 3–0 and tied Sewanee 6–6. 1927—8–0–1. Bible's 3rd unbeaten team and 5th conference champion outscored foes 262–32 as Hunt (19 TDs) starred again; tie was with TCU 0–0. 1931—7–3–0. Shut out 5 and lost none by more than 8 points. 1936—8–3–1. Homer Norton's 3rd team won 3 by TD or less as linemen Joe Routt, Charles DeWare and Roy Young starred. 1939—10–0–0. Led nation in total defense and rushing defense while outscoring opponents 198–18 behind T Joe Boyd and FB John Kimbrough; won national championship and beat undefeated Tulane in Sugar Bowl 14–13. 1940—8–1–0. Again led nation in rushing defense as Kimbrough starred again along with G Marshall Robnett and E James Sterling; lost only to Texas 7–0 in finale, then beat Fordham in Cotton Bowl 13–12. 1941—9–1–0. Shut out 6 and won 3rd straight SWC title behind C Bill Sibley (who intercepted 10 passes on defense) and Sterling; lost only to Texas (23–0), then to Alabama in Cotton Bowl 29–21. 1943—7–1–1. Shut out 6 but lost finale to Texas 27–13; lost to LSU in Orange Bowl 19–14. 1955—7–2–1. Bear Bryant's 1st A&M team lost only to UCLA in opener and Texas in finale as Gene Stallings starred at E. 1956—9–0–1. Won SWC behind linemen Charles Krueger and Dennis Goehring and backs John David Crow (10 TDs) and Jack Pardee; tie was with Houston 14–14. 1957—8–2–0. Bryant's last A&M team again starred Crow (Heisman Trophy winner) and Krueger along with E Bobby Marks; lost last 2 games to Rice 7–6 and Texas 9–7, then lost to Tennessee in Gator Bowl 3–0. 1967—6–4–0. Lost first 4 (3 by less than TD) but then swept 6 straight to take SWC title as LB Bill Hobbs starred; beat Alabama in Cotton Bowl 20–16. 1974—8–3–0. Emory Bellard's 3rd team won 7 of first 8 as Pat Thomas starred at DB. 1975—10–1–0. Led nation in total defense and rushing defense behind Thomas, LB Ed Simonini and LB Garth TenNapel; lost only to Arkansas 31–6 in finale, then to Southern California in Liberty Bowl 20–0. 1976—9–2–0. Scored 290 as George Woodard ran for 1,153 yards and 17 TDs and Tony Franklin led nation with 17 FGs while LB Robert Jackson and S Lester Hayes sparked defense; won last 6, then beat Florida in Sun Bowl 37–14. 1977—8–3–0. Scored 322 behind Woodard (1,107 yards and 13 TDs), Curtis Dickey (1,510 yards in all-purpose running) and Franklin (16 FGs); lost to Southern California in Bluebonnet Bowl 47–21.

BOWL RECORD

Bluebonnet 0–1–0; Cotton 2–1–0; Dixie Classic 1–0–0; Gator 0–1–0; Hall of Fame 1–0–0; Independence 1–0–0; Liberty 0–1–0; Orange 0–1–0; Presidential Cup 1–0–0; Sugar 1–0–0; Sun 1–0–0.

CONFERENCE TITLES

Southwest 1917, 1919, 1921, 1925, 1927, 1939, 1940*, 1941, 1956, 1967, 1975*.

TOP 10 AP & UPI RANKING

1939	1	1956	5–5
1940	6	1957	9–10
1941	9	1976	7–8

MAJOR RIVALS

Aggies have played at least 15 games with Arkansas (20–34–3), Baylor (45–27–8), Houston (9–10–3), LSU (14–22–3), Rice (38–27–3), SMU (32–28–6), Southwestern (18–0–0), TCU (43–29–7), Texas (22–63–5), Texas Tech (23–18–1), Trinity (18–1–2) and Tulane (10–5–0).

COACHES

Homer H. Norton was dean of A&M coaches with record of 82–53–9 for 1934–47, including 3 conference titles, 4 bowl teams and 1 undefeated national champion. Dana X. Bible was 72–19–9 for 1917 and 1919–28 with 5 conference titles, 1 bowl champion and 3 unbeaten teams. Other top records were by Charles B. Moran, 38–8–4 for 1909–14 with 1 unbeaten team; Paul (Bear) Bryant, 25–14–2 for 1955–57 with 1 conference title, 1 bowl team and 1 unbeaten team; and Emory Bellard, 48–27–0 for 1972 to mid-1978 with 1 conference title and 3 bowl teams. Bear Bryant tops college coaches in all-time victories with Dana Bible ranking in top 10. Bryant and Charles Moran rank in top 20 in all-time winning percentage.

MISCELLANEA

First game was 14–6 win over Galveston H.S. in 1894 . . . 1st win over college foe was 22–4 over Austin College in 1896 . . . highest score was

110–0 over Daniel Baker in 1920 . . . highest since W.W. II was 61–22 over Texas-Arlington in 1982 . . . biggest margin of victory since W.W. II was 58–0 over Memphis St. in 1978 . . . worst defeat was 48–0 by Texas in 1898 . . . worst since 1900 was 46–0 by Baylor in 1901 . . . worst since W.W. II was 56–13 by Ohio St. in 1970 . . . highest ever against Aggies was 57–28 by Texas in 1977 . . . longest unbeaten string of 20 in 1938–40 ended by Texas 7–0 . . . unbeaten string of 18 in 1918–20 ended by Texas 7–3 and in 1956–57 ended by Rice 7–6 . . . longest winless string of 15 in 1947–49 broken with 26–7 win over Texas Tech . . . consensus All America players were Joe Routt, G, 1937; John Kimbrough, B, 1939–40; Marshall Robnett, G, 1940; John David Crow, B, 1957; Dave Elmendorf, DB, 1970; Pat Thomas, DB, 1974–75; Ed Simonini, LB, 1975; Tony Franklin, K, and Robert Jackson, LB, 1976 . . . Academic All America choices were Jack Pardee, B, 1956; Bill Luebbehusen, LB, 1971; and Kevin Monk, LB, 1976–77 . . . John David Crow, HB, won Heisman Trophy in 1957.

Texas Christian (Horned Frogs; Purple & White) (Southwest)

NOTABLE TEAMS

1912—8–1–0. Scored 230 and shut out 5, losing only to Texas 30–10 in 2nd game. 1916—6–2–1. Lost to Southwestern and Baylor. 1917—8–2–0. Shut out 5, losing only to Rice and 2nd Texas 132nd Infantry. 1920—9–0–0. Won 3 by less than TD; lost to Centre in Fort Worth Classic 63–7. 1925—7–1–1. Matty Bell's 3rd team shut out 5 behind T Harold Brewster and C Johnny Washmon; lost only to Oklahoma St. 22–7 and tied Baylor 7–7. 1926— 6–1–2. Won 4 by TD or less, losing only to SMU 14–13 in finale. 1928— 8–2–0. Bell's last team shut out 5 and lost only to Baylor 7–6 and Texas 6–0 behind linemen Mike Brumbelow and Jake Williams. 1929—9–0–1. Francis Schmidt's 1st team scored 249 and shut out 6, taking 1st Southwest Conference title as Cy Leland scored 13 TDs and ran for 680 yards and Howard Grubbs passed for 836 yards; tie was 7–7 with SMU in finale. 1930—9–2–1. Scored 298 and shut out 9 as Leland scored 10 TDs and Hubert Dennis intercepted 6 passes. 1931—9–2–1. Shut out 7 behind G Johnny Vaught, but lost to Tulsa and Texas. 1932—10–0–1. Outscored foes 283–23, shutting out 7 and winning SWC title as Vaught starred again along with Richard Oliver (12 TDs); tie was with LSU 3–3 in 2nd game. 1933—9–2–1. Schmidt's last team lost only to Arkansas and Baylor (7–0) as Charlie Casper caught 17 passes and scored 10 TDs. 1935—11–1–0. Dutch Meyer's 2nd team lost only to unbeaten SMU 20–14 as C Darrell Lester became TCU's 1st consensus All America player and other stars were Jimmy Lawrence (23 pass receptions and 7 interceptions) and Sammy Baugh (1,240 yards and 18 TDs passing, and a 43-yard average on 66 punts); beat LSU in Sugar Bowl 3–2. 1936—8–2–2. Baugh passed for 1,261 yards and 11 TDs behind C Ki Aldrich; Frogs were unbeaten in last 7, then beat Marquette in Cotton Bowl 16–6. 1938—10–0–0. Outscored foes 254–53 and led nation in passing as Heisman winner Davey O'Brien led nation in total offense (1,847 yards) and passing (1,457 yards) behind Aldrich, and also intercepted 6 passes; won national championship and beat Carnegie Tech in Sugar Bowl 15–7. 1941—7–3–0. Won 4 by TD or less; lost to Georgia in Orange Bowl 40–26. 1942—7–3–0. Again won 4 by TD or less behind T Derrell Palmer and E Bruce Alford. 1944—7–2–1. Won 4 by TD or less and won SWC title as T Clyde Flowers starred; lost to Oklahoma St. in Cotton Bowl 34–0. 1951—6–4–0. Scored in double figures in all and won 5th SWC title behind QB Ray McKown; lost to Kentucky in Cotton Bowl 20–7. 1955—9–1–0. Abe Martin's 3rd team scored 293 and lost only to Texas A&M 19–16 as Jim Swink led nation in scoring (125 points) and all-purpose running (1,702 yards) behind C Hugh Pitts; lost to Mississippi in Cotton Bowl 14–13. 1956—7–3–0. Swink ran for 669 yards and caught 19 passes for 390 more; beat Syracuse in Cotton Bowl 28–27. 1958—8–2–0. T Don Floyd led Frogs to SWC title; lost only to national co-champ Iowa and SMU (20–13), then tied unbeaten Air Force in Cotton Bowl 0–0. 1959—8–2–0. Won share of SWC title behind tackles Floyd and Bob Lilly and FB Jack Spikes; won last 7 but lost to Clemson in Bluebonnet Bowl 23–7.

BOWL RECORD

Bluebonnet 0–1–0; Cotton 2–3–1; Delta 0–1–0; Fort Worth Classic 0–1–0; Orange 0–1–0; Sugar 2–0–0; Sun 0–1–0.

CONFERENCE TITLES

Southwest 1929, 1932, 1938, 1944, 1951, 1955, 1958, 1959*.

TOP 10 AP & UPI RANKING

1938	1	1958	10–9
1951	U–10	1959	7–8
1955	5–6		

MAJOR RIVALS

TCU has played at least 15 games with Arkansas (21–37–2), Austin College (18–5–0), Baylor (43–40–7), Daniel Baker (11–4–0), Kansas (15–5–4), Oklahoma St. (6–10–2), Rice (32–27–3), SMU (28–31–7), Texas (19–49–1), Texas A&M (29–43–7), Texas Tech (19–18–3) and Trinity (15–4–2).

COACHES

Dean of TCU coaches was Dutch Meyer with record of 109–79–13 for 1934–52, including 3 conference titles, 7 bowl teams and 1 unbeaten national champion. Abe Martin was 74–64–7 for 1953–66 with 3 conference titles and 5 bowl teams. Other top records were by Madison A. Bell, 33–17–5 for 1923–28; and Francis Schmidt, 46–6–5 for 1929–33 with 2 conference titles and 2 unbeaten teams.

MISCELLANEA

First game was 8–6 win over Toby's Business College in 1896 . . . 1st win over college foe was 6–0 over Dallas University in 1897 . . . highest score was 68–0 over Austin in 1932 . . . highest since W.W. II was 47–0 over Trinity in 1952 . . . worst defeat was 72–0 by Texas in 1915 . . . worst since W.W. II was 81–16 by Texas in 1974 . . . longest unbeaten string of 20 in 1928–30 ended by Texas 7–0 . . . winning streak of 14 in 1937–38 ended by UCLA 6–3 in 1939 . . . longest losing string of 20 in 1974–75 broken with 28–21 win over Rice . . . consensus All America players were Darrell Lester, C, 1935; Sammy Baugh, B, 1936; Ki Aldrich, C, and Davey O'Brien, B, 1938; Jim Swink, B, 1955; Don Floyd, T, 1959; and Bob Lilly, T, 1960 . . . Academic All America selections were Marshall Harris, T, 1952; Hugh Pitts, C, 1955; Jim Swink, B, 1955–56; John Nikkel, E, 1957; Jim Ray, OG, 1968; Scott Walker, C, 1972; Terry Drannan, DB, 1974; and John McClean, DL, 1980 . . . Davey O'Brien, QB, won Heisman Trophy in 1938.

Texas–El Paso (Miners; Orange, White & Blue) (WAC)

NOTABLE TEAMS

1925—5–1–1. Lost opener to Sul Ross 31–7 and tied New Mexico St. 6–6. 1929—6–1–2. Mack Saxon's 1st team shut out 5 and lost only to Arizona St. 19–0. 1930—7–1–1. Again shut out 5, losing only to Texas 28–0 in opener and tying Arizona 0–0 in finale. 1931—7–1–0. Lost only to Hardin-Simmons 45–0. 1932—7–2–0. Lost to Arizona St. (15–14) and Oklahoma St.; lost to SMU in El Paso Charity Classic 26–0. 1937—7–1–2. QB Kenneth Heineman led Miners to wins over all but New Mexico St. (14–0 loss in opener). 1948 —8–1–1. Scored 349 and led nation in rushing as Fred Wendt led nation in rushing (1,570 yards) and scoring (152 points on 20 TDs and 32 extra points) behind linemen Ray Evans and Ernest Keily; lost only to Texas Tech (46–6), but lost to West Virginia in Sun Bowl 21–12. 1949—7–2–1. Jack Curtice's last team again led nation in rushing as Pug Gabrel ran for 886 yards and 11 TDs behind Keily and C Wayne Hansen; beat Georgetown in Sun Bowl 33–20. 1950—7–3–0. Mike Brumbelow's 1st team scored 279 as E J.D. Partridge starred. 1953—7–2–0. Lost only to Texas Tech and Hardin-Simmons (14–13); beat Southern Mississippi in Sun Bowl 37–14. 1954— 7–3–0. John Howle caught 27 passes and Jess Whittenton starred at QB; beat Florida St. in Sun Bowl 47–20. 1956—9–1–0. Scored 305 and lost only to North Texas St. 13–6 while winning Border Conference as Jimmy Bevers ran for 606 yards and 9 TDs; lost to George Washington in Sun Bowl 13–0. 1965—7–3–0. Bobby Dobbs' 1st team scored 304 as soph Billy Stevens passed for 3,032 yards and 21 TDs and Chuck Hughes caught 80 for 1,519 yards and 12 TDs; beat TCU in Sun Bowl 13–12. 1967—6–2–1. Scored 323 and led nation in passing and scoring average as Stevens passed for 1,365 yards and Volly Murphy caught 40 for 747 yards; lost only to Arizona St. 33–32 and unbeaten Wyoming 21–19, and beat Mississippi in Sun Bowl 14–7.

BOWL RECORD

El Paso Charity 0–1–0; Sun 5–3–0.

CONFERENCE TITLES

Border 1956.

TOP 10 AP & UPI RANKING

None.

MAJOR RIVALS

Miners have played at least 15 games with Arizona (11–36–2), Arizona St. (13–30–3), Brigham Young (5–16–1), Colorado St. (6–14–0), Hardin-Simmons (10–18–1), New Mexico (21–31–3), New Mexico Military (12–5–1), New Mexico St. (35–26–2), North Texas St. (5–13–3), Sul Ross St. (10–4–1), Texas Tech (6–9–1), Utah (4–14–0), West Texas St. (15–9–1) and Wyoming (5–17–0).

COACHES

Dean of Texas-El Paso coaches was Mack Saxon with record of 66–43–9 for 1929–41, including 2 bowl teams. Mike Brumbelow was 46–24–3 for 1950–56 with 1 conference title and 3 Sun Bowl teams. Other top records were by Jack Curtice, 24–13–3 for 1946–49 with 2 Sun Bowl teams; and Bobby Dobbs, 41–35–2 for 1965–72 with 2 Sun Bowl champions.

MISCELLANEA

First game was 7–6 win over YMCA in 1914 . . . 1st win over college foe was 3–0 over Daniel Baker in 1922 . . . highest score was 92–7 over New Mexico St. in 1948 . . . worst defeat was 79–0 by New Mexico Military in 1916 . . . worst since W.W. II was 83–7 by Brigham Young in 1980 (highest ever against Miners) . . . margin was equalled by Utah 82–6 in 1973 . . . longest unbeaten string of 12 in 1937–38 ended by Texas Tech 14–7 . . . longest losing string of 14 in 1976–77 broken with 23–21 win over New Mexico St. . . . . Texas-El Paso has had no consensus All America players and no Academic All America selections.

Texas Tech (Red Raiders; Scarlet & Black) (Southwest)

NOTABLE TEAMS

1925—6–1–2. First varsity team lost only to Howard Payne 29–0. 1926— 6–1–3. Shut out 5, losing only to TCU 28–16. 1932—10–2–0. Pete Cawthon's 3rd team outscored foes 382–35, losing only to Texas A&M 7–0 and Hardin-Simmons 13–12, and won 1st Border Conference title. 1933—8– 1–0. Shut out 6 and took conference again as E Elva Baker starred; lost only to SMU 14–0 in opener. 1934—7–2–1. C Lawrence Priddy and HB Glynn Dowell led Red Raiders to 3rd straight Border title; lost to Texas 12–6 in opener and to Loyola 12–7. 1937—8–3–0. Elmer Tarbox picked off 6 passes and helped Raiders win Border title along with E Herschel Ramsey and G Floyd Owens; won last 7 (4 by shutout) but lost to West Virginia in Sun Bowl 7–6. 1938—10–0–0. Outscored foes 274–35, winning 4 by TD or less as Tarbox led nation with 11 interceptions; lost to St. Mary's in Cotton Bowl 20–13. 1940—9–1–1. Cawthon's last team won 5 by TD or less, losing only to New Mexico 19–14 and tying Oklahoma St. 6–6. 1941—9–1–0. Dell Morgan's 1st team outscored foes 226–30 but lost to Miami (Fla.) 6–0; lost to Tulsa in Sun Bowl 6–0. 1946—8–3–0. Won 4 by TD margin. 1948— 7–3–0. Lost only to Rice 14–7 in last 5; won 8th Border title. 1953—10–1–0. Scored 428 and led nation in scoring average behind Bobby Cavazos (747 yards rushing) while winning 11th Border title; lost only to Texas A&M 27–14 and beat Auburn in Gator Bowl 35–13. 1954—7–2–1. Scored 367 but lost successive games to LSU 20–13 and Pacific 20–7. 1955—7–2–1. Won 3rd straight (and last) Border title behind T Jerry Walker and FB Jim Sides; lost to Wyoming in Sun Bowl 21–14. 1965—8–2–0. Tom Wilson passed for 2,119 yards and 18 TDs and Donny Anderson ran for 705 yards and caught 60 passes for 797 yards (scoring 17 TDs in all) as Red Raiders lost only to Texas and unbeaten Arkansas; lost to Georgia Tech in Gator Bowl 31–21. 1970—8–3–0. Jim Carlen's 1st team won 5 by TD or less as Doug McCutchen ran for 1,068 yards; lost to Georgia Tech in Sun Bowl 17–9. 1972—8–3–0. George Smith ran for 740 yards and Joe Barnes passed for 1,142; lost to North Carolina in Sun Bowl 32–28. 1973—10–1–0. Scored 314 as Barnes ran and passed for 1,546 yards and Andre Tillman caught 26 passes for 428 yards; lost only to Texas 28–12, and beat Tennessee in Gator Bowl 28–19. 1976—10–1–0. Steve Sloan's 2nd team scored 312 as Rod Allison passed for 1,458 yards, Sammy Williams caught 32 for 601 yards and

Brian Hall kicked 15 FGs while LB Thomas Howard sparked defense; lost only to Houston 27–19 and got share of Southwest Conference title, but lost to Nebraska in Bluebonnet Bowl 27–24.

BOWL RECORD

Bluebonnet 0–1–0; Cotton 0–1–0; Gator 2–1–0; Peach 0–0–1; Raisin 0–1–0; Sun 1–7–0; Tangerine 0–1–0.

CONFERENCE TITLES

Border 1932, 1933, 1934, 1937, 1942*, 1944, 1947, 1948, 1949, 1951, 1953, 1954, 1955. Southwest 1976*.

TOP 10 AP & UPI RANKING

1965	U–10

MAJOR RIVALS

Texas Tech has played at least 15 games with Arizona (25–3–2), Arkansas (4–23–0), Baylor (17–24–1), Hardin-Simmons (14–7–3), Houston (4–12–0), New Mexico (23–4–2), Oklahoma St. (11–7–3), Rice (17–16–1), SMU (18–13–0), TCU (18–19–3), Texas (6–27–), Texas A&M (18–23–1), Texas-El Paso (11–6–1), Tulsa (8–12–0) and West Texas St. (20–7–0).

COACHES

Dean of Texas Tech coaches was Pete Cawthon with record of 76–32–6 for 1930–40, including 4 conference titles, 2 bowl teams and 1 team unbeaten in regular season. Dell Morgan was 55–49–3 for 1941–50 with 5 conference titles and 3 bowl teams. Other top records were by E.Y. Freeland, 21–10–6 for 1925–28; DeWitt Weaver, 49–51–5 for 1951–60 with 4 conference titles and 3 bowl teams; J.T. King, 44–45–3 for 1961–69 with 2 bowl teams; Jim Carlen, 37–20–2 for 1970–74 with 4 bowl teams; and Steve Sloan, 23–12–0 for 1975–77 with 1 conference title and 2 bowl teams.

MISCELLANEA

First game was 0–0 tie with McMurry in 1925 . . . 1st win was 30–0 over Montezuma same year . . . highest score was 120–0 over Wayland in 1925 . . . highest since W.W. II was 71–0 over New Mexico St. in 1953 . . . worst defeat was 43–0 by Texas in 1949 . . . highest against Red Raiders was 59–20 by Tulsa in 1983 . . . longest unbeaten string of 13 in 1973–74 ended by Texas A&M 28–7 . . . longest losing string of 8 in 1956–57 broken with 21–12 win over Colorado . . . consensus All America players were E.J. Holub, C, 1960; Donny Anderson, B, 1965; Dan Irons, T, 1977; and Gabriel Rivera, DL, 1982 . . . Academic All America choices were Jeff Lobe, E, 1972; Maury Buford, P, 1979; and Chuck Alexander, DB, 1983.

Tulane (Green Wave; Olive Green & Sky Blue) (Independent)

NOTABLE TEAMS

1900—5–0–0. Blanked opponents 105–0. 1901—5–1–0. Lost only to Mobile 2–0. 1904—5–2–0. Shut out 5, but lost to Sewanee and Alabama (5–0). 1908—7–1–0. Shut out 5, losing only to Baylor 6–0. 1919—6–2–1. Unbeaten till losing to LSU and Washington & Lee (7–0) in last 2. 1920—6–2–1. Shut out 7 but lost to Michigan and Detroit (7–0). 1924—8–1–0. Lost only to Mississippi St. 14–0 as G Milton Levy and B Charles Flournoy starred. 1925—9–0–1. Clark Shaughnessy's best team outscored foes 246–32 behind Levy and Flournoy (19 TDs and 128 points); tie was with Missouri 6–6 in 2nd game. 1929—9–0–0. Bernie Bierman's 3rd team scored 297 behind B Willis Banker (13 TDs and 21 extra points) and shut out 5 while winning 1st Southern Conference title. 1930—8–1–0. Scored 263 and shut out 6, losing only to Northwestern 14–0 in 2nd game; C Lloyd Roberts and E Jerry Dalrymple helped Green Wave win 2nd straight conference title. 1931—11–0–0. Bierman's last team outscored foes 338–35, shutting out 7, as Don Zimmerman had 1,885 yards in all-purpose running and Dalrymple became Tulane's 1st consensus All America choice; won 3rd straight Southern title but lost to Southern California in Rose Bowl 21–12. 1932—6–2–1. Ted Cox's 1st team won 3 by TD or less as Zimmerman starred again. 1934 —9–1–0. Back Claude Simons Jr. led Green Wave to wins over all but Colgate (20–6 loss); got share of first SEC title and beat Temple in inaugural Sugar Bowl 20–14. 1938—7–2–1. Lost only to Clemson 13–10 in opener and Alabama 3–0 behind B Warren Brunner. 1939—8–0–1. Won 3rd SEC crown as Bobby Kellogg averaged 38.2 yards on 6 kickoff returns and T Harley McCollum and E Ralph Wenzel starred on line; tied North Carolina 14–14 in 4th game and lost to unbeaten national champion Texas A&M in Sugar Bowl 14–13. 1948—9–1–0. Henry Frnka's 3rd team lost only to Georgia Tech 13–7 in 2nd game as Eddie Price ran for 1,178 yards behind

T Paul Lea. 1949—7–2–1. Price ran for 1,137 yards behind Lea and Jimmy Glisson intercepted 9 passes as Green Wave won last SEC title; lost only to unbeaten national champion Notre Dame and LSU. 1950—6–2–1. Scored 260 behind tackles Lea and Jerome Helluin; unbeaten in last 6 after losses to Alabama and Notre Dame (13–9). 1973—9–2–0. DT Charles Hall and DE Mike Traux led defense as Green Wave lost only to Kentucky and Maryland; lost to Houston in Bluebonnet Bowl 47–7. 1979—9–2–0. Scored 314 as Rodney Holman caught 47 passes for 477 yards and QB Roch Hontas directed attack; lost only to Rice 21–17 and West Virginia 27–17, then to Penn St. in Liberty Bowl 9–6.

BOWL RECORD

Bluebonnet 0–1–0; Hall of Fame 0–1–0; Liberty 1–1–0; Rose 0–1–0; Sugar 1–1–0.

CONFERENCE TITLES

Southern 1929, 1930*, 1931. Southeastern 1934*, 1935*, 1939*, 1949.

TOP 10 AP & UPI RANKING

1939	5

MAJOR RIVALS

Tulane has played at least 15 games with Alabama (10–23–3), Auburn (17–13–6), Florida (6–12–2), Georgia (10–13–1), Georgia Tech (13–35–0), LSU (23–51–7), Mississippi (27–28–0), Mississippi St. (22–19–2), Rice (8–10–1), Sewanee (13–6–0), Texas (1–15–1), Texas A&M (5–10–0) and Vanderbilt (24–16–3).

COACHES

Dean of Tulane coaches was Clark Shaughnessy with record of 57–28–7 for 1915–20 and 1922–26, including 1 unbeaten team. Bernie Bierman was 36–10–2 for 1927–31 with 3 conference titles, 1 bowl team and 2 teams unbeaten in regular season. Other top records were by Ted Cox, 28–10–2 for 1932–35 with 2 conference titles and 1 bowl team; Lowell Dawson, 36–19–4 for 1936–41 with 1 conference title, 1 bowl team and 1 team unbeaten in regular season; and Henry E. Frnka, 31–23–4 for 1946–51 with 1 conference title.

MISCELLANEA

First game was 12–0 loss to Southern A.C. in 1893 . . . 1st win was 34–0 over LSU same year . . . highest score was 95–0 over Southwestern Louisiana in 1912 . . . highest since W.W. II was 64–0 over Louisiana College in 1950 . . . worst defeat was 62–0 by LSU in 1958, 1961 and 1965 . . . highest against Green Wave ever was 63–47 by Virginia in 1968 . . . longest winning streak of 18 in 1930–31 ended by Southern California 21–12 in Rose Bowl . . . longest losing string of 17 in 1961–63 broken with 20–7 win over South Carolina . . . consensus All America players were Jerry Dalrymple, E, 1931; Don Zimmerman, B, 1932; Harley McCollum, T, 1939; and Ernie Blandin, T, 1941 . . . Dave Hebert, DB, was Academic All America in 1971.

Tulsa (Golden Hurricane; Old Gold, Royal Blue & Crimson) (MVC)

NOTABLE TEAMS

1913—5–1–0. Scored 270 and shut out 5, losing only to Pittsburg Teachers 32–25. 1914—6–2–0. Sam McBirney's 1st team scored 272 and shut out 6. 1915—6–1–1. Scored 256 and lost only to unbeaten Oklahoma 14–13 while tying Oklahoma St. 0–0. 1916—10–0–0. McBirney's last team outscored foes 566–50 and beat Oklahoma for first time, 16–0. 1919—8–0–1. Francis Schmidt's 1st team outscored foes 592–27; tie was with Oklahoma St. 7–7. 1920—10–0–1. Outscored foes 622–28, shutting out 8; tie was with Phillips 0–0. 1922—7–0–0. Scored in double figures in all, winning 3 by TD or less. 1925—6–2–0. Elmer Henderson's 1st team lost only to Haskell and Arkansas. 1926—7–2–0. Shut out 5. 1927—8–1–0. Lost only to Phillips 13–7. 1928—7–2–1. Shut out 5 but lost successive heartbreakers to unbeaten Detroit 19–14 and Phillips 27–26. 1930—7–2–0. Won first 7 before losing to Haskell and Oklahoma St. 1931—8–3–0. Won first 7 and shut out 6. 1932 —7–1–1. Shut out 5, including 0–0 tie with Oklahoma St., and lost only to Oklahoma 7–0. 1933—6–1–0. Won 4 by TD or less, losing only to Oklahoma St. 7–0. 1937—6–2–2. Won 3rd straight Missouri Valley Conference title, losing only to TCU 20–13 and Arkansas. 1940—7–3–0. Won 3 by TD or less and took 5th MVC title as Dick Morgan led nation with 7 interceptions. 1941—7–2–0. Henry Frnka's 1st team lost only to TCU 6–0 in opener and to Arkansas 13–6 in finale as Bobby Dobbs starred at FB; beat Texas

Tech in Sun Bowl 6–0. 1942—10–0–0. Outscored foes 422–32 behind E Johnny Green and B Cal Purdin and led nation in passing, scoring and scoring defense; shut out 7 and won 3rd straight MVC title but lost to Tennessee in Sugar Bowl 14–7. 1943—6–0–1. Outscored foes 251–32 behind T C.G. Stanley and B Charley Mitchell and won MVC again; tied Southwestern (Texas) 6–6 and lost squeaker to Georgia Tech in Sugar Bowl 20–18. 1944—7–2–0. Scored 354 and led nation in total offense and passing behind G Carl Buda and Mitchell; beat Georgia Tech in Orange Bowl 26–12. 1945—8–2–0. Frnka's last team lost only to unbeaten Indiana 7–2 and unbeaten Oklahoma St. 12–6 in successive games; lost to Georgia in Oil Bowl 20–6. 1946—9–1–0. J.O. Brothers' 1st team scored 295 behind C Bob Hellinghausen and FB Hardy Brown, losing only to Detroit 20–14. 1950— 9–1–1. Scored 339 as Jake Roberts ran for 954 yards and 12 TDs and Jack Crocker scored 10 TDs; lost only to San Francisco 23–14 in 2nd game and tied Detroit 13–13. 1951—9–2–0. Scored 371 and led nation in total offense as Howie Waugh ran for 1,118 yards and Ronnie Morris ran and passed for 1,572. 1952—8–1–1. Brothers' last team scored 328 and led nation in total offense, rushing, passing and scoring as Waugh led nation's rushers with 1,372 yards and scored 10 TDs and Morris ran and passed for 1,571 yards and 23 TDs; lost only to Houston (33–7), but lost to Florida in Gator Bowl 14–13. 1956—7–2–1. Lost only to Cincinnati 7–6 and Houston 14–0. 1958 —7–3–0. Won 3 by TD or less as Bob Brumble starred at FB. 1964—8–2–0. Scored 384 and led nation in total offense as Jerry Rhome topped nation's passers with 2,870 yards (and 32 TDs) and led in total offense (3,128 yards) while Howard Twilley led nation's receivers with 95 catches for 1,178 yards and 13 TDs; lost to unbeaten national champion Arkansas 31–22 in opener and to Cincinnati 28–23 but beat Mississippi in Bluebonnet Bowl 14–7. 1965 —8–2–0. Led nation in total offense and passing as Bill Anderson led in same categories (3,343 yards in total offense and 3,464 in passing with 30 TDs) and Twilley led in receiving (NCAA record 134 receptions for 1,779 yards and 16 TDs) and scoring (127 points); won last 7 to take MVC but lost to Tennessee in Bluebonnet Bowl 27–6. 1967—7–3–0. Scored 304 as Rick Eber caught 78 passes for 1,168 yards and 12 TDs and LB Bob Junko led defense. 1974—8–3–0. Won last 7 to take MVC title as Jeb Blount (1,860 yards and 15 TDs passing) teamed with Steve Largent (52 catches for 844 yards and 14 TDs) to lead offense. 1978—9–2–0. QB Dave Rader directed Golden Hurricane to wins over all but Arkansas (21–13 loss) and New Mexico St. (23–20 defeat) in John Cooper's 2nd year. 1980—8–3–0. Won 4 by TD or less and took MVC title. 1982—10–1–0. Scored 342 behind Michael Gunter (1,464 yards rushing and 11 TDs) and Ken Lacy (1,097 yards and 12 TDs rushing) while losing only to Arkansas (38–0 in 2nd game). 1983—8–3–0. Won 23rd MVC title as Gunter ran for 1,198 yards and 14 TDs.

BOWL RECORD

Bluebonnet 1–1–0; Gator 0–1–0; Independence 0–1–0; Oil 0–1–0; Orange 1–0–0; Sugar 0–2–0; Sun 1–0–0.

CONFERENCE TITLES

Missouri Valley 1935*, 1936*, 1937, 1938, 1940, 1941, 1942, 1943, 1946, 1947, 1950, 1951, 1962, 1965, 1966*, 1973*, 1974, 1975, 1976*, 1980, 1981*, 1982, 1983.

TOP 10 AP & UPI RANKING

1942   4

MAJOR RIVALS

Tulsa has played at least 15 games with Arkansas (15–43–3), Cincinnati (16–9–2), Detroit (6–10–1), Houston (11–14–0), Kansas St. (9–6–1), Louisville (11–7–0), New Mexico St. (13–2–0), North Texas St. (13–6–0), Oklahoma (6–8–1), Oklahoma St. (22–25–5) and Texas Tech (12–8–0).

COACHES

Dean of Tulsa coaches was Elmer Henderson with record of 70–25–5 for 1925–35, including 1 conference title. John Cooper had record of 50–27–0 for 1977–83 with 4 conference titles. J.O. Brothers was 45–25–4 for 1946–52 with 4 conference titles and 1 bowl team. Glenn Dobbs was 45–37–0 for 1961–68 with 3 conference titles and 2 bowl teams. Other top records were by Sam McBirney, 22–3–1 for 1914–16 with 1 unbeaten team; Francis Schmidt, 24–3–2 for 1919–21 with 2 unbeaten teams; Henry Frnka, 40–9–1 for 1941–45 with 3 conference titles, 5 bowl teams and 2 teams unbeaten in regular season; Bobby Dobbs, 30–28–2 for 1955–60; and F.A. Dry, 31–17–1 for 1972–76 with 4 conference titles and 1 bowl team.

MISCELLANEA

First game was win over Bacone Indians in 1895 (no score recorded) . . . 1st win over college foe was over Arkansas in 1898 (no score recorded)

... highest score was 152–0 over Oklahoma Baptist in 1919 ... highest since W.W. II was 77–0 over Tampa in 1967 ... worst defeat was 100–6 by Houston in 1968 ... longest unbeaten string of 23 in 1919–21 ended by TCU 16–0 ... longest losing string of 15 in 1953–55 broken with 41–19 win over Hardin-Simmons ... only consensus All America player was Howard Twilley, E, 1965 ... Academic All America choices were Twilley, E, 1964–65; and Mack Lancaster, DT, 1974 ... Tulsa ranks in top 30 in all-time winning percentage.

UCLA (Bruins; Navy Blue & Gold) (Pacific-10)

NOTABLE TEAMS

1927—6–2–1. William Spaulding's 3rd team shut out 5, losing only to Arizona 16–13 and Drake. 1934—7–3–0. Shut out 5. 1935—8–2–0. HB Chuck Cheshire led Bruins to share of 1st Pacific Coast Conference title; lost only to California and unbeaten SMU. 1939—6–0–4. Kenny Washington ran for 812 yards and passed for 582 to lead nation in total offense while Jackie Robinson starred on punt returns; tied 3 of last 4 foes. 1942—7–3–0. Bob Waterfield passed for 1,095 yards and 12 TDs behind G Jack Lescoulie and Bruins won 7 of last 8 to take PCC; lost to Georgia in Rose Bowl 9–0. 1946 —10–0–0. Outscored foes 313–72 as Ernie Case passed for 1,033 yards and E Burr Baldwin became UCLA's 1st consensus All America choice; lost to Illinois in Rose Bowl 45–14. 1952—8–1–0. Red Sanders' 4th team lost only to Southern California 14–12 in finale behind LB Don Moomaw and Bill Stits (8 interceptions). 1953—8–1–0. Lost only to Stanford 21–20 and won PCC behind tackles Chuck Doud and Jack Ellena and HB Paul Cameron (1,143 yards total offense and 13 TDs); lost to Michigan St. in Rose Bowl 28–20. 1954—9–0–0. Outscored foes 367–40 and led nation in scoring, rushing defense and scoring defense behind Ellena and FB Bob Davenport (11 TDs); shut out 5 and earned share of national championship. 1955—9–1–0. Scored 285 and shut out 5 behind G Hardiman Cureton, HB Sam Brown (892 yards rushing) and Davenport; lost only to unbeaten Maryland 7–0 in 2nd game, then to Michigan St. in Rose Bowl 17–14. 1956—7–3–0. Won 4 by TD or less. 1957—8–2–0. Sanders' last team lost only to Oregon and Stanford as Dick Wallen caught 20 passes and intercepted 4. 1960—7–2–1. Bill Kilmer led nation in total offense with 1,889 yards as Bruins lost only to Washington 10–8 and USC. 1961—7–3–0. Mike Haffner ran for 703 yards and UCLA won 6 of last 7 to take AAWU title; lost to Minnesota in Rose Bowl 21–3.

1965—7–2–1. Tommy Prothro's 1st team won 3rd and last AAWU title as Mel Farr ran for 821 yards and Gary Beban had 2,073 yards of total offense; upset unbeaten national champion Michigan St. in Rose Bowl 14–12 after losing to Spartans 13–3 in season opener. 1966—9–1–0. Scored 281 behind Beban (1,697 yards total offense) and Farr (809 yards rushing) while losing only to Washington 16–3. 1967—7–2–1. Scored 284 behind Heisman winner Beban (1,586 yards total offense) while LB Don Manning led defense; lost to national champion USC 21–20 and Syracuse. 1969—8–1–1. Scored 329 as Greg Jones ran for 761 yards and Dennis Dummit passed for 1,963 yards and 15 TDs while LB Mike Ballou anchored defense; lost only to USC 14–12 in finale and tied Stanford 20–20. 1972—8–3–0. Scored 351 as Kermit Johnson ran for 952 yards and Mark Harmon ran and passed for 1,018. 1973—8–2–1. Led nation in rushing and scored 470 points behind Johnson (1,129 yards rushing) as DE Fred McNeil and DB Jimmy Allen led defense. 1975—8–2–1. Scored 326 as Wendell Tyler ran for 1,388 yards and John Sciarra ran and passed for 2,100; upset unbeaten Ohio St. in Rose Bowl 23–10 after losing to Buckeyes 41–20 in regular season. 1976—9–1–1. Terry Donahue's 1st team scored 385 behind Theotis Brown (1,092 yards rushing) while LB Jerry Robinson led defense; lost only to USC in finale 24–14 and tied Ohio St. 10–10, but lost to Alabama in Liberty Bowl 36–6. 1978—8–3–0. Lost no game by more than 7 as Robinson and safety Kenny Easley (7 interceptions) sparked defense while Brown ran for 1,283 yards; tied Arkansas in Fiesta Bowl 10–10. 1980—9–2–0. Scored 306 behind Freeman McNeil (1,105 yards rushing) and Cormac Carney (33 receptions for 581 yards) while Easley again starred on defense; lost successive games to Arizona 23–17 and Oregon 20–14. 1982—9–1–1. Scored 375 as Tom Ramsey led nation in passing efficiency (2,824 yards and 21 TDs); lost only to Washington 10–7 and tied Arizona 24–24 while winning PAC-10 and beating Michigan in Rose Bowl 24–14 (after beating Wolverines 31–27 in regular season). 1983—6–4–1. Won 6 of last 7 to take PAC-10 again behind Rick Neuheisel (1,947 yards passing) and DB Don Rogers; beat Illinois in Rose Bowl 45–9.

BOWL RECORD

Bluebonnet 0–1–0; Fiesta 0–0–1; Liberty 0–1–0; Rose 4–5–0.

CONFERENCE TITLES

Pacific Coast 1935*, 1939*, 1942, 1946, 1953, 1954, 1955. AAWU 1959*, 1961, 1965. Pacific-8 1975*. Pacific-10 1982, 1983.

TOP 10 AP & UPI RANKING

1946	4	1954	2–1	1966	5–5	1973	U–9
1952	6–6	1955	4–4	1967	U–10	1975	5–5
1953	5–4	1965	4–5	1969	U–10	1982	5–5

MAJOR RIVALS

UCLA has played at least 15 games with California (35–18–1), Oregon (29–13–0), Oregon St. (23–9–4), Stanford (29–22–3), Southern California (17–30–6), Washington (23–22–1) and Washington St. (26–7–1).

COACHES

Dean of UCLA coaches was William Spaulding with record of 72–51–8 for 1925–38, including 1 conference title. Henry (Red) Sanders was 66–19–1 for 1949–57 with 3 conference titles, 2 Rose Bowl teams and 1 unbeaten national champion. He was national coach of the year in 1954. Other top records were by Tommy Prothro, national coach of the year in 1965, 41–18–3 for 1965–70 with 1 conference title and 1 Rose Bowl champion; and Terry Donahue, 62–26–5 for 1976–83 with 2 conference titles and 5 bowl teams.

MISCELLANEA

First game was 74–0 loss to Manual Arts H.S. in 1919 . . . 1st win was 7–2 over Occidental freshmen same year . . . 1st win over college varsity was 24–6 over San Diego St. in 1922 . . . highest score was 72–0 over Stanford in 1954 . . . worst defeat was 103–0 by Whittier in 1920 . . . worst since W.W. II was 61–20 by Washington in 1970 . . . longest unbeaten string of 14 in 1975–76 ended by USC 24–14 . . . longest losing string of 16 in 1919–21 broken with 24–6 win over San Diego St. in 1922 . . . UCLA has had 16 consensus All America players since 1946 . . . multi-year choices were Jerry Robinson, LB, 1976–78; and Kenny Easley, DB, 1978–80 . . . unanimous choices for 1 year were Burr Baldwin, E, 1946; Gary Beban, B, 1967; and Tim Wrightman, TE, 1981 . . . other choices since 1960 were Mel Farr, B, 1966; Don Manning, LB, 1967; Mike Ballou, LB, 1969; Kermit Johnson, B, 1973; John Sciarra, QB, 1975; and Don Rogers, DB, 1983 . . . Academic All America selections were Ed Flynn, G, and Donn Moomaw, LB, 1952; Ira Pauley, C, 1953; Sam Boghosian, G, 1954; Ray Armstrong, E, 1966; John Sciarra, QB, 1975; John Fowler, LB, 1977; Tim Wrightman, TE, 1981; and Cormac Carney, WR, 1981–82 . . . Gary Beban, QB, won Heisman Trophy in 1967.

Utah (Utes; Crimson & White) (WAC)

NOTABLE TEAMS

1904—6-1-0. Joseph Maddock's 1st team lost only to Colorado 32–6 in opener; blanked others 251–0. 1905—6-2-0. Scored 260 but lost to Colorado and Colorado Mines. 1906—4-1-0. Lost opener to Colorado College 6–0 but shut out others 111–0. 1909—5-1-0. Maddock's last team lost only to Colorado Mines 14–8. 1911—6-1-1. Shut out 7, losing only to unbeaten Colorado 9–0. 1912—5-1-1. Yielded just 16 points; tied Utah St. 7–7 in opener and lost only to Colorado 3–0. 1915—6-2-0. Lost to Colorado A.C. and Colorado College. 1922—7-1-0. Shut out 5, losing only to Idaho 16–0, and won 1st Rocky Mountain Conference title. 1925—6-2-0. Ike Armstrong's 1st team lost opener to Southern California 28–2 and finale to Utah St. 10–6. 1926—7-0-0. Outscored foes 164–23; won Rocky Mountain title. 1928—5-0-2. T Alton Carman led Utes to wins over all but Creighton (7–7) and Brigham Young (0–0). 1929—7-0-0. Outscored foes 219–23 and won 2nd straight Rocky Mountain title behind FB Earl Pomeroy. 1930—8-0-0. Armstrong's 4th unbeaten team outscored foes 340–20 to win 5th Rocky Mountain crown behind C Marwin Jonas and E George Watkins. 1931—7-2-0. Scored 301 and shut out 5, losing only to Washington 7–6 in opener and Oregon St. 12–0 in finale. 1932—5-1-1. Lost opener to unbeaten Southern California 35–0 and tied Nevada-Reno 6–6 in 2nd game but blanked others 102–0. 1938—7-1-2. Shut out 6 and lost only to Idaho 16–6 as T Bernard McGarry starred; won 1st Mountain States Conference title and beat New Mexico in Sun Bowl 26–0. 1939—6-1-2. Scored 261, losing only to Colorado 21–14. 1940—7-2-0. Won last 5 to take Mountain States title. 1941—6-0-2. Armstrong's 5th unbeaten team won conference again behind T Floyd Spendlove; ties were with Brigham Young 6–6 and Denver 0–0. 1946—8-3-0. No loss by more than 8 points. 1947—8-1-1. Won 5th and last Mountain States title as Frank Nelson ran and passed for 1,109 yards; lost only to Idaho 13–6 and tied Arizona 20–20. 1948—8-1-1. Lost opener to Southern California 27–0 and tied Oregon St. 20–20. 1953—8-2-0. Won 3rd straight Skyline 8 title under Jack Curtice as Don Petersen ran for 720 yards; lost only to Washington 21–14 and Colorado. 1960—7-3-0. Ray Nagel's 3rd team lost 2 by TD or less. 1964—8-2-0. Won last 6 to earn share of Western Athletic Conference title as Roy Jefferson starred at E; beat West Virginia in Liberty Bowl 32–6. 1969—8-2-0. Lost only to Oregon (28–17 in opener) and Arizona 17–16 as

Craig Smith starred as DB and punter. 1978—8–3–0. Wayne Howard's 2nd team won 4 by less than TD. 1981—8–2–1. Howard's last team scored 322 behind Del Rogers (1,127 yards and 13 TDs rushing) while DT Steve Clark anchored defense; lost only to Arizona St. and Brigham Young.

BOWL RECORD

Liberty 1–0–0; Sun 1–0–0.

CONFERENCE TITLES

Rocky Mountain 1922, 1926, 1928, 1929, 1930, 1931, 1932, 1933*. Mountain States 1938, 1940, 1941, 1942*, 1947. Skyline 8 1951, 1952, 1953, 1957. Western Athletic 1964*.

TOP 10 AP & UPI RANKING

None.

MAJOR RIVALS

Utah has played at least 15 games with Arizona (16–13–2), Arizona St. (6–12–0), Brigham Young (38–16–4), Colorado (24–30–3), Colorado St. (38–13–2), Colorado College (14–11–0), Denver (28–9–5), Hawaii (11–4–0), Idaho (14–11–2), New Mexico (15–7–2), Oregon (5–14–0), Texas-El Paso (13–4–0) and Utah St. (51–26–4).

COACHES

Dean of Utah coaches was Ike Armstrong with record of 140–57–13 for 1925–49, including 12 conference titles, 1 Sun Bowl champion and 5 unbeaten teams. Jack Curtice was 45–32–4 for 1950–57 with 4 conference titles. Other top records were by Joseph H. Maddock, 31–10–1 for 1904–09; Fred Bennion, 16–7–3 for 1910–13; Thomas Fitzpatrick, 23–17–3 for 1919–24 with 1 conference title; Ray Nagel, 42–39–1 for 1958–65 with 1 conference title and 1 Liberty Bowl champion; and Wayne Howard, 30–24–2 for 1977–81.

MISCELLANEA

First game was 12–0 loss to Utah St. in 1892 . . . 1st win was 4–0 over YMCA same year . . . 1st win over college foe was 21–0 over Utah St. in 1900 . . . highest score was 129–0 over Fort Douglas in 1905 . . . highest since

W.W. II was 82–6 over Texas-El Paso in 1973 . . . worst defeat was 64–0
by Colorado College in 1943 . . . worst since W.W. II was 54–0 by Colorado
in 1951 . . . highest against Utes ever was 66–16 by UCLA in 1973 . . .
longest unbeaten string of 24 in 1927–30 ended by Washington 7–6 in 1931
. . . longest losing string of 9 in 1973–74 broken with 21–10 win over New
Mexico . . . Utah has had no consensus All America players . . . Academic
All America choices were Mel Carpenter, T, 1964; Scott Robbins, DB, 1971;
Steve Odom, RB, 1973; and Dick Graham, E, 1976.

Utah State (Aggies, Utags, Big Blue; Navy Blue & White) (PCAA)

NOTABLE TEAMS

1907—7–0–0. Outscored foes 207–25 with 1 score unrecorded. 1910—
5–1–0. Yielded only 12 points, half in 6–0 loss to Utah in finale. 1911—
5–0–0. Blanked foes 156–0. 1917—7–0–1. Outscored foes 267–26; tie was
7–7 with Montana St. 1919—5–2–0. Lowell Romney's 1st team outscored
foes 234–44 but lost to Colorado St. and Utah. 1921—7–1–0. Lost only to
Nevada-Reno (41–0); won 1st Rocky Mountain Conference title. 1923—
5–2–0. Lost to Denver and Colorado St. 1925—6–1–0. Lost only to
Colorado St. 13–0. 1926—5–1–2. Shut out 5 and gave up only 9 points
before losing finale to unbeaten Utah 34–0. 1931—6–2–0. Won first 5
before losing to Brigham Young 6–0 and Utah. 1934—5–1–1. Tied
Colorado St. 21–21 and lost only to Utah in finale 14–7. 1936—7–0–1. Shut
out all but Colorado (14–13), including 0–0 tie with Denver, and won 3rd
and last Rocky Mountain title. 1946—7–1–1. Lost only to Colorado 6–0 (in
2nd game) and tied Brigham Young 0–0 while earning share of Mountain
States Conference title behind FB Frank Williams and linemen George Nelson and Ralph Maughan; lost to San Jose St. in Raisin Bowl 20–0. 1953—
8–3–0. Won 4 by TD or less and Earl Lindley led nation in scoring with 81
points (13 TDs). 1960—9–1–0. John Ralston's 2nd team scored 261 and led
nation in rushing as Tom Larscheid ran for 1,044 yards; lost only to Utah 6–0
in finale, then lost to unbeaten New Mexico St. in Sun Bowl 20–13. 1961
—9–0–1. Outscored foes 387–78, leading nation in scoring average, as
Larscheid ran for 773 yards and T Merlin Olsen became Aggies' 1st consensus All America player; got share of 2nd straight Skyline 8 title despite 6–6
tie with Wyoming, but lost to Baylor in Gotham Bowl 24–9. 1962—8–2–0.
Ralston's last team scored 273 and Steve Shafer intercepted 6 passes; lost only

to New Mexico 14–13 and Arizona St. 1963—8–2–0. Tony Knap's 1st team scored 317 and led nation in total offense and scoring average as Bill Munson passed for 1,699 yards and 12 TDs; lost close ones to Wyoming 21–14 and Utah 25–23. 1965—8–2–0. Scored 271 as Ron Edwards passed for 1,095 yards and 12 TDs and Roy Shivers ran for 1,138 yards; lost successive late-season games to Memphis St. 7–0 and Wichita St. 21–19. 1967—7–2–1. Chuck Mills' 1st team lost only to New Mexico St. 10–9 and Colorado St. 17–14 behind John Pappas (1,424 yards passing), Altie Taylor (717 yards rushing) and Mike O'Shea (41 receptions for 599 yards). 1968—7–3–0. No game decided by margin of more than 10 points as Pappas passed for 1,647 yards and 16 TDs, Taylor ran for 929 yards and O'Shea caught 56 passes for 1,077 yards and 11 TDs. 1971—8–3–0. Won 4 by 8 points or less as Tony Adams passed for 2,035 yards and Bob Wicks caught 58 for 862 yards. 1972 —8–3–0. Mills' last team scored 329 behind Adams (2,797 yards and 22 TDs passing) and Tom Forzani (nation's leading pass receiver with 85 catches for 1,169 yards and 8 TDs). 1974—8–3–0. Won 4 by TD or less as Louie Giammona led nation's rushers with 1,534 yards. 1979—7–3–1 (9–2–0 by forfeit). Scored 347 as Eric Hipple passed for 1,924 yards, Rick Parros ran for 1,236 and James Murphy caught 63 passes for 1,067 yards; won PCAA title for 2nd straight year.

BOWL RECORD

Gotham 0–1–0; Grape 0–1–0; Raisin 0–1–0; Sun 0–1–0.

CONFERENCE TITLES

Rocky Mountain 1921, 1935*, 1936. Mountain States 1946*. Skyline 8 1960*, 1961*. Pacific Coast Athletic Association 1978*, 1979.

TOP 10 AP & UPI RANKING

1961	10–10

MAJOR RIVALS

Utah St. has played at least 15 games with Brigham Young (32–24–3), Colorado St. (30–32–2), Denver (13–19–3), Idaho (11–11–2), Montana (26–8–0), Montana St. (21–6–6), New Mexico (7–8–0), Pacific (11–5–0), San Jose St. (8–8–1), Utah (26–51–4) and Wyoming (34–20–4).

COACHES

Dean of Utah State coaches was E. Lowell Romney with record of 128–91–16 for 1919–48, including 4 conference titles, 2 bowl teams and 1 unbeaten team. Chuck Mills was 39–22–1 for 1967–72; and Bruce Snyder was 39–37–1 for 1976–82 with 2 conference titles. Other top records were by John Ralston, 31–11–1 for 1959–62 with 2 conference titles, 2 bowl teams and 1 team unbeaten in regular season; and Tony Knap, 25–14–1 for 1963–66.

MISCELLANEA

First game was 12–0 win over Utah in 1892 . . . highest score was 136–0 over Idaho St. in 1919 . . . highest since W.W. II was 76–0 over New Mexico St. in 1964 . . . worst defeat was 72–3 by Oklahoma in 1974 . . . longest unbeaten string of 14 in 1935–37 ended by Colorado 33–0 . . . longest winless string of 9 in 1904–05 broken with 21–0 win over Ogden H.S. . . . consensus All America players were Merlin Olsen, T, 1961; and Phil Olsen, DE, 1969 . . . Academic All America choices were Merlin Olsen, T, 1961; Gary Anderson, LB, 1969; and Randy Stockham, DE, 1974–75 . . . Merlin Olsen, T, won Outland Trophy in 1961.

Vanderbilt (Commodores; Black & Gold) (SEC)

NOTABLE TEAMS

1893—6–1–0. Lost only to Auburn 30–10. 1894—7–1–0. Outscored foes 246–20, shutting out 5 and losing only to Louisville A.C. 10–8. 1897—6–0–1. Blanked foes 141–0; tie was 0–0 with Virginia in finale. 1899—7–2–0. Shut out 6 but lost to Cincinnati 6–0 and Indiana. 1901—6–1–1. Lost only to Washington (Mo.) 12–11; shut out others, including 0–0 tie with Sewanee. 1902—8–1–0. Lost only to Sewanee 11–5 in finale. 1903—6–1–1. Yielded just 16 points as FB John Tigert starred; lost opener to Cumberland 6–0 and tied Texas 5–5. 1904—9–0–0. Dan McGugin's 1st team outscored foes 474–4 (only Missouri Mines scored) behind C J.N. Stone, G J.H. Brown and HB Honus Craig. 1905—7–1–0. Outscored foes 372–22, shutting out 6 and losing only to Michigan 18–0. 1906—8–1–0. Shut out 7, losing only to Michigan 10–4 as B Owsley Manier starred. 1907—5–1–1. Lost only to Michigan 8–0 and tied Navy 6–6 as Stone and Craig starred for 3rd straight year. 1908—7-2-1. Shut out 5, but lost to Michigan and Ohio St. 1909—7-3-0. Again shut out 5 behind T Ewing Freeland and G W.E. Metzger. 1910—8-0-1. Outscored foes 166-8, shutting out 7 as Metzger starred again; tie was with Yale 0-0. 1911—8-1-0. Outscored foes 259-9, yielding all points in 9-8 loss to Michigan; Freeland and Metzger starred for 3rd year, QB Ray Morrison for 4th. 1912—8-1-1. Outscored foes 391-19, shutting out 7, behind HB Lewie Hardage; lost only to unbeaten national champion Harvard 9-3 and tied Auburn 7-7. 1915—9-1-0. Outscored foes 514-38, shutting out 8 behind T Josh Cody and losing only to Virginia 35-10. 1916 —7-1-1. Outscored foes 328-25, shutting out 6 as Rabbit Curry starred in backfield; lost only to Tennessee 10-6 and tied Sewanee 0-0. 1919—5-1-2. Lost only to Georgia Tech 20-0 as Josh Cody starred again. 1921—7-0-1. Outscored foes 161-21, shutting out 6; tie was with Georgia 7-7. 1922—8-0-1. McGugin's 4th unbeaten team shut out 7 as Lynn Bomar starred at E; tie was 0-0 with Michigan. 1926—8-1-0. Shut out 5 and lost only to unbeaten Alabama 19-7 behind QB Bill Spears, FB Bill Hendrix and T Fred McKibbon. 1927—8-1-2. Spears starred again as Commodores lost only to Texas 13-6. 1928—8-2-0. Won 4 by TD or less behind G John Brown; lost only to unbeaten national champion Georgia Tech and Tennessee 6-0. 1929 —7-2-0. Brown led team to wins over all but Minnesota and Tennessee. 1930—8-2-0. Shut out 5, losing only to unbeaten Alabama 12-7 and Tennessee. 1932—6-1-2. Lost only to Alabama 20-0 in finale as Pete Gracey starred at C. 1935—7-3-0. Ray Morrison's 1st team lost none by more than 6 as E Willie Geny starred. 1937—7-2-0. C Carl Hinkle led Commodores to wins over all but Georgia Tech and unbeaten Alabama 9-7. 1941—8-2-0. Red Sanders' 2nd team scored 260 behind C Bob Gude, losing only to Tulane and Tennessee. 1943—5-0-0. Outscored slate of small college and service teams 145-33. 1948—8-2-1. Sanders' last team scored 328 behind C John Clark while Lee Nalley led nation as punt returner; won last 8 after losses to Georgia Tech and Mississippi. 1955—7-3-0. Art Guepe's 3rd team lost 2 by TD or less as Phil King ran for 628 yards and Charles Horton scored 12 TDs; beat Auburn in Gator Bowl 25-13. 1982 —8-3-0. Whit Taylor ran and passed for 2,481 yards and 24 TDs while Allama Matthews caught 61 passes for 797 yards and 14 TDs and Jim Arnold was All America punter; won last 5 but lost to Air Force in Hall of Fame Bowl 36-28.

BOWL RECORD

Gator 1–0–0; Hall of Fame 0–1–0; Peach 0–0–1.

CONFERENCE TITLES

Southern 1923.

TOP 10 AP & UPI RANKING

None.

MAJOR RIVALS

Vanderbilt has played at least 15 games with Alabama (17–40–4), Auburn (19–9–1), Central (Ky.) (13–1–1), Chattanooga (16–1–0), Florida (8–13–2), Georgia (15–28–1), Georgia Tech (15–16–3), Kentucky (28–24–4), LSU (6–13–1), Mississippi (28–28–2), Sewanee (40–8–4), Tennessee (27–46–5), Tulane (16–24–3) and Virginia (12–7–2).

COACHES

Dean of Vanderbilt coaches was Dan McGugin with record of 197–55–19 for 1904–17 and 1919–34, including 1 conference title and 4 unbeaten teams. He ranks in top 10 in total coaching victories and in top 25 in all-time winning percentage. Red Sanders was 36–22–2 for 1940–42 and 1946–48. Ray Morrison was 29–22–2 for 1918 and 1935–39. Second in years coached was Art Guepe with record of 39–54–7 for 1953–62, including 1 Gator Bowl champion.

MISCELLANEA

First game was 40–0 win over Nashville in 1890 . . . highest score was 105–0 over Bethel in 1912 . . . highest since W.W. II was 68–0 over Tennessee Tech in 1947 . . . worst defeat was 83–0 by Georgia Tech in 1917 . . . worst since W.W. II was 66–3 by Alabama in 1979 . . . longest unbeaten streak of 21 in 1920–23 ended by Michigan 3–0 . . . unbeaten string of 18 in 1903–05 ended by Michigan 18–0 . . . longest losing string of 16 in 1961–62 broken with 20–0 win over Tulane . . . consensus All America players were Henry Wakefield, E, 1924; Pete Gracey, C, 1932; George Deiderich, G, 1958; and Jim Arnold, P, 1982 . . . Academic All America selections were Ben Donnell, C, 1958; Jim Burns, DB, 1968; Doug Martin, E, 1974; Damen Regen, LB, 1975; Greg Martin, K, 1977; and Phil Roach, WR, 1983.

Virginia (Cavaliers, Wahoos; Orange & Blue) (ACC)

NOTABLE TEAMS

1890—5–2–0. Lost only to Pennsylvania and Princeton. 1893—8–3–0. Lost 2 by TD or less and shut out last 5 foes. 1894—8–2–0. Outscored foes 414–30, shutting out 7 and losing only to Princeton and unbeaten Penn. 1895—9–2–0. Shut out 6 and won last 6 after losses to Princeton and unbeaten national champion Penn. 1896—7–2–2. Shut out 6 but again lost to Penn and Princeton. 1897—6–2–1. Shut out 5, losing only to unbeaten national champion Penn and Navy 4–0. 1900—7–2–1. Shut out 6, losing only to Carlisle Indians and Georgetown. 1901—8–2–0. Shut out 6 but lost to Penn and Georgetown 17–16. 1902—8–1–1. Shut out 7, losing only to Lehigh (34–6) and tying North Carolina 12–12. 1903—7–2–1. Shut out 6 but lost to Navy 6–5 and North Carolina. 1906—7–2–2. Shut out 7 but lost to Bucknell 12–5 and Carlisle 18–17. 1908—7–0–1. Shut out 7, including 0–0 tie with Sewanee. 1909—7–1–0. Lost only to Lehigh 11–7 and shut out others. 1910—6–2–0. Shut out 6 but lost successive games to Carlisle and Georgetown. 1911—8–2–0. Shut out 6, losing only to Swarthmore 9–8 and Georgetown 9–0. 1913—7–1–0. Outscored foes 265–28, losing only to Georgetown 8–7. 1914—8–1–0. Scored 363 as Gene Mayer scored 142 (including 21 TDs); shut out 6 and lost only to Yale 21–0 in 2nd game. 1915 —8–1–0. Shut out 6, losing only to Harvard 9–0, as Mayer became Cavaliers' 1st consensus All America player. 1925—7–1–1. Greasy Neale's 3rd team shut out 5, losing only to Washington & Lee 12–0 and tying North Carolina 3–3. 1926—6–2–2. Shut out 5; unbeaten in last 5 after losses to Georgia and Virginia Tech. 1941—8–1–0. Scored 279 as Bill Dudley led nation in scoring (134 points) and all-purpose running (1,674 yards) while rolling up 1,824 yards in total offense and running and passing for 29 TDs; team shut out 5 and lost only to Yale 21–19. 1944—6–1–2. Led nation in total defense and lost only to North Carolina St. 13–0 in 2nd game. 1945—7–2–0. Frank Murray's last team won first 7 before losing to Maryland 19–13 and North Carolina. 1947—7–3–0. Art Guepe's 2nd team lost only to unbeaten Penn in first 8. 1949—7–2–0. John Papit ran for 1,214 yards and Cavaliers swept first 7 before losing to Tulane 28–14 and North Carolina 14–7. 1950— 8–2–0. Papit ran for 949 yards, Rufus Barkley passed for 16 TDs and Gene Schroeder caught 35 passes for 552 yards and 7 scores as Cavaliers scored 260, losing only to Penn and Tulane. 1951—8–1–0. Scored 278 and lost only to Washington & Lee (42–14 in 3rd game). 1952—8–2–0. Guepe's last team scored 297 and led nation in pass defense as Billy King intercepted 6; lost successive games to Duke 21–7 and South Carolina 21–14. 1968— 7–3–0. Scored 328 as Frank Quayle ran for 1,213 yards and caught 30 passes for another 426 and Gene Arnette passed for 1,463 yards and 17 TDs; Billy Schmidt intercepted 6 passes.

BOWL RECORD

None.

CONFERENCE TITLES

None.

TOP 10 AP & UPI RANKING

None.

MAJOR RIVALS

Virginia has played at least 15 games with Clemson (0–23–0), Duke (12– 23–0), Georgetown (7–7–2), George Washington (12–2–1), Georgia (6– 6–3), Hampden-Sydney (17–1–2), Maryland (15–31–2), Navy (5–25–0), North Carolina (34–51–3), North Carolina St. (7–25–1), Pennsylvania (1– 15–0), Randolph-Macon (21–0–1), Richmond (21–2–2), St. John's (Md.) (17–0–0), South Carolina (10–19–1), Vanderbilt (7–12–2), VMI (51–23– 3), Virginia Tech (27–33–5), Wake Forest (14–11–0), Washington & Lee (21–13–1), West Virginia (9–10–1) and William & Mary (20–4–1).

COACHES

Most successful Cavalier coach was Art Guepe with record of 47–17–2 for 1946–52. Longest tenure was by Frank Murray with record of 41–34–5 for 1937–45. Earle (Greasy) Neale was 28–22–5 for 1923–28.

MISCELLANEA

First game was 20–0 win over Pantops Academy in 1888 . . . 1st win over college foe was 32–0 over Georgetown in 1889 . . . highest score was 136–0 over Randolph-Macon in 1890 . . . highest since 1900 was 88–0 over St. John's in 1914 . . . highest since W.W. II was 71–0 over Hampden-Sydney in 1946 . . . worst defeat was 115–0 by Princeton in 1890 . . . worst since 1900 was 75–0 by Ohio St. in 1933 . . . worst since W.W. II was 68–0 by

Texas in 1977 . . . longest unbeaten string of 14 in 1944–45 ended by Maryland 19–13 . . . longest losing string of 28 in 1958–60 broken with 21–6 win over William & Mary in 1961 . . . consensus All America players were Eugene Mayer, B, 1915; and Bill Dudley, B, 1941 . . . Academic All America choices were Tom Kennedy, OG, 1972; and Bob Meade, DT, 1975.

Virginia Military Institute (Keydets; Red, White & Yellow) (Southern)

NOTABLE TEAMS

1892—4-0-1. Tie was with unbeaten Wake Forest 12–12. 1894—5-0-0. Blanked all but Virginia Tech (10–6 in finale). 1895—5-1-0. Outscored first 5 foes 160–6 but lost finale to Virginia Tech 6–4. 1900—4-1-2. Lost only to Georgetown 16–11; shut out others. 1911—7-1-0. Scored 203 and shut out 6, losing only to Virginia 22–6. 1912—7-1-0. Lost to St. John's 25–3 but gave up only 11 more points. 1913—7-1-2. Shut out 6, losing only to Virginia (38–7). 1915—6-2-1. Won 3 by TD or less, losing only to Virginia and Virginia Tech. 1919—6-2-0. Lost successive games to Virginia 7–0 and North Carolina St. 21–0. 1920—9-0-0. B.B. Clarkson's 1st team, known as the "Flying Squadron," outscored foes 431–20 and shut out 6. 1922—7-2-0. Scored 291 and shut out 6, losing only to North Carolina 9–7 and Virginia Tech 7–3. 1923—9-1-0. Shut out 7, losing only to Georgia Tech 10–7 in 3rd game. 1929—8-2-0. Won 3 by TD or less, losing only to Florida 12–7 and Kentucky 23–12. 1938—6-1-4. Lost only to Navy 26–0 as Paul Shu starred in backfield. 1940—7-2-1. Shut out 6, losing only to Duke and Richmond 9–7. 1951—7-3-0. Lost only to unbeaten Georgia Tech in last 5 and earned share of 1st Southern Conference title as Tom Brehany passed for 1,206 yards and 14 TDs. 1957—9-0-1. Won Southern Conference title behind tackles Jim McFalls and Lou Farmer and backs Sam Woolwine and Bobby Jordan; tie was with Holy Cross 21–21 in 2nd game. 1958—6-2-2. Unbeaten in first 8 before losing to The Citadel 14–6 and Virginia Tech 21–16; McFalls starred again, along with C Jerry Borst and RB Sam Horner. 1959—8-1-1. Howard Dyer passed for 1,072 yards and Dick Evans caught 35 for 698 yards as Keydets won last 7 after losing to Penn St. 21–0 and tying Richmond 14–14; won 3rd Southern Conference title. 1960—7-2-1. Repeated as conference champions behind Dyer (1,222 yards passing), Stinson Jones (26 receptions for 394 yards) and G Lou Shuba.

BOWL RECORD

None.

CONFERENCE TITLES

Southern 1951*, 1957, 1959, 1960, 1962, 1974, 1977*.

TOP 10 AP & UPI RANKING

None.

MAJOR RIVALS

VMI has played at least 15 games with The Citadel (23–19–1), Davidson (33–17–3), George Washington (12–7–1), Hampden-Sydney (18–0–1), Kentucky (4–12–0), Maryland (10–14–2), North Carolina (6–14–1), North Carolina St. (11–7–1), Richmond (38–24–5), Roanoke (20–1–0), Virginia (23–51–3), Virginia Tech (25–48–5), Washington & Lee (15–0–1) and William & Mary (32–27–2).

COACHES

Dean of VMI coaches was John McKenna with record of 62–60–8 for 1953–65, including 4 conference titles and 1 unbeaten team. Tied with McKenna in tenure was Bob Thalman with record of 53–85–3 for 1971–83, including 2 conference titles. B.B. Clarkson was 44–21–2 for 1920–26 with 1 perfect season.

MISCELLANEA

First game was 6–0 win over Washington & Lee in 1891 . . . highest score was 136–0 over Hampden-Sydney in 1920 . . . highest since W.W. II was 69–0 over Central Florida in 1982 . . . worst defeat was 67–0 by Cincinnati in 1953 . . . highest against Keydets was 70–12 by Virginia Tech in 1966 . . . longest unbeaten string of 18 in 1957–58 ended by The Citadel 14–6 . . . winning streak of 16 in 1919–21 ended by Virginia 14–7 . . . longest losing string of 18 in 1971–72 broken with 31–3 win over Furman . . . VMI has had no consensus All America players . . . Craig Jones, K, was Academic All America in 1978–79.

Virginia Tech (Gobblers, Hokies; Chicago Maroon & Burnt Orange) (Independent)

NOTABLE TEAMS

1894—4–1–0. Shut out first 4 but lost finale to unbeaten VMI 10–6. 1897 —5–2–0. Shut out 5 but lost to Maryland and Tennessee. 1899—4–1–0. Shut out 4, losing only to Virginia 28–0. 1901—6–1–0. Lost only to Virginia 16–0. 1903—5–1–0. Lost to Virginia 21–0 but shut out others. 1905— 9–1–0. Outscored foes 305–24, shutting out 7; lost only to Navy 12–6. 1907 —7–2–0. Shut out 6 but lost to Davidson and Navy. 1909—6–1–0. B.B. Bocock's 1st team lost only to Princeton 8–6 in 2nd game. 1910—6–2–0. Lost close ones to Navy 3–0 and North Carolina St. 5–3. 1911—6–1–2. Shut out 5 but lost to Yale 33–0. 1913—7–1–1. Lost only to Washington & Lee 21–0 and tied VMI 6–6. 1914—6–2–1. Shut out 5, losing only to West Virginia Wesleyan 13–0 and unbeaten Washington & Lee 7–6. 1916— 7–2–0. Shut out 5 but lost successive games to West Virginia and Yale. 1917 —6–2–1. C.A. Bernier's 1st team lost only to Georgetown and West Virginia. 1918—7–0–0. Outscored foes 152–13, shutting out 5. 1921—7–3–0. B.C. Cubbage's 1st team lost 2 by 3-point margins. 1922—8–1–1. Shut out 5, losing only to Centre 10–6 and tying Davidson 7–7. 1928—7–2–0. Andy Gustafson's best Tech team lost only to Colgate and VMI. 1932—8–1–0. H.B. Redd's 1st team shut out 5 and lost only to Alabama 9–6. 1942— 7–2–1. Lost only to William & Mary and Army. 1954—8–0–1. Frank Moseley's 4th team won 3 by TD margins as Dickie Beard had 730 yards total offense and handled place kicking; tie was with William & Mary 7–7. 1956 —7–2–1. Scored 264 as Jimmy Lugar directed attack; lost only to Tulane 21–14 and Clemson. 1963—8–2–0. Jerry Claiborne's 3rd team won Southern Conference title as Bob Schweickert ran and passed for 1,526 yards and Tommy Marvin caught 28 passes; lost to Kentucky and North Carolina St. 13–7. 1965—7–3–0. Won 4 by 8 points or less as Bobby Owens ran and passed for 1,417 yards. 1966—8–1–1. Won last 7 after losing opener to Tulane 13–0 and tying West Virginia 13–13; lost to Miami (Fla.) in Liberty Bowl 14–7. 1967—7–3–0. Won first 7 and lost 2 by TD or less as DB Frank Loria became Gobblers' 1st consensus All America player. 1968—7–3–0. Two of losses by TD or less; won last 5 but lost to Mississippi in Liberty Bowl 34–17. 1975—8–3–0. Jimmy Sharpe's best team lost only to West Virginia 10–7 in last 9; Roscoe Coles ran for 1,045 yards and 10 TDs. 1980—8–3–0. Bill Dooley's 3rd team won 6 of first 7 behind Steve Casey (1,119 yards and

13 TDs passing), Cyrus Lawrence (1,221 yards rushing) and Sidney Snell (43 receptions for 568 yards and 8 TDs); lost to Miami (Fla.) in Peach Bowl 20–10. 1983—9–2–0. Scored 301 and led nation in rushing defense and scoring defense; lost only to Wake Forest 13–6 in opener and West Virginia 13–0.

BOWL RECORD

Liberty 0–2–0; Peach 0–1–0; Sun 0–1–0.

CONFERENCE TITLES

Southern 1963.

TOP 10 AP & UPI RANKING

None.

MAJOR RIVALS

VPI has played at least 15 games with Clemson (6–12–1), Florida St. (10–14–1), George Washington (11–8–0), Hampden-Sydney (24–0–0), Kentucky (5–10–2), Maryland (12–16–0), North Carolina (13–7–6), North Carolina St. (20–16–3), Richmond (35–9–4), Roanoke (25–0–2), Virginia (33–27–5), VMI (48–25–5), Wake Forest (19–11–1), Washington & Lee (23–20–5), West Virginia (9–19–1) and William & Mary (37–18–4).

COACHES

Top VPI coaches were Jerry Claiborne, 61–39–2 for 1961–70 with 1 conference title and 2 bowl teams; and Frank Moseley, 54–42–4 for 1951–60 with 1 unbeaten team. Other top records were by B.B. Bocock, 34–14–2 for 1909–10 and 1912–15; C.A. Bernier, 18–6–1 for 1917–19 with 1 perfect record; B.C. Cubbage, 30–12–6 for 1921–25; Andy Gustafson, 22–13–1 for 1926–29; H.B. Redd, 43–37–8 for 1932–40; and Bill Dooley, 40–27–0 for 1978–83 with 1 bowl team.

MISCELLANEA

First game was 14–10 win over St. Albans in 1892 . . . highest score was 99–0 over Emory & Henry in 1919 . . . highest since W.W. II was 70–12 over VMI in 1966 . . . worst defeat was 77–6 by Alabama in 1973 . . . longest unbeaten string of 12 in 1917–19 ended by Georgetown 33–7 . . . longest

winless string of 18 in 1947–49 broken with 28–13 win over Richmond
. . . only consensus All America player was Frank Loria, DB, 1967 . . .
Academic All America choices were Loria, DB, 1967; and Tommy Car-
penito, LB, 1972.

Wake Forest (Demon Deacons; Old Gold & Black) (ACC)

NOTABLE TEAMS

1892—4–0–1. Tie was with unbeaten VMI 12–12. 1924—7–2–0. Hank
Garrity's 2nd team lost only to South Carolina 7–0 and Florida. 1925—
6–2–1. Garrity's last team shut out 5, losing only to Florida and North
Carolina St. 6–0. 1939—7–3–0. Peahead Walker's 3rd team led nation in
rushing as John Polanski led individual rushers with 882 yards. 1940—
7–3–0. Won 2 by TD or less as B Tony Gallovich starred. 1942—6–2–1.
Linemen Pat Preston and Buck Jones and B Red Cochran starred as Deacons
lost only to North Carolina 6–0 and Boston College. 1944—8–1–0. Won 4
by TD or less behind B Nick Sacrinty and 4 All-Southern Conference linemen; lost only to Duke 34–0. 1950—6–1–2. Walker's last team won 4 by
TD or less, losing only to unbeaten Clemson 13–12, and led nation in total
defense behind linemen Jim Staton, Bob Auffarth, Jack Lewis and Ed Lis-
topad. 1979—8–3–0. All wins by 8 points or less as James McDougald ran
for 1,231 yards and 13 TDs, Jay Venuto passed for 2,597 yards and 17 TDs
and Wayne Baumgardner caught 61 for 1,128 yards and 9 scores; lost to LSU
in Tangerine Bowl 34–10.

BOWL RECORD

Dixie 0–1–0; Gator 1–0–0; Tangerine 0–1–0.

CONFERENCE TITLES

Atlantic Coast 1970.

TOP 10 AP & UPI RANKING

None.

MAJOR RIVALS

Wake Forest has played at least 15 games with Clemson (11–37–1), Davidson (11–15–4), Duke (17–45–2), Furman (7–11–0), Maryland (8–23–1),
North Carolina (25–53–2), North Carolina St. (27–44–6), Richmond (7–
7–1), South Carolina (20–32–2), Virginia (11–14–0), Virginia Tech (11–
19–1) and William & Mary (8–9–1).

COACHES

Dean of Wake Forest coaches was D.C. (Peahead) Walker with record of
77–50–6 for 1937–50, including 2 bowl teams. Only other with winning
record for at least 3 years was Hank Garrity, 19–7–1 for 1923–25.

MISCELLANEA

First game was 6–4 win over North Carolina in 1888 . . . highest score was
80–0 over Florence YMCA in 1915 . . . highest since W.W. II was 66–21
over Virginia in 1975 . . . biggest margin of victory since W.W. II was 56–6
over Richmond in 1951 . . . worst defeat was 76–0 by North Carolina St.
in 1908 . . . worst since W.W. II was 63–0 by Oklahoma in 1974 . . . most
points ever against Deacons was 82–24 by Clemson in 1981 . . . longest
unbeaten string of 9 in 1945–46 ended by North Carolina St. 14–6 . . .
longest losing string of 18 in 1962–63 broken with 20–19 win over South
Carolina . . . only consensus All America player was Bill Armstrong, DB,
1976 . . . Wake Forest has had no Academic All America selections.

Washington (Huskies; Purple & Gold) (Pacific-10)

NOTABLE TEAMS

1895—4–0–1. Tied Seattle A.C. 0–0. 1899—4–1–1. Lost to Pt. Townsend
A.C. 11–0 and tied All-Seattle 5–5. 1902—5–1–0. Lost only to Multnomah
A.C. 7–0. 1903—6–1–0. Shut out 5, losing only to Multnomah A.C. 6–0 in
finale. 1908—6–0–1. Gil Dobie's 1st team yielded just 15 points; tie was with
Washington St. 6–6. 1909—7–0–0. Scored 214 and blanked all but Oregon
(20–6 in finale). 1910—6–0–0. Shut out all but Whitman (12–8). 1911—
7–0–0. Outscored foes 277–9, shutting out first 5. 1912—6–0–0. Scored 190
and shut out 4. 1913—7–0–0. Outscored foes 266–20. 1914—6–0–1. Shut
out 5, including 0–0 tie with Oregon St. (1st non-victory in 6 years). 1915

—7–0–0. Outscored foes 274–14, blanking 5. 1916—6–0–1. Dobie's last team (9th consecutive undefeated one) outscored foes 189–16 and won 1st Pacific Coast Conference championship behind G Louis Seagraves; tie was with Oregon 0–0. 1919—5–1–0. Lost to Oregon 24–13 but gave up only 7 other points and got share of PCC title. 1922—6–1–1. Enoch Bagshaw's 2nd team lost only to unbeaten California (45–7) and tied Oregon 3–3. 1923— 10–1–0. Shut out 6 and lost only to California 9–0 behind G James Bryan and HB George Wilson; tied Navy in Rose Bowl 14–14. 1924—8–1–1. Outscored foes 355–24, shutting out 6, as Wilson scored 13 TDs; lost only to Oregon 7–3 and tied California 7–7. 1925—10–0–1. Outscored foes 461–39, shutting out 6, as Wilson scored 14 TDs and became Huskies' 1st consensus All America player; tied Nebraska 6–6 but won PCC, then lost to unbeaten Alabama in Rose Bowl 20–19. 1926—8–2–0. Shut out 5, losing only to Washington St. 9–6 and unbeaten national champion Stanford. 1927 —9–2–0. Shut out 7 and HB Chuck Carroll scored 15 TDs as Huskies lost only to Stanford 13–7 and Southern California. 1932—6–2–2. James Phelan's 3rd team lost only to California 7–6 and unbeaten USC 9–6 as E Dave Nisbet starred. 1934—6–1–1. Lost only to Stanford 24–0 and tied Washington St. 0–0. 1936—7–1–1. Shut out 6 and won PCC behind G Max Starcevich and HB Jim Cain; lost only to national champion Minnesota 14–7 in opener and tied Stanford 14–14, but lost to Pittsburgh in Rose Bowl 21–0. 1937—7–2–2. Shut out 5 behind T Vic Markov but lost close ones to Oregon St. 6–3 and Stanford 13–7. 1940—7–2–0. C Rudy Mucha and G Ray Frankowski led Huskies to wins over all but unbeaten teams, national champion Minnesota 19–14 in opener and Stanford 20–10. 1943—4–0–0. Outscored foes 150–32 and Jay Stoves led nation with 7 interceptions in war-shortened schedule; lost to USC in Rose Bowl 29–0. 1950—8–2–0. Howard Odell's best team scored 265 behind nation's leading passer Don Heinrich (1,846 yards and 14 TDs) and FB Hugh McElhenny (1,107 yards rushing and 14 TDs) while Dick Sprague intercepted 7 passes; lost only to Illinois 20–13 and unbeaten California 14–7. 1952—7–3–0. Heinrich again led nation in passing (1,647 yards and 13 TDs) while George Black caught 42 for 637 yards and 7 TDs; won 5 of last 6. 1959—9–1–0. QB Bob Schloredt directed Huskies to wins over all but USC (22–15 loss) and intercepted 6 passes (as did George Fleming); got share of AAWU and beat Wisconsin in Rose Bowl 44–8. 1960—9–1–0. Linemen Roy McKasson, Chuck Allen and Kurt Gegner led team to wins over all but Navy (15–14 loss in 3rd game) and won AAWU again; beat Minnesota in Rose Bowl 17–7. 1962—7–1–2. Lost only to unbeaten national champion USC 14–0 behind C Ray Mansfield and G Rick Redman. 1963—6–4–0. Won 6 of last 7 to win AAWU behind Bill

Douglas (1,242 yards total offense) and Redman; lost to Illinois in Rose Bowl 17-7. 1971—8-3-0. Scored 357 as Sonny Sixkiller passed for 2,068 yards and 13 TDs and Tom Scott caught 35 for 820 yards and 6 scores; lost 2 by total of 3 points. 1972—8-3-0. Jim Owens' last notable team won 5 by 8 points or less behind defense led by LB Gordy Guinn and DB's Cal Jones and Tony Bonwell (7 interceptions). 1977—7-4-0 (9-2-0 by forfeit). Don James' 3rd team scored 317 and won PAC-8 title as Warren Moon ran and passed for 1,850 yards and Joe Steele ran for 865 yards and 13 TDs; beat Michigan in Rose Bowl 27-20. 1979—8-3-0 (9-2-0 by forfeit). Scored 307 behind Steele (12 TDs) and Paul Skansi (31 receptions) while DT Doug Martin and LB Bruce Harrell led defense; beat Texas in Sun Bowl 14-7. 1980—9-2-0. Scored 327 and won PAC-10 as Tom Flick passed for 2,178 yards and 15 TDs and Chuck Nelson kicked 18 FGs; lost to Michigan in Rose Bowl 23-6. 1981—9-2-0. Won PAC-10 again as Nelson kicked 16 FGs; beat Iowa in Rose Bowl 28-0. 1982—9-2-0. Scored 333 behind receivers Skansi (50 receptions for 631 yards) and Anthony Allen (42 for 558) and Nelson's 25 FGs; lost to Stanford and Washington St. 24-20, but beat Maryland in inaugural Aloha Bowl 21-20. 1983—8-3-0. Steve Pelluer ran and passed for 2,376 yards and Jeff Jaeger kicked 20 FGs; lost to Penn St. in Aloha Bowl 13-10.

BOWL RECORD

Aloha 1-1-0; Rose 4-5-1; Sun 1-0-0.

CONFERENCE TITLES

Pacific Coast 1916, 1919*, 1925, 1936. AAWU 1959*, 1960, 1963. Pacific-8 1977. Pacific-10 1980, 1981.

TOP 10 AP & UPI RANKING

1936	5	1977	10-9
1959	8-7	1981	10-7
1960	6-5	1982	7-7

MAJOR RIVALS

Huskies have played at least 15 games with California (30-32-4), Idaho (30-2-2), Minnesota (7-10-0), Montana (16-1-1), Oregon (46-26-5), Oregon St. (41-24-4), Stanford (24-31-4), UCLA (23-22-1), USC (19-34-3), Washington St. (48-22-6) and Whitman (29-2-3).

COACHES

Most successful Washington coach was Gilmour Dobie with amazing record of 58-0-3 for 1908-16 with 9 unbeaten teams and 6 perfect records. He ranks in top 20 both in total coaching victories and all-time winning percentage. Most wins and longest tenure were by Jim Owens with record for 1957-74 of 99-82-6, including 3 conference titles and 3 Rose Bowl teams. Other top records were by Enoch Bagshaw, 63-22-6 for 1921-29 with 1 conference title and 2 Rose Bowl teams; James M. Phelan, 65-37-8 for 1930-41 with 1 conference title and 1 Rose Bowl team; and Don James, 75-30-0 for 1975-83 with 3 conference titles and 6 bowl teams (4 winners). He was national coach of the year in 1977.

MISCELLANEA

First game was 7-0 loss to Alumni in 1889 . . . 1st win was 14-0 over Seattle A.C. in 1892 . . . 1st win over college foe was 46-0 over Whitman in 1894 . . . highest score was 120-0 over Whitman in 1919 . . . highest since W.W. II was 66-0 over Oregon in 1974 . . . worst defeat was 72-3 by California in 1921 . . . worst since W.W. II was 58-0 by Oregon in 1973 . . . highest against Huskies since W.W. II was 62-13 by UCLA in 1973 . . . longest unbeaten string of 63 (NCAA record) in 1907-17 ended by California 27-0 . . . unbeaten string of 14 in 1924-25 ended by Alabama 20-19 in Rose Bowl . . . longest losing string of 10 in 1968-69 broken with 30-21 win over Washington St. . . . consensus All America players were George Wilson, B, 1925; Charles Carroll, B, 1928; Max Starcevich, G, 1936; Rudy Mucha, C, 1940; Ray Frankowski, G, 1941; Rick Redman, G, 1963-64; Tom Greenlee, DT, 1966; Al Worley, DB, 1968; and Chuck Nelson, K, 1982 . . . Academic All America choices were Jim Houston, E, 1955; Mike Briggs, T, 1963; Rick Redman, G, 1964; Steve Bramwell, DB, 1965; Bruce Harrell, LB, 1979; Mark Jerue, LB, 1981; and Chuck Nelson, K, 1981-82 . . . Washington ranks in top 25 in all-time winning percentage.

Washington State (Cougars; Crimson & Gray) (Pacific-10)

NOTABLE TEAMS

1900—4-0-1. Tied Washington 5-5 and shut out others. 1901—4-1-0. Lost only to Idaho 5-0. 1906—6-0-0. Blanked foes 44-0. 1907—7-1-0. Outscored foes 282-18, losing only to Idaho 5-4. 1908—4-0-2. Outscored foes 202-10; ties were with Washington 6-6 and Idaho 4-4. 1909—4-1-0. Lost only to Denver 11-6 in finale. 1915—7-0-0. William Dietz' 1st team outscored foes 190-10; beat Brown in Rose Bowl 14-0. 1917—6-0-1. Tied 362nd Infantry 0-0 in opener; gave up only 3 points and won 1st Pacific Coast Conference championship behind linemen Walter Herried and Silas Stites, E Clarence Zimmerman and B Benton Bangs. 1919—5-2-0. Returned to football after year's layoff during W.W. I and lost only to Washington 13-7 and Oregon St. 6-0. 1920—5-1-0. Lost only to unbeaten national champion California (49-0) behind C Earl Dunlap and FB Lloyd Gillis. 1926 —6-1-0. O.E. Hollingbery's 1st team won 4 by TD or less, losing only to USC 16-7 in 2nd game. 1928—7-3-0. Won 7 of first 8 behind T Mel Dressel. 1929—10-2-0. Shut out 6, losing only to California and USC as Elmer Schwartz starred at FB. 1930—9-0-0. Outscored foes 218-32 behind C Mel Hein, G Harold Ahlskog and T Turk Edwards; shut out 5 and won PCC title but lost to unbeaten Alabama in Rose Bowl 24-0. 1932—7-1-1. Shut out 6, losing only to unbeaten USC 20-0 and tying Washington 0-0 behind HB George Sander. 1942—6-2-2. Hollingbery's last team lost only to USC and Texas A&M as FB Bob Kennedy ran for 813 yards and 11 TDs. 1945—6-2-1. Lost only to Washington 6-0 and Oregon St. following 2-year layoff during W.W. II; Bill Lippincott intercepted 7 passes. 1951—7-3-0. Scored 280 as Ed Barker caught 46 passes for 864 yards and 9 TDs and Bud Roffler scored 9 TDs and kicked 26 extra points. 1958—7-3-0. Jim Sutherland's 3rd team won 4 by TD or less behind FB Chuck Morrell and G Marv Nelson. 1965—7-3-0. Won 4 by TD or less as DT Wayne Foster and DB Bill Gaskins (5 interceptions) led defense and Larry Eilmes (818 yards rushing) and Doug Flansburg (46 receptions for 578 yards) paced offense. 1981 —8-2-1. Scored in double figures in all but lost to USC and Washington; lost to Brigham Young in Holiday Bowl 38-36.

BOWL RECORD

Holiday 0–1–0; Rose 1–1–0.

CONFERENCE TITLES

Pacific Coast 1917, 1930.

TOP 10 AP & UPI RANKING

None.

MAJOR RIVALS

Cougars have played at least 15 games with California (13–32–4), Gonzaga (18–5–3), Idaho (61–14–3), Montana (30–2–0), Oregon (30–25–7), Oregon St. (33–36–3), Southern California (4–37–4), Stanford (16–20–1), UCLA (8–25–1), Washington (22–48–6) and Whitman (18–3–1).

COACHES

Dean of Washington State coaches was O.E. Hollingbery with record of 93–53–14 for 1926–42, including 1 conference title and 1 Rose Bowl team. William H. Dietz was 17–2–1 for 1915–17 with 1 conference title, 1 Rose Bowl champion and 2 unbeaten teams. Other long-time coaches were Jim Sutherland, 37–39–4 for 1956–63; and Jim Sweeney, 26–59–1 for 1968–75.

MISCELLANEA

First game was 10–0 win over Idaho in 1894 . . . highest score was 86–0 over Blair Business College in 1907 . . . highest since W.W. II was 84–27 over Idaho in 1975 . . . worst defeat was 61–0 by California in 1922 . . . worst since W.W. II was 62–3 by UCLA in 1976 . . . highest ever against Cougars was 70–33 by USC in 1970 . . . longest unbeaten string of 14 in 1907–09 ended by Denver 11–6 . . . unbeaten string of 13 in 1916–19 ended by Washington 13–7 . . . longest losing string of 11 in 1970–71 broken with 31–20 win over Minnesota . . . Washington State has had no consensus All America players and no Academic All America choices.

West Virginia (Mountaineers; Old Gold & Blue) (Independent)

NOTABLE TEAMS

1895—5–1–0. Yielded just 10 points; lost to Washington & Jefferson 4–0 and beat Pittsburgh 8–0 in 1st meeting. **1898**—6–1–0. Shut out 5, losing only to Pittsburgh A.C. 18–0. **1903**—7–1–0. Shut out 5, losing only to Ohio State (34–6). **1905**—8–1–0. Shut out 6 but lost to Penn St. 6–0. **1919**—8–2–0. Outscored foes 326–47, shutting out 7, as FB Ira (Rat) Rodgers scored 147 points (including 19 TDs) and became Mountaineers' 1st consensus All America player; lost only to Pitt and Centre. **1922**—9–0–1. Dr. Clarence Spears' 2nd team outscored foes 246–18, shutting out 8, behind T Russ Meredith, G Joe Setron and HB Nick Nardacci; beat Gonzaga 21–13 in San Diego East-West Christmas Classic. **1923**—7–1–1. Outscored foes 296–41, losing only to Washington & Jefferson 7–2 in finale and tying Penn St. 13–13. **1924**—8–1–0. Spears' last team outscored foes 282–47 behind G Red Mahan and E Fred Graham, losing only to Pitt 14–7 in 3rd game. **1925**—8–1–0. Ira Rodgers' 1st team shut out 7 as Mahan starred again; beat Penn St. for 1st time 14–0 but lost to Pitt 15–7. **1928**—8–2–0. Shut out 5, losing only to Davis & Elkins 7–0 in opener and to Georgetown 12–0. **1937**—7–1–1. HB Harry Clarke ran for 816 yards as Mountaineers shut out 6, losing only to national champion Pitt 20–0 and tying Georgetown 6–6; beat Texas Tech in Sun Bowl 7–6. **1948**—8–3–0. Jimmy Walthall passed for 1,222 yards and 13 TDs and Vic Bonfili ran for 535 yards and caught 24 passes for 244 more; won 5 of last 6, then beat Texas-El Paso in Sun Bowl 21–12. **1952**—7–2–0. Art Lewis' 3rd team won last 6 after losses to Furman 22–14 in opener and Penn St. as freshman QB Fred Wyant ran and passed for 1,049 yards and 13 TDs and E Paul Bischoff caught 31 passes for 402 yards. **1953**—8–1–0. Scored 290 behind C Bob Orders, G Gene Lamone and T Bruce Bosley while losing only to South Carolina 20–14; won first Southern Conference title but lost to Georgia Tech in Sugar Bowl 42–19. **1954**—8–1–0. Wyant ran and passed for 12 TDs as Mountaineers lost only to Pitt 13–10. **1955**—8–2–0. Scored 285 as Bob Moss ran for 807 yards and 10 TDs and tackles Bruce Bosley and Sam Huff starred both offensively and defensively; won 3rd straight Southern Conference title, losing only to Pitt and Syracuse 20–13 after winning first 7. **1957**—7–2–1. Won 6 of last 7, losing only to Wisconsin and Penn St. during year. **1962**—8–2–0. Jerry Yost ran and passed for 1,361 yards and 16 TDs to lead Mountaineers to wins over all but Oregon St. and Penn St. 1964—7–3–0. Allen McCune passed for 1,034 yards and 11 TDs and Milt Clegg caught 31 for 437 yards; won 5 of last 6 to take 6th Southern Conference title, but lost to Utah in Liberty Bowl 32–6. 1968—7–3–0. Jim Carlen's 3rd team scored in double figures in all behind Mike Sherwood (1,998 yards and 12 TDs passing) and Oscar Patrick (50 receptions for 770 yards). 1969—9–1–0. Scored 288 as Bob Gresham ran for 1,155 yards and caught 15 passes for 147 more and Jim Braxton scored 113 points (including 13 TDs and 26–30 extra points) while MG Carl Crennel and DB Mike Slater (7 interceptions) sparked defense; lost only to unbeaten Penn St. 20–0 and beat South Carolina in Peach Bowl 14–3. 1970 —8–3–0. Bobby Bowden's 1st team scored 311 as Sherwood passed for 1,550 yards and 15 TDs, Gresham ran for 866 yards and Braxton starred at TE while LB Dale Farley sparked defense. 1972—8–3–0. Scored 402 as Bernie Galiffa passed for 2,496 yards and 17 TDs, Marshall Mills caught 39 for 659 yards and Kerry Marbury ran for 775 yards and scored 18 TDs while Tom Geishauser intercepted 7 passes; lost 2 by TD or less, but lost to North Carolina St. in Peach Bowl 49–13. 1975—8–3–0. Bowden's last team lost 2 by less than 3 points as Dan Kendra passed for 1,315 yards, Artie Owens ran for 1,055 yards and Ron Lee scored 10 TDs; beat North Carolina St. in Peach Bowl 13–10. 1981—8–3–0. Don Nehlen's 2nd team was sparked by QB Oliver Luck (2,448 yards and 16 TDs passing) and TE Mark Raugh (64 receptions for 601 yards) along with LBs Darryl Talley and Dennis Fowlkes; upset Florida in Peach Bowl 26–6. 1982—9–2–0. QB Jeff Hostetler ran and passed for 1,853 yards, Raugh caught 32 passes for 423 yards, Paul Woodside led nation with NCAA record 28 FGs (in 31 tries), and Talley, Fowlkes and DB Tim Agee sparked defense as Mountaineers lost only to Pitt 16–13 and Penn St.; lost to Florida St. in Gator Bowl 31–12. 1983—8–3–0. Scored 302 behind Hostetler (2,257 yards and 14 TDs passing) and Woodside (19 FGs in 23 tries) while Agee again sparked defense along with DB Steve Newberry and MG Dave Oblak; beat Kentucky in Hall of Fame Bowl 20–16.

BOWL RECORD

Gator 0–1–0; Hall of Fame 1–0–0; Liberty 0–1–0; Peach 3–1–0; San Diego Christmas Classic 1–0–0; Sugar 0–1–0; Sun 2–0–0.

CONFERENCE TITLES

Southern 1953, 1954, 1955, 1956, 1958, 1964, 1965, 1967.

TOP 10 AP & UPI RANKING

1953   10–U

MAJOR RIVALS

West Virginia has played at least 15 games with George Washington (17–7–0), Kentucky (8–11–1), Marietta (16–6–1), Maryland (10–9–2), Penn St. (7–41–2), Pittsburgh (23–52–1), Richmond (21–3–1), Syracuse (12–19–0), Temple (11–10–0), Virginia (10–9–1), Virginia Tech (19–9–1), Washington & Jefferson (12–20–2), Washington & Lee (27–6–4), Waynesburg (16–1–0), West Virginia Wesleyan (29–4–1) and William & Mary (15–0–1).

COACHES

Dean of Mountaineer coaches was Art (Pappy) Lewis with record of 58–38–2 for 1950–59, including 5 conference titles and 1 bowl team. Dr. Clarence Spears was 30–6–3 for 1921–24 with 1 unbeaten bowl team. Other top records were by Mont McIntire, 24–11–4 for 1916–17 and 1919–20; Ira E. Rodgers, 44–31–8 for 1925–30 and 1943–45; Bill Kern, 24–23–1 for 1940–42 and 1946–47; Jim Carlen, 25–13–3 for 1966–69 with 1 conference title and 1 bowl champion; Bobby Bowden, 42–26–0 for 1970–75 with 2 bowl teams; and Don Nehlen, 33–15–0 for 1980–83 with 3 bowl teams.

MISCELLANEA

First game was 72–0 loss to Washington & Jefferson in 1891 . . . 1st win was 12–2 over Uniontown Independents in 1893 . . . 1st win over college foe was 6–0 over Bethany (W.Va.) in 1894 . . . highest score was 92–6 over Marshall in 1915 . . . highest since W.W. II was 89–0 over Geneva in 1951 . . . worst defeat was 130–0 by Michigan in 1904 . . . worst since W.W. II was 62–14 by Penn St. in 1973 . . . longest unbeaten string of 19 in 1922–23 ended by Washington & Jefferson 7–2 . . . winning streak of 13 in 1952–53 ended by South Carolina 20–14 . . . longest winless string of 18 in 1959–61 broken with 28–0 win over Virginia Tech . . . consensus All America players were Ira Rodgers, B, 1919; Bruce Bosley, T, 1955; and Darryl Talley, LB, 1982 . . . Academic All America choices were Paul Bischoff, E, 1952; Fred Wyant, QB, 1954; Sam Huff, T, 1955; Kim West, K, 1970; Oliver Luck, QB, 1980–81; and Jeff Hostetler, QB, 1983.

William & Mary (Indians; Green, Gold & Silver) (Independent)

NOTABLE TEAMS

1923—7–3–0. J.W. Tasker's 1st team shut out 6; lost only to Roanoke 9–7 in last 7 games. 1924—6–2–1. Unbeaten in last 6 after successive losses to Navy 14–7 and Syracuse 24–7. 1926—7–3–0. Shut out 5; lost only to Columbia 13–10 in last 6. 1929—8–2–0. Branch Bocock's 2nd team won last 6 after losses to Navy and Virginia Tech. 1930—7–2–1. Shut out 7; lost early-season games to Navy 19–6 and Virginia Tech 7–6. 1939—6–2–1. Carl Voyles' 1st team lost only to Navy and Virginia. 1940—6–2–1. Lost only to North Carolina St. and Navy. 1941—8–2–0. Shut out 5 and lost only to Navy and North Carolina St. behind G Buster Ramsey and B Harvey Johnson. 1942—9–1–1. Shut out 5 and won 1st Southern Conference title as Ramsey and Johnson starred again along with T Marvin Bass and E Glenn Knox; lost only to North Carolina Pre-Flight 14–0 and tied Harvard 7–7. 1946— 8–2–0. Rube McCray's 3rd team outscored foes 347–71, shutting out 5, behind G Knox Ramsey and FB Jack Cloud; lost only to Miami (Fla.) and North Carolina. 1947—9–1–0. Scored 301 and won Southern Conference behind Cloud (17 TDs), Ramsey, C Tommy Thompson and E Bob Steckroth while Jack Bruce led nation with 9 interceptions; lost only to North Carolina 13–7, then lost to Arkansas in Dixie Bowl 21–19. 1948—6–2–2. Unbeaten in last 5 after losses to Wake Forest 21–12 and St. Bonaventure 7–6 as Cloud and Thompson starred again; beat Oklahoma St. in Delta Bowl 20–0. 1951 —7–3–0. Outscored by rivals overall, but won 4 by TD or less as B Ed Mioduszewski starred.

BOWL RECORD

Delta 1–0–0; Dixie 0–1–0; Tangerine 0–1–0.

CONFERENCE TITLES

Southern 1942, 1947, 1970.

TOP 10 AP & UPI RANKING

None.

MAJOR RIVALS

Indians have played at least 15 games with The Citadel (17–6–0), East Carolina (4–11–1), George Washington (12–9–2), Hampden-Sydney (18–19–1), Navy (4–35–1), North Carolina St. (8–8–0), Randolph-Macon (20–20–1), Richmond (43–45–5), Virginia (4–20–1), VMI (27–32–2), Virginia Tech (18–37–4), Wake Forest (9–8–1) and West Virginia (0–15–1).

COACHES

Most successful William & Mary coaches were Rube McCray, 44–21–3 for 1944–50 with 1 conference title and 2 bowl teams; and Carl M. Voyles, 29–7–3 for 1939–42 with 1 conference title. Other top records were by J.W. Tasker, 31–17–2 for 1923–27; and Branch Bocock, 26–20–3 for 1928–30 and 1936–37. Jim Root had longest tenure with record of 39–48–1 for 1972–79.

MISCELLANEA

First game was 16–0 loss to Norfolk YMCA in 1893 . . . 1st win was 6–4 over Capital City A.C. same year . . . 1st win over college foe was 5–0 over Randolph-Macon in 1898 . . . highest score was 95–0 over Bridgewater in 1931 . . . highest since W.W. II was 61–0 over Ft. McClelland in 1946 . . . worst defeat was 93–0 by Delaware in 1915 . . . worst since W.W. II was 57–7 by Cincinnati in 1953 and 56–6 by West Virginia in 1958 . . . highest against Indians since W.W. II was 62–21 by Delaware in 1982 . . . longest unbeaten string of 9 in 1942 ended by North Carolina Pre-Flight 14–0 . . . longest winless string of 15 in 1955–57 broken with 13–7 win over Virginia Tech . . . William & Mary has had no consensus All America players . . . Academic All America choices were John Gerdelman, RB, 1974; Ken Smith, DB, 1975 and 1977; and Robert Musculus, TE, 1978.

Wisconsin (Badgers; Cardinal & White) (Big 10)

NOTABLE TEAMS

1894—6–1–0. Shut out last 5 after forfeiting to Purdue. **1896**—7–1–1. Phil King's 1st team shut out 6; lost only to Carlisle Indians 18–8 in finale and tied Northwestern 6–6. **1897**—9–1–0. Shut out 8 and won 1st Big 10 title, losing only to Alumni 6–0. **1898**—9–1–0. Again shut out 8 and scored 318, losing only to Chicago 6–0. 1899—9–2–0. Shut out 7 but lost to Yale 6–0 and Chicago. 1900—8–1–0. Scored 300 and shut out 7, losing only to Minnesota 6–5. 1901—9–0–0. Outscored foes 317–5 and got share of Big 10 title. 1905—8–2–0. King's last team shut out 7, losing only to unbeaten national champion Chicago 4–0 and Michigan 12–0. 1906—5–0–0. Outscored foes 78–15 and got share of Big 10 title. 1908—5–1–0. Lost only to Chicago in finale 18–12. 1911—5–1–1. J.R. Richards' 1st team won first 5 before tying Minnesota 6–6 and losing to Chicago 5–0. 1912—7–0–0. Outscored foes 246–29 and won Big 10 as T Robert Butler became Badgers' 1st consensus All America player. 1919—5–2–0. C Charles Carpenter led team to wins over all but Minnesota and Ohio St. (0–3). 1920—6–1–0. Lost only to unbeaten Ohio St. 13–7 as E Frank Weston and T Ralph Scott starred. 1921—5–1–1. Backs Guy Sundt and Alvah Elliott led Badgers to wins in first 5; tied Michigan 7–7 and lost to Chicago 3–0. 1925—6–1–1. Lost only to Michigan 21–0 and tied Minnesota 12–12. 1928—7–1–1. Shut out 5, losing only to Minnesota 6–0 in finale and tying Purdue 19–19 as QB Bo Cuisinier and G John Parks starred. 1930—6–2–1. Scored 227 and shut out 5 behind T Milo Lubratovich; lost only to Purdue 7–6 and Northwestern. 1932—6–1–1. Clarence Spears' 1st team lost only to Purdue 7–6 and tied Ohio St. 7–7 as Mickey McGuire starred at HB. 1942—8–1–1. E David Schreiner and FB Pat Harder led Badgers to wins over all but Notre Dame (7–7) and Iowa (6–0 defeat). 1951—7–1–1. Led nation in total defense and scoring defense behind DE's Harold Faverty and Pat O'Donahue as Alan Ameche ran for 824 yards and John Coatta passed for 1,154; won last 6 after losing to Illinois 14–10 and tying Ohio St. 6–6. 1952—6–2–1. Ameche ran for 946 yards and Jim Haluska passed for 1,410 yards and 12 TDs behind T Dave Suminski while DE Don Voss sparked defense; won share of Big 10 but lost to Southern California in Rose Bowl 7–0. 1953—6–2–1. Ameche ran for 801 yards as Badgers lost only to UCLA 13–0 and Ohio St. 20–19. 1954—7–2–0. Heisman winner Ameche ran for 641 yards and 9 TDs behind C Gary Messner and Jim Miller intercepted 6 passes as Badgers lost only to unbeaten national champion Ohio St. and Iowa 13–7.1958—7–1–1. Milt Bruhn's 3rd team lost only to national champion Iowa 20–9 and tied Ohio St. 7–7 as QB Dale Hackbart scored 9 TDs and intercepted 7 passes. 1959—7–2–0. Won Big 10 despite losses to Purdue and Illinois 9–6 as Hackbart ran and passed for 955 yards behind T Dan Lanphear; lost to Washington in Rose Bowl 44–8. 1962—8–1–0. Scored 285 and led nation in scoring average as Ron VanderKelen passed for 1,181 yards and 12 TDs and Pat Richter caught 38 for 531 yards and 5 TDs; won Big 10 despite 14–7 loss to Ohio St. but lost to unbeaten national champion Southern California in Rose Bowl 42–37.

BOWL RECORD

Garden State 0–1–0; Independence 1–0–0; Rose 0–3–0.

CONFERENCE TITLES

Big 10 1897, 1901*, 1906*, 1912, 1952*, 1959, 1962.

TOP 10 AP & UPI RANKING

1942	3	1958	7–6
1951	8–8	1959	6–6
1952	U–10	1962	2–2
1954	9–10		

MAJOR RIVALS

Wisconsin has played at least 15 games with Beloit (16–1–0), Chicago (19–16–5), Illinois (23–25–6), Indiana (23–11–2), Iowa (34–26–1), Marquette (32–4–0), Michigan (8–34–1), Michigan St. (11–15–0), Minnesota (36–49–8), Notre Dame (6–8–2), Northwestern (44–22–5), Ohio St. (9–40–4) and Purdue (30–22–7).

COACHES

Most wins were by Phil King with record of 65–11–1 for 1896–1902 and 1905, including 2 Big 10 titles and 1 perfect record. Longest tenure was by Harry Stuhldreher with record of 45–62–6 for 1936–48, including 1 national title. Other top records were by J.R. Richards, 29–9–4 for 1911, 1917 and 1919–22; Ivan Williamson, 41–19–4 for 1949–55 with 1 Big 10 title and 1 Rose Bowl team; and Milt Bruhn, 52–45–6 for 1956–66 with 2 Big 10 titles and 2 Rose Bowl teams.

MISCELLANEA

First game was 27–0 loss to Calumet Club in 1889 . . . 1st win was 106–0 over Whitewater Normal in 1890 . . . highest score also was in 1st win . . . highest since 1900 was 87–0 over Beloit in 1903 . . . highest since W.W. II was 69–13 over New Mexico St. in 1962 . . . worst defeat was 63–0 by Minnesota in 1890 . . . worst since 1900 was 59–0 by Ohio St. in 1979 . . . highest against Badgers since 1900 was 62–7 by Ohio St. in 1969 . . . longest winning streak of 17 in 1900–02 ended by Michigan 6–0 . . . longest winless string of 23 in 1967–69 broken with 23–17 win over Iowa

. . . Wisconsin has had 13 consensus All America players since 1912 . . . unanimous choices were Dave Schreiner, E, 1942; Alan Ameche, B, 1954; and Dan Lanphear, T, 1959 . . . others selected since W.W. II were Pat Richter, E, 1962; Dennis Lick, T, 1975; and Tim Krumrie, DL, 1981 . . . Academic All America selections were Bob Kennedy, G, 1952; Alan Ameche, B, 1953–54; Jon Hobbs, B, 1958; Dale Hackbart, B, 1959; Pat Richter, E, 1962; Ken Bowman, C, 1963; Rufus Ferguson, RB, 1972; and Kyle Borland, LB, 1982 . . . Alan Ameche, FB, won Heisman Trophy in 1954.

Wyoming (Cowboys, Pokes; Brown & Yellow) (WAC)

NOTABLE TEAMS

1904— 4–1–1. Lost only to Utah 23–0 and tied Colorado St. 6–6. 1949— 9–1–0. Bowden Wyatt's 3rd team scored 375 (leading nation in scoring average) and shut out 6, losing only to Baylor 32–7. 1950—9–0–0. Outscored foes 343–53 as Eddie Talboom scored 15 TDs, passed for 8 more and kicked 40 extra points; won Skyline 6 and beat Washington & Lee in Gator Bowl 20–7. 1951—7–2–1. Dewey McConnell led nation's pass receivers with 47 receptions for 725 yards and 9 TDs and Harry Geldien scored 11 TDs as Cowboys lost only to Florida 13–0 in opener and Colorado St. 14–7. 1955—7–3–0. Phil Dickens' 3rd team lost 2 by 3 points or less as Jerry Jester ran for 696 yards; beat Texas Tech in Sun Bowl 21–14. 1956—10–0–0. Won 4 by 8 points or less as Jim Crawford led nation's runners with 1,104 yards and 14 TDs; won Skyline 8 championship. 1958—7–3–0. Bob Devaney's 2nd team won 5 by 8 points or less and took Skyline 8 title; beat Hardin-Simmons in Sun Bowl 14–6. 1959—9–1–0. Outscored foes 287–62 and repeated as conference champs, losing only to Air Force 20–7 in 2nd game. 1960—8–2–0. Led nation in total defense and rushing defense and Jerry Hill ran for 636 yards as Cowboys won 3rd straight Skyline 8 title; lost only to Arizona 21–19 and Utah St. 17–13. 1961—6–1–2. Devaney's last team won 6th and last Skyline title, losing only to Arizona 20–15. 1964—6–2–2. Lloyd Eaton's 3rd team lost only to Arizona and New Mexico behind linemen Herm Memmelaar and Bill Levine. 1966—9–1–0. Scored 327 and led nation in rushing defense while winning 1st Western Athletic Conference title behind Jerry DePoyster (nation's leading FG kicker with 13), HB Vic Washington (nation's leading punt returner) and linemen Ron Billingsley and

Dave Rupp; lost only to Colorado St. 12–10, and beat Florida St. in Sun Bowl 28–20. **1967—10–0–0.** Again led nation in rushing defense behind T Mike Dirks as Paul Toscano ran and passed for 1,915 yards and 22 TDs and DePoyster kicked 15 FGs; won 2nd straight WAC title but lost to LSU in Sugar Bowl 20–13. **1968—7–3–0.** All losses by TD or less as Cowboys led nation in total defense and Bob Jacobs led nation in FGs with 14 (and also averaged 42.1 yards per punt); won 3rd straight WAC title. **1976—8–3–0.** Scored in double figures in all behind T Dennis Baker and won 5 by TD or less in 2nd and last year under Fred Akers; won share of WAC but lost to Oklahoma in Fiesta Bowl 41–7. **1981—8–3–0.** Scored 344 in Al Kincaid's 1st year, losing 2 by less than TD.

BOWL RECORD

Fiesta 0–1–0; Gator 1–0–0; Sugar 0–1–0; Sun 3–0–0.

CONFERENCE TITLES

Skyline 6 1950. Skyline 8 1956, 1958, 1959, 1960*, 1961*. Western Athletic 1966, 1967, 1968, 1976*.

TOP 10 AP & UPI RANKING

1967   6–5

MAJOR RIVALS

Wyoming has played at least 15 games with Air Force (9–10–3), Arizona (10–12–0), Arizona St. (6–9–0), Brigham Young (26–25–3), Colorado (2–21–1), Colorado College (1–16–1), Colorado Mines (9–16–2), Colorado St. College (17–5–3), Colorado State U. (30–40–5), Denver (11–32–2), Montana St. (11–6–0), New Mexico (21–19–0), Texas-El Paso (17–5–0), Utah (21–36–1) and Utah St. (20–34–4).

COACHES

Dean of Wyoming coaches was Lloyd W. Eaton with record of 57–33–2 for 1962–70, including 3 conference titles, 2 bowl teams and 1 team unbeaten in regular season. Bowden Wyatt was 39–17–1 for 1947–52 with 1 conference title and 1 unbeaten bowl champion. Bob Devaney was 35–10–5 for 1957–61 with 4 conference titles and 1 bowl champion. He ranks among top 15 coaches in all-time winning percentage. Other top records were by William McMurray, 15–11–1 for 1900–06; and Phil Dickens, 29–11–1 for 1953–56 with 1 conference title, 1 bowl champion and 1 unbeaten team.

MISCELLANEA

First game was 14–0 win over Cheyenne H.S. in 1893 . . . 1st win over college foe was 34–0 over Colorado St. in 1895 . . . highest score was 103–0 over Northern Colorado in 1949 . . . worst defeat was 79–0 by Utah in 1923 . . . worst since W.W. II was 66–7 by LSU in 1977 . . . highest against Cowboys since W.W. II was 69–14 by Utah in 1983 . . . longest unbeaten string of 16 in 1956–57 ended by Utah 23–15 . . . longest winless string of 12 in 1929–30 broken with 21–6 win over Colorado St. . . . Jack Weil, P, was consensus All America in 1983 . . . Academic All America choices were Bob Dinges, DE, 1965; George Mills, OG, 1967; and Mike Lopiccolo, OT, 1973.

Yale (Bulldogs, Elis; Yale Blue & White) (Ivy)

NOTABLE TEAMS

1878—4–1–1. Lost only to unbeaten Princeton 1–0 in finale. 1879—3–0–2. Had 0–0 ties with Harvard and Princeton. 1880—4–0–1. Tie was 0–0 with Princeton in finale. 1881—5–0–1. Unscored-on but had 0–0 tie with Princeton in finale. 1882—8–0–0. Shut out first 7 and beat Princeton 2–1 in finale. 1883—8–0–0. Buried opponents 485–2. 1884—8–0–1. Outscored foes 495–10; tie was 0–0 with Princeton in finale. 1885—7–1–0. Outscored foes 366–11 but lost to unbeaten Princeton 6–5. 1886—9–0–1. Clobbered foes 687–4; tie was with Princeton 0–0 in finale. 1887—9–0–0. Outscored foes 515–12, shutting out 7. 1888—13–0–0. Walter Camp's 1st team blanked opponents 698–0. 1889—15–1–0. Shut out 12 and outscored foes 665–31 as E Amos Alonzo Stagg, G Pudge Heffelfinger and T Charles Gill made 1st All America team; lost only to unbeaten national champion Princeton 10–0 in finale. 1890—13–1–0. Outscored foes 486–18, shutting out 12 and losing only to unbeaten national champion Harvard 12–6 as Heffelfinger, HB Thomas McClung and T William Rhodes starred. 1891—13–0–0. Blanked foes 488–0 and won 1st national championship behind Heffelfinger, McClung, T Wallace Winter and ends Frank Hinkey and John Hartwell. 1892—13–0–0. Camp's last team blanked foes 435–0 and took 2nd straight national title behind Hinkey, T Hamilton Wallis and QB Vance McCormick. 1893—10–1–0. Outscored foes 330–12, shutting out 9 and losing only to unbeaten national champion Princeton 6–0 in finale as Hinkey, FB Frank Butterworth and G William Hickok starred. 1894—16–0–0. Outscored foes 485–13, shutting out 13 and winning 3rd national championship behind

Hinkey, Butterworth, Hickok, QB George Adee and C Phillip Stillman. 1895—13-0-2. Scored 316 and shut out 10; ties were with Boston A.C. 0-0 and Brown 6-6. 1896—13-1-0. Shut out 9 but lost finale to unbeaten national champion Princeton 24-6. 1897—9-0-2. Shut out 7 behind T Burr Chamberlin and G Gordon Brown; ties were 6-6 with Army and 0-0 with Harvard. 1898—9-2-0. Won first 9, shutting out 7, then lost to Princeton 6-0 and unbeaten national champion Harvard 17-0 as Chamberlin, Brown and FB Malcolm McBride starred. 1899—7-2-1. Shut out 8 and lost close ones to Columbia 5-0 and Princeton 11-10 as Brown, McBride, HB Albert Sharpe and T George Stillman starred. 1900—12-0-0. Outscored foes 336-10, shutting out 10, and won national title behind 7 All America players (including Brown, Stillman, FB Perry Hale, HB George Chadwick and T James Bloomer). 1901—11-1-1. Shut out 9, losing only to unbeaten Harvard 22-0 in finale and tying Army 5-5 as C Henry Holt starred. 1902—11-0-1. Shut out 8 as Holt and 6 others (including Chadwick, T James Hogan and E Thomas Shevlin) made All America; tie was with Army 6-6. 1903—11-1-0. Outscored foes 312-26, shutting out 9, and lost only to unbeaten national champion Princeton 11-6 behind Hogan, HB Ledyard Mitchell, G James Bloomer and E Charles Rafferty. 1904—10-1-0. Shut out 9 and lost only to Army 11-6 as Hogan, Shevlin, G Ralph Kinney and QB Foster Rockwell starred. 1905—10-0-0. Shut out all but Princeton (23-4) while outscoring foes 227-4 behind Shevlin, HB Howard Roome, QB Guy Hutchinson and G Roswell Tripp. 1906—9-0-1. Shut out all but Army (10-6) and tied national champion Princeton 0-0 behind E Robert Forbes, HB William Knox, FB Paul Veeder and T Horatio Biglow. 1907—9-0-1. Shut out all but Princeton (12-10) and won 5th national championship despite 0-0 tie with Army as Biglow, E Clarence Alcott, QB T.A.D. Jones and FB Edward Coy starred. 1908—7-1-1. Shut out first 6 but tied Brown 10-10 and lost finale to Harvard 4-0 as Coy starred again. 1909—10-0-0. Blanked foes 209-0 under Howard Jones and won national championship behind Coy, T Henry Hobbs, G Hamlin Andrus, C Carroll Cooney, E John Kilpatrick and HB Stephen Philbin. 1910—6-2-2. Shut out 6 but lost to Army 9-3 and Brown as Kilpatrick starred again. 1911—7-1-2. Shut out 8 and lost only to unbeaten national champion Princeton 6-3 behind QB Arthur Howe, E Douglass Bomeisler and C Henry Ketcham. 1912—7-1-1. Won first 7 before tying Princeton 6-6 and losing to unbeaten national champion Harvard 20-0 as Bomeisler and Ketcham starred again. 1914—7-2-0. HB Harry Legore led Bulldogs to wins over all but Washington & Jefferson (7-13) and Harvard. 1916—8-1-0. T.A.D. Jones' 1st team lost only to Brown 21-6 as G Clinton Black and ends George Moseley and

Charles Comerford starred. 1921—8–1–0. Shut out 5, losing only to Harvard 10–3 in finale as Malcolm Aldrich starred at HB. 1923—8–0–0. Scored 230 and shut out 5 behind FB William Mallory and T Century Milstead. 1924—6–0–2. HB Raymond Pond, E Richard Luman and C Winslow Lovejoy led Bulldogs to wins over all but Dartmouth (14–14) and Army (7–7). 1927—7–1–0. Jones' last team lost only to Georgia 14–10 in 2nd game as HB Bruce Caldwell starred behind linemen Sidney Quarrier, William Webster and J.D. Charlesworth. 1931—5–1–2. Lost only to Georgia 26–7 in 2nd game. 1936—7–1–0. Won 4 by TD or less behind E Larry Kelley (Heisman Trophy winner) and HB Clint Frank (7 interceptions); lost only to Dartmouth 11–7. 1937—6–1–1. Frank ran and passed for 1,156 yards and 16 TDs and won Heisman as Bulldogs lost only to Harvard 13–6 in finale and tied Dartmouth 9–9. 1944—7–0–1. Howard Odell's 3rd team won 3 by TD or less as E Paul Walker starred; tie was 6–6 with Virginia in finale. 1946 —7–1–1. Scored 272 as Levi Jackson ran for 806 yards and John Roderick caught 26 passes for 418 yards and 5 TDs; won last 5 after losing to Columbia 28–20 and tying Cornell 6–6. 1952—7–2–0. Jordan Oliver's 1st team scored 240 as Ed Molloy passed for 1,305 yards and 15 TDs and Ed Woodsum caught 40 for 633 yards and 11 scores; lost to Navy and Princeton 27–21. 1955—7–2–0. Lost only to Colgate 7–0 and Princeton 13–0. 1956—8–1–0. Scored 246 as Denny McGill ran for 639 yards; lost only to Colgate 14–6 and won inaugural formal Ivy League championship. 1957—6–2–1. Scored in double figures in all as Dick Winterbauer directed attack. 1960—9–0–0. Outscored foes 253–73 to take Ivy League and share of Lambert Trophy behind G Ben Balme. 1964—6–2–1. Unbeaten in first 7 before losing to Princeton and Harvard 18–14 as Chuck Mercein ran for 755 yards. 1967— 8–1–0. Carmen Cozza's 3rd team scored 278 and lost only to Holy Cross 26–14 in opener; won 3rd Ivy title. 1968—8–0–1. Scored 317 as Brian Dowling passed for 1,554 yards and 19 TDs and led nation in passing efficiency while Calvin Hill ran for 680 yards and 14 TDs; tied Harvard 29–29 in finale but got share of Ivy title. 1969—7–2–0. Joe Massey passed for 1,280 yards and soph Rich Maher caught 30 as Bulldogs got share of 3rd straight Ivy title; lost only to Connecticut 19–15 in opener and to Dartmouth. 1970—7–2–0. Dick Jauron ran for 962 yards to lead Bulldogs to wins over all but unbeaten Dartmouth (10–0 loss) and Harvard (14–12 defeat). 1972 —7–2–0. Jauron ran for 1,055 yards and 13 TDs as Yale scored 283 and lost only to Cornell and Penn. 1974—8–1–0. Rudy Green ran for 759 yards and 12 TDs and Gary Fencik caught 32 passes for 491 yards as Bulldogs got share of Ivy title; lost only to Harvard 21–16 in finale. 1975—7–2–0. Don Gesicki ran for 873 yards and Fencik caught 42 passes for 729 yards; lost only to

Brown and Harvard 10–7. **1976—8–1–0.** John Pagliaro ran for 1,023 yards and 16 TDs to lead Elis to share of Ivy title; lost only to Brown 14–6 in opener. **1977—7–2–0.** Won last 5 to take Ivy title after losses to Miami (0.) 28–14 and Dartmouth 3–0; Pagliaro ran for 1,159 yards and 14 TDs and John Spagnola caught 35 passes for 593 yards. **1979—8–1–0.** Won 3 by less than TD while leading nation in total defense and rushing defense and lost only to Harvard 22–7 in finale; John Stratton caught 33 passes for 629 yards to lead Bulldogs to Ivy title. **1980—8–2–0.** Lost only to Boston College and Cornell and repeated as Ivy champs behind Rich Diana (1,074 yards rushing) and Curtis Grieve (32 receptions for 580 yards and 8 TDs). **1981—9–1–0.** Scored 285 as Diana ran for 1,442 yards and 15 TDs, John Rogan passed for 1,267 yards and Grieve caught 51 for 791 yards and 12 scores; won share of 11th formal Ivy title despite 35–31 loss to Princeton.

BOWL RECORD

None.

CONFERENCE TITLES

Ivy (informal) 1900, 1905*, 1923, 1927, 1946*, 1954*. Ivy (formal) 1956, 1960, 1967, 1968*, 1969*, 1974*, 1976*, 1977, 1979, 1980, 1981*.

TOP 10 AP & UPI RANKING

None.

MAJOR RIVALS

Yale has played at least 15 games with Amherst (22–0–1), Army (21–12–8), Brown (64–20–4), Colgate (21–7–3), Columbia (46–14–2), Connecticut (30–5–0), Cornell (30–14–2), Dartmouth (38–24–5), Harvard (54–38–8), Holy Cross (14–3–0), Pennsylvania (36–14–1), Princeton (58–38–10), Trinity (18–0–0), Wesleyan (46–0–0) and Williams (16–0–0).

COACHES

Dean of Yale coaches was Carmen Cozza with record of 119–53–3 for 1965–83, including 9 Ivy League titles and 1 unbeaten team. Walter Camp was 67–2–0 for 1888–92 with 3 unbeaten, unscored-on teams. T.A.D. Jones was 60–15–4 for 1916–17 and 1920–27 with 2 unofficial Ivy titles and 3 unbeaten teams. Other top records were by Marvin Stevens, 21–11–8 for

1928–32; Howard Odell, 35–15–2 for 1942–47 with 1 unofficial Ivy title and 1 unbeaten team; and Jordan Olivar, 61–32–6 for 1952–62 with 3 Ivy titles and an unbeaten Lambert Trophy winner.

MISCELLANEA

First game was 3–0 win over Columbia in 1872 . . . highest score was 136–0 over Wesleyan in 1886 . . . highest since 1900 was 89–0 over Vermont in 1929 . . . highest since W.W. II was 56–15 over Dartmouth in 1967 . . . biggest margin of victory since W.W. II was 54–0 over Harvard in 1957 and over Lehigh in 1964 . . . worst defeat was 50–7 by Penn in 1940 . . . worst since W.W. II was 48–7 by Army in 1954 . . . highest score against Bulldogs since W.W. II was 50–14 by Princeton in 1958 . . . longest unbeaten string of 48 in 1885–89 ended by Princeton 10–0 . . . unbeaten string of 47 in 1879–85 ended by Princeton 6–5 . . . unbeaten string of 44 in 1894–96 ended by Princeton 24–6 . . . unbeaten string of 42 in 1904–08 ended by Harvard 4–0 . . . winning streak of 37 in 1890–93 ended by Princeton 6–0 . . . unbeaten string of 18 in 1923–25 ended by Penn 16–13 . . . longest losing string of 7 in 1941 broken with 33–6 win over Lehigh in 1942 . . . Yale has had 69 consensus All America players (most of any school) since 1889 . . . multi-year choices were Pudge Heffelfinger, G, 1889–91; Thomas McClung, B, 1890–91; Frank Hinkey, E, 1891–94; William Hickok, G, 1893–94; Frank Butterworth, B, 1893–94; Fred Murphy, T, 1895–96; Burr Chamberlin, T, 1897–98; Gordon Brown, G, 1897–1900; Malcolm McBride, B, 1898–99; George Stillman, T, 1899–1900; James Bloomer, T, 1900, and G, 1903; George Chadwick, B, 1900, 1902; Henry Holt, C, 1901–02; Thomas Shevlin, E, 1902, 1904–05; Ralph Kinney, T, 1902, and G, 1904; James Hogan, T, 1902–04; Foster Rockwell, B, 1902, 1904; L. Horatio Biglow, T, 1906–07; Edward Coy, B, 1907–09; Hamlin Andrus, G, 1908–09; John Kilpatrick, E, 1909–10; Douglass Bomeisler, E, 1911–12; and Henry Ketcham, C, 1911–12 . . . Clint Frank, B, was unanimous choice in 1937 . . . last Yale consensus All America was Paul Walker, E, 1944 . . . Academic All America choices were Fred Morris, C, 1968; Tom Neville, DT, 1970; William Crowley, LB, 1978; and Rich Diana, RB, and Frederick Leone, DL, 1981 . . . Larry Kelley, E, won Heisman Trophy in 1936 and Clint Frank, B, won in 1937 . . . Yale leads nation in total victories and ranks 2nd in winning percentage.

All-Time
Bowl Records

YEAR	RECORD	BOWL	RESULT	OPPONENT (RECORD)
AIR FORCE (2–2–1)				
1958	(9–0–1)	Cotton	0–0	Texas Christian (8–2–0)
1963	(7–3–0)	Gator	0–35	North Carolina (8–2–0)
1970	(9–2–0)	Sugar	13–34	Tennessee (10–1–0)
1982	(7–5–0)	Hall of Fame	36–28	Vanderbilt (8–3–0)
1983	(9–2–0)	Independence	9–3	Mississippi (6–5–0)
ALABAMA (20–14–3)				
1925	(9–0–0)	Rose	20–19	Washington (10–0–1)
1926	(9–0–0)	Rose	7–7	Stanford (10–0–0)
1930	(9–0–0)	Rose	24–0	Washington St. (9–0–0)
1934	(9–0–0)	Rose	29–13	Stanford (9–0–1)
1937	(9–0–0)	Rose	0–13	California (9–0–1)
1941	(8–2–0)	Cotton	29–21	Texas A&M (9–2–0)
1942	(7–3–0)	Orange	37–21	Boston College (8–1–0)
1944	(5–1–2)	Sugar	26–29	Duke (5–4–0)
1945	(9–0–0)	Rose	34–14	Southern California (7–3–0)
1947	(8–2–0)	Sugar	7–27	Texas (9–1–0)
1952	(9–2–0)	Orange	61–6	Syracuse (7–2–0)
1953	(6–2–3)	Cotton	6–28	Rice (8–2–0)
1959	(7–1–2)	Liberty	0–7	Penn State (8–2–0)

YEAR	RECORD	BOWL	RESULT	OPPONENT (RECORD)
1960	(8–1–1)	Bluebonnet	3–3	Texas (7–3–0)
1961	(10–0–0)	Sugar	10–3	Arkansas (8–2–0)
1962	(9–1–0)	Orange	17–0	Oklahoma (8–2–0)
1963	(8–2–0)	Sugar	12–7	Mississippi (7–0–2)
1964	(10–0–0)	Orange	17–21	Texas (9–1–0)
1965	(8–1–1)	Orange	39–28	Nebraska (10–0–0)
1966	(10–0–0)	Sugar	34–7	Nebraska (9–1–0)
1967	(8–1–1)	Cotton	16–20	Texas A&M (6–4–0)
1968	(8–2–0)	Gator	10–35	Missouri (7–3–0)
1969	(6–4–0)	Liberty	33–47	Colorado (7–3–0)
1970	(6–5–0)	Bluebonnet	24–24	Oklahoma (7–4–0)
1971	(11–0–0)	Orange	6–38	Nebraska (12–0–0)
1972	(10–1–0)	Cotton	13–17	Texas (9–1–0)
1973	(11–0–0)	Sugar	23–24	Notre Dame (10–0–0)
1974	(11–0–0)	Orange	11–13	Notre Dame (9–2–0)
1975	(10–1–0)	Sugar	13–6	Penn State (9–2–0)
1976	(8–3–0)	Liberty	36–6	UCLA (9–1–1)
1977	(10–1–0)	Sugar	35–6	Ohio State (9–2–0)
1978	(10–1–0)	Sugar	14–7	Penn State (11–0–0)
1979	(11–0–0)	Sugar	24–9	Arkansas (10–1–0)
1980	(9–2–0)	Cotton	30–2	Baylor (10–1–0)
1981	(9–1–1)	Cotton	12–14	Texas (9–1–1)
1982	(7–4–0)	Liberty	21–15	Illinois (7–4–0)
1983	(7–4–0)	Sun	28–7	Southern Methodist (10–1–0)

ARIZONA (0–4–0)

YEAR	RECORD	BOWL	RESULT	OPPONENT (RECORD)
1921	(7–1–0)	San Diego Classic	0–38	Centre (9–0–0)
1948	(6–4–0)	Salad	13–14	Drake (6–3–0)
1968	(8–2–0)	Sun	10–34	Auburn (6–4–0)
1979	(6–4–1)	Fiesta	10–16	Pittsburgh (10–1–0)

ARIZONA STATE (7–4–1)

YEAR	RECORD	BOWL	RESULT	OPPONENT (RECORD)
1939	(8–2–0)	Sun	0–0	Catholic U. (8–1–0)
1940	(7–1–2)	Sun	13–26	Western Reserve
1949	(7–2–0)	Salad	21–33	Xavier (Ohio) (9–1–0)
1950	(9–1–0)	Salad	21–34	Miami (Ohio) (8–1–0)

YEAR	RECORD	BOWL	RESULT	OPPONENT (RECORD)
1970	(10–0–0)	Peach	48–26	North Carolina (8–3–0)
1971	(10–1–0)	Fiesta	45–38	Florida St. (8–3–0)
1972	(9–2–0)	Fiesta	49–35	Missouri (6–5–0)
1973	(10–1–0)	Fiesta	28–7	Pittsburgh (6–4–1)
1975	(11–0–0)	Fiesta	17–14	Nebraska (10–1–0)
1977	(9–2–0)	Fiesta	30–42	Penn State (10–1–0)
1978	(8–3–0)	Garden State	34–18	Rutgers (9–2–0)
1982	(9–2–0)	Fiesta	32–21	Oklahoma (8–3–0)

ARKANSAS (8–9–3)

YEAR	RECORD	BOWL	RESULT	OPPONENT (RECORD)
1933	(7–3–0)	Dixie Classic	7–7	Centenary
1946	(6–3–1)	Cotton	0–0	Louisiana St. (9–1–0)
1947	(5–4–1)	Dixie	21–19	William & Mary (9–1–0)
1954	(8–2–0)	Cotton	6–14	Georgia Tech (7–3–0)
1959	(8–2–0)	Gator	14–7	Georgia Tech (6–4–0)
1960	(8–2–0)	Cotton	6–7	Duke (7–3–0)
1961	(8–2–0)	Sugar	3–10	Alabama (10–0–0)
1962	(9–1–0)	Sugar	13–17	Mississippi (9–0–0)
1964	(10–0–0)	Cotton	10–7	Nebraska (9–1–0)
1965	(10–0–0)	Cotton	7–14	Louisiana St. (7–3–0)
1968	(9–1–0)	Sugar	16–2	Georgia (8–0–2)
1969	(9–1–0)	Sugar	22–27	Mississippi (7–3–0)
1971	(8–2–1)	Liberty	13–14	Tennessee (9–2–0)
1975	(9–2–0)	Cotton	31–10	Georgia (9–2–0)
1977	(10–1–0)	Orange	31–6	Oklahoma (10–1–0)
1978	(9–2–0)	Fiesta	10–10	UCLA (8–3–0)
1979	(10–1–0)	Sugar	9–24	Alabama (11–0–0)
1980	(6–5–0)	Hall of Fame	34–15	Tulane (7–4–0)
1981	(8–3–0)	Gator	27–31	North Carolina (9–2–0)
1982	(8–2–1)	Bluebonnet	28–24	Florida (8–3–0)

ARMY (1–0–0)

YEAR	RECORD	BOWL	RESULT	OPPONENT (RECORD)
1930	(8–1–1)	New York Charity	6–0	Navy (6–4–0)

YEAR	RECORD	BOWL	RESULT	OPPONENT (RECORD)
AUBURN (8–7–1)				
1936	(7–2–1)	Bacardi	7–7	Villanova (7–2–0)
1937	(5–2–3)	Orange	6–0	Michigan St. (8–2–0)
1953	(7–2–1)	Gator	13–35	Texas Tech (10–1–0)
1954	(7–3–0)	Gator	33–13	Baylor (7–3–0)
1955	(8–1–1)	Gator	13–25	Vanderbilt (7–3–0)
1963	(9–1–0)	Orange	7–13	Nebraska (9–1–0)
1965	(5–4–1)	Liberty	7–13	Mississippi (6–4–0)
1968	(6–4–0)	Sun	34–10	Arizona (8–2–0)
1969	(8–2–0)	Bluebonnet	7–36	Houston (8–2–0)
1970	(8–2–0)	Gator	35–28	Mississippi (7–3–0)
1971	(9–1–0)	Sugar	22–40	Oklahoma (10–1–0)
1972	(9–1–0)	Gator	24–3	Colorado (8–3–0)
1973	(6–5–0)	Sun	17–34	Missouri (7–4–0)
1974	(9–2–0)	Gator	27–3	Texas (8–3–0)
1982	(8–3–0)	Tangerine	33–26	Boston College (8–2–1)
1983	(10–1–0)	Sugar	9–7	Michigan (9–2–0)
BAYLOR (5–6–0)				
1948	(5–3–2)	Dixie	20–7	Wake Forest (6–3–0)
1951	(8–1–1)	Orange	14–17	Georgia Tech (10–0–1)
1954	(7–3–0)	Gator	13–33	Auburn (7–3–0)
1956	(8–2–0)	Sugar	13–7	Tennessee (10–0–0)
1960	(8–2–0)	Gator	12–13	Florida (8–2–0)
1961	(5–5–0)	Gotham	24–9	Utah St. (9–0–1)
1963	(7–3–0)	Bluebonnet	14–7	Louisiana St. (7–3–0)
1974	(8–3–0)	Cotton	20–41	Penn State (9–2–0)
1979	(7–4–0)	Peach	24–18	Clemson (8–3–0)
1980	(10–1–0)	Cotton	2–30	Alabama (9–2–0)
1983	(7–3–1)	Bluebonnet	14–24	Oklahoma St. (7–4–0)
BOSTON COLLEGE (1–4–0)				
1939	(9–1–0)	Cotton	3–6	Clemson (8–1–0)
1940	(10–0–0)	Sugar	19–13	Tennessee (10–0–0)
1942	(8–1–0)	Orange	21–37	Alabama (7–3–0)

YEAR	RECORD	BOWL	RESULT	OPPONENT (RECORD)
1982	(8–2–1)	Tangerine	26–33	Auburn (8–3–0)
1983	(9–2–0)	Liberty	18–19	Notre Dame (6–5–0)

BRIGHAM YOUNG (3–5–0)

YEAR	RECORD	BOWL	RESULT	OPPONENT (RECORD)
1974	(7–3–1)	Fiesta	6–16	Oklahoma St. (6–5–0)
1976	(9–2–0)	Tangerine	21–49	Oklahoma St. (8–3–0)
1978	(9–3–0)	Holiday	16–23	Navy (8–3–0)
1979	(11–0–0)	Holiday	37–38	Indiana (7–4–0)
1980	(11–1–0)	Holiday	46–45	Southern Methodist (8–3–0)
1981	(10–2–0)	Holiday	38–36	Washington St. (8–2–1)
1982	(8–3–0)	Holiday	17–47	Ohio State (8–3–0)
1983	(10–1–0)	Holiday	21–17	Missouri (7–4–0)

BROWN (0–1–0)

YEAR	RECORD	BOWL	RESULT	OPPONENT (RECORD)
1915	(5–3–1)	Rose	0–14	Washington St. (6–0–0)

CALIFORNIA (2–6–1)

YEAR	RECORD	BOWL	RESULT	OPPONENT (RECORD)
1920	(8–0–0)	Rose	28–0	Ohio State (7–0–0)
1921	(9–0–0)	Rose	0–0	Washington & Jefferson (10–0–0)
1928	(6–1–2)	Rose	7–8	Georgia Tech (9–0–0)
1937	(9–0–1)	Rose	13–0	Alabama (9–0–0)
1948	(10–0–0)	Rose	14–20	Northwestern (7–2–0)
1949	(10–0–0)	Rose	14–17	Ohio State (6–1–2)
1950	(9–0–1)	Rose	6–14	Michigan (5–3–1)
1958	(7–3–0)	Rose	12–38	Iowa (7–1–1)
1979	(6–5–0)	Garden State	17–28	Temple (9–2–0)

CLEMSON (6–5–0)

YEAR	RECORD	BOWL	RESULT	OPPONENT (RECORD)
1939	(8–1–0)	Cotton	6–3	Boston College (9–1–0)
1948	(10–0–0)	Gator	24–23	Missouri (8–2–0)
1950	(8–0–1)	Orange	15–14	Miami (Fla.) (9–0–1)
1951	(7–2–0)	Gator	0–14	Miami (Fla.) (7–3–0)

YEAR	RECORD	BOWL	RESULT	OPPONENT (RECORD)
1956	(7–1–2)	Orange	21–27	Colorado (7–2–1)
1958	(8–2–0)	Sugar	0–7	Louisiana St. (10–0–0)
1959	(8–2–0)	Bluebonnet	23–7	Texas Christian (8–2–0)
1977	(8–2–1)	Gator	3–34	Pittsburgh (8–2–1)
1978	(10–1–0)	Gator	17–15	Ohio State (7–3–1)
1979	(8–3–0)	Peach	18–24	Baylor (7–4–0)
1981	(11–0–0)	Orange	22–15	Nebraska (9–2–0)

COLORADO (4–6–0)

YEAR	RECORD	BOWL	RESULT	OPPONENT (RECORD)
1937	(8–0–0)	Cotton	14–28	Rice (5–3–2)
1956	(7–2–1)	Orange	27–21	Clemson (7–1–2)
1961	(9–1–0)	Orange	7–25	Louisiana St. (9–1–0)
1967	(8–2–0)	Bluebonnet	31–21	Miami (Fla.) (7–3–0)
1969	(7–3–0)	Liberty	47–33	Alabama (6–4–0)
1970	(6–4–0)	Liberty	3–17	Tulane (7–4–0)
1971	(9–2–0)	Bluebonnet	29–17	Houston (9–2–0)
1972	(8–3–0)	Gator	3–24	Auburn (9–1–0)
1975	(9–2–0)	Bluebonnet	21–38	Texas (9–2–0)
1976	(8–3–0)	Orange	10–27	Ohio State (8–2–1)

COLORADO STATE (0–1–0)

YEAR	RECORD	BOWL	RESULT	OPPONENT (RECORD)
1948	(8–2–0)	Raisin	20–21	Occidental (8–0–0)

COLUMBIA (1–0–0)

YEAR	RECORD	BOWL	RESULT	OPPONENT (RECORD)
1933	(7–1–0)	Rose	7–0	Stanford (8–1–1)

DUKE (3–3–0)

YEAR	RECORD	BOWL	RESULT	OPPONENT (RECORD)
1938	(9–0–0)	Rose	3–7	Southern California (8–2–0)
1941	(9–0–0)	Rose	16–20	Oregon St. (7–2–0)
1944	(5–4–0)	Sugar	29–26	Alabama (5–1–2)
1954	(7–2–1)	Orange	34–7	Nebraska (6–4–0)
1957	(6–2–2)	Orange	21–48	Oklahoma (9–1–0)
1960	(7–3–0)	Cotton	7–6	Arkansas (8–2–0)

YEAR	RECORD	BOWL	RESULT	OPPONENT (RECORD)
EAST CAROLINA (3–0–0)				
1964	(8–1–0)	Tangerine	14–13	Massachusetts (8–1–0)
1965	(8–1–0)	Tangerine	31–0	Maine (8–1–0)
1978	(8–3–0)	Independence	35–13	Louisiana Tech (6–4–0)
FLORIDA (7–8–0)				
1952	(7–3–0)	Gator	14–13	Tulsa (8–1–1)
1958	(6–3–1)	Gator	3–7	Mississippi (8–2–0)
1960	(8–2–0)	Gator	13–12	Baylor (8–2–0)
1962	(6–4–0)	Gator	17–7	Penn State (9–1–0)
1965	(7–3–0)	Sugar	18–20	Missouri (7–2–1)
1966	(8–2–0)	Orange	27–12	Georgia Tech (9–1–0)
1969	(8–1–1)	Gator	14–13	Tennessee (9–1–0)
1973	(7–4–0)	Tangerine	7–16	Miami (Ohio) (10–0–0)
1974	(8–3–0)	Sugar	10–13	Nebraska (8–3–0)
1975	(9–2–0)	Gator	0–13	Maryland (8–2–1)
1976	(8–3–0)	Sun	14–37	Texas A&M (9–2–0)
1980	(7–4–0)	Tangerine	35–20	Maryland (8–3–0)
1981	(7–4–0)	Peach	6–26	West Virginia (8–3–0)
1982	(8–3–0)	Bluebonnet	24–28	Arkansas (8–2–1)
1983	(8–2–1)	Gator	14–6	Iowa (9–2–0)
FLORIDA STATE (4–7–1)				
1954	(8–3–0)	Sun	20–47	Texas-El Paso (7–3–0)
1958	(7–3–0)	Bluegrass	6–15	Oklahoma St. (7–3–0)
1964	(8–1–1)	Gator	36–19	Oklahoma (6–3–1)
1966	(6–4–0)	Sun	20–28	Wyoming (9–1–0)
1967	(7–2–1)	Gator	17–17	Penn State (8–2–0)
1968	(8–2–0)	Peach	27–31	Louisiana St. (7–3–0)
1971	(8–3–0)	Fiesta	38–45	Arizona St. (10–1–0)
1977	(9–2–0)	Tangerine	40–17	Texas Tech (7–4–0)
1979	(11–0–0)	Orange	7–24	Oklahoma (10–1–0)
1980	(10–1–0)	Orange	17–18	Oklahoma (9–2–0)
1982	(8–3–0)	Gator	31–12	West Virginia (9–2–0)

YEAR	RECORD	BOWL	RESULT	OPPONENT (RECORD)
1983	(6–5–0)	Peach	28–3	North Carolina (8–3–0)

FRESNO STATE (2–1–0)

YEAR	RECORD	BOWL	RESULT	OPPONENT (RECORD)
1945	(4–5–2)	Raisin	12–13	Drake (4–4–1)
1961	(9–0–0)	Mercy	36–6	Bowling Green (8–1–0)
1982	(10–1–0)	California	29–28	Bowling Green (7–4–0)

FULLERTON STATE (0–1–0)

YEAR	RECORD	BOWL	RESULT	OPPONENT (RECORD)
1983	(7–4–0)	California	13–20	Northern Illinois (9–2–0)

GEORGIA (11–11–1)

YEAR	RECORD	BOWL	RESULT	OPPONENT (RECORD)
1941	(8–1–1)	Orange	40–26	Texas Christian (7–3–0)
1942	(10–1–0)	Rose	9–0	UCLA (7–3–0)
1945	(8–2–0)	Oil	20–6	Tulsa (8–2–0)
1946	(10–0–0)	Sugar	20–10	North Carolina (8–1–1)
1947	(7–4–0)	Gator	20–20	Maryland (7–2–1)
1948	(9–1–0)	Orange	28–41	Texas (6–3–1)
1950	(6–2–3)	Presidential Cup	20–40	Texas A&M (6–4–0)
1959	(9–1–0)	Orange	14–0	Missouri (6–4–0)
1964	(6–3–1)	Sun	7–0	Texas Tech (6–3–1)
1966	(9–1–0)	Cotton	24–9	Southern Methodist (8–2–0)
1967	(7–3–0)	Liberty	7–14	North Carolina St. (8–2–0)
1968	(8–0–2)	Sugar	2–16	Arkansas (9–1–0)
1969	(5–4–1)	Sun	6–45	Nebraska (8–2–0)
1971	(10–1–0)	Gator	7–3	North Carolina (9–2–0)
1973	(6–4–1)	Peach	17–16	Maryland (8–3–0)
1974	(6–5–0)	Tangerine	10–21	Miami (Ohio) (9–0–1)

YEAR	RECORD	BOWL	RESULT	OPPONENT (RECORD)
1975	(9–2–0)	Cotton	10–31	Arkansas (9–2–0)
1976	(10–1–0)	Sugar	3–27	Pittsburgh (11–0–0)
1978	(9–1–1)	Bluebonnet	22–25	Stanford (7–4–0)
1980	(11–0–0)	Sugar	17–10	Notre Dame (9–1–1)
1981	(10–1–0)	Sugar	20–24	Pittsburgh (10–1–0)
1982	(11–0–0)	Sugar	23–27	Penn State (10–1–0)
1983	(9–1–1)	Cotton	10–9	Texas (11–0–0)

GEORGIA TECH (14–8–0)

YEAR	RECORD	BOWL	RESULT	OPPONENT (RECORD)
1928	(9–0–0)	Rose	8–7	California (6–1–2)
1939	(7–2–0)	Orange	21–7	Missouri (9–1–0)
1942	(9–1–0)	Cotton	7–14	Texas (8–2–0)
1943	(7–3–0)	Sugar	20–18	Tulsa (6–0–1)
1944	(8–2–0)	Orange	12–26	Tulsa (7–2–0)
1946	(8–2–0)	Oil	41–19	St. Mary's (6–2–0)
1947	(9–1–0)	Orange	20–14	Kansas (8–0–2)
1951	(10–0–1)	Orange	17–14	Baylor (8–1–1)
1952	(11–0–0)	Sugar	24–7	Mississippi (8–0–2)
1953	(8–2–1)	Sugar	42–19	West Virginia (8–1–0)
1954	(7–3–0)	Cotton	14–6	Arkansas (8–2–0)
1955	(8–1–1)	Sugar	7–0	Pittsburgh (7–3–0)
1956	(9–1–0)	Gator	21–14	Pittsburgh (7–2–1)
1959	(6–4–0)	Gator	7–14	Arkansas (8–2–0)
1961	(7–3–0)	Gator	15–30	Penn State (7–3–0)
1962	(7–2–1)	Bluebonnet	10–14	Missouri (7–1–2)
1965	(6–3–1)	Gator	31–21	Texas Tech (8–2–0)
1966	(9–1–0)	Orange	12–27	Florida (8–2–0)
1970	(8–3–0)	Sun	17–9	Texas Tech (8–3–0)
1971	(6–5–0)	Peach	18–41	Mississippi (9–2–0)
1972	(6–4–1)	Liberty	31–30	Iowa St. (5–5–1)
1978	(7–4–0)	Peach	21–41	Purdue (8–2–1)

HARVARD (1–0–0)

YEAR	RECORD	BOWL	RESULT	OPPONENT (RECORD)
1919	(8–0–1)	Rose	7–6	Oregon (5–2–0)

HOLY CROSS (0–1–0)

YEAR	RECORD	BOWL	RESULT	OPPONENT (RECORD)
1945	(8–1–0)	Orange	6–13	Miami (Fla.) (8–1–1)

YEAR	RECORD	BOWL	RESULT	OPPONENT (RECORD)
HOUSTON (7–3–1)				
1951	(5–5–0)	Salad	26–21	Dayton (7–2–0)
1962	(6–4–0)	Tangerine	49–21	Miami (Ohio) (8–1–1)
1969	(8–2–0)	Bluebonnet	36–7	Auburn (8–2–0)
1971	(9–2–0)	Bluebonnet	17–29	Colorado (9–2–0)
1973	(10–1–0)	Bluebonnet	47–7	Tulane (9–2–0)
1974	(8–3–0)	Bluebonnet	31–31	North Carolina St. (9–2–0)
1976	(9–2–0)	Cotton	30–21	Maryland (11–0–0)
1978	(9–2–0)	Cotton	34–35	Notre Dame (8–3–0)
1979	(10–1–0)	Cotton	17–14	Nebraska (10–1–0)
1980	(6–5–0)	Garden State	35–0	Navy (8–3–0)
1981	(7–3–1)	Sun	14–40	Oklahoma (6–4–1)
ILLINOIS (3–2–0)				
1946	(7–2–0)	Rose	45–14	UCLA (10–0–0)
1951	(8–0–1)	Rose	40–7	Stanford (9–1–0)
1963	(7–1–1)	Rose	17–7	Washington (6–4–0)
1982	(7–4–0)	Liberty	15–21	Alabama (7–4–0)
1983	(10–1–0)	Rose	9–45	UCLA (6–4–1)
INDIANA (1–1–0)				
1967	(9–1–0)	Rose	3–14	Southern California (9–1–0)
1979	(7–4–0)	Holiday	38–37	Brigham Young (11–0–0)
IOWA (3–2–0)				
1956	(8–1–0)	Rose	35–19	Oregon St. (7–2–1)
1958	(7–1–1)	Rose	38–12	California (7–3–0)
1981	(8–3–0)	Rose	0–28	Washington (9–2–0)
1982	(7–4–0)	Peach	28–22	Tennessee (6–4–1)
1983	(9–2–0)	Gator	6–14	Florida (8–2–1)
IOWA STATE (0–4–0)				
1971	(8–3–0)	Sun	15–33	Louisiana St. (8–3–0)
1972	(5–5–1)	Liberty	30–31	Georgia Tech (6–4–1)

YEAR	RECORD	BOWL	RESULT	OPPONENT (RECORD)
1977	(8–3–0)	Peach	14–24	North Carolina St. (7–4–0)
1978	(8–3–0)	Hall of Fame	12–28	Texas A&M (7–4–0)

KANSAS (1–5–0)

1947	(8–0–2)	Orange	14–20	Georgia Tech (9–1–0)
1961	(6–3–1)	Bluebonnet	33–7	Rice (7–3–0)
1968	(9–1–0)	Orange	14–15	Penn State (10–0–0)
1973	(7–3–1)	Liberty	18–31	North Carolina St. (8–3–0)
1975	(7–4–0)	Sun	19–33	Pittsburgh (7–4–0)
1981	(8–3–0)	Hall of Fame	0–10	Mississippi St. (7–4–0)

KANSAS STATE (0–1–0)

1982	(6–4–1)	Independence	3–14	Wisconsin (6–5–0)

KENTUCKY (4–2–0)

1947	(7–3–0)	Great Lakes	24–14	Villanova (6–2–1)
1949	(9–2–0)	Orange	13–21	Santa Clara (7–2–1)
1950	(10–1–0)	Sugar	13–7	Oklahoma (10–0–0)
1951	(7–4–0)	Cotton	20–7	Texas Christian (6–4–0)
1976	(7–4–0)	Peach	21–0	North Carolina (9–2–0)
1983	(6–4–1)	Hall of Fame	16–20	West Virginia (8–3–0)

LONG BEACH STATE (0–0–1)

1970	(9–2–0)	Pasadena	24–24	Louisville (8–3–0)

LOUISIANA STATE (10–12–1)

1935	(9–1–0)	Sugar	2–3	Texas Christian (11–1–0)
1936	(9–0–1)	Sugar	14–21	Santa Clara (8–1–0)
1937	(9–1–0)	Sugar	0–6	Santa Clara (8–0–0)
1943	(5–3–0)	Orange	19–14	Texas A&M (7–1–1)
1946	(9–1–0)	Cotton	0–0	Arkansas (6–3–1)
1949	(8–2–0)	Sugar	0–35	Oklahoma (10–0–0)

YEAR	RECORD	BOWL	RESULT	OPPONENT (RECORD)
1958	(10–0–0)	Sugar	7–0	Clemson (8–2–0)
1959	(9–1–0)	Sugar	0–21	Mississippi (9–1–0)
1961	(9–1–0)	Orange	25–7	Colorado (9–1–0)
1962	(8–1–1)	Cotton	13–0	Texas (9–0–1)
1963	(7–3–0)	Bluebonnet	7–14	Baylor (7–3–0)
1964	(7–2–1)	Sugar	13–10	Syracuse (7–3–0)
1965	(7–3–0)	Cotton	14–7	Arkansas (10–0–0)
1967	(6–3–1)	Sugar	20–13	Wyoming (10–0–0)
1968	(7–3–0)	Peach	31–27	Florida St. (8–2–0)
1970	(9–2–0)	Orange	12–17	Nebraska (10–0–1)
1971	(8–3–0)	Sun	33–15	Iowa St. (8–3–0)
1972	(9–1–1)	Bluebonnet	17–24	Tennessee (9–2–0)
1973	(9–2–0)	Orange	9–16	Penn State (11–0–0)
1977	(8–3–0)	Sun	14–24	Stanford (8–3–0)
1978	(8–3–0)	Liberty	15–20	Missouri (7–4–0)
1979	(6–5–0)	Tangerine	34–10	Wake Forest (8–3–0)
1982	(8–2–1)	Orange	20–21	Nebraska (11–1–0)

LOUISVILLE (1–1–1)

YEAR	RECORD	BOWL	RESULT	OPPONENT (RECORD)
1957	(8–1–0)	Sun	34–20	Drake (7–1–0)
1970	(8–3–0)	Pasadena	24–24	Long Beach St. (9–2–0)
1977	(7–3–1)	Independence	14–24	Louisiana Tech (8–1–2)

MARYLAND (4–9–1)

YEAR	RECORD	BOWL	RESULT	OPPONENT (RECORD)
1947	(7–2–1)	Gator	20–20	Georgia (7–4–0)
1949	(8–1–0)	Gator	20–7	Missouri (7–3–0)
1951	(9–0–0)	Sugar	28–13	Tennessee (10–0–0)
1953	(10–0–0)	Orange	0–7	Oklahoma (8–1–1)
1955	(10–0–0)	Orange	6–20	Oklahoma (10–0–0)
1973	(8–3–0)	Peach	16–17	Georgia (6–4–1)
1974	(8–3–0)	Liberty	3–7	Tennessee (6–3–2)
1975	(8–2–1)	Gator	13–0	Florida (9–2–0)
1976	(11–0–0)	Cotton	21–30	Houston (9–2–0)
1977	(7–4–0)	Hall of Fame	17–7	Minnesota (7–4–0)
1978	(9–2–0)	Sun	0–42	Texas (8–3–0)
1980	(8–3–0)	Tangerine	20–35	Florida (7–4–0)

YEAR	RECORD	BOWL	RESULT	OPPONENT (RECORD)
1982	(8–3–0)	Aloha	20–21	Washington (9–2–0)
1983	(8–3–0)	Florida Citrus	23–30	Tennessee (8–3–0)

MEMPHIS STATE (1–0–0)

YEAR	RECORD	BOWL	RESULT	OPPONENT (RECORD)
1971	(4–6–0)	Pasadena	28–9	San Jose St. (5–5–1)

MIAMI (FLA.) (5–5–0)

YEAR	RECORD	BOWL	RESULT	OPPONENT (RECORD)
1934	(5–2–1)	Orange	0–26	Bucknell (5–2–2)
1945	(8–1–1)	Orange	13–6	Holy Cross (8–1–0)
1950	(9–0–1)	Orange	14–15	Clemson (8–0–1)
1951	(7–3–0)	Gator	14–0	Clemson (7–2–0)
1961	(7–3–0)	Liberty	14–15	Syracuse (7–3–0)
1962	(7–3–0)	Gotham	34–36	Nebraska (8–2–0)
1966	(7–2–1)	Liberty	14–7	Virginia Tech (8–1–1)
1967	(7–3–0)	Bluebonnet	21–31	Colorado (8–2–0)
1980	(8–3–0)	Peach	20–10	Virginia Tech (8–3–0)
1983	(10–1–0)	Orange	31–30	Nebraska (12–0–0)

MIAMI (OHIO) (5–1–0)

YEAR	RECORD	BOWL	RESULT	OPPONENT (RECORD)
1947	(8–0–1)	Sun	13–12	Texas Tech (6–4–0)
1950	(8–1–0)	Salad	34–21	Arizona St. (9–1–0)
1962	(8–1–1)	Tangerine	21–49	Houston (6–4–0)
1973	(10–0–0)	Tangerine	16–7	Florida (7–4–0)
1974	(9–0–1)	Tangerine	21–10	Georgia (6–5–0)
1975	(10–1–0)	Tangerine	20–7	South Carolina (7–4–0)

MICHIGAN (6–9–0)

YEAR	RECORD	BOWL	RESULT	OPPONENT (RECORD)
1901	(10–0–0)	Rose	49–0	Stanford (3–1–2)
1947	(9–0–0)	Rose	49–0	Southern California (7–1–1)
1950	(5–3–1)	Rose	14–6	California (9–0–1)
1964	(8–1–0)	Rose	34–7	Oregon St. (8–2–0)
1969	(8–2–0)	Rose	3–10	Southern California (9–0–1)
1971	(11–0–0)	Rose	12–13	Stanford (8–3–0)

YEAR	RECORD	BOWL	RESULT	OPPONENT (RECORD)
1975	(8–1–2)	Orange	6–14	Oklahoma (10–1–0)
1976	(10–1–0)	Rose	6–14	Southern California (10–1–0)
1977	(10–1–0)	Rose	20–27	Washington (9–2–0)
1978	(10–1–0)	Rose	10–17	Southern California (11–1–0)
1979	(8–3–0)	Gator	15–17	North Carolina (7–3–1)
1980	(9–2–0)	Rose	23–6	Washington (9–2–0)
1981	(8–3–0)	Bluebonnet	33–14	UCLA (7–3–1)
1982	(8–3–0)	Rose	14–24	UCLA (9–1–1)
1983	(9–2–0)	Sugar	7–9	Auburn (10–1–0)

MICHIGAN STATE (2–2–0)

YEAR	RECORD	BOWL	RESULT	OPPONENT (RECORD)
1937	(8–2–0)	Orange	0–6	Auburn (5–2–3)
1953	(8–1–0)	Rose	28–20	UCLA (8–1–0)
1955	(8–1–0)	Rose	17–14	UCLA (9–1–0)
1965	(10–0–0)	Rose	12–14	UCLA (7–2–1)

MINNESOTA (1–2–0)

YEAR	RECORD	BOWL	RESULT	OPPONENT (RECORD)
1960	(8–1–0)	Rose	7–17	Washington (9–1–0)
1961	(7–2–0)	Rose	21–3	UCLA (7–3–0)
1977	(7–4–0)	Hall of Fame	7–17	Maryland (7–4–0)

MISSISSIPPI (11–10–0)

YEAR	RECORD	BOWL	RESULT	OPPONENT (RECORD)
1935	(9–2–0)	Orange	19–20	Catholic U. (7–1–0)
1947	(8–2–0)	Delta	13–9	Texas Christian (4–4–2)
1952	(8–0–2)	Sugar	7–24	Georgia Tech (11–0–0)
1954	(9–1–0)	Sugar	0–21	Navy (7–2–0)
1955	(9–1–0)	Cotton	14–13	Texas Christian (9–1–0)
1957	(8–1–1)	Sugar	39–7	Texas (6–3–1)
1958	(8–2–0)	Gator	7–3	Florida (6–3–1)
1959	(9–1–0)	Sugar	21–0	Louisiana St. (9–1–0)
1960	(9–0–1)	Sugar	14–6	Rice (7–3–0)

YEAR	RECORD	BOWL	RESULT	OPPONENT (RECORD)
1961	(9–1–0)	Cotton	7–12	Texas (9–1–0)
1962	(9–0–0)	Sugar	17–13	Arkansas (9–1–0)
1963	(7–0–2)	Sugar	7–12	Alabama (8–2–0)
1964	(5–4–1)	Bluebonnet	7–14	Tulsa (8–2–0)
1965	(6–4–0)	Liberty	13–7	Auburn (5–4–1)
1966	(8–2–0)	Bluebonnet	0–19	Texas (6–4–0)
1967	(6–3–1)	Sun	7–14	Texas-El Paso (6–2–1)
1968	(6–3–1)	Liberty	34–17	Virginia Tech (7–3–0)
1969	(7–3–0)	Sugar	27–22	Arkansas (9–1–0)
1970	(7–3–0)	Gator	28–35	Auburn (8–2–0)
1971	(9–2–0)	Peach	41–18	Georgia Tech (6–5–0)
1983	(6–5–0)	Independence	3–9	Air Force (9–2–0)

MISSISSIPPI STATE (4–2–0)

YEAR	RECORD	BOWL	RESULT	OPPONENT (RECORD)
1936	(7–2–1)	Orange	12–13	Duquesne (7–2–0)
1940	(9–0–1)	Orange	14–7	Georgetown (8–1–0)
1963	(6–2–2)	Liberty	16–12	North Carolina St. (8–2–0)
1974	(8–3–0)	Sun	26–24	North Carolina (7–4–0)
1980	(9–2–0)	Sun	17–31	Nebraska (9–2–0)
1981	(7–4–0)	Hall of Fame	10–0	Kansas (8–3–0)

MISSOURI (8–11–0)

YEAR	RECORD	BOWL	RESULT	OPPONENT (RECORD)
1924	(7–1–0)	Los Angeles Christmas Festival	7–20	Southern California (8–2–0)
1939	(9–1–0)	Orange	7–21	Georgia Tech (8–2–0)
1941	(8–1–0)	Sugar	0–2	Fordham (7–1–0)
1945	(6–3–0)	Cotton	27–40	Texas (9–1–0)
1948	(8–2–0)	Gator	23–24	Clemson (10–0–0)
1949	(7–3–0)	Gator	7–20	Maryland (8–1–0)
1959	(6–4–0)	Orange	0–14	Georgia (9–1–0)
1960	(9–1–0)	Orange	21–14	Navy (9–1–0)
1962	(7–1–2)	Bluebonnet	14–10	Georgia Tech (7–2–1)
1965	(7–2–1)	Sugar	20–18	Florida (7–3–0)
1968	(7–3–0)	Gator	35–10	Alabama (8–2–0)
1969	(9–1–0)	Orange	3–10	Penn State (10–0–0)

YEAR	RECORD	BOWL	RESULT	OPPONENT (RECORD)
1972	(6–5–0)	Fiesta	35–49	Arizona St. (9–2–0)
1973	(7–4–0)	Sun	34–17	Auburn (6–5–0)
1978	(7–4–0)	Liberty	20–15	Louisiana St. (8–3–0)
1979	(6–5–0)	Hall of Fame	24–14	South Carolina (8–3–0)
1980	(8–3–0)	Liberty	25–28	Purdue (8–3–0)
1981	(7–4–0)	Tangerine	19–17	Southern Mississippi (9–1–1)
1983	(7–4–0)	Holiday	17–21	Brigham Young (10–1–0)

NAVY (3–5–1)

YEAR	RECORD	BOWL	RESULT	OPPONENT (RECORD)
1923	(5–1–2)	Rose	14–14	Washington (10–1–0)
1930	(6–4–0)	New York Charity	0–6	Army (9–1–1)
1954	(7–2–0)	Sugar	21–0	Mississippi (9–1–0)
1957	(8–1–1)	Cotton	20–7	Rice (7–3–0)
1960	(9–1–0)	Orange	14–21	Missouri (9–1–0)
1963	(9–1–0)	Cotton	6–28	Texas (10–0–0)
1978	(8–3–0)	Holiday	23–16	Brigham Young (9–3–0)
1980	(8–3–0)	Garden State	0–35	Houston (6–5–0)
1981	(7–3–1)	Liberty	28–31	Ohio State (8–3–0)

NEBRASKA (12–10–0)

YEAR	RECORD	BOWL	RESULT	OPPONENT (RECORD)
1940	(8–1–0)	Rose	13–21	Stanford (9–0–0)
1954	(6–4–0)	Orange	7–34	Duke (7–2–1)
1962	(8–2–0)	Gotham	36–34	Miami (Fla.) (7–3–0)
1963	(9–1–0)	Orange	13–7	Auburn (9–1–0)
1964	(9–1–0)	Cotton	7–10	Arkansas (10–0–0)
1965	(10–0–0)	Orange	28–39	Alabama (8–1–1)
1966	(9–1–0)	Sugar	7–34	Alabama (10–0–0)
1969	(8–2–0)	Sun	45–6	Georgia (5–4–1)
1970	(10–0–1)	Orange	17–12	Louisiana St. (9–2–0)
1971	(12–0–0)	Orange	38–6	Alabama (11–0–0)
1972	(8–2–1)	Orange	40–6	Notre Dame (8–2–0)
1973	(8–2–1)	Cotton	19–3	Texas (8–2–0)
1974	(8–3–0)	Sugar	13–10	Florida (8–3–0)

YEAR	RECORD	BOWL	RESULT	OPPONENT (RECORD)
1975	(10–1–0)	Fiesta	14–17	Arizona St. (11–0–0)
1976	(7–3–1)	Bluebonnet	27–24	Texas Tech (10–1–0)
1977	(8–3–0)	Liberty	21–17	North Carolina (8–2–1)
1978	(9–2–0)	Orange	24–31	Oklahoma (10–1–0)
1979	(10–1–0)	Cotton	14–17	Houston (10–1–0)
1980	(9–2–0)	Sun	31–17	Mississippi St. (9–2–0)
1981	(9–2–0)	Orange	15–22	Clemson (11–0–0)
1982	(11–1–0)	Orange	21–20	Louisiana St. (8–2–1)
1983	(12–0–0)	Orange	30–31	Miami (Fla.) (10–1–0)

NEW MEXICO (2–2–1)

YEAR	RECORD	BOWL	RESULT	OPPONENT (RECORD)
1938	(8–2–0)	Sun	0–26	Utah (7–1–2)
1943	(3–1–0)	Sun	0–7	Southwestern (9–1–1)
1945	(5–1–1)	Sun	34–24	Denver (4–4–1)
1946	(5–5–1)	Harbor	13–13	Montana St. (5–3–1)
1961	(6–4–0)	Aviation	28–12	Western Michigan (5–3–1)

NEW MEXICO STATE (2–0–1)

YEAR	RECORD	BOWL	RESULT	OPPONENT (RECORD)
1935	(7–1–1)	Sun	14–14	Hardin-Simmons (6–3–0)
1959	(7–3–0)	Sun	28–8	North Texas St. (9–1–0)
1960	(10–0–0)	Sun	20–13	Utah St. (9–1–0)

NORTH CAROLINA (6–9–0)

YEAR	RECORD	BOWL	RESULT	OPPONENT (RECORD)
1946	(8–1–1)	Sugar	10–20	Georgia (10–0–0)
1948	(9–0–1)	Sugar	6–14	Oklahoma (9–1–0)
1949	(7–3–0)	Cotton	13–27	Rice (9–1–0)
1963	(8–2–0)	Gator	35–0	Air Force (7–3–0)
1970	(8–3–0)	Peach	26–48	Arizona St. (10–0–0)
1971	(9–2–0)	Gator	3–7	Georgia (10–1–0)
1972	(10–1–0)	Sun	32–28	Texas Tech (8–3–0)
1974	(7–4–0)	Sun	24–26	Mississippi St. (8–3–0)
1976	(9–2–0)	Peach	0–21	Kentucky (7–4–0)
1977	(8–2–1)	Liberty	17–21	Nebraska (8–3–0)

YEAR	RECORD	BOWL	RESULT	OPPONENT (RECORD)
1979	(7–3–1)	Gator	17–15	Michigan (8–3–0)
1980	(10–1–0)	Bluebonnet	16–7	Texas (7–4–0)
1981	(9–2–0)	Gator	31–27	Arkansas (8–3–0)
1982	(7–4–0)	Sun	26–10	Texas (9–2–0)
1983	(8–3–0)	Peach	3–28	Florida St. (6–5–0)

NORTH CAROLINA STATE (5–3–1)

YEAR	RECORD	BOWL	RESULT	OPPONENT (RECORD)
1946	(8–2–0)	Gator	13–34	Oklahoma (7–3–0)
1963	(8–2–0)	Liberty	12–16	Mississippi St. (6–2–2)
1967	(8–2–0)	Liberty	14–7	Georgia (7–3–0)
1972	(7–3–1)	Peach	49–13	West Virginia (8–3–0)
1973	(8–3–0)	Liberty	31–18	Kansas (7–3–1)
1974	(9–2–0)	Bluebonnet	31–31	Houston (8–3–0)
1975	(7–3–1)	Peach	10–13	West Virginia (8–3–0)
1977	(7–4–0)	Peach	24–14	Iowa St. (8–3–0)
1978	(8–3–0)	Tangerine	30–17	Pittsburgh (8–3–0)

NORTHWESTERN (1–0–0)

YEAR	RECORD	BOWL	RESULT	OPPONENT (RECORD)
1948	(7–2–0)	Rose	20–14	California (10–0–0)

NOTRE DAME (8–3–0)

YEAR	RECORD	BOWL	RESULT	OPPONENT (RECORD)
1924	(9–0–0)	Rose	27–10	Stanford (7–0–1)
1969	(8–1–1)	Cotton	17–21	Texas (10–0–0)
1970	(9–1–0)	Cotton	24–11	Texas (10–0–0)
1972	(8–2–0)	Orange	6–40	Nebraska (8–2–1)
1973	(10–0–0)	Sugar	24–23	Alabama (11–0–0)
1974	(9–2–0)	Orange	13–11	Alabama (11–0–0)
1976	(8–3–0)	Gator	20–9	Penn State (7–4–0)
1977	(10–1–0)	Cotton	38–10	Texas (11–0–0)
1978	(8–3–0)	Cotton	35–34	Houston (9–2–0)
1980	(9–1–1)	Sugar	10–17	Georgia (11–0–0)
1983	(6–5–0)	Liberty	19–18	Boston College (9–2–0)

OHIO STATE (9–9–0)

YEAR	RECORD	BOWL	RESULT	OPPONENT (RECORD)
1920	(7–0–0)	Rose	0–28	California (8–0–0)
1949	(6–1–2)	Rose	17–14	California (10–0–0)

YEAR	RECORD	BOWL	RESULT	OPPONENT (RECORD)
1954	(9–0–0)	Rose	20–7	Southern California (8–3–0)
1957	(8–1–0)	Rose	10–7	Oregon (7–3–0)
1968	(9–0–0)	Rose	27–16	Southern California (9–0–1)
1970	(9–0–0)	Rose	17–27	Stanford (8–3–0)
1972	(9–1–0)	Rose	17–42	Southern California (11–0–0)
1973	(9–0–1)	Rose	42–21	Southern California (9–1–1)
1974	(10–1–0)	Rose	17–18	Southern California (9–1–1)
1975	(11–0–0)	Rose	10–23	UCLA (8–2–1)
1976	(8–2–1)	Orange	27–10	Colorado (8–3–0)
1977	(9–2–0)	Sugar	6–35	Alabama (10–1–0)
1978	(7–3–1)	Gator	15–17	Clemson (10–1–0)
1979	(11–0–0)	Rose	16–17	Southern California (10–0–1)
1980	(9–2–0)	Fiesta	19–31	Penn State (9–2–0)
1981	(8–3–0)	Liberty	31–28	Navy (7–3–1)
1982	(8–3–0)	Holiday	47–17	Brigham Young (8–3–0)
1983	(8–3–0)	Fiesta	28–23	Pittsburgh (8–2–1)

OKLAHOMA (16–7–1)

YEAR	RECORD	BOWL	RESULT	OPPONENT (RECORD)
1938	(10–0–0)	Orange	0–17	Tennessee (10–0–0)
1946	(7–3–0)	Gator	34–13	North Carolina St. (8–2–0)
1948	(9–1–0)	Sugar	14–6	North Carolina (9–0–1)
1949	(10–0–0)	Sugar	35–0	Louisiana St. (8–2–0)
1950	(10–0–0)	Sugar	7–13	Kentucky (10–1–0)
1953	(8–1–1)	Orange	7–0	Maryland (10–0–0)
1955	(10–0–0)	Orange	20–6	Maryland (10–0–0)
1957	(9–1–0)	Orange	48–21	Duke (6–2–2)
1958	(9–1–0)	Orange	21–6	Syracuse (8–1–0)
1962	(8–2–0)	Orange	0–17	Alabama (9–1–0)
1964	(6–3–1)	Gator	19–36	Florida St. (8–1–1)

YEAR	RECORD	BOWL	RESULT	OPPONENT (RECORD)
1967	(9–1–0)	Orange	26–24	Tennessee (9–1–0)
1968	(7–3–0)	Bluebonnet	27–28	Southern Methodist (7–3–0)
1970	(7–4–0)	Bluebonnet	24–24	Alabama (6–5–0)
1971	(10–1–0)	Sugar	40–22	Auburn (9–1–0)
1972	(10–1–0)	Sugar	14–0	Penn State (10–1–0)
1975	(10–1–0)	Orange	14–6	Michigan (8–1–2)
1976	(8–2–1)	Fiesta	41–7	Wyoming (8–3–0)
1977	(10–1–0)	Orange	6–31	Arkansas (10–1–0)
1978	(10–1–0)	Orange	31–24	Nebraska (9–2–0)
1979	(10–1–0)	Orange	24–7	Florida St. (11–0–0)
1980	(9–2–0)	Orange	18–17	Florida St. (10–1–0)
1981	(6–4–1)	Sun	40–14	Houston (7–3–1)
1982	(8–3–0)	Fiesta	21–32	Arizona St. (9–2–0)

OKLAHOMA STATE (6–2–0)

YEAR	RECORD	BOWL	RESULT	OPPONENT (RECORD)
1944	(7–1–0)	Cotton	34–0	Texas Christian (7–2–1)
1945	(8–0–0)	Sugar	33–13	St. Mary's (7–1–0)
1948	(6–3–0)	Delta	0–20	William & Mary (6–2–2)
1958	(7–3–0)	Bluegrass	15–6	Florida St. (7–3–0)
1974	(6–5–0)	Fiesta	16–6	Brigham Young (7–3–1)
1976	(8–3–0)	Tangerine	49–21	Brigham Young (9–2–0)
1981	(7–4–0)	Independence	16–33	Texas A&M (6–5–0)
1983	(7–4–0)	Bluebonnet	24–14	Baylor (7–3–1)

OREGON (2–4–0)

YEAR	RECORD	BOWL	RESULT	OPPONENT (RECORD)
1916	(6–0–1)	Rose	14–0	Pennsylvania (7–2–1)
1919	(5–1–0)	Rose	6–7	Harvard (8–0–1)
1948	(9–1–0)	Cotton	13–21	Southern Methodist (8–1–1)
1957	(7–3–0)	Rose	7–10	Ohio State (8–1–0)
1960	(7–2–1)	Liberty	12–41	Penn State (6–3–0)
1963	(7–3–0)	Sun	21–14	Southern Methodist (4–6–0)

YEAR	RECORD	BOWL	RESULT	OPPONENT (RECORD)
OREGON STATE (2–2–0)				
1941	(7–2–0)	Rose	20–16	Duke (9–0–0)
1956	(7–2–1)	Rose	19–35	Iowa (8–1–0)
1962	(8–2–0)	Liberty	6–0	Villanova (7–2–0)
1964	(8–2–0)	Rose	7–34	Michigan (8–1–0)
PACIFIC (3–1–1)				
1947	(8–1–0)	Grape	35–21	Utah St. (6–4–0)
1947		Raisin	26–14	Wichita St. (7–3–0)
1948	(7–1–1)	Grape	35–35	Hardin-Simmons (6–2–2)
1951	(6–4–0)	Sun	14–25	Texas Tech (6–4–0)
1952	(6–3–1)	Sun	26–7	Southern Mississippi (10–1–0)
PENNSYLVANIA (0–1–0)				
1916	(7–2–1)	Rose	0–14	Oregon (6–0–1)
PENN STATE (14–6–2)				
1922	(6–3–1)	Rose	3–14	Southern California (9–1–0)
1947	(9–0–0)	Cotton	13–13	Southern Methodist (9–0–1)
1959	(8–2–0)	Liberty	7–0	Alabama (7–1–2)
1960	(6–3–0)	Liberty	41–12	Oregon (7–2–1)
1961	(7–3–0)	Gator	30–15	Georgia Tech (7–3–0)
1962	(9–1–0)	Gator	7–17	Florida (6–4–0)
1967	(8–2–0)	Gator	17–17	Florida St. (7–2–1)
1968	(10–0–0)	Orange	15–14	Kansas (9–1–0)
1969	(10–0–0)	Orange	10–3	Missouri (9–1–0)
1971	(10–1–0)	Cotton	30–6	Texas (8–2–0)
1972	(10–1–0)	Sugar	0–14	Oklahoma (10–1–0)
1973	(11–0–0)	Orange	16–9	Louisiana St. (9–2–0)
1974	(9–2–0)	Cotton	41–20	Baylor (8–3–0)
1975	(9–2–0)	Sugar	6–13	Alabama (10–1–0)
1976	(7–4–0)	Gator	9–20	Notre Dame (8–3–0)
1977	(10–1–0)	Fiesta	42–30	Arizona St. (9–2–0)

YEAR	RECORD	BOWL	RESULT	OPPONENT (RECORD)
1978	(11–0–0)	Sugar	7–14	Alabama (10–1–0)
1979	(7–4–0)	Liberty	9–6	Tulane (9–2–0)
1980	(9–2–0)	Fiesta	31–19	Ohio State (9–2–0)
1981	(9–2–0)	Fiesta	26–10	Southern California (9–2–0)
1982	(10–1–0)	Sugar	27–23	Georgia (11–0–0)
1983	(7–4–1)	Aloha	13–10	Washington (8–3–0)

PITTSBURGH (7–9–0)

YEAR	RECORD	BOWL	RESULT	OPPONENT (RECORD)
1927	(8–0–1)	Rose	6–7	Stanford (7–2–1)
1929	(9–0–0)	Rose	14–47	Southern California (9–2–0)
1932	(8–0–2)	Rose	0–35	Southern California (9–0–0)
1936	(7–1–1)	Rose	21–0	Washington (7–1–1)
1955	(7–3–0)	Sugar	0–7	Georgia Tech (8–1–1)
1956	(7–2–1)	Gator	14–21	Georgia Tech (9–1–0)
1973	(6–4–1)	Fiesta	7–28	Arizona St. (10–1–0)
1975	(7–4–0)	Sun	33–19	Kansas (7–4–0)
1976	(11–0–0)	Sugar	27–3	Georgia (10–1–0)
1977	(8–2–1)	Gator	34–3	Clemson (8–2–1)
1978	(8–3–0)	Tangerine	17–30	North Carolina St. (8–3–0)
1979	(10–1–0)	Fiesta	16–10	Arizona (6–4–1)
1980	(10–1–0)	Gator	37–9	South Carolina (8–3–0)
1981	(10–1–0)	Sugar	24–20	Georgia (10–1–0)
1982	(9–2–0)	Cotton	3–7	Southern Methodist (10–0–1)
1983	(8–2–1)	Fiesta	23–28	Ohio State (8–3–0)

PURDUE (4–0–0)

YEAR	RECORD	BOWL	RESULT	OPPONENT (RECORD)
1966	(8–2–0)	Rose	14–13	Southern California (7–3–0)
1978	(8–2–1)	Peach	41–21	Georgia Tech (7–4–0)
1979	(9–2–0)	Bluebonnet	27–22	Tennessee (7–4–0)
1980	(8–3–0)	Liberty	28–25	Missouri (8–3–0)

YEAR	RECORD	BOWL	RESULT	OPPONENT (RECORD)
RICE (4–3–0)				
1937	(5–3–2)	Cotton	28–14	Colorado (8–0–0)
1946	(8–2–0)	Orange	8–0	Tennessee (9–1–0)
1949	(9–1–0)	Cotton	27–13	North Carolina (7–3–0)
1953	(8–2–0)	Cotton	28–6	Alabama (6–2–3)
1957	(7–3–0)	Cotton	7–20	Navy (8–1–1)
1960	(7–3–0)	Sugar	6–14	Mississippi (9–0–1)
1961	(7–3–0)	Bluebonnet	7–33	Kansas (6–3–1)
RUTGERS (0–1–0)				
1978	(9–2–0)	Garden State	18–34	Arizona St. (8–3–0)
SAN DIEGO STATE (1–1–0)				
1947	(7–2–1)	Harbor	0–53	Hardin-Simmons (7–3–0)
1969	(10–0–0)	Pasadena	28–7	Boston University (9–1–0)
SAN JOSE STATE (2–2–0)				
1946	(8–1–1)	Raisin	20–0	Utah St. (7–1–1)
1949	(8–4–0)	Raisin	20–13	Texas Tech (7–4–0)
1971	(5–5–1)	Pasadena	9–28	Memphis St. (4–6–0)
1981	(9–2–0)	California	25–27	Toledo (8–3–0)
SOUTH CAROLINA (0–5–0)				
1945	(2–3–3)	Gator	14–26	Wake Forest (4–3–1)
1969	(7–3–0)	Peach	3–14	West Virginia (9–1–0)
1975	(7–4–0)	Tangerine	7–20	Miami (Ohio) (10–1–0)
1979	(8–3–0)	Hall of Fame	14–24	Missouri (6–5–0)
1980	(8–3–0)	Gator	9–37	Pittsburgh (10–1–0)

YEAR	RECORD	BOWL	RESULT	OPPONENT (RECORD)
SOUTHERN CALIFORNIA (20–7–0)				
1922	(9–1–0)	Rose	14–3	Penn State (6–3–1)
1924	(8–2–0)	Los Angeles Christmas Festival	20–7	Missouri (7–1–0)
1929	(9–2–0)	Rose	47–14	Pittsburgh (9–0–0)
1931	(9–1–0)	Rose	21–12	Tulane (11–0–0)
1932	(9–0–0)	Rose	35–0	Pittsburgh (8–0–2)
1938	(8–2–0)	Rose	7–3	Duke (9–0–0)
1939	(7–0–2)	Rose	14–0	Tennessee (10–0–0)
1943	(7–2–0)	Rose	29–0	Washington (4–0–0)
1944	(7–0–2)	Rose	25–0	Tennessee (7–0–1)
1945	(7–3–0)	Rose	14–34	Alabama (9–0–0)
1947	(7–1–1)	Rose	0–49	Michigan (9–0–0)
1952	(9–1–0)	Rose	7–0	Wisconsin (6–2–1)
1954	(8–3–0)	Rose	7–20	Ohio State (9–0–0)
1962	(10–0–0)	Rose	42–37	Wisconsin (8–1–0)
1966	(7–3–0)	Rose	13–14	Purdue (8–2–0)
1967	(9–1–0)	Rose	14–3	Indiana (9–1–0)
1968	(9–0–1)	Rose	16–27	Ohio State (9–0–0)
1969	(9–0–1)	Rose	10–3	Michigan (8–2–0)
1972	(11–0–0)	Rose	42–17	Ohio State (9–1–0)
1973	(9–1–1)	Rose	21–42	Ohio State (9–0–1)
1974	(9–1–1)	Rose	18–17	Ohio State (10–1–0)
1975	(7–4–0)	Liberty	20–0	Texas A&M (10–1–0)
1976	(10–1–0)	Rose	14–6	Michigan (10–1–0)
1977	(7–4–0)	Bluebonnet	47–21	Texas A&M (8–3–0)
1978	(11–1–0)	Rose	17–10	Michigan (10–1–0)
1979	(10–0–1)	Rose	17–16	Ohio State (11–0–0)
1981	(9–2–0)	Fiesta	10–26	Penn State (9–2–0)
SOUTHERN METHODIST (4–6–1)				
1924	(5–0–4)	Dixie Classic	7–9	W.Va. Wesleyan (8–2–0)
1932	(2–7–2)	El Paso Charity	26–0	Texas-El Paso (7–2–0)
1935	(12–0–0)	Rose	0–7	Stanford (7–1–0)
1947	(9–0–1)	Cotton	13–13	Penn State (9–0–0)

YEAR	RECORD	BOWL	RESULT	OPPONENT (RECORD)
1948	(8–1–1)	Cotton	21–13	Oregon (9–1–0)
1963	(4–6–0)	Sun	14–21	Oregon (7–3–0)
1966	(8–2–0)	Cotton	9–24	Georgia (9–1–0)
1968	(7–3–0)	Bluebonnet	28–27	Oklahoma (7–3–0)
1980	(8–3–0)	Holiday	45–46	Brigham Young (11–1–0)
1982	(10–0–1)	Cotton	7–3	Pittsburgh (9–2–0)
1983	(10–1–0)	Sun	7–28	Alabama (7–4–0)

SOUTHERN MISSISSIPPI (1–5–0)

YEAR	RECORD	BOWL	RESULT	OPPONENT (RECORD)
1952	(10–1–0)	Sun	7–26	Pacific (6–3–1)
1953	(9–1–0)	Sun	14–37	Texas-El Paso (7–2–0)
1956	(7–1–1)	Tangerine	13–20	West Texas St. (7–2–0)
1957	(8–2–0)	Tangerine	9–10	East Texas St. (8–1–0)
1980	(8–3–0)	Independence	16–14	McNeese St. (10–1–0)
1981	(9–1–1)	Tangerine	17–19	Missouri (7–4–0)

STANFORD (7–5–1)

YEAR	RECORD	BOWL	RESULT	OPPONENT (RECORD)
1901	(3–1–2)	Rose	0–49	Michigan (10–0–0)
1924	(7–0–1)	Rose	10–27	Notre Dame (9–0–0)
1926	(10–0–0)	Rose	7–7	Alabama (9–0–0)
1927	(7–2–1)	Rose	7–6	Pittsburgh (8–0–1)
1933	(8–1–1)	Rose	0–7	Columbia (7–1–0)
1934	(9–0–1)	Rose	13–29	Alabama (9–0–0)
1935	(7–1–0)	Rose	7–0	Southern Methodist (12–0–0)
1940	(9–0–0)	Rose	21–13	Nebraska (8–1–0)
1951	(9–1–0)	Rose	7–40	Illinois (8–0–1)
1970	(8–3–0)	Rose	27–17	Ohio State (9–0–0)
1971	(8–3–0)	Rose	13–12	Michigan (11–0–0)
1977	(8–3–0)	Sun	24–14	Louisiana St. (8–3–0)
1978	(7–4–0)	Bluebonnet	25–22	Georgia (9–1–1)

SYRACUSE (3–5–0)

YEAR	RECORD	BOWL	RESULT	OPPONENT (RECORD)
1952	(7–2–0)	Orange	6–61	Alabama (9–2–0)

YEAR	RECORD	BOWL	RESULT	OPPONENT (RECORD)
1956	(7–1–0)	Cotton	27–28	Texas Christian (7–3–0)
1958	(8–1–0)	Orange	6–21	Oklahoma (9–1–0)
1959	(10–0–0)	Cotton	23–14	Texas (9–1–0)
1961	(7–3–0)	Liberty	15–14	Miami (Fla.) (7–3–0)
1964	(7–3–0)	Sugar	10–13	Louisiana St. (7–2–1)
1966	(8–2–0)	Gator	12–18	Tennessee (7–3–0)
1979	(6–5–0)	Independence	31–7	McNeese St. (11–0–0)

TEMPLE (1–1–0)

YEAR	RECORD	BOWL	RESULT	OPPONENT (RECORD)
1934	(7–0–2)	Sugar	14–20	Tulane (10–1–0)
1979	(9–2–0)	Garden State	28–17	California (6–5–0)

TENNESSEE (13–13–0)

YEAR	RECORD	BOWL	RESULT	OPPONENT (RECORD)
1931	(8–0–1)	New York Charity	13–0	New York University (6–3–1)
1938	(10–0–0)	Orange	17–0	Oklahoma (10–0–0)
1939	(10–0–0)	Rose	0–14	Southern California (7–0–2)
1940	(10–0–0)	Sugar	13–19	Boston College (10–0–0)
1942	(8–1–1)	Sugar	14–7	Tulsa (10–0–0)
1944	(7–0–1)	Rose	0–25	Southern California (7–0–2)
1946	(9–1–0)	Orange	0–8	Rice (8–2–0)
1950	(10–1–0)	Cotton	20–14	Texas (9–1–0)
1951	(10–0–0)	Sugar	13–28	Maryland (9–0–0)
1952	(8–1–1)	Cotton	0–16	Texas (8–2–0)
1956	(10–0–0)	Sugar	7–13	Baylor (8–2–0)
1957	(7–3–0)	Gator	3–0	Texas A&M (8–2–0)
1965	(7–1–2)	Bluebonnet	27–6	Tulsa (8–2–0)
1966	(7–3–0)	Gator	18–12	Syracuse (8–2–0)
1967	(9–1–0)	Orange	24–26	Oklahoma (9–1–0)
1968	(8–1–1)	Cotton	13–36	Texas (8–1–1)
1969	(9–1–0)	Gator	13–14	Florida (8–1–1)
1970	(10–1–0)	Sugar	34–13	Air Force (9–2–0)
1971	(9–2–0)	Liberty	14–13	Arkansas (8–2–1)
1972	(9–2–0)	Bluebonnet	24–17	Louisiana St. (9–1–1)

YEAR	RECORD	BOWL	RESULT	OPPONENT (RECORD)
1973	(8–3–0)	Gator	19–28	Texas Tech (10–1–0)
1974	(6–3–2)	Liberty	7–3	Maryland (8–3–0)
1979	(7–4–0)	Bluebonnet	22–27	Purdue (9–2–0)
1981	(7–4–0)	Garden State	28–21	Wisconsin (7–4–0)
1982	(6–4–1)	Peach	22–28	Iowa (7–4–0)
1983	(8–3–0)	Florida Citrus	30–23	Maryland (8–3–0)

TEXAS (15–13–2)

YEAR	RECORD	BOWL	RESULT	OPPONENT (RECORD)
1942	(8–2–0)	Cotton	14–7	Georgia Tech (9–1–0)
1943	(7–1–0)	Cotton	7–7	Randolph Field (9–1–0)
1945	(9–1–0)	Cotton	40–27	Missouri (6–3–0)
1947	(9–1–0)	Sugar	27–7	Alabama (8–2–0)
1948	(6–3–1)	Orange	41–28	Georgia (9–1–0)
1950	(9–1–0)	Cotton	14–20	Tennessee (10–1–0)
1952	(8–2–0)	Cotton	16–0	Tennessee (8–1–1)
1957	(6–3–1)	Sugar	7–39	Mississippi (8–1–1)
1959	(9–1–0)	Cotton	14–23	Syracuse (10–0–0)
1960	(7–3–0)	Bluebonnet	3–3	Alabama (8–1–1)
1961	(9–1–0)	Cotton	12–7	Mississippi (9–1–0)
1962	(9–0–1)	Cotton	0–13	Louisiana St. (8–1–1)
1963	(10–0–0)	Cotton	28–6	Navy (9–1–0)
1964	(9–1–0)	Orange	21–17	Alabama (10–0–0)
1966	(6–4–0)	Bluebonnet	19–0	Mississippi (8–2–0)
1968	(8–1–1)	Cotton	36–13	Tennessee (8–1–1)
1969	(10–0–0)	Cotton	21–17	Notre Dame (8–1–1)
1970	(10–0–0)	Cotton	11–24	Notre Dame (9–1–0)
1971	(8–2–0)	Cotton	6–30	Penn State (10–1–0)
1972	(9–1–0)	Cotton	17–13	Alabama (10–1–0)
1973	(8–2–0)	Cotton	3–19	Nebraska (8–2–1)
1974	(8–3–0)	Gator	3–27	Auburn (9–2–0)
1975	(9–2–0)	Bluebonnet	38–21	Colorado (9–2–0)
1977	(11–0–0)	Cotton	10–38	Notre Dame (10–1–0)
1978	(8–3–0)	Sun	42–0	Maryland (9–2–0)
1979	(9–2–0)	Sun	7–14	Washington (9–2–0)
1980	(7–4–0)	Bluebonnet	7–16	North Carolina (10–1–0)

YEAR	RECORD	BOWL	RESULT	OPPONENT (RECORD)
1981	(9–1–1)	Cotton	14–12	Alabama (9–1–1)
1982	(9–2–0)	Sun	10–26	North Carolina (7–4–0)
1983	(11–0–0)	Cotton	9–10	Georgia (9–1–1)

TEXAS A&M (8–5–0)

YEAR	RECORD	BOWL	RESULT	OPPONENT (RECORD)
1921	(5–1–2)	Dixie Classic	22–14	Centre (9–0–0)
1939	(10–0–0)	Sugar	14–13	Tulane (8–1–1)
1940	(8–1–0)	Cotton	13–12	Fordham (7–1–0)
1941	(9–1–0)	Cotton	21–29	Alabama (8–2–0)
1943	(7–1–1)	Orange	14–19	Louisiana St. (5–3–0)
1950	(6–4–0)	Presidential Cup	40–20	Georgia (6–2–3)
1957	(8–2–0)	Gator	0–3	Tennessee (7–3–0)
1967	(6–4–0)	Cotton	20–16	Alabama (8–1–1)
1975	(10–1–0)	Liberty	0–20	Southern California (7–4–0)
1976	(9–2–0)	Sun	37–14	Florida (8–3–0)
1977	(8–3–0)	Bluebonnet	21–47	Southern California (7–4–0)
1978	(7–4–0)	Hall of Fame	28–12	Iowa St. (8–3–0)
1981	(6–5–0)	Independence	33–16	Oklahoma St. (7–4–0)

TEXAS CHRISTIAN (4–8–1)

YEAR	RECORD	BOWL	RESULT	OPPONENT (RECORD)
1920	(9–0–0)	Fort Worth Classic	7–63	Centre (7–2–0)
1935	(11–1–0)	Sugar	3–2	Louisiana St. (9–1–0)
1936	(8–2–2)	Cotton	16–6	Marquette (7–1–0)
1938	(10–0–0)	Sugar	15–7	Carnegie Tech (7–1–0)
1941	(7–3–0)	Orange	26–40	Georgia (8–1–1)
1944	(7–2–1)	Cotton	0–34	Oklahoma St. (7–1–0)
1947	(4–4–2)	Delta	9–13	Mississippi (8–2–0)
1951	(6–4–0)	Cotton	7–20	Kentucky (7–4–0)
1955	(9–1–0)	Cotton	13–14	Mississippi (9–1–0)
1956	(7–3–0)	Cotton	28–27	Syracuse (7–1–0)
1958	(8–2–0)	Cotton	0–0	Air Force (9–0–1)

YEAR	RECORD	BOWL	RESULT	OPPONENT (RECORD)
1959	(8–2–0)	Bluebonnet	7–23	Clemson (8–2–0)
1965	(6–4–0)	Sun	12–13	Texas-El Paso (7–3–0)

TEXAS–EL PASO (5–4–0)

YEAR	RECORD	BOWL	RESULT	OPPONENT (RECORD)
1932	(7–2–0)	El Paso Charity	0–26	Southern Methodist (2–7–2)
1936	(5–2–1)	Sun	6–34	Hardin-Simmons (8–2–0)
1948	(8–1–1)	Sun	12–21	West Virginia (8–3–0)
1949	(7–2–1)	Sun	33–20	Georgetown (5–4–0)
1953	(7–2–0)	Sun	37–14	Southern Mississippi (9–1–0)
1954	(7–3–0)	Sun	47–20	Florida St. (8–3–0)
1956	(9–1–0)	Sun	0–13	George Washington (7–1–1)
1965	(7–3–0)	Sun	13–12	Texas Christian (6–4–0)
1967	(6–2–1)	Sun	14–7	Mississippi (6–3–1)

TEXAS TECH (3–12–1)

YEAR	RECORD	BOWL	RESULT	OPPONENT (RECORD)
1937	(8–3–0)	Sun	6–7	West Virginia (7–1–1)
1938	(10–0–0)	Cotton	13–20	St. Mary's (6–2–0)
1941	(9–1–0)	Sun	0–6	Tulsa (7–2–0)
1947	(6–4–0)	Sun	12–13	Miami (Ohio) (8–0–1)
1949	(7–4–0)	Raisin	13–20	San Jose St. (8–4–0)
1951	(6–4–0)	Sun	25–14	Pacific (6–4–0)
1953	(10–1–0)	Gator	35–13	Auburn (7–2–1)
1955	(7–2–1)	Sun	14–21	Wyoming (7–3–0)
1964	(6–3–1)	Sun	0–7	Georgia (6–3–1)
1965	(8–2–0)	Gator	21–31	Georgia Tech (6–3–1)
1970	(8–3–0)	Sun	9–17	Georgia Tech (8–3–0)
1972	(8–3–0)	Sun	28–32	North Carolina (10–1–0)
1973	(10–1–0)	Gator	28–19	Tennessee (8–3–0)
1974	(6–4–1)	Peach	6–6	Vanderbilt (7–3–1)
1976	(10–1–0)	Bluebonnet	24–27	Nebraska (7–3–1)
1977	(7–4–0)	Tangerine	17–40	Florida St. (9–2–0)

YEAR	RECORD	BOWL	RESULT	OPPONENT (RECORD)
TULANE (2–5–0)				
1931	(11–0–0)	Rose	12–21	Southern California (9–1–0)
1934	(10–1–0)	Sugar	20–14	Temple (7–0–2)
1939	(8–0–1)	Sugar	13–14	Texas A&M (10–0–0)
1970	(7–4–0)	Liberty	17–3	Colorado (6–4–0)
1973	(9–2–0)	Bluebonnet	7–47	Houston (10–1–0)
1979	(9–2–0)	Liberty	6–9	Penn State (7–4–0)
1980	(7–4–0)	Hall of Fame	15–34	Arkansas (6–5–0)
TULSA (3–6–0)				
1941	(7–2–0)	Sun	6–0	Texas Tech (9–1–0)
1942	(10–0–0)	Sugar	7–14	Tennessee (8–1–1)
1943	(6–0–1)	Sugar	18–20	Georgia Tech (7–3–0)
1944	(7–2–0)	Orange	26–12	Georgia Tech (8–2–0)
1945	(8–2–0)	Oil	6–20	Georgia (8–2–0)
1952	(8–1–1)	Gator	13–14	Florida (7–3–0)
1964	(8–2–0)	Bluebonnet	14–7	Mississippi (5–4–1)
1965	(8–2–0)	Bluebonnet	6–27	Tennessee (7–1–2)
1976	(7–3–1)	Independence	16–20	McNeese St. (9–2–0)
UCLA (4–7–1)				
1942	(7–3–0)	Rose	0–9	Georgia (10–1–0)
1946	(10–0–0)	Rose	14–45	Illinois (7–2–0)
1953	(8–1–0)	Rose	20–28	Michigan St. (8–1–0)
1955	(9–1–0)	Rose	14–17	Michigan St. (8–1–0)
1961	(7–3–0)	Rose	3–21	Minnesota (7–2–0)
1965	(7–2–1)	Rose	14–12	Michigan St. (10–0–0)
1975	(8–2–1)	Rose	23–10	Ohio State (11–0–0)
1976	(9–1–1)	Liberty	6–36	Alabama (8–3–0)
1978	(8–3–0)	Fiesta	10–10	Arkansas (9–2–0)
1981	(7–3–1)	Bluebonnet	14–33	Michigan (8–3–0)
1982	(9–1–1)	Rose	24–14	Michigan (8–3–0)
1983	(6–4–1)	Rose	45–9	Illinois (10–1–0)

YEAR	RECORD	BOWL	RESULT	OPPONENT (RECORD)
UTAH (2–0–0)				
1938	(7–1–2)	Sun	26–0	New Mexico (8–2–0)
1964	(8–2–0)	Liberty	32–6	West Virginia (7–3–0)
UTAH STATE (0–4–0)				
1946	(7–1–1)	Raisin	0–20	San Jose St. (8–1–1)
1947	(6–4–0)	Grape	21–35	Pacific (8–1–0)
1960	(9–1–0)	Sun	13–20	New Mexico St. (10–0–0)
1961	(9–0–1)	Gotham	9–24	Baylor (5–5–0)
VANDERBILT (1–1–1)				
1955	(7–3–0)	Gator	25–13	Auburn (8–1–1)
1974	(7–3–1)	Peach	6–6	Texas Tech (6–4–1)
1982	(8–3–0)	Hall of Fame	28–36	Air Force (7–5–0)
VIRGINIA TECH (0–4–0)				
1946	(3–3–3)	Sun	6–18	Cincinnati (8–2–0)
1966	(8–1–1)	Liberty	7–14	Miami (Fla.) (7–2–1)
1968	(7–3–0)	Liberty	17–34	Mississippi (6–3–1)
1980	(8–3–0)	Peach	10–20	Miami (Fla.) (8–3–0)
WAKE FOREST (1–2–0)				
1945	(4–3–1)	Gator	26–14	South Carolina (2–3–3)
1948	(6–3–0)	Dixie	7–20	Baylor (5–3–2)
1979	(8–3–0)	Tangerine	10–34	Louisiana St. (6–5–0)
WASHINGTON (6–6–1)				
1923	(10–1–0)	Rose	14–14	Navy (5–1–2)
1925	(10–0–1)	Rose	19–20	Alabama (9–0–0)
1936	(7–1–1)	Rose	0–21	Pittsburgh (7–1–1)
1943	(4–0–0)	Rose	0–29	Southern California (7–2–0)
1959	(9–1–0)	Rose	44–8	Wisconsin (7–2–0)
1960	(9–1–0)	Rose	17–7	Minnesota (8–1–0)
1963	(6–4–0)	Rose	7–17	Illinois (7–1–1)

YEAR	RECORD	BOWL	RESULT	OPPONENT (RECORD)
1977	(7–4–0)	Rose	27–20	Michigan (10–1–0)
1979	(9–2–0)	Sun	14–7	Texas (9–2–0)
1980	(9–2–0)	Rose	6–23	Michigan (9–2–0)
1981	(9–2–0)	Rose	28–0	Iowa (8–3–0)
1982	(9–2–0)	Aloha	21–20	Maryland (8–3–0)
1983	(8–3–0)	Aloha	10–13	Penn State (7–4–1)

WASHINGTON STATE (1–2–0)

1915	(6–0–0)	Rose	14–0	Brown (5–3–1)
1930	(9–0–0)	Rose	0–24	Alabama (9–0–0)
1981	(8–2–1)	Holiday	36–38	Brigham Young (10–2–0)

WEST VIRGINIA (7–4–0)

1922	(9–0–1)	San Diego Christmas Classic	21–13	Gonzaga (5–2–0)
1937	(7–1–1)	Sun	7–6	Texas Tech (8–3–0)
1948	(8–3–0)	Sun	21–12	Texas-El Paso (8–1–1)
1953	(8–1–0)	Sugar	19–42	Georgia Tech (8–2–1)
1964	(7–3–0)	Liberty	6–32	Utah (8–2–0)
1969	(9–1–0)	Peach	14–3	South Carolina (7–3–0)
1972	(8–3–0)	Peach	13–49	North Carolina St. (7–3–1)
1975	(8–3–0)	Peach	13–10	North Carolina St. (7–3–1)
1981	(8–3–0)	Peach	26–6	Florida (7–4–0)
1982	(9–2–0)	Gator	12–31	Florida St. (8–3–0)
1983	(8–3–0)	Hall of Fame	20–16	Kentucky (6–4–1)

WILLIAM & MARY (1–2–0)

1947	(9–1–0)	Dixie	19–21	Arkansas (5–4–1)
1948	(6–2–2)	Delta	20–0	Oklahoma St. (6–3–0)
1970	(5–6–0)	Tangerine	12–40	Toledo (11–0–0)

YEAR	RECORD	BOWL	RESULT	OPPONENT (RECORD)
WISCONSIN (1–4–0)				
1952	(6–2–1)	Rose	0–7	Southern California (9–1–0)
1959	(7–2–0)	Rose	8–44	Washington (9–1–0)
1962	(8–1–0)	Rose	37–42	Southern California (10–0–0)
1981	(7–4–0)	Garden State	21–28	Tennessee (7–4–0)
1982	(6–5–0)	Independence	14–3	Kansas St. (6–4–1)
WYOMING (4–2–0)				
1950	(9–0–0)	Gator	20–7	Washington & Lee (8–2–0)
1955	(7–3–0)	Sun	21–14	Texas Tech (7–2–1)
1958	(7–3–0)	Sun	14–6	Hardin-Simmons (6–4–0)
1966	(9–1–0)	Sun	28–20	Florida St. (6–4–0)
1967	(10–0–0)	Sugar	13–20	Louisiana St. (6–3–1)
1976	(8–3–0)	Fiesta	7–41	Oklahoma (8–2–1)